Foreword

It is surprisingly fun to know
you do so, learn new knowledg   .e answers are there in ... ...   just read!

Originally written simply to encourage reading for knowledge. The comprehension questions are at the heart of what the book does. They provide good and manageable coverage of the topics that **all** students can access to feel that sense of achievement. These questions are available as **printable gapped handouts** for students to stick into their books at www.nextpagescience.com . The book is also available as a **comprehension only** version that students can keep and work through as their own.

The additional tasks in this edition are designed to:

1. Consolidate content and important relationships
2. Stretch ideas further without putting them out of reach
3. Provoke thought and discussion on topics
4. Introduce further content
5. Practise skills such as graph plotting, numeracy and planning

Additional tasks are designed with enough guidance that the majority of students can access them even when introducing new ideas which overlap with KS4. Also available to download and print at www.nextpagescience.com .

What the book does:

*   Provides the basis of a lesson
*   Covers the subject content of Key Stage 3 Science in a question and answer style approach
*   Enables 1:1 work with no specialist knowledge required
*   Extends coverage through the additional tasks
*   Encourages the essential skill of reading for knowledge
*   Is written in Comic Sans to aid any reader with dyslexia
*   Has 'WHAT?' facts on each page to provide a sense of awe alongside the subject content
*   Is great as a revision tool. Can you answer the comprehension questions without looking?
*   And fun

Enjoy.

Contents

BIOLOGY

The Light Microscope: Seeing Cells

The smallest things that humans could see before lenses and microscopes was limited by the naked eye. This allows us to see objects about 0.1mm (1/10th of a millimetre) across. Living organisms are made from small units called cells. The average size of a cell is about 0.01mm, too small to be seen with an unaided eye.

A **magnifying lens** is the simplest microscope and makes objects look bigger. A compound microscope uses **two magnifying lenses** to make objects look even bigger. The lens nearest to the object is called the **objective lens**. The lens that you look through is called the **eyepiece lens**. Magnification is how much bigger something looks. This is found by dividing the image size (usually measured from an image on a photograph) by the object's size (the real size of the object). The lens opposite has a magnification of X5 because **20 ÷ 4 = 5**.

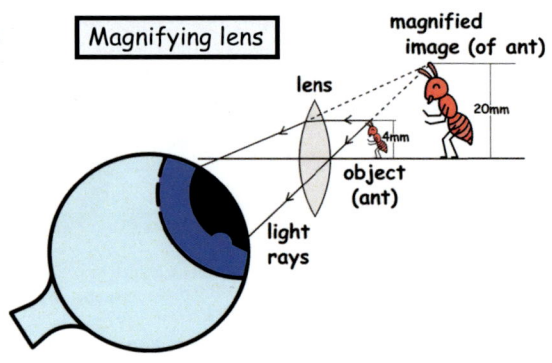
Magnifying lens

Eyepiece lenses on microscopes often have a magnification of X10 (times 10). To get the total magnification of a microscope we multiply the eyepiece lens magnification by the objective lens magnification. The lowest power objective lens often has a value of X4, so the **total magnification** would be **4 x 10 = 40** times bigger.

Preparing a Cheek Cell Slide

- Use a cotton bud to wipe the inside of your cheek

- Smear the bud over a microscope slide

- Add a drop of dye and place a cover slip on top

Using a Microscope

1. Place a slide on the stage and clip it in place using the stage clips.

2. Select the lowest power objective lens first.

3. To begin with adjust the coarse focus so that the objective lens is positioned as near to the slide as possible **without touching.**

4. Look down the eyepiece lens and adjust the coarse focus **away from** the slide up until the object is seen.

5. Adjust the fine focus to obtain the clearest image possible, voila!

WHAT?

The smallest thing that can be seen with a light microscope is about 1/2000th the size of a full stop on a piece of paper. Microscopes that use electrons to 'see' can image the individual atoms and molecules that a substance is made from. The image is formed on a fluorescent screen that emits light when the electrons hit the screen after passing through the specimen.

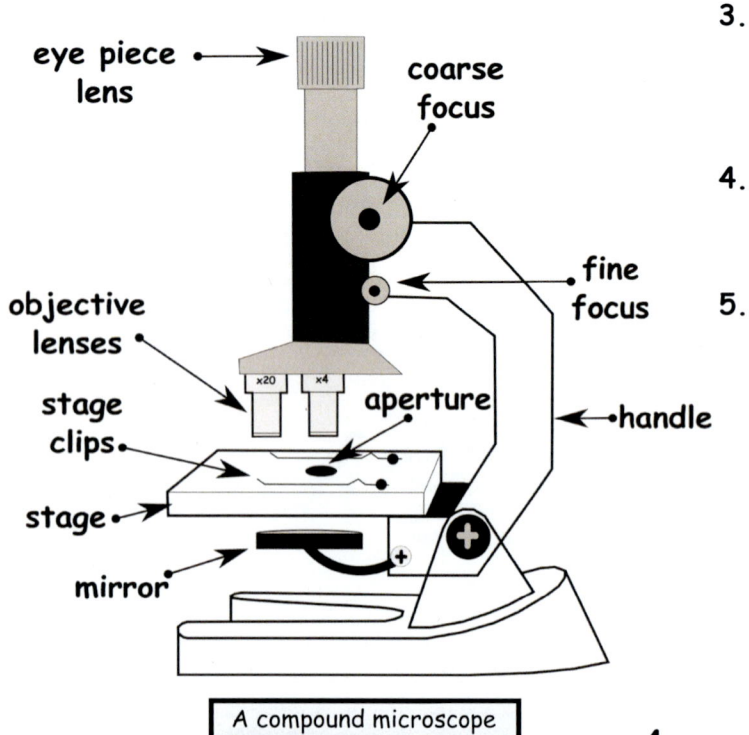

A compound microscope

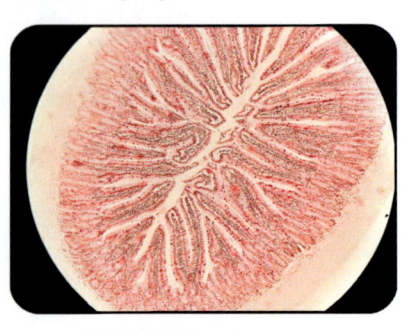

Intestinal 'villi' cells

Questions on The Light Microscope

Comprehension

1. What used to be the limit of what humans can see?

2. About how small an object can you see with the naked eye?

3. What are living organisms made from?

4. What is the average size of a cell?

5. What could we say is the simplest microscope?

6. What does a compound microscope use to make objects look even bigger?

7. What is the lens that you look through called?

8. How do you calculate magnification?

9. What magnification do eyepiece lenses often have?

10. How do we get the **total magnification** of a microscope?

11. What do we use to hold the slide in place?

12. When using a microscope, which power lens should you use first?

13 To begin with, where should the objective lens be positioned?

14. Which way should you move the objective lens when beginning to focus?

15. What should you adjust to obtain the clearest image possible?

Additional tasks

1. Label and memorise the parts of the microscope opposite.

2. Calculate the magnification of the cell images below.

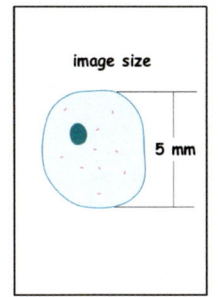

image size

5 mm

object size
0.1mm

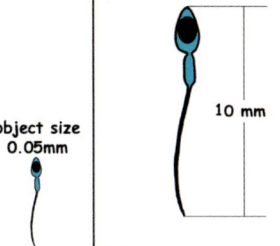

image size

10 mm

object size
0.05mm

_____   _____

magnification   magnification

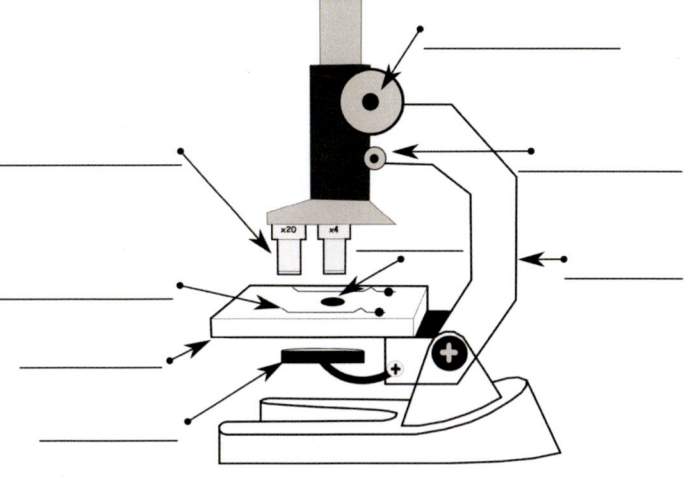

3. Calculate the **total magnification** when using a compound microscope with the following eyepiece and objective lenses.

a.	Eyepiece lens X10, objective lens X10	_____
b.	Eyepiece lens X10, objective lens X20	_____
c.	Eyepiece lens X10, objective lens X40	_____
d.	Eyepiece lens X5, objective lens X100	_____
e.	Eyepiece lens X5, objective lens X50	_____

4. Calculate the 'real' object size (O) using the magnification and image size in the table below;

Magnification	Image size on paper (mm)	Object size (mm)
40	40	1.
100	20	2.
250	5	3.
50	1	4.

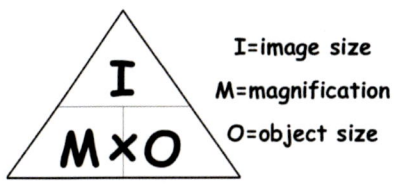

I=image size
M=magnification
O=object size

Cells

Living things are made from cells. Cells are the tiny individual units of life that larger organisms like us are made from. All animals and plants are made from cells. Plant and animal cells have slightly different organelles (specialised structures) that make up the cell.

Animal cell   **Plant cell**

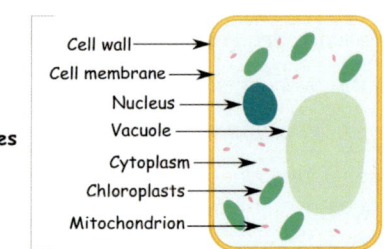

Both **plant** and **animal** cells have a membrane, cytoplasm, nucleus and mitochondria. The **cell membrane** controls what goes in and out of the cell; the **cytoplasm** is where chemical reactions take place; the **nucleus** contains the DNA (instructions for making new cells) and the **mitochondrion** is where energy is released by respiration. **Plant** cells also have a **cell wall** for support, so they are not floppy (flaccid), a **vacuole** that contains sap and **chloroplasts** containing chlorophyll for photosynthesis.

Cells are small but vary in size, a red blood cell is about 0.008 (8/1000) of a millimetre, whilst a woman's egg cells are about 0.2 (1/5) of a millimetre.

Specialised Cells

Sperm cells are specially adapted for their job. They have a long tail for swimming to the egg and special enzymes to get through the egg's membrane.

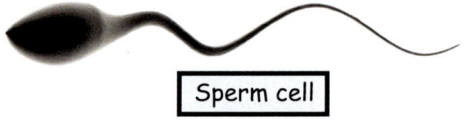

Red blood cells have no nucleus so they can carry more oxygen.

Root hair cells stick out from a plant's roots, this gives them a large surface area for absorbing water and nutrients.

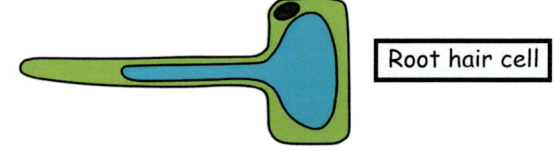

Muscle cells are adapted to contract rapidly.

Tissues, Organs and Organ Systems

Cells carrying out a similar function can group together to form **tissue**, like muscle cells in muscles. Different types of tissues can work together to form an **organ**. Different organs can work together to form an **organ system** e.g. the digestive system. Finally different organ systems can combine to produce an **organism** like humans (animals) or trees (plants).

> **WHAT?**
>
> The largest cell in the human body is an egg cell, it is just visible with the naked eye at nearly 0.2 mm in diameter (across). The smallest cell is the male sperm cell! Approximately 60 billion cells in the human body die every day.

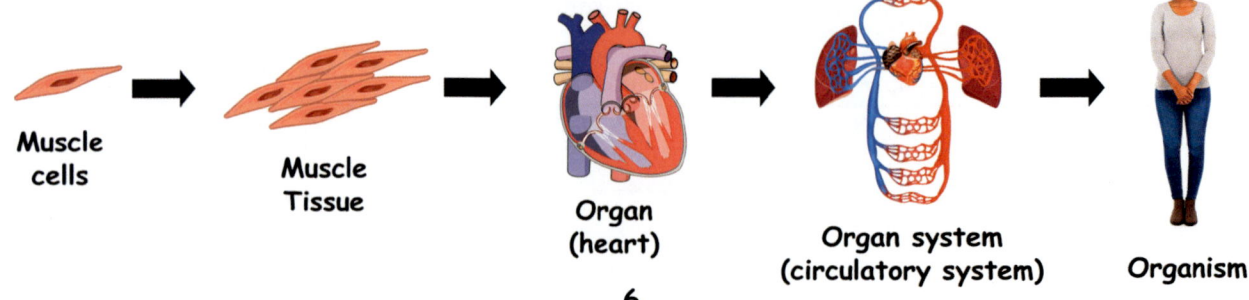

Muscle cells → Muscle Tissue → Organ (heart) → Organ system (circulatory system) → Organism

Questions on Cells

Comprehension

1. What are living things made from?
2. What are cells?
3. What are the specialised structures that make up the cell called?
4. What do plant and animal cells both have in common?
5. What does the cell membrane control?
6. Chemical reactions happen in the ....?
7. Where is the DNA stored and what does it do?
8. What stops plant cells being floppy (flaccid)?
9. Where is cell sap contained?
10. What is in the chloroplasts and what is it used for?
11. How are sperm cells specially adapted?
12. What do root hair cells have for absorbing water and nutrients?
13. How is tissue formed?
14. When different types of tissues work together what is formed?
15. What is an organ system?
16. What happens if different organ systems combine?

Additional tasks

1. Label and memorise the parts of a plant and animal cell below.

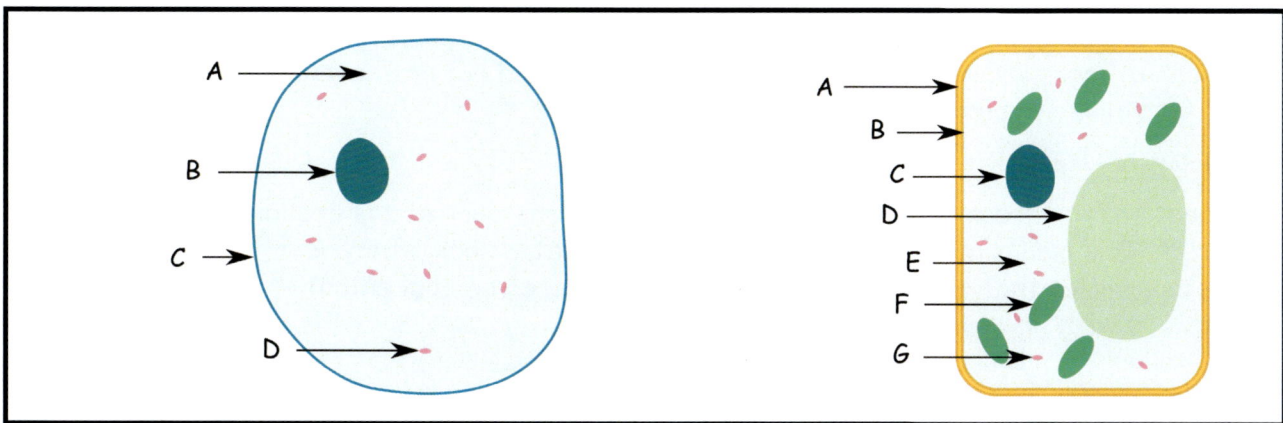

2. Complete the flow diagram showing how **cells** can group together, finally forming an **organism.**

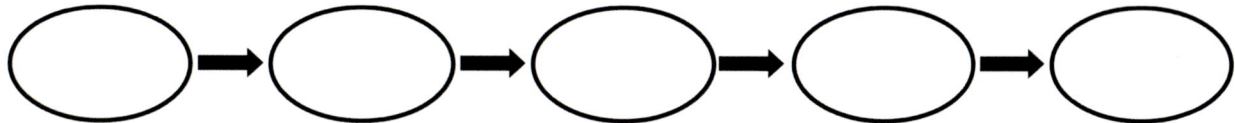

3. Match the organ (s) below to their organ systems.

1.	Ear canal, ear drum, ossicles	Digestive system
2.	Mouth, gullet, small intestines	Female reproductive system
3.	Pupil, lens, retina	Nervous system
4.	Lungs and wind pipe	Respiratory system (breathing)
5.	Blood vessels	Male reproductive system
6.	Penis and testes	Visual system
7.	Spinal cord	Hearing (auditory) system
8.	Ovaries, oviduct, womb	Circulatory system

4. Rearrange the jumbled up letters to reveal the names of the cell organelles and write next to the organelle, **plant only** or **animal and plant.**

LECL BRNEAMEM _____   LSUECNU _____

PSTLSAOLROHC _____   ALCOVUE _____

CPOTSMALY _____   ELCL LLWA _____

CHOTIMRIODNON _____

Diffusion

We all quickly realise it's our favourite dinner when we smell chips frying in a pan. The chips haven't moved, but the smell spreads through a process called **diffusion**. Particles (very small bits) of the food are released during cooking, they mix with the air and spread out. We can think of diffusion as mixing without stirring. The particles always spread out from where there are more (**high concentration**) to where there are less (**low concentration**). You see this if you make orange squash by adding the squash after the water. The squash slowly spreads out without stirring, the particles of squash are diffusing through the water until they are evenly spread.

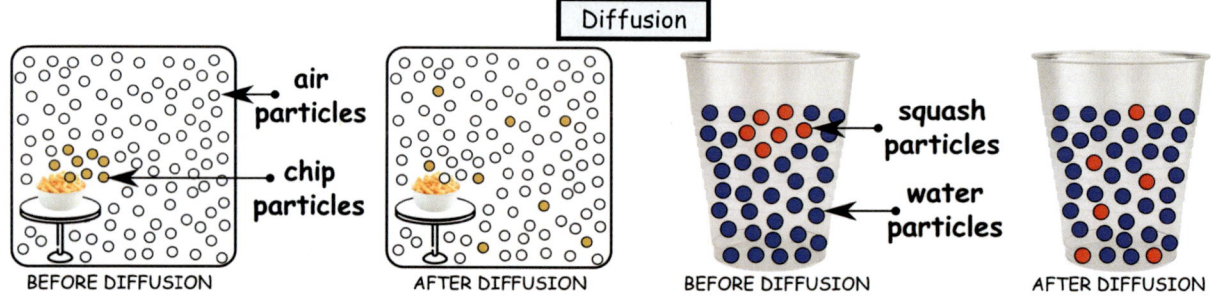

Diffusion happens in gases and liquids due to the random motion of the particles. They bump into each other, causing the high concentration to spread out until evenly distributed and the diffusion is complete.

Diffusion is Useful

In digestion (the breaking down of food for absorption), our food is broken up into tiny particles. This means inside our bodies (in the small intestines) there is a high concentration of food particles that can diffuse into our blood, where the concentration is lower. This provides us with energy and nutrients.

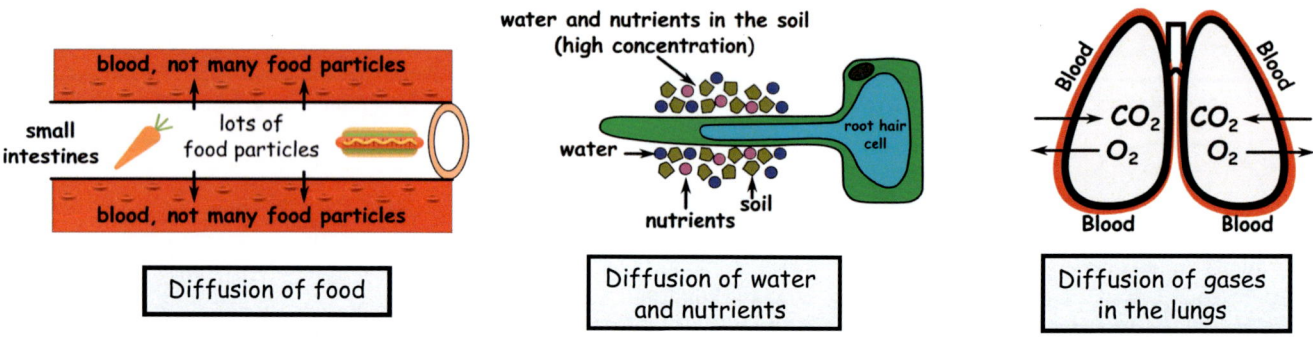

Diffusion of food

Diffusion of water and nutrients

Diffusion of gases in the lungs

WHAT?

Sharks are thought to be able to detect a drop of blood from a quarter of a mile away through diffusion but this has not been proved and the chance of suffering a shark attack are less than 1 in 10,000,000!

Due to diffusion, smells (pleasant or unpleasant) travel about 5 centimetres every second.

In plants the large surface area of the adapted 'sticking out' root hair cells allows water and nutrients to be absorbed through diffusion. There is a higher concentration of water and nutrients in the soil than in the root hair cell. In breathing, oxygen in the air we inhale is able to move from a higher concentration, in our lungs, to a lower concentration, in our blood. Also, carbon dioxide that has built up in our blood through respiration (the release of energy from food), diffuses from the blood to the lungs to be breathed out (exhaled). The diagram opposite shows the stages of a blue dye diffusing in a jar of water.

Questions on Diffusion

Comprehension

1. What do we call the process of 'smells spreading out'?

2. How can we think of diffusion?

3. From where to where do the particles diffuse?

4. When would the particles of orange squash stop diffusing?

5. In what sort of substances does diffusion happen?

6. In what sort of motion do the particles move?

7. What is digestion?

8. What happens to the high concentration of food particles in our small intestines?

9. What does the large surface area of root hair cells allow?

10. How does the concentration of water and nutrients in the soil compare to the root hair cell?

11. Where does the oxygen in the air we breathe end up?

12. Why does carbon dioxide build up in our blood?

13. What is respiration?

14. What happens to the carbon dioxide that has built up in the blood?

Additional tasks

Glucose with a higher concentration in the blood can diffuse into a red blood cell with a lower concentration.

1. Complete the diagram below to show what things look like after diffusion (it looks just like the squash and chips opposite). Any colour is fine.

2. Where have some of the glucose molecules ended up?!

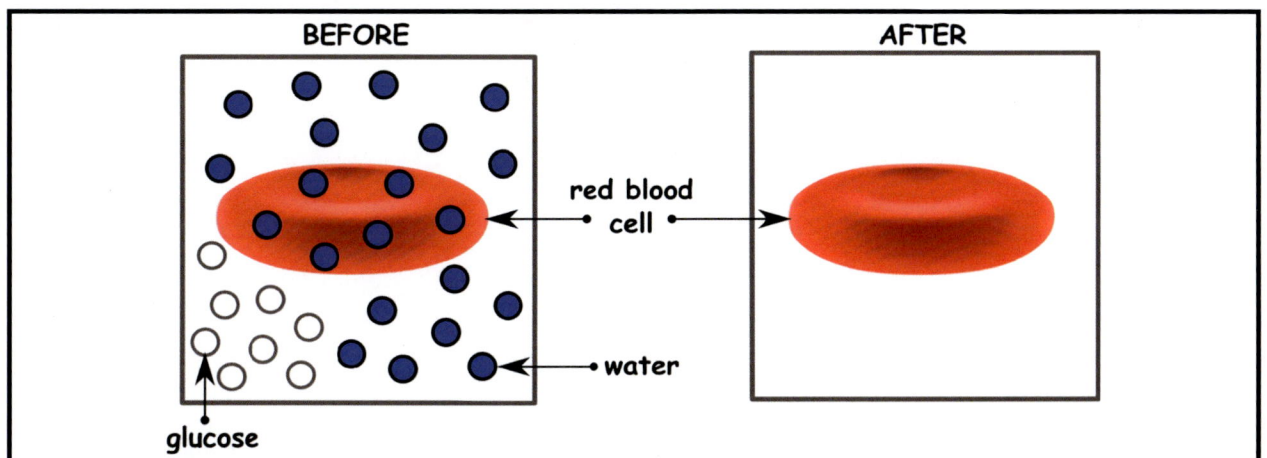

3. Hydrochloric acid particles and ammonia particles diffuse through the tube of air. When they meet they react to form ammonium chloride, a **white solid**. This happens nearer to where the hydrochloric acid particles came from. They diffuse slower because they are heavier and move more slowly than ammonia particles. Complete the gapped exercise below to explain what is happening. Choose from the words in bold.

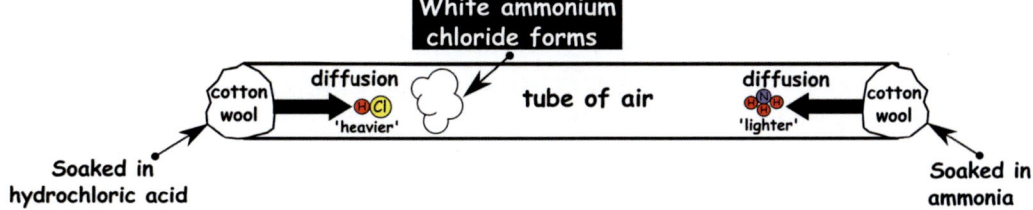

> **quickly, particles, diffuse, ammonium chloride, meet, heavier, faster, white solid, more slowly, Heavier, slowly**
>
> Hydrochloric acid (HCl) and ammonia (NH_3) _____ both _____ through the tube. When they _____ they form _____, this _____ _____ forms nearer to where the hydrochloric acid particles came from. Hydrochloric acid particles are _____ and move _____ _____ then ammonia particles. _____ and slower particles diffuse more _____. Lighter _____ moving particles diffuse more _____.

The Skeleton and Muscles

A human skeleton has 206 bones, snakes can have as many as 1800 bones. Bones need to be hard so are made mostly from a mineral called calcium. Humans have an endoskeleton, this is the name given to animals that have their bones on the inside of the body. Some animals, such as insects, have an exoskeleton, this is where the bones are on the outside of the body. The bones of insects' are made from a substance called chitin.

The Purpose of the Skeleton

The human skeleton has **four** main jobs. It supports your body, it protects organs (like your skull protects your brain from injury), it enables you to move through bone joints and it makes blood. The elbow is a '**hinge joint'**, the top of your spine a '**pivot joint'**, for turning your head. The shoulder has a '**ball and socket**' joint. Ball and socket joints allow limbs to rotate in a circle, really useful! Inside your bones is bone marrow, it makes your blood cells. **Red cells** for carrying **oxygen**, **white cells** for **fighting infection** and disease and **platelets** to **stop bleeding** by clotting cuts and wounds.

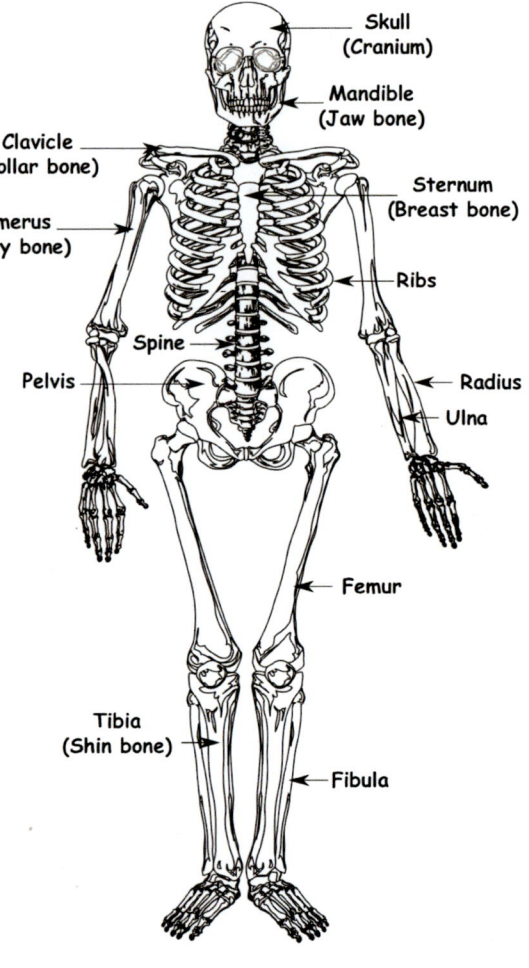

Skull (Cranium)
Mandible (Jaw bone)
Clavicle (Collar bone)
Sternum (Breast bone)
Humerus (Funny bone)
Ribs
Spine
Pelvis
Radius
Ulna
Femur
Tibia (Shin bone)
Fibula

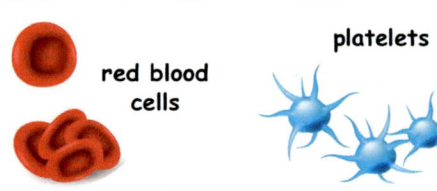

red blood cells

platelets

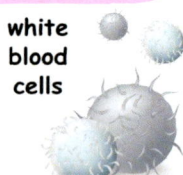

white blood cells

Movement

Muscles are made from cells that are good at contracting (becoming shorter). Muscles are held to the bone by non-stretchy tissues called **tendons**. Bones are held together by fibrous tissues called **ligaments**. Muscles can work together in pairs to create movement. When you lift an object with your arm, your biceps fatten and contract and your triceps relax, staying their normal length. Muscles working together in this way are called **antagonistic**, the action of one muscle affects what the other muscle does (relax or contract). Put the **back** of your hand **on a table** and push down, feel your triceps contract. Now put the **palm** of your hand **under** the table and push up, feel your biceps contract.

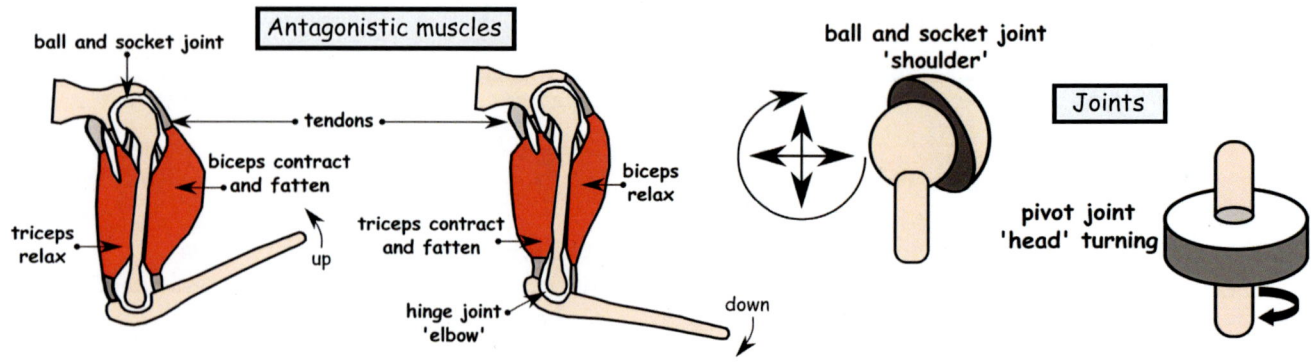

Antagonistic muscles

ball and socket joint
tendons
biceps contract and fatten
triceps relax
up
biceps relax
triceps contract and fatten
hinge joint 'elbow'
down

ball and socket joint 'shoulder'

Joints

pivot joint 'head' turning

Questions on the Skeleton and Muscles

Comprehension

1. How many bones does a human skeleton have?
2. Why are bones made mostly from calcium?
3. What is an endoskeleton?
4. What sort of skeleton do insects have?
5. What is chitin?
6. What are the four main jobs of the human skeleton?
7. What is the purpose of the skull?
8. What do bone joints do?
9. What sort of joint does your shoulder have?
10. Why are ball and socket joints really useful?
11. What is made inside of bones?
12. What do red blood cells carry?
13. What holds the muscles to the bones?
14. What do ligaments do?
15. What happens to your triceps when your biceps contract?
16. What do we call muscles that work in pairs contracting and relaxing?

Additional tasks

1. Name and memorise the bones below.

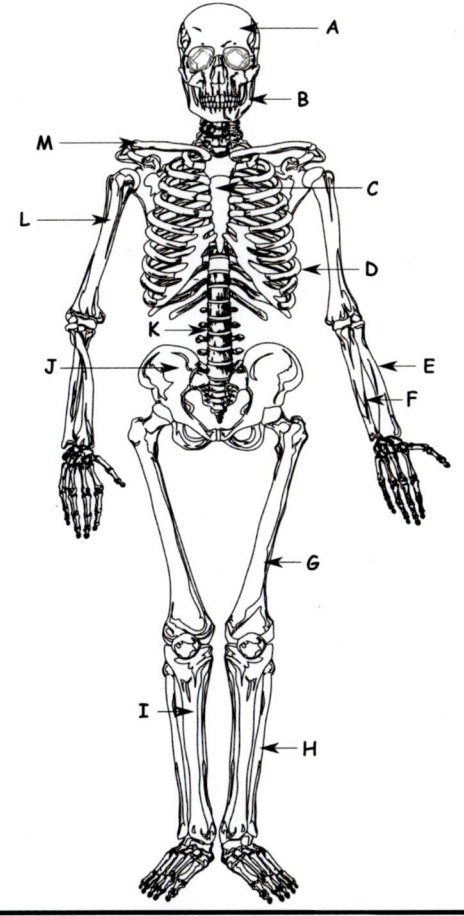

A. CRANIUM	B. MANDIBLE
C. STERNUM	D. RIBS
E. RADIUS	F. ULNA
G. FEMUR	H. FIBULA
I. TIBIA	J. PELVIS
K. SPINE	L. HUMERUS
M. CLAVICLE	

2. Below are examples of where we find **pivot joints** (for rotation), **hinge joints** (for bending and straightening) or **ball and socket joints** for movement in most directions. For each one write down which type of joint you think they are.

   a. the hip joint
   b. the knee joint
   c. the finger joints
   d. the ankle joint
   e. the joint connecting the head to the neck

3. Write down next to the animal's name below, whether you think they have an exoskeleton or endoskeleton.

   WASPS exoskel   FISH endoskel
   BEARS endoskel   HORSES endoskel
   CRABS endoskel   CENTIPEDES exoskel
   BIRDS endoskel   BEETLES exoskel
   LIZARDS exoskel   GRASSHOPPERS exoske

    animals    insects

4. 100 children test their bicep strength by **pushing up** on a **force meter** fixed under a desk. The results are shown below. Plot a histogram of the results (see pg50).

Force (N)	101-110	111-120	121-130	131-140	141-150
Number of pupils	10	15	50	15	10

5. Explain what you think the job of the rib cage and the spine is.

   Can you explain the job of any other bones?

The Healthy Human Diet

A healthy diet is all about consuming the right amount of the seven food groups. Too much (excessive) or too little (insufficient) of any of the groups can lead to disease (abnormal function of an organism). There isn't a single food that contains everything we need, so having a balanced diet (the right mixture of all the groups) is essential for good health.

The Seven Food Groups

Carbohydrates provide energy.

Proteins are used to help you grow and repair tissue.

Fats or lipids, their main role is as an energy store.

Minerals are essential inorganic (don't contain carbon) compounds containing elements needed by the body, e.g. calcium for strong bones and iron for making blood.

Vitamins are essential organic compounds (contain carbon) needed in small quantities for normal growth and health. Vitamin C is well known, it helps wounds to heal and keeps your skin healthy.

Fibre is undigested food, it gives your waste 'bulk' to help it pass through the large intestine better.

Water is needed to hydrate (provide water for) our cells and aids with digestion.

Where to get the Food Groups and how much of each

An 'eat well' plate shows you roughly how much of each food group you should be eating. **Carbohydrates (starches and sugars)** come mainly from grain based foods such as bread, pasta, cereals and also potatoes. **Fats** are found in oils, butter, cheese, meats and nuts. Good

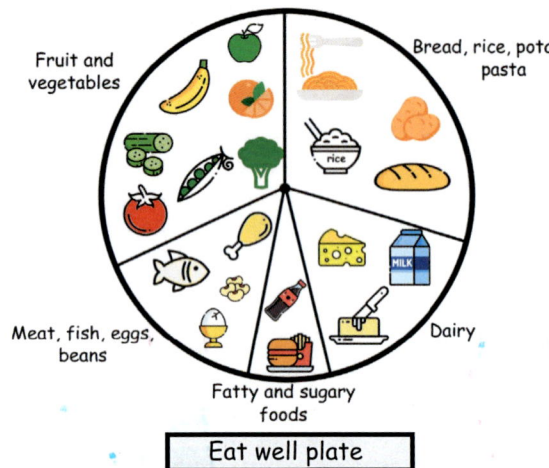

Eat well plate

sources of **protein** are meats, eggs, pulses (edible seeds), nuts, cheese and fish. **Vitamins** and **minerals** come from many sources e.g. iron from leafy or green vegetables, vitamin C from fruit and vegetables and calcium from dairy products. Wholegrain foods along with fruit, vegetables and beans are good sources of **fibre**. Eating about 33% bread, rice, potatoes and pasta; 33% fruit and vegetables; 15% dairy; 12% meat, fish, eggs and beans and finally only 7% of our diets being made up from fatty and sugary food, will mean that we are getting the right amount of all the food groups for a healthy diet.

Diseases due to Deficiency (not enough)

Scurvy is a disease caused by the lack of vitamin C, symptoms include bleeding gums and terrible pain in the joints. Not enough vitamin A can cause *Night Blindness*, not being able to see well at night. Lack of calcium and vitamin D can cause *Rickets*, weak and underdeveloped bones. Iron deficiency causes *Anaemia*, symptoms are tiredness and lethargy (a lack of energy).

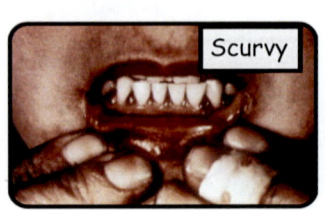

Scurvy

WHAT?
A portion of broccoli has as much vitamin C as a whole orange. The mushroom is the only plant based source of vitamin D. The banana is classed as a berry, but strawberries, raspberries and blackberries aren't! McDonald's sell about 70 hamburgers per second (don't eat too many!). White spots on your nails are not usually caused by calcium deficiency, they are normally just nail bruises.

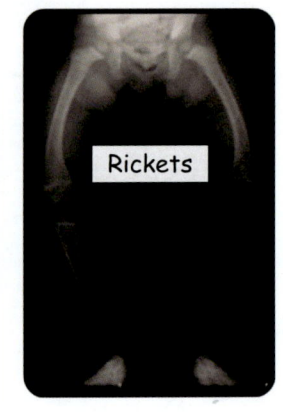

Rickets

Questions on the Healthy Human Diet

Comprehension

1.	What is a healthy diet all about?	9.	Where do starchy foods mainly come from?
2.	Complete the sentence; There isn't a............... food that contains everything we need.	10.	What are pulses and what food group are they a good source of?
3.	What do carbohydrates do?	11.	What kind of vegetables are a good source of iron?
4.	What is the main role of lipids?	12.	What causes scurvy?
5.	What helps you grow and repair tissue?	13.	What are the symptoms of scurvy?
6.	Give two examples of minerals needed by the body?	14.	What is night blindness?
7.	In what quantities are vitamins needed?	15.	What does lack of calcium and vitamin D cause?
8.	What is fibre and what does it do?		

Additional tasks

1. Match the food groups below to their use and memorise.

Carbohydrates	are used to help you grow and repair tissue
Fats or lipids	are essential organic (contain carbon) compounds needed for good health
Proteins	is needed to hydrate (provide water for) our cells and aids with digestion
Minerals	their main role is as an energy store
Vitamins	is undigested food, it provides your waste with bulk
Fibre	essential inorganic (don't contain carbon) compounds needed for good health
Water	provide energy

2. a. Use the Eat Well Plate to write down in order the types of foods we should eat most of, to the types of food we should eat least of.

   b. Write down which food groups you would get too much of and which too little of if you ate the following:

   i. Only fruit and vegetables

   ii. Only dairy foods

   iii. Only meat, fish, eggs and beans

3. Match the vitamins and minerals below to what they help keep healthy.

VITAMIN C	healthy bones
IRON	healthy vision
VITAMIN D	healthy blood
CALCIUM	healthy bones
VITAMIN A	healthy skin

4. Design a healthy diet for the five days of the working week to include breakfast, lunch, dinner and a snack. Choose from the foods below or use your own.

Breakfast;

Two pieces of toast, bowl of cereal, two crumpets, bowl of porridge, bacon sandwich, sausage sandwich, egg sandwich, full English, crisps, chocolate bar, can of pop.

Lunch;

Cheese sandwich, fish and chips, toasted sandwich, ham sandwich, tuna sandwich, burritos, beans on toast, sausage roll, chips, sausages, spaghetti bolognese, lasagne, chilli con carne, curry and rice, pizza, pasta, baked potato with topping, apple, banana, orange, grapes, pear, packet of crisps, chocolate bar, can of pop, apple pie and custard, slice of cake, snack bar, biscuits.

Dinner;

Fish and chips, curry and rice, chilli con carne, beans on toast, mashed potatoes, meat and vegetables, chips, pizza, baked potato with topping, salad, noodles, pasta, spaghetti bolognese, cheese on toast, burritos, lasagne, burger and chips, ribs, fish pie, spaghetti on toast, cheese and potato pie, chicken and chips.

Food Fuel

Food literally (meaning really) is our fuel. A fuel is something we burn to provide heat. Humans slowly burn food through respiration in our cells, producing the heat we need to stay alive. Humans have to maintain a body temperature of 37°C.

If humans consume more energy from food than they use in daily activities, they gain weight. If they consume less energy from food than they use in daily activities, they lose weight. Energy is measured in joules, but for foods we use kilojoules (kJ). Kilo means thousand, kilojoules are thousands of joules. 1 kJ is 1000J, 5kJ is 5000J etc. Using kilojoules is easier than millions of joules (1000kJ is 1 million joules). An **average adult** requires about **8,400kJ** of energy per day. An average child a bit less, apart from in their teenage years when they are growing quickly. These averages also vary a lot depending on what activities we do.

Pen Hadow, an arctic explorer consumed **22,000kJ** a day on his expedition to the North Pole, but burnt **30,000kJ** a day. He lost 17kg (nearly 3 stones). An adult just sitting and watching television all day still uses around **8,000kJ.** You don't need to make sure that you eat exactly the same amount each day, but you do have to be careful not to overeat (put on weight) or undereat (lose weight) for long periods of time.

North pole expedition required a lot of energy

Food Labels: Comparing Energy Values

Nutritional information usually tells you how much energy, protein, fat, carbohydrates, fibre and salt is in the food. This is often given per item (like a biscuit), per 100g or as a percentage reference intake. Percentage reference intake (%RI), tells us the **percentage** of the **maximum** amount an adult should eat for that food group **per day**. The daily reference intake of fat, for example, is a maximum of 70g for an adult. Using the food label below for **fat**, 100g of **chocolate biscuits** gives 28 ÷ 70 = 0.40 or 40% of our %RI of fat. An adult eating chocolate biscuits alone would need to eat 8400KJ ÷ 220KJ = 38 biscuits to gain their daily energy requirements. However, this would mean they are eating too much fat and not enough protein, carbohydrate, fibre or salt. If they did the same with **boiled potatoes** they would have to eat nearly 2.5kg to gain their daily energy requirement.

Nutritional information;	chocolate	biscuits	% RI
	Per biscuit	Per 100g	Per 100g
Energy	220 kJ	2200 kJ	26%
Protein	.54 g	5.4 g	11%
Fat	2.8 g	28 g	40%
of which are Saturated fats	1.4 g	14 g	
Carbohydrates	6.2 g	62 g	24%
of which are sugars	4.4 g	44 g	
Dietary fibre	0.4 g	4.0 g	13%
Sodium (salt)	.08 g	0.8g	13%

Nutritional information;	boiled potatoes	% RI
	Per 100g	Per 100g
Energy	340 kJ	4%
Protein	1.9 g	3.8%
Fat	0.1 g	0.1%
of which are Saturated fats	0 g	
Carbohydrates	20 g	7.7%
of which are sugars	1 g	
Dietary fibre	1.8 g	6%
Sodium (salt)	0.007 g	0.12%

This would have far too many carbohydrates, too much fibre and not enough protein, fat or salt. Clearly we need a balanced diet to be healthy, this means eating a bit of all types of food is really important and looking at the eat well plate helps us with this (pg12).

WHAT?

Your brain is the organ that uses the most energy, 20%, so thinking, reading and doing homework helps burn energy. Unsurprisingly fat has the most energy out of the food groups so cutting down on fat is a good way to lose weight.

Swimming
3000KJ per hour

Running
3800KJ per hour

Walking
1400KJ per hour

Questions on Food Fuel

Comprehension

1. What is a fuel?

2. Through what process do humans slowly burn their food?

3. What happens if humans consume more energy than they use in daily activities?

4. What is energy measured in?

5. What does Kilo mean?

6. How many joules are in 5kJ?

7. What does the value of 8400kJ tell us?

8. In which years does a child need more energy and why?

9. What does the nutritional information on food labels usually tell us?

10. How is this information often given?

11. What does %RI tell us?

12. If an adult just ate biscuits, which food group would they be eating too much of?

13. What wouldn't they get enough of?

14. What do we mean by a balanced diet?

Additional tasks

1. Use a calculator to complete the %RI columns for **100g** of the **Multigrain cereal** and the **Cheese and onion sandwich** below. The reference intakes are;

   energy 8400kJ, protein 50g, fat 70g, carbohydrate 260g, fibre 30g, Sodium (salt) 6g.

   <u>Example (boiled potatoes opposite page);</u>

   *%RI **energy** = 340 ÷ **8400** = 0.04 (x by 100 to get 4%)*

   *%RI **protein** = 1.9 ÷ **50** = 0.038 (x by 100 to get 3.8%)*

   *%RI **carbohydrates** = 20 ÷ **260** = 0.077 (x by 100 to get 7.7%)*

Nutritional information;	Multigrain cereal	% RI
	Per 100g	Per 100g
Energy	1500 kJ	
Protein	9.3 g	
Fat	2.9 g	
of which are saturated fats	0.6g	
Carbohydrates	69 g	
of which are sugars	17g	
Dietary fibre	12 g	
Sodium (salt)	0.5 g	

Nutritional information;	Cheese and onion sandwich brown bread	% RI
	Per 100g	Per 100g
Energy	1200 kJ	
Protein	10 g	
Fat	16.5 g	
of which are saturated fats	0.6g	
Carbohydrates	42g	
of which are sugars	2 g	
Dietary fibre	6 g	
Sodium (salt)	1.7 g	

2. One of the ways to measure the amount of energy in foods is to burn the food and use the flame to heat up water. To calculate the energy value (in joules) of the food you've burned, just multiply the **mass of the water (in grams)** by the **temperature change of the water (in °C)** and then **multiply by 4.2**.

a. Explain how you could measure the mass of water in the test tube (what mass will you measure first?).

b. Explain how you could measure the temperature change of the water.

c. **Dividing** the **energy value found from burning the food**, by the **mass of food burned** tells us the *energy value per gram* of that food, the **energy density**. Calculate the energy densities of some common foods in the table below.

	Potatoes	Biscuits	Crisps	Peanuts	Cereal	Banana
Energy found by burning food (J)	17,000	40,000	70,000	100,000	15,000	14,000
Mass of food burned (g)	5	2	3	4	1	4
Energy density (J/g)						

The Human Digestive System

We can 'think' of the digestion process as starting on your plate, here food is cut into smaller pieces.

The purpose of digestion is to turn large insoluble pieces of food into the smaller soluble molecules that it is made from. This provides nutrition and energy for our bodies. Digestion really starts in our mouths where the food is broken up, ground down and digestive juices from saliva are added. It ends with our faeces (waste matter) in the rectum, where this indigestible food is stored. Finally, our waste is excreted (the process of expelling waste) from the anus.

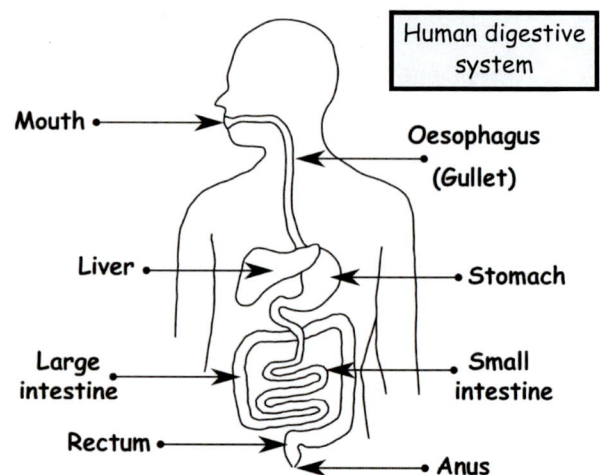

Human digestive system

Mouth • Oesophagus (Gullet) • Liver • Stomach • Large intestine • Small intestine • Rectum • Anus

The Order of Events

1. Food is chewed in our mouth and the digestive juice **saliva** is added before being swallowed.

2. The food passes down the gullet where it is helped on its way by **peristalsis** (muscle contractions pushing the food along the gullet). This is similar to squashing toothpaste out of a tube.

Peristalsis

3. On entering the stomach, the food is churned (squashed and mixed through contractions) with strong hydrochloric acid (pH 1-2). The acidic conditions kill bacteria and help the digestive juices to work well.

4. In the **small intestine** more digestive juices are added, also **bile** from the **liver** to help break down fats. The broken down food is absorbed into the blood here.

5. The food (now mostly undigestible waste) then passes into the **large intestine** where the only thing left to **absorb** is **water**.

6. After the water is absorbed, our waste faeces (poo) is more solid. The faeces passes to the rectum for storage before we go to the toilet and excrete it through the anus.

Bacteria are Important too

Our digestive system contains trillions of micro-organisms, living organisms so small you need a microscope to see them. So many they would weigh about 1kg. The waste **they** produce makes up about half of our faeces. They help us produce some important vitamins and absorb some nutrients. A healthy digestive system needs these bacteria and foods that boost gut bacteria are called **probiotics**.

Gut bacteria

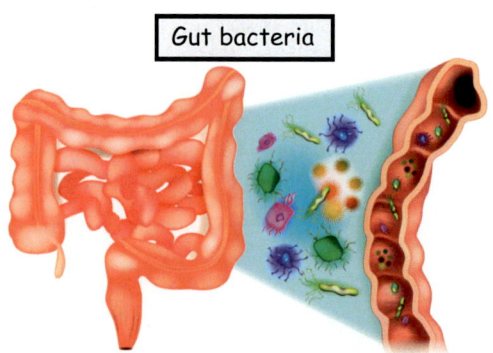

Probiotic yogurt

WHAT?

Your entire digestive system is about 10 metres long! Food takes about 5 seconds to reach your stomach. Peristalsis means if you ate upside down food would still get to your stomach. Our mouths make about one litre of saliva every day. The digestive system contains about 500 different bacteria all playing their part.

Questions on the Human Digestive System

Comprehension

1.	Why can we 'think' of digestion as starting on the plate?
2.	What is the purpose of digestion?
3.	Where does digestion really start?
4.	Where does digestion end?
5.	What does excretion mean?
6.	What is saliva an example of?
7.	Where does food go after entering the mouth and before reaching the stomach?
8.	What helps it on its way and what is it similar to?
9.	What does churned in the stomach mean?
10.	Why are the acidic conditions useful?
11.	What does bile do and where does it come from?
12.	What happens to the broken down food in the small intestines?
13.	How could the food be described in the large intestine?
14.	What is the only thing left to absorb in the large intestine?
15.	What is another word for waste faeces?
16.	Why is it more solid at this stage?
17.	What is the name for the part of the digestive system where faeces is stored?
18.	Where are faeces finally excreted?

Additional tasks

1. Label and memorise the names of the organs in the human digestive system shown below.

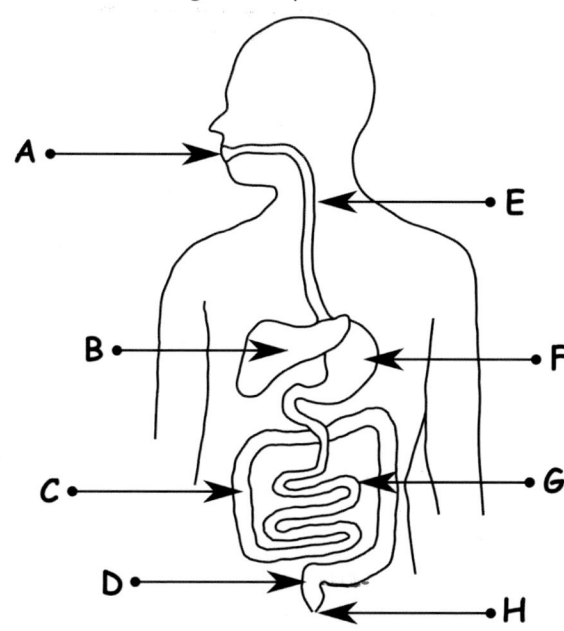

A. Mouth
B. Liver
C. Large intestine
D. Rectum
E. Gullet (Osophagus).
F. Stomach
G. Small intestine.
H. Anus

2. Write **1** to **11** next to the mixed up order of events for digestion to put them in their correct order. 1 first, 11 last

_1_ water is absorbed from the faeces
_2_ food moves down the gullet
_3_ food is chewed
_4_ food enters the stomach
_5_ saliva is added
_6_ food is churned
_7_ faeces is stored in the rectum
_8_ food moves to small intestine
_9_ faeces excreted from anus
_10_ bile is added
_11_ undigestible food moves to large intestine

3. Write about why 'bacteria are important too', include the words; **micro-organism, faeces, vitamins, nutrients, gut bacteria, probiotics.**

Bacteria are important too

Enzymes, their Role in Digestion and Other Uses

Enzymes act as catalysts. Catalysts speed up chemical reactions without being 'used up'. Enzymes are called **biological catalysts** because they speed up chemical reactions in living organisms. They are produced by the organism itself. No enzymes would mean no living humans! They are vital in allowing chemical reactions to proceed fast enough to keep us alive, for example, digesting our food.

Digestive Enzymes

There are three main types of enzyme in the human digestive system. **Protease** for breaking down proteins, **carbohydrase** for breaking down carbohydrates and **lipase** for breaking down fats (lipids). **Amylase** is a well known **carbohydrase** and **pepsin** a well know **protease**. A little like using scissors to cut up a paper chain, enzymes break down longer undigestible food molecules into smaller digestible ones. **Starch** is a **long carbohydrate** molecule made from connected **sugar** molecules (blue circles). It is broken down by the enzyme amylase, like in the diagram shown below. The sugar molecules are then able to be absorbed into the blood through the gut wall in the small intestines.

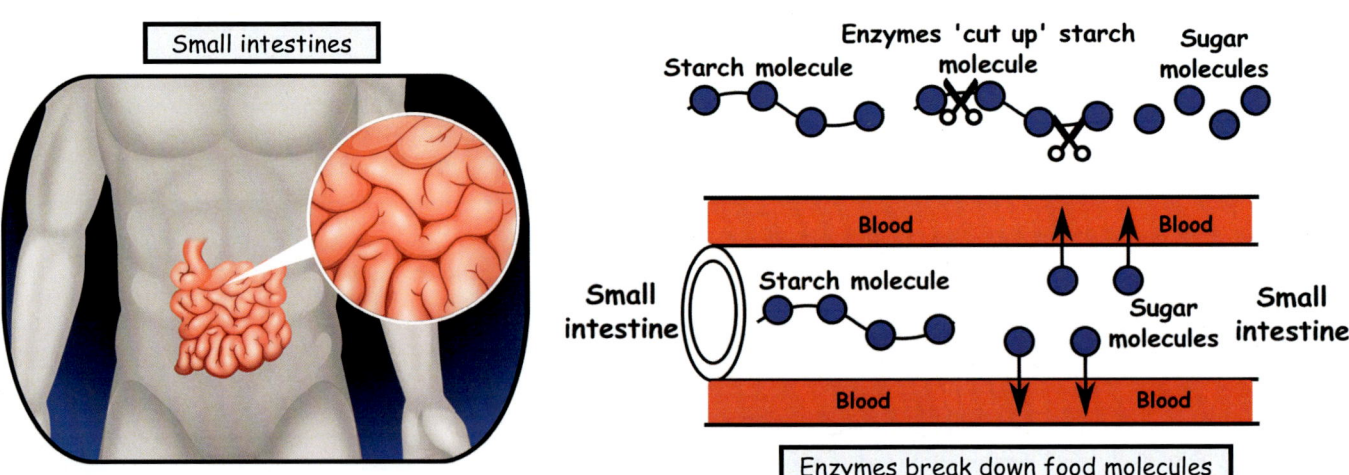

Other Uses of Enzymes

Protease can be added to washing powder, this can help it to break down stains that may contain protein, such as blood stains, stains from baby foods or dairy products. Protease is also used in baby foods to help break down proteins to make it easier for the baby to digest the food. Another example is using enzymes in making chocolates, **invertase** is an enzyme used for breaking down sugar and is injected into chocolates to give them a soft centre. An enzyme called **rennet** is used to thicken milk to make cheese. Enzymes in **yeast** convert sugar into alcohol and carbon dioxide giving us fizzy booze!

Enzymes in yeast can produce alcohol

Invertase gives chocolates a soft centre

Rennet is used to make cheese

Enzymes in washing powder breakdown stains

WHAT?

Enzymes are secreted (produced) by the mouth, stomach (and bacteria in the stomach too!), pancreas, and small intestines. Unfortunately, even if you're hungry eating grass is pointless, humans don't produce an enzyme called cellulase to be able to break down cellulose in grass. Cows do though and they have specially adapted stomachs.

Questions on Enzymes

Comprehension

1.	What do enzymes do? *they speed up chemical reactions speed them up*	9.	What is starch?
2.	What do catalysts do to chemical reactions?	10.	Which well known enzyme breaks down starch into simple sugars?
3.	Why are enzymes called biological catalysts?	11.	What does adding protease to washing powder help with?
4.	What produces the enzymes?	12.	Protease in baby foods breaks down protein, how is this helpful?
5.	How many main types of enzyme are there in the human digestive system?	13.	Why is invertase injected into chocolates?
6.	Which enzyme breaks down proteins?	14.	What can enzymes in yeast do?
7.	What does lipase do?	15.	Which enzyme is used in cheese making?
8.	What do enzymes act like in breaking down undigestible food molecules?		

Additional tasks

1. Match the words below to their meanings and memorise.

Catalysts	enzymes that break down carbohydrates
Enzymes	enzyme for breaking down sugar (sucrose)
Carbohydrase	substances that speed up chemical reactions without being used up
Protease	enzymes that break down fats (lipids)
Lipase	enzymes that break down proteins
Invertase	biological catalysts

2. Complete the gap filling exercise below on enzymes. Choose from the words in bold.

carbohydrase, soluble, chemical, used, digest, insoluble, protease, sugars, catalysts, fats, amino, lipase, oils, proteins

Enzymes are biological _____. This means they speed up _____ reactions without being _____ up. Enzymes help us _____ our food. They breakdown larger _____ molecules into smaller _____ ones. _____ enzymes break down _____ into _____ acids, _____ enzymes break down carbohydrates into _____ and _____ enzymes break down _____ and _____.

3. Write a few sentences about how our lives are made better because of enzymes (NB: the petrol that we put in our cars is 5% alcohol).

4. **Proteins** are **big molecules** made from **smaller molecules** linked together called **amino acids** (shown as triangles below). Complete the diagram below (exactly the same as the one of starch being broken down into sugar opposite), showing proteins being broken down into **amino acids** by the enzyme **protease**. Don't forget the scissors showing the protein molecule being cut into amino acids.

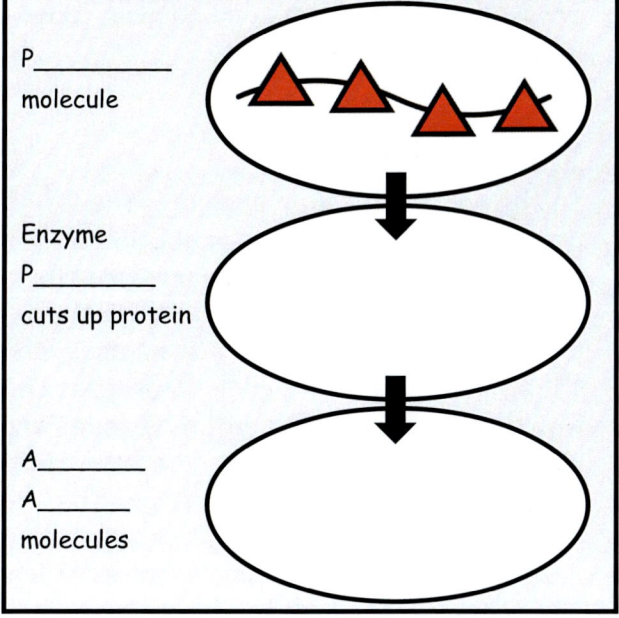

P_____ molecule

Enzyme P_____ cuts up protein

A_____
A_____ molecules

Plants and Energy Flow: Food Chains and Webs

No plants, no animal life. Plants are known as the **producers** because they are able to make (produce) their own food using the energy from sunlight. All animals on the other hand are **consumers** (eaters) of the food made by plants. These can be animals like **herbivores**, that eat plants only, or **carnivores** that eat other animals only, or **omnivores** that eat other animals **and** plants like humans.

Food Chains

Plants use the solar energy (light) from the sun to make glucose (sugar) and grow. This energy is passed along from producer to consumer in a **food chain.** The arrow shows the direction of energy flow. Animals that eat plants only (herbivores) are known as **primary consumers**. Animals that eat primary consumers are called **secondary consumers**. Secondary consumers can be carnivores or omnivores.

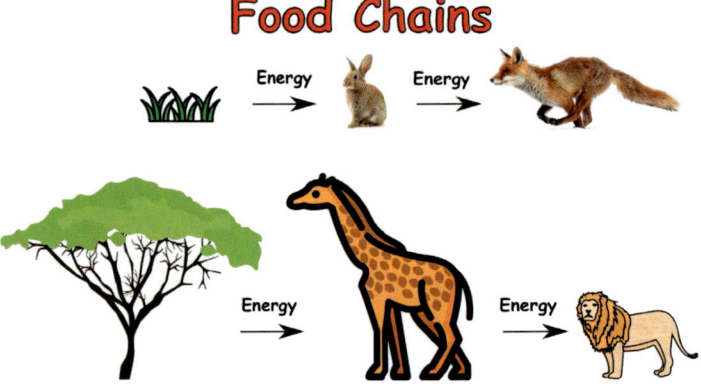

Food Chains

> ### WHAT?
>
> Apex predators are predators at the top of a food chain and have no natural predators in that ecosystem, a killer whale is an example. The position an organism occupies in a food chain is called a trophic level. Trophic level 1 is the producers.
>
> Only about 10% of the energy in a food chain is passed to the next level as an animal's biomass (amount of living material). Energy is lost as heat, faeces and for movement.

Food Webs

Since animals usually eat more than one thing, food webs can show how many food chains can connect to each other (interlink). Food webs can get complicated when there are a lot of animals and plants in an **ecosystem**. An ecosystem is the plants and animals found in a certain location.

A pond ecosystem

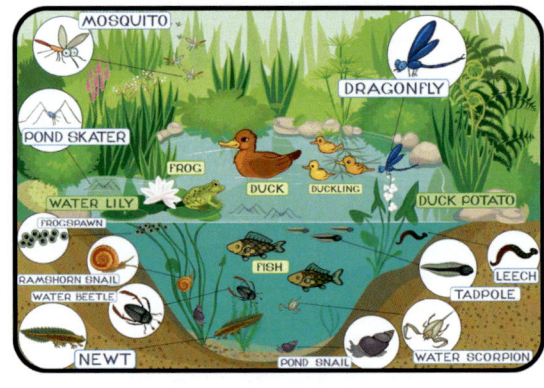

Predators and Prey

In the food web shown opposite, the primary consumers are the rabbit and sheep. The secondary consumers are the wolf and the fox (predators). If another predator like a hawk entered the ecosystem, the number of rabbits could decrease. This would mean more sheep eaten by foxes and wolves. This could bring them into conflict (a competition over who should get the available food). If there isn't enough available resources, one of the animals may even leave the ecosystem to look for food elsewhere.

Food Web

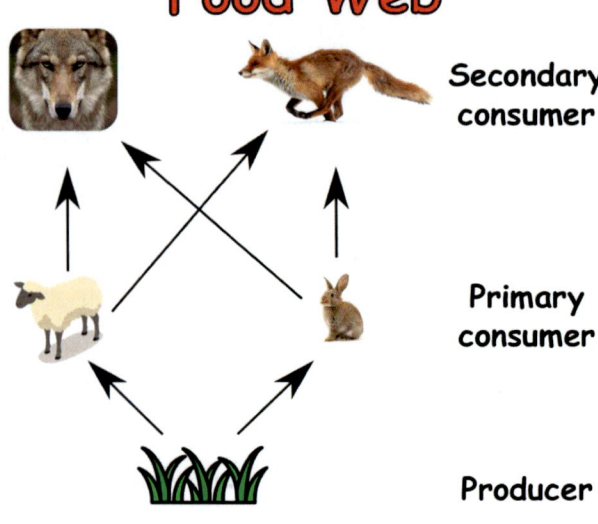

Secondary consumer

Primary consumer

Producer

Questions on Plants and Energy Flow: Food Chains and Webs

Comprehension

1.	What would happen to animal life with no plants?
2.	Why are plants called producers?
3.	What do herbivores eat?
4.	What do animals called omnivores eat?
5.	What is the name of an animal that eats only other animals?
6.	What do plants use light for?
7.	What happens to the energy in a food chain?
8.	What do primary consumers eat?
9.	What do food webs show?
10.	What do we call the plants and animals found in a certain location?
11.	What would happen if a hawk entered the ecosystem?
12.	What might the foxes and wolves do if this happened?
13.	What do we mean by conflict?
14.	What might one of the animals do to avoid this conflict?
15.	What are predators at the top of the food chain called? (WHAT? box)
16.	How is energy 'lost' as it moves between levels in a food chain? (WHAT? box)

Additional tasks

1. Match and memorise the words below.

Producer	animals that eat meat (other animals) only
Consumers	animals that eat plants only
Glucose	amount of living material
Biomass	a sugar
Herbivores	animals that eat plants and meat (other animals)
Carnivores	the animals
Omnivores	the plants

2. Draw food chains for the following *jumbled up* producers and consumers.

a. ***rabbit, grass, snake***

b. ***mouse, seeds, hawk***

c. aphids, leaf, ladybirds

d. hawk, caterpillar, robin, cabbage

e. tuna, zooplankton (tiny ocean animals), herring, shark

f. humans, cow, grass

g. greenfly, spider, leaf, ladybird

h. grass, hawk, snake, vole

3. Write the food chains **a** and **b** above side by side and show how they can connect to form a **food web** like the one opposite (pg20).

4. Write down **four** food chains from the food web opposite (pg20).

5. Out of the two food chains shown below, which is best for the planet and wastes least energy? Explain why. (The WHAT? box opposite helps)

Wheat ⟶ Humans

Wheat ⟶ Cows ⟶ Humans

6. Complete the food chain word search below.

TROPHICLEVEL, ECOSYSTEM, HERBIVORE, OMNIVORE, CONSUMER, BIOMASS, ENERGYFLOW, PHOTOSYNTHESIS, CARNIVORE, PRODUCER

```
T R O P H I C L E V E L A B C
D E F H G H I J K B L M N O P
Q R S O T U V W X I Y Z Z C M
W T V T W L B N H O A N T A Q
Q R F O G A E O U M V A U R E
L V P S O P J C Y A K O Z N Q
M J V Y B X H T O S D H P I C
E A V N E B H E P S O X K V D
L C P T J E N E R G Y F L O W
A V N H X Y C C O B F S R R A
F V K E Y Q A S D S I E T E B
C O N S U M E R U H U V U E J
N B K I N D W E C K U L O A M
C G F S J M Z Y E J V Z G R X
P G O M N I V O R E J K T X E
```

The Respiratory System: Breathing

To respire means to breathe. This means getting air into and out of our lungs. We respire so that our cells can get the **oxygen** (O_2) they need for respiration. **Respiration** is a chemical reaction which **releases energy**. As well as inhaling (breathing in) to get oxygen, we also exhale (breathe out) to get rid of the waste gas from respiration.

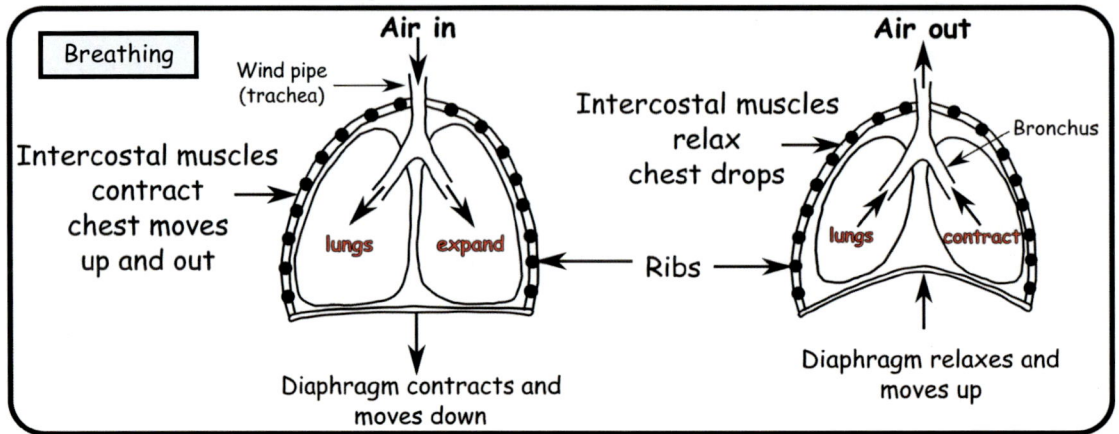

The waste gas is carbon dioxide (CO_2). The air we breathe in contains about **21%** oxygen. The air we breathe out contains about **16.5%** oxygen and **4.5%** carbon dioxide. This tells us that oxygen is taken in by the lungs and carbon dioxide is removed.

How it happens

Breathing in: A thin muscle at the bottom of your chest called the **diaphragm** contracts (shortens) and moves down. Muscles called **intercostal muscles** in the ribcage also contract making the chest move up and out. This causes the space inside the lungs to increase. This means that the air pressure **inside** the lungs is **less** than **outside**, so air is **pushed** into the lungs.

Breathing out: The diaphragm muscle relaxes (lengthens) and the intercostal muscles also relax causing the rib cage to drop down and the chest to contract at the same time. This decreases the space inside the lungs, increases the air pressure and pushes the air out of the lungs.

Gas Exchange

By this we mean getting oxygen in and carbon dioxide out of the blood. This process happens through tiny air sacs in the lungs called **alveoli**. There are a lot of them (about 600 million) and each one is in contact (touching) with a very thin blood vessel called a **capillary**. Blood where the oxygen has been used up is pumped to the lungs and travels through the capillaries where it absorbs oxygen through diffusion. There is a higher concentration of oxygen in the lungs than the capillaries. Carbon dioxide moves the other way through diffusion, because there is more carbon dioxide in the blood (capillaries) than the lungs.

WHAT?

The average person breathes more than 5 litres of air every minute. The alveoli of the lungs can stretch to the size of a tennis court. This large surface area improves oxygen absorption. The right lung is bigger than the left lung which has to make room for the heart. We breathe out nearly half a litre of water every day! Women and children breath faster than men.

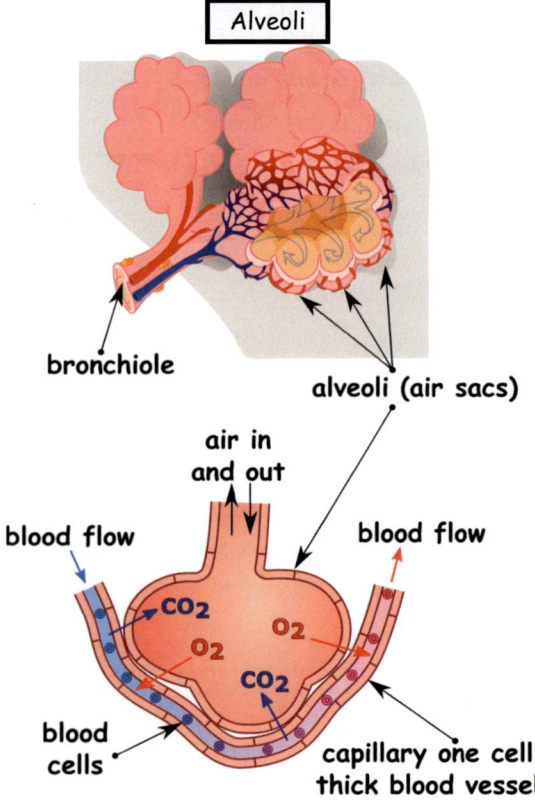

22

Questions on The Respiratory System: Breathing

Comprehension

1. What does respire mean?
2. Why do we respire?
3. What does respiration do?
4. What is the waste gas from respiration?
5. How much oxygen is in the air we breathe in and how much in what we breathe out?
6. What does this tell us?
7. What is the diaphragm?
8. What does contract mean?
9. What happens to the space inside the lungs when we breath in?
10. What does this do to the air pressure inside the lungs?
11. What does this mean will happen?
12. In breathing out what does the increase in pressure in the lungs do?
13. What do we mean by gas exchange?
14. What are the tiny air sacs in the lungs called?
15. How many are there?
16. What are the alveoli touching?
17. Through what process is oxygen absorbed into the capillaries?
18. Why does carbon dioxide move the other way?

Additional tasks

1. Put the descriptions below in the correct order to describe **breathing in** and **breathing out**.

Breathing in

Diaphragm contracts, lung space increases, air pushed into lungs, air pressure inside lungs decreases, intercostal muscles contract

_____ → _____ → _____
→ _____ → _____

Breathing out

intercostal muscles relax, air pushed out of lungs, Diaphragm relaxes, air pressure inside lungs increases, lung space decreases

_____ → _____ → _____
→ _____ → _____

2. Label your own version of the alveoli (air sac) below using the diagram opposite.

3. Below is a model of the lungs, when the rubber balloon (diaphragm) is pulled down the lungs inflate. When it is released they deflate. Explain why.

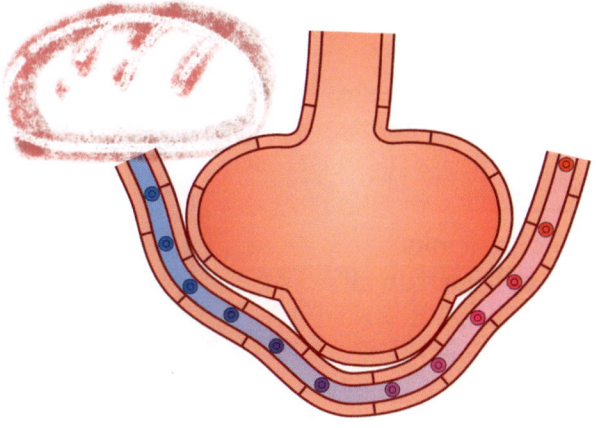

Aerobic and Anaerobic Respiration

Aerobic means involving oxygen, anaerobic means not involving oxygen. All living things are made up of cells and these cells **release energy** through a process called **respiration**. Respiration can happen with or without oxygen. If it happens **with oxygen**, it is called **aerobic respiration**, if it happens **without oxygen** it is called **anaerobic respiration**. The energy comes from the food that we have digested (chemical energy), most of this is in the form of glucose. Glucose is a simple sugar molecule, we can think of glucose as the body's fuel. The chemical reaction between glucose and oxygen in respiration releases energy. This energy fuels our life processes such as growth, reproduction and movement amongst others. The products of aerobic respiration are carbon dioxide gas and water. These are expelled (forced out) from the body through the lungs when we breathe.

The word equation below summarises the reaction for aerobic respiration.

| Glucose + Oxygen ⟶ Carbon dioxide + Water + Energy |
| (Reactants)   (Products) |

This is the same equation as for combustion (burning) of a fuel. This is why aerobic respiration is sometimes called '**slow burning**'.

Not Enough Oxygen?

If the blood cannot supply enough oxygen to our cells for aerobic respiration and we are asking our bodies to do a lot of work, for example, running, our cells can release energy through anaerobic respiration too. This doesn't work as well (is less efficient) as aerobic respiration but does make more energy available if not enough oxygen is present.

Unfortunately there is a down side to anaerobic respiration, **lactic acid** is produced. This leads to **muscle pain** and causes our muscles to 'burn' and feel very tired (fatigued). The equation for anaerobic respiration is shown below.

| Glucose ⟶ Lactic acid + Energy |

Ouch!

Fermentation (brewing) and Baking

Louis Pasteur discovered that yeast (a single celled organism, part of the fungus family) could undergo aerobic and anaerobic respiration. Aerobic respiration is used in making **bread** because a lot of carbon dioxide gas is given off which makes the bread rise. This part of the bread making process is called **proofing**.

| Glucose + Oxygen $\xrightarrow{yeast}$ Carbon dioxide + Water + Energy |

Anaerobic respiration is used in **brewing**, the products are carbon dioxide and ethanol (alcohol). This process is called **fermentation**.

| Glucose $\xrightarrow{yeast}$ Carbon dioxide + Ethanol (alcohol) |

The carbon dioxide produced, helps to make many alcoholic drinks fizzy. Champagne is fermented twice. The first time, yeast uses up all the sugars from the grapes and fermentations stops. The second fermentation happens in the bottle, more yeast and some sugar is added to the bottle, it is then sealed. The carbon dioxide produced in the bottle cannot escape and this makes champagne fizzy and gives us the celebratory pop.

Questions on Aerobic and Anaerobic Respiration

Comprehension

1. What does aerobic mean?
2. Through what process do cells release energy?
3. What is respiration without oxygen called?
4. In what form does most of our energy come from?
5. Give three examples of life processes.
6. What are the products of aerobic respiration?
7. What does expelled mean?
8. Why is respiration sometimes called slow burning?
9. When might our bodies require anaerobic respiration?
10. What is the downside to anaerobic respiration?
11. What does this lead to?
12. What did Louis Pasteur discover?
13. What is yeast?
14. Why is aerobic respiration used in bread making?
15. What is another word for ethanol?
16. What are the products of fermentation?

Additional tasks

1. Match the words below to their meanings and memorise.

Aerobic	the release of energy in a cell
Anaerobic	single celled organism used in brewing and baking
Respiration	involving oxygen
Lactic acid	anaerobic respiration by yeast producing alcohol and carbon dioxide
Yeast	not involving oxygen
Fermentation	an acid produced during anaerobic respiration that causes muscle 'burn'

2. 130 Year 8 students see how many push ups they can do before lactic acid causes enough pain that they have to stop. Plot a bar chart of the results with number of students on the y-axis (vertical) and number of push ups on the x-axis (horizontal). See pg50 for example bar chart.

Number of students	1	2	4	8	15	24	28	22	12	7	4	2	1
Number of push ups	4	5	6	7	8	9	10	11	12	13	14	15	16

3. a. The following are the chemical formulae for carbon dioxide, oxygen, water, glucose, ethanol and lactic acid (they are not in order!). O_2, $C_6H_{12}O_6$, CO_2, H_2O, $C_3H_6O_3$, C_2H_5OH (ethanol). All apart from lactic acid can be found in the book (use the index). Select the correct formula and write it in the correct place to make a formula equation for the following:

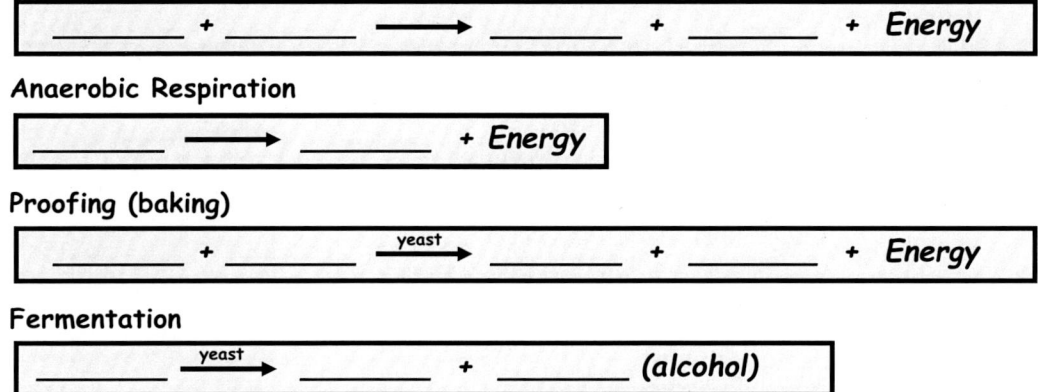

Aerobic Respiration

_____ + _____ ⟶ _____ + _____ + *Energy*

Anaerobic Respiration

_____ ⟶ _____ + *Energy*

Proofing (baking)

_____ + _____ --yeast--> _____ + _____ + *Energy*

Fermentation

_____ --yeast--> _____ + _____ (alcohol)

b. The equations are **not** balanced. Use the anaerobic respiration equation to explain what we mean by this.

Exercise, Asthma and Smoking

Exercise is an activity which requires physical effort. Humans deliberately exercise to improve their health and fitness. Exercise helps strengthen your heart, increases your lung capacity and can improve blood circulation. It is also known to reduce the risk of heart disease, strokes, diabetes and cancer. On top of these benefits it also helps reduce stress (a state caused by demanding activities such as a test), puts us in a better mood, improves our energy levels and how well we sleep. Many of us don't get enough exercise, 5 to 18 year olds are recommended to have about an hour of exercise a day!

Immediate Effects of Exercise on the Body

Sweating

These are the things that happen straight away or during exercise. They include, the heart beating faster, an increase in body temperature and more blood pumped to the muscles instead of other parts of the body, for example, the digestive system. Also, blood flows near to our skin's surface to help us cool down, this is why we look red.

WHAT?

Over 5 million people in the UK are treated for asthma. Unfortunately, about three people per day die from asthma attacks.

As well as nicotine, tar and carbon monoxide, cigarette smoke contains over 4000 chemicals! Stopping smoking reduces your risk of a heart attack by half, one year after giving up.

Longer Term Effects on the Body

If you exercise regularly the longer term (weeks and months) effects are as follows: your muscles grow in size and strength, your tendons (hold muscles to the bone) and ligaments (hold bones together) get stronger, your heart becomes stronger, your resting pulse rate is slower and you recover from exertion faster. Bone density increases (meaning your bones are less likely to break) and you become more flexible. Your ability to sustain (keep going) physical effort also improves, called **stamina.**

Exercise builds muscles

strong

Asthma

Asthma is a disease (abnormal function) of the airways. It is a **chronic** condition (meaning it is **long term**, or constantly recurring). Symptoms are breathlessness and wheezing. It is caused by narrowing of a person's airways in the lungs and the build up of mucus. Attacks are triggered differently from person to person but exposure to traffic fumes, dust, pollen, animal hair and exercise are common causes. Sufferers who have asthma attacks can suddenly become short of breath, if this happens they need to use their reliever inhaler or if this does not help, call an ambulance.

Asthma

Smoking

Smoking cigarettes is **addictive** (difficult to stop once you've started), this is because of the drug **nicotine**. However, nicotine itself is not thought to be harmful but the tar and carbon monoxide gas from smoking is. **Tar exposure** is strongly linked to cancer and stops **cilia** (tiny hairs in our lungs that sweep out unwanted dust etc) from working properly. The **carbon monoxide** gas in smoke is **poisonous** and reduces the ability of our blood to transport oxygen around the body.

Tar damaged lung (right)

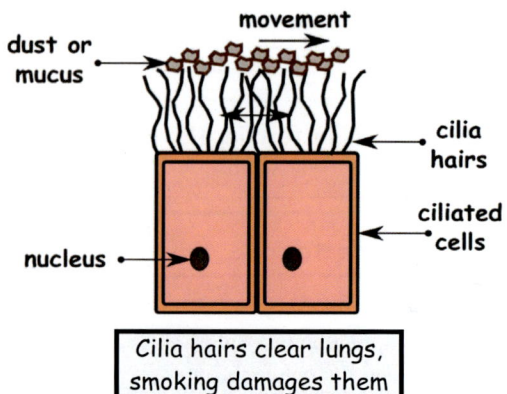

movement

dust or mucus

cilia hairs

ciliated cells

nucleus

Cilia hairs clear lungs, smoking damages them

Questions on Exercise, Asthma and Smoking

Comprehension

1. What do we mean by exercise?
2. Why do humans exercise?
3. What diseases is exercise known to reduce the risk of?
4. What does exercise do for our energy levels?
5. How much exercise is recommended for 5 to 18 year olds?
6. How is more blood pumped to the muscles during exercise?
7. What is the long term effect of exercise on your muscles?
8. What do your tendons do?
9. What holds your bones together?
10. Why is an increase in bone density good?
11. What does the condition asthma affect?
12. What does chronic mean?
13. What are the symptoms of asthma?
14. What can happen to a person's airways who has asthma?
15. What should someone who is having an asthma attack do?
16. Why is smoking addictive?
17. What is tar exposure linked to?
18. What are cilia and what do they do?
19. What is the negative (bad) effect of carbon monoxide?

Additional tasks

1. Match the words to their meanings below and memorise.

Exercise	the addictive drug from smoking
Stress	a disease of the airways leading to breathlessness and wheezing
Nicotine	an activity that requires physical effort
Asthma	a state caused by demanding activities
Tar	a toxic gas from smoking that reduces the ability of the blood to carry oxygen
Carbon monoxide	a sticky brown substance from smoking and the main cause of throat and lung cancer

2. Design a five day exercise regime for a 12 year old who should do about **one hour** of exercise per day.

Monday	Tuesday	Wednesday	Thursday	Friday

3. One of the ways to measure fitness is your **recovery heart rate**. This is the amount of time that it takes your heart rate (**beats per minute**) to return to its resting value after exercise. The table below gives data for the recovery rate of **six 40 year olds** asked to **run** at the **same speed** for **10 minutes**.

   a. Which adults do you think are 'fit'?

   b. Why do you think they were asked to run at the same speed for the same time?

Adult	1	2	3	4	5	6
Recovery time (mins)	1.5	8	2	10	7.5	9

   c. What would you advise the 'unfit' 40 year olds to do?

   d. What 'things' doesn't the data tell you that may affect the results?

Reproduction in Humans: Women

Sex cells are called **gametes** and are made in our reproductive organs. A woman's gametes (the eggs) are made in the ovaries and a man's gametes (the sperm) are made in the testes. If reproduction is to happen the sperm has to meet the egg. This type of reproduction is called **sexual reproduction,** half of the genes (information for making new cells) come from the woman and half from the man. All sexual reproduction has this in common, even in plants. Girls become sexually mature (able to release eggs) at about 14 years old. Chemical messengers called hormones stimulate the release of an egg about **once every 28 days**, this happens in the **middle** of the menstrual cycle, **day 14.**

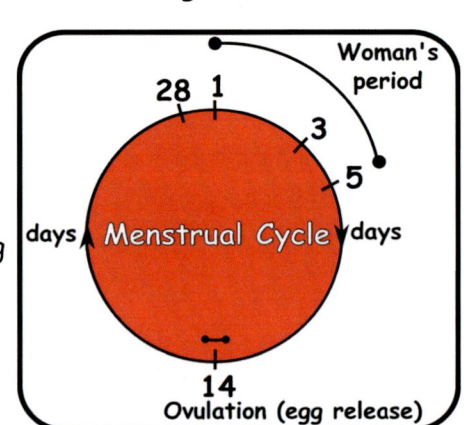

Fallopian tubes (oviducts)

Uterus (womb)

Ovary

Cervix

Vagina

Female reproductive system

The Menstrual Cycle

This describes how a woman's fertility changes over approximately one month. Starting at menstruation (when a woman's uterus lining breaks down and she bleeds, also called **having a period**) and calling this **day 1,** a woman will **bleed** for between **3-5 days.** At about day 14, hormone changes in a woman's body causes the ovaries to release a mature **egg** (called **ovulation**). The egg travels down the fallopian tube (oviduct) towards the uterus (or womb). The **egg** will stay **alive** in the fallopian tube and capable of being fertilised for about **12-24 hours.** Sperm must 'meet' the egg in the fallopian tube during this time for a woman to become pregnant. **Sperm** can live inside the woman for up to **5 days.** If the egg is not fertilised during this time it dies. **14 days** after ovulation (egg release) **day 28**, hormones cause the lining of the uterus to begin to break down again and **we are back at day 1** having another period. The main hormones involved in a woman's menstrual cycle are **estrogen** and **progesterone.**

Woman's period

28 1

3

5

days Menstrual Cycle days

14
Ovulation (egg release)

Fertilisation (Congratulations!)

Fertilisation means the fusion (joining) of sperm and egg. If this happens around day 14 of the cycle then a fertilised egg begins to grow. It grows by cell division: 1 cell becomes 2, 2 becomes 4, 4 becomes 8 etc, until we have a **ball of cells** called an **embryo.** The embryo moves along the fallopian tube and becomes implanted (fixed in position) on the lining of the uterus. Here it continues to grow forming a **placenta,** the placenta allows for nutrients and oxygen to pass from the mother to the baby and waste products to pass from the baby to the mother. After about eight weeks or so the embryo starts to develop **human features** that we recognise, we now call the embryo a **foetus.**

WHAT?

The name of a fertilised egg from a sperm is called a **zygote**, it is one cell containing half of the genes from the male and half from the female. When born a human baby is made from around 200 million cells. A baby's heart starts beating at about week six of pregnancy. A baby's heart beats about twice as fast as an adults.

Cell division

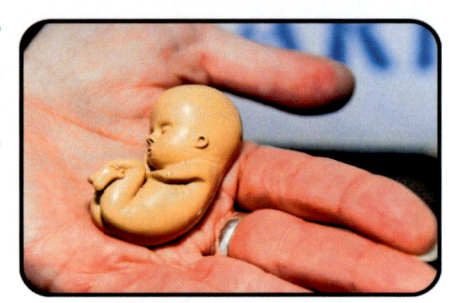

Life size foetus model

28

Questions on Reproduction in Humans: Women

Comprehension

1. What are gametes?
2. Where are a woman's gametes made?
3. What is made in the testes?
4. What is the name of the type of reproduction where sperm and egg meet?
5. What are hormones?
6. On what day is the egg released?
7. What does the menstrual cycle describe?
8. What happens when a woman's uterus lining breaks down?
9. What do we call this?
10. How long does a woman's period last?
11. What is the release of a mature egg called?
12. Where does the egg go after release from the ovaries?
13. How long does the egg stay alive?
14. What happens if the egg is not fertilised by a sperm?
15. What are the main hormones involved in a woman's menstrual cycle?
16. What does fertilisation mean?
17. How does the fertilised egg grow?
18. What does the placenta do?
19. What do we call the embryo after it starts to develop human features?

Additional tasks

1. Label and memorise the parts of a woman's reproductive system below.

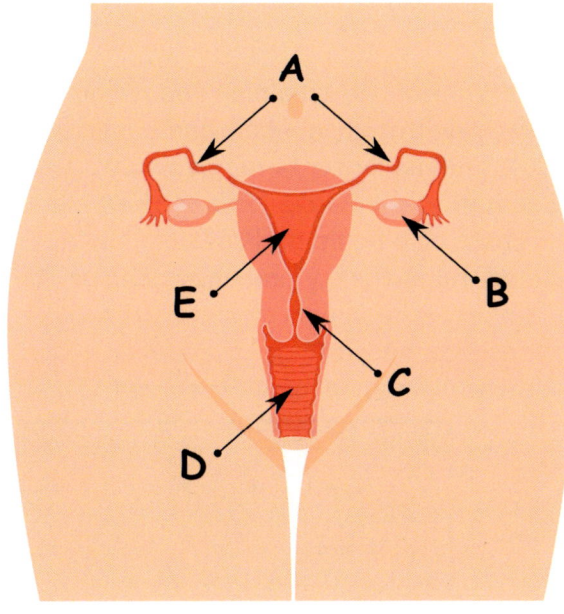

2. Solve the jumbled up letters to reveal words relating to the female reproductive system.

ESTRMUALN	_____
IOAREVS	_____
RUTESU	_____
FALTULOPANIBES	_____
GVAAIN	_____
TESOERNG	_____
EPORGTRONEES	_____
GAETESM	_____
ONUAVTILO	_____
OMWB	_____
ZOTEYG	_____

3. 'Join the dots' to show how the levels of progesterone and estrogen change during the menstrual cycle.

a. What do you think the rise in estrogen causes?

b. What do you think the drop in progesterone? causes?

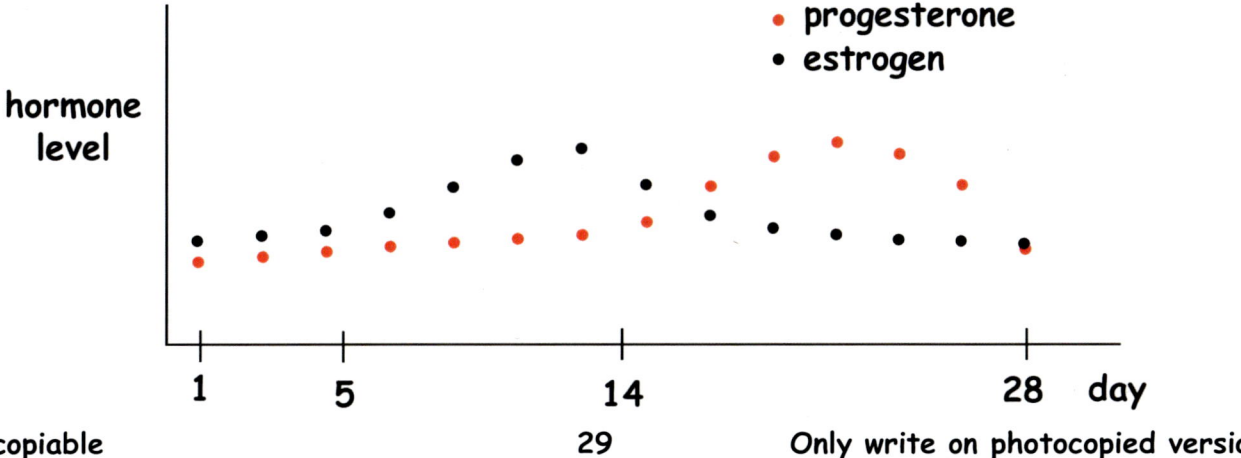

- progesterone
- estrogen

Reproduction in Humans: Men

In women the hormones which control the reproductive organs are **estrogen** and **progesterone**. In men the hormone is **testosterone** and is made in the **testes**. The testes (the often used slang term is balls) are found in a sac of skin called the **scrotum**. Boys become sexually mature (are able to release sperm) around age thirteen. The main job of the testes is to produce sperm (a male's gametes or sex cells) and testosterone. They produce sperm better at a temperature below our normal body temperature of 37°C (about 35°C is best). That is why they are kept in the scrotum which is outside of a man's body.

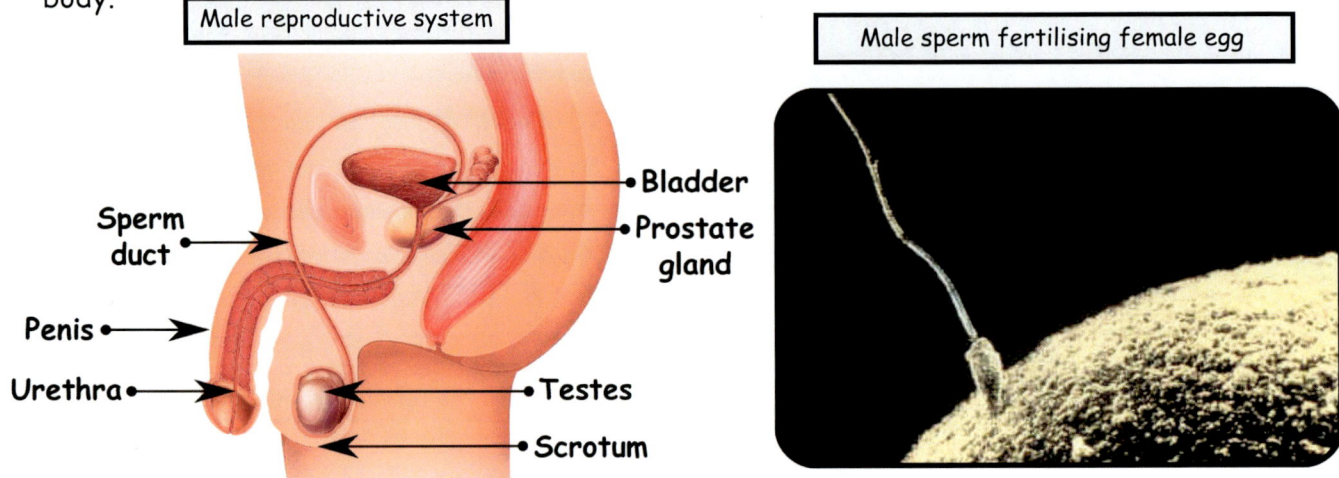

Male reproductive system

- Bladder
- Prostate gland
- Sperm duct
- Penis
- Urethra
- Testes
- Scrotum

Male sperm fertilising female egg

Sexual Intercourse

To have a baby, a man and a woman must have sexual intercourse. When a man and a woman both want to have sex they become aroused. A woman's vagina becomes moist and a man gets an erection (his penis fills with blood and becomes stiff). The man inserts his penis into the woman's vagina and the back and forth movement causes him to **ejaculate** (this is the pumping of semen into a woman's vagina). **Semen** is a mixture of a liquid and sperm. The liquid is made in the **prostate gland**. The liquid part of semen contains energy and enzymes for the sperm to do its job of reaching and fertilising the egg (ovum). The sperm swims up through the cervix and uterus into the fallopian tube where an egg may be waiting. If a sperm reaches the egg and fuses (joins together) with it, then the woman becomes pregnant. This normally happens around day 14 of a woman's cycle.

Pregnancy and Lifestyle

If a woman becomes pregnant her **gestation** period (time between becoming pregnant and giving birth) is about 9 months (around 40 weeks). During this time she will provide the baby with everything it needs, namely oxygen and food. A healthy diet becomes even more important and

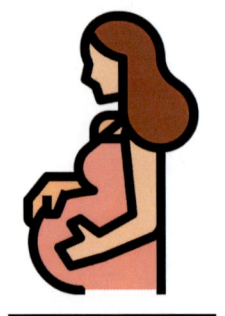

Pregnant woman

pregnant women do need more protein, iron, calcium and folic acid during pregnancy. **Folic acid** (vitamin B9), is particularly important since it reduces the risk of babies developing defects. Women normally take supplements of this before and during pregnancy. Substances such as chemicals from cigarette smoke and alcohol, can harm a baby because they can pass across the placenta into the baby's blood. Some babies are born addicted to drugs like heroin that the mother was using during pregnancy.

> **WHAT?**
>
> The sperm cell is the smallest cell in the human body. Men produce approximately 150 million sperms in one ejaculation! They are not 'fast' swimmers by our standards, they can swim about 20cm in one hour, although this is about 4000 times their own length. Sperm that is made by the testes but not ejaculated is just re-absorbed into the body.

Questions on Reproduction in Humans: Men

Comprehension

1. Which hormone controls the reproductive system in men?
2. Where is testosterone made?
3. What is the main job of the testes?
4. Where are a man's testes kept?
5. Why is it important that this is outside of the body?
6. To have a baby what must happen?
7. What happens to a woman's vagina before wanting sex?
8. What happens to a man's penis to get an erection?
9. What causes a man to ejaculate during sex?
10. Where is semen made?
11. What does the liquid part of semen contain?
12. What happens when an egg and sperm fuse?
13. What do we mean by gestation period?
14. How long is the gestation period for women?
15. What does the woman provide the baby with during pregnancy?
16. What does a woman need more of during pregnancy?
17. Why is folic acid important?
18. Why are alcohol and cigarette smoke harmful during pregnancy?
19. Why are some babies born addicted to drugs?

Additional tasks

1. Label and memorise the parts of a man's reproductive system below.

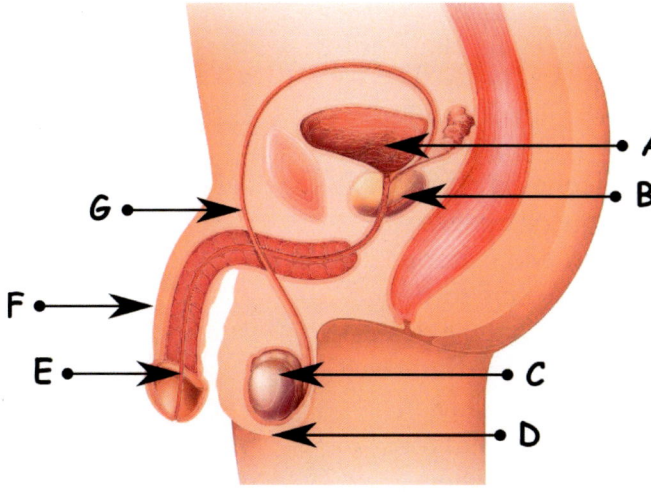

2. Complete the gap filling exercise on 'making a baby'.
   Choose from the words in bold below.

   pregnant, stimulates, ejaculate, sperm, egg, fallopian tube, penis, moist, sexually mature, ejaculate, cervix, fuses, ejaculate, periods

   To make a baby both a man and a woman must be _____ _____. This means that a man must be able to _____ and a woman must have started her _____.

   If a man can _____ he can release _____.

(CONTINUED)

If a woman has started her periods she is able to release an _____. If a man and woman are aroused, a man's _____ becomes hard and a woman's vagina _____. This allows for the penis to enter the vagina. On inserting his penis the man's back and forth motion _____ him to _____. On ejaculation sperm is released and swims up through the _____ and uterus into the _____ _____ where an egg may be waiting. If the sperm meets an egg and _____ the woman becomes _____.

3. Write down some ideas about why it is important for a woman to stay healthy during pregnancy.

4. Design a healthy diet for ONE DAY for a pregnant woman remembering that she will need more protein, iron and calcium. You can use the healthy human diet page to help (pg12).

Healthy diet

Drugs and their Impact

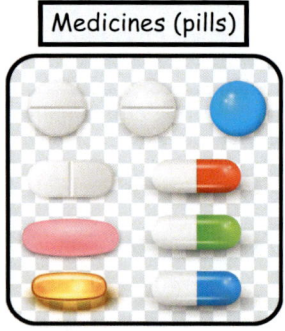
Medicines (pills)

A drug is a chemical substance that affects the way your body works. Drugs that help us get better from illness are called **medicines**. People also use **recreational** drugs for **pleasure**, because it makes them feel good. All drugs (medicines or recreational) can have side effects. Usually these are undesirable effects of the drug, for example, chemotherapy drugs can help us recover fully from cancer treatment, but one of the undesirable effects is that a person's hair may fall out. This can be a small price to pay for recovering from cancer but sometimes the negative side effects have to be carefully considered against the benefits.

Helpful Drugs (Medicines)

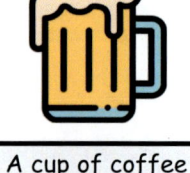
Headache

There are many commonly used medicines and our lives are better because of them. **Pain relief** medicines are an obvious example, **paracetamol** and **ibuprofen** are widely used. Operations are made painless by the use of **anaesthetics** (drugs that cause **loss of sensation**), these drugs can **stop the pain** from certain areas of the body or make us unconscious during an operation or relieve pain during childbirth. A well known anaesthetic is **morphine**. **Antibiotics** are drugs used to **kill bacterial infections**. They have enabled operations to be carried out with little risk of infection, before antibiotics many people died from infections following an operation. Antibiotics can treat many bacterial conditions such as kidney infections, pneumonia, conjunctivitis (eye infection) and some STDs (sexually transmitted diseases). However, antibiotics don't help colds and flu, these are caused by viruses and antibiotics have no effect on viruses. Overuse of antibiotics is worrying the medical profession because some bacteria are becoming resistant to their effects.

Recreational Drugs and their Harm

Alcohol (beer)

Recreational drugs are taken for enjoyment only. **Alcohol** is an example of a **legal** recreational drug, it is a **depressant**. This means nerve activity is slowed down and it can affect your feelings and reaction speed (slower, although many people convince themselves they can do things better with alcohol). Long term overuse of alcohol causes liver damage. Getting drunk is also dangerous because people can choke on their own vomit. **Heroin** is an example of an **illegal** depressant, it is highly addictive and once 'hooked' nothing else in life can seem to matter other than taking the drug. Drugs called *stimulants* increase nerve activity and mean that people **react quicker**. **Caffeine** and **nicotine** are examples of legal stimulants. A well known **illegal** stimulant is **ecstasy**; often taken as a pill, people feel energised and happy. It is often taken at night clubs and parties because of this. Long term mental health problems such as anxiety can occur. Another **illegal** stimulant is **cocaine** (called **crack** in its rock form). Highly addictive with many negative long term side effects such as; nose damage through 'snorting' and bowel problems such as diarrhoea or vomiting.

A cup of coffee

WHAT?

Cannabis is the most widely used illegal recreational drug. Heroin is considered the worst drug in terms of its effects on health and society, it is also the most addictive. Alcohol, a legal drug, kills more people than all the illegal drugs combined.

Cannabis leaf

Heroin addiction can ruin lives

Questions on Drugs and their Impact

Comprehension

1. What is a drug?
2. Why do people use recreational drugs?
3. What can happen with all drugs?
4. What is an obvious example of a good medicine?
5. What is an anaesthetic?
6. Give an example of a use for an anaesthetic.
7. What do antibiotics do?
8. What often happened to people after operations before antibiotics?
9. Why are many infections becoming resistant to antibiotics?
10. What kind of drug is alcohol?
11. What happens to your nerve activity after drinking alcohol?
12. What is a side effect of long term overuse of alcohol?
13. What's one of the reasons that getting drunk is dangerous?
14. Give an example of an illegal depressant.
15. Why can getting 'hooked' on heroin be bad?
16. What does a stimulant do?
17. What are the two legal stimulants mentioned?
18. What are some of the long term side effects of cocaine use?

Additional tasks

1. Match the words below and memorise.

Medicines	drugs taken for enjoyment
Recreational drugs	slows down nerve activity
Anaesthetic	drugs that help us get better from illness
Antibiotics	speeds up nerve activity
Depressant	drugs that cause loss of sensation
Stimulant	drugs taken to treat bacterial infections

2. List as many medicines as you can and write down what they are used for. Ask a friend or adult if you don't know any.

Medicines

3. Below are some 'claimed' pros (positives) and cons (negatives) of alcohol. Write down whether you think alcohol is good or bad for society.

In moderation alcohol has health benefits, the beverage industry employs a lot of people, it makes people happier, it helps people to socialise, it helps people to sleep, it provides a lot of money to government through taxes.

Too much alcohol is bad for your health, it makes people do stupid things, some people become violent, it can cause accidents and death, gives you a hangover, it is addictive, people 'waste' their money on alcohol.

4. Put the following results of drinking alcohol in order of severity (getting worse). You may debate these!

DRUNK	MORE RELAXED THAN NORMAL
VERY RELAXED	
DEATH	DIFFICULT TO WALK IN A STRAIGHT LINE
SOME SLURRED SPEECH	PASS OUT

Reproduction in Plants

Plants that produce a flower reproduce sexually. This means there is a male sex cell (its name is pollen and is made in the **anther**) and a female sex cell called the ovule. Just as is the case for humans, the female sex cell and male must join. In plants this begins with pollination, a **pollen** grain landing on the **stigma** of the flower. This can be from the same plant (self pollination) or another plant of the same species (cross pollination). The pollen cell grows a tube down to the **ovule** where its nucleus is able to join with the ovule's nucleus, this is **fertilisation**. This produces a **seed**. After fertilisation the **ovary** becomes a **fruit** and the seeds are contained inside it, for example, an apple.

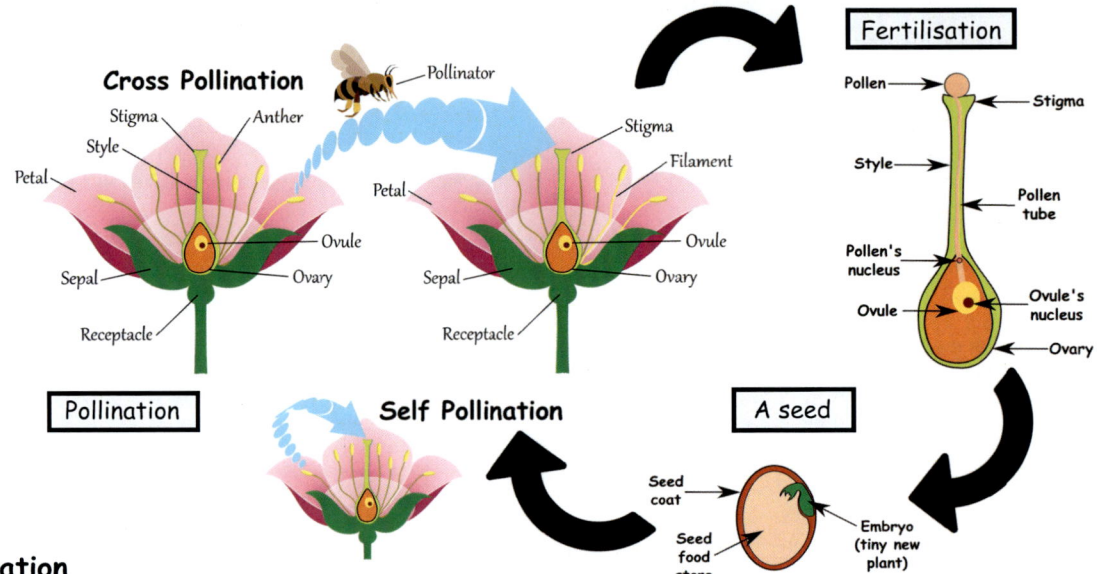

Pollination

Most plants require pollination. This happens usually by wind (pollen particles are very small and light) or by being carried by insects such as bees. To increase the chances of pollination plants produce a **sugary** liquid called **nectar** to attract insects. They also produce **a lot** of pollen and some plants produce flowers that mimic (imitate/look like) female insects to attract the male. They also produce scents (smells) and have bright colours to attract insects.

Bee orchids mimic bees

Seed Dispersal (Spreading)

Seeds can be spread by **four** main methods: the **wind**, carried by **animals**, transported by **water** or **thrown** by seed pods suddenly opening (exploding). Dispersal is important so that the seeds aren't too close together competing for available light, water and nutrients. The growing conditions directly under a tree or plant may be poor and reduce the number of successful germinations.

Dandelion: wind seed dispersal

Germination

This is the name given to a seed that begins to grow. A seed contains a protective coating, inside is an embryo (the beginnings of a new plant) ready to begin growing. The seed also has a food store to provide the seedling (a developing young plant) with what it needs to begin growing.

Germination

WHAT?

About 85% of plant life is actually in the oceans! The tallest living tree is about 116 metres high. There are more than 200,000 different plants. Trees live longer than any other organism on earth. The suicide plant from Australia produces a sting that is painful for so long people have been known to take their own lives because of the pain.

Questions on Reproduction in Plants

Comprehension

1. How do plants that produce a flower reproduce?
2. What is the male sex cell called?
3. What is the ovule?
4. What do we mean by pollination?
5. Pollination in the same plant is called what?
6. How is the nucleus of the pollen cell able to join with the ovule?
7. What does this produce?
8. What does the ovule become after fertilisation?
9. By what two methods does pollination usually happen?
10. Why do plants produce a sugary liquid called nectar?
11. What else do flowers produce to attract insects?
12. What are the four main methods of seed dispersal?
13. Why is it important that seeds are dispersed?
14. What is germination?
15. What is the embryo inside a seed's protective coating?
16. What percentage of plant life is actually in the oceans? (WHAT? box)

Additional tasks

1. Label and memorise the parts of a flower below.

Parts of a flower

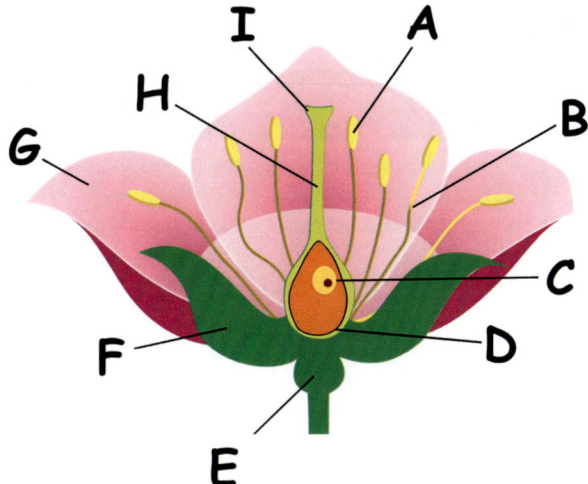

A. _____

B. _____

C. _____

D. _____

E. _____

F. _____

G. _____

H. _____

I. _____

2. On a calm day 100 seeds fall from a tree and land close together near to the trunk. On a windy day 100 seeds fall from the tree and are scattered far apart and away from the tree's trunk.

   Write down which seeds are more likely to grow and reasons why.

   Seeds most likely to grow and why

3. Put the following statements in the correct order for a plant that undergoes **cross pollination** with another plant of the same species.

   __ bee flies to another plant

   __ pollen is made in the anther

   __ plant is fertilised to produce a seed

   __ pollen accidentally sticks to bee

   __ pollen grains move from bee to stigma

   __ pollen collects on top of the anther

   __ pollen grows a tube down to the ovule

   __ nucleus of pollen and ovule fuse

   __ bee visits flower to collect nectar

Photosynthesis

Photo refers to light and synthesise means to make, so photosynthesis means to use light to make food. Light provides the energy to synthesise (make) glucose (the food). The two reactants (chemicals that change to form the products) are water (chemical formula, H_2O) and carbon dioxide (chemical formula, CO_2). The word equation for photosynthesis is below.

$$\textbf{Carbon dioxide} \ + \ \textbf{Water} \ \xrightarrow[\textbf{chlorophyll}]{\textbf{light}} \ \textbf{Glucose} \ + \ \textbf{Oxygen}$$

One of the products glucose, (chemical formula $C_6H_{12}O_6$) is an example of a sugar. Glucose dissolves, so plants **store the food** they make as **starch**. Starch is a long molecule made from lots of glucose molecules, it **doesn't dissolve**. The other product, oxygen, is equally important for life, we breathe it in when we inhale and it allows respiration (the release of energy from food) to take place in our cells. Plants are the producers of our food and oxygen, without them life as we know it would not exist. They also affect the amount of carbon dioxide in the atmosphere by absorbing it during photosynthesis. Carbon dioxide contributes to global warming so plants help reduce this. However plants also respire, especially at night, but lucky for us they produce more O_2 through photosynthesis than CO_2 from respiration.

Photosynthesis

Sun

Light

CO_2 + H_2O → Chlorophyll → $C_6H_{12}O_6$ + O_2

Planting trees helps reduce global warming by absorbing carbon dioxide. Get planting and save the planet!

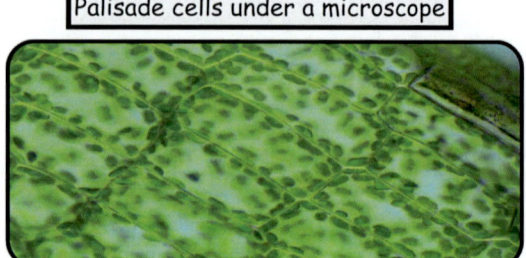

WHAT?

Half of the world's oxygen is produced by phytoplankton, mostly single celled algae that live in the sea and produce food through photosynthesis. It takes **six** molecules of carbon dioxide and **six** molecules of water to produce **one** glucose molecule. Plants stop making chlorophyll in the winter and that's why their leaves change colour.

The Leaf

You will have noticed most leaves are green, this is because they contain **chlorophyll** (a green pigment). Chlorophyll has the ability to absorb light and use the energy for photosynthesis. Most chlorophyll is contained in cells called **palisade** cells near to the surface of the leaf. To allow gases in and out, **stomata**, pores or 'holes' mainly on the underside of a leaf, can open or close. During the day time the stomata will open to let in carbon dioxide and let out oxygen. At night they will close to prevent water loss from the plant. The cells that control this opening and closing of stomata are called **guard cells**.

Another feature of a leaf that reduces water loss is the **waxy cuticle** (waxy layer) on the top of the leaf. The leaf is well adapted to do its job.

Palisade cells under a microscope

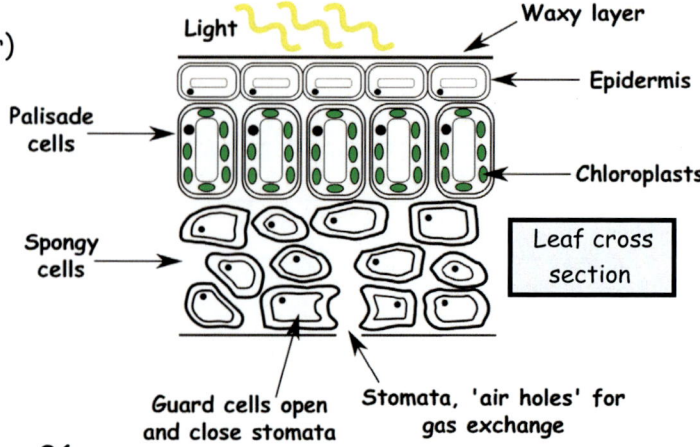

Light

Waxy layer

Epidermis

Palisade cells

Chloroplasts

Spongy cells

Leaf cross section

Guard cells open and close stomata

Stomata, 'air holes' for gas exchange

Questions on Photosynthesis

Comprehension

1. What does the 'photo' in photosynthesis refer to?	10. What do plants do especially at night?
2. What does photosynthesis mean?	11. Why are leaves green?
3. What are the two reactants of photosynthesis?	12. What is chlorophyll able to do?
4. What are the chemical formulae of water and carbon dioxide?	13. Which cells contain most of the chlorophyll?
	14. What are stomata?
5. What is glucose an example of?	15. What happens to the stomata during the day time?
6. How is glucose stored?	16. What is the name of the cells that control the opening and closing of stomata?
7. What does oxygen allow the body's cells to do?	
8. What would happen without plants?	17. Why do the stomata close at night?
9. What does carbon dioxide contribute to?	18. What else helps reduce water loss?

Additional tasks

1. Match and memorise the words and chemical formulae below.

Chlorophyll	a gas produced by photosynthesis, chemical formula O_2
Stomata	a liquid absorbed through photosynthesis, chemical formula H_2O
Oxygen	a gas absorbed through photosynthesis, chemical formula CO_2
Carbon dioxide	a green pigment found in leaves for photosynthesis
Water	a sugar produced through photosynthesis, chemical formula $C_6H_{12}O_6$
Glucose	pores on the underside of a leaf to control gas exchange

2. Label the leaf cross section below.

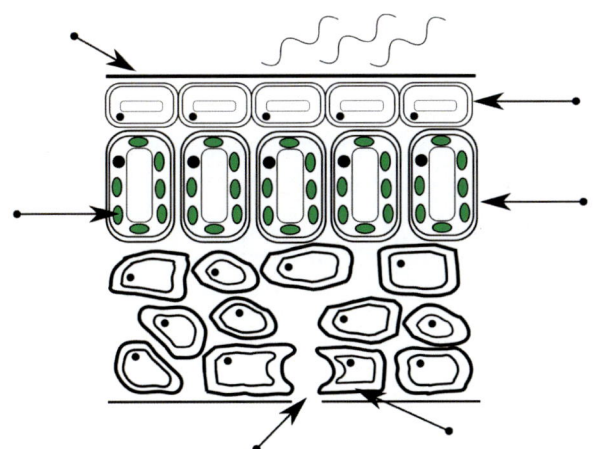

Photosynthesis experiment

3. The **number of bubbles** of **oxygen** released in **one hour** were **counted** from a photosynthesising pond plant placed in a test tube. The brightness of light was varied. The results are shown below.

a. Plot a graph of Number of bubbles in one hour on the y-axis (vertical) against light brightness on the x-axis (horizontal) and draw a smooth line.

Light brightness (lux)	100	200	300	400	500	600	700	800	900	1000
Number of bubbles in one hour	10	19	28	36	42	46	49	50	50	50

b. Label three parts to the line with, **FAST CHANGE, SLOW CHANGE, NO CHANGE** as the brightness increases.

Genetics and Inheritance

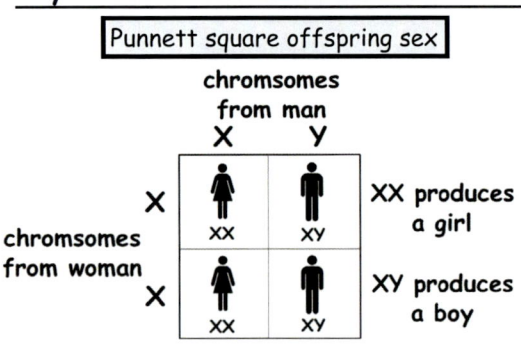

Chromosome DNA Gene

In biology inheritance is the passing of genetic characteristics from parent to offspring. Our characteristics, brown hair, blue eyes etc are influenced by the genes we get from our parents, half from mom and half from dad. Two genes for each characteristic. The genetic information is carried by chromosomes that look like two long balloons tied in the middle. A human cell has 46 chromosomes, 23 from each parent. Each chromosome is made from a long thread like molecule called DNA. Sections of the chromosome that carry information for how we grow are called **genes**. DNA molecules have the famous double helix shape shown opposite, the shape is like a spiral staircase.

Boy or Girl? It's the Man that Decides!

Punnett square offspring sex

chromsomes from man

X   Y

chromsomes from woman

X — XX / XY — XX produces a girl

X — XX / XY — XY produces a boy

The chromosomes that determine your sex are the X and Y chromosomes. Half of male sperms carry X and half Y. Womens' eggs only carry X chromosomes. **XY** means the baby is a **boy**, **XX** means the baby is a **girl**. A punnett square shows that the combinations possible mean a boy and a girl are equally likely, that is why the population is half male and half female. It is a gene on the Y chromosome that decides the sex is male. A gene that determines a characteristics is called a **dominant (stronger) gene**, the other gene is called a **recessive (weaker) gene**. A similar thing happens with inherited characteristics, parents with freckles mostly have kids with freckles, the freckle gene is dominant. The punnett square opposite shows the outcome for offspring from a mom and dad that carry both brown eye and blue eye genes.

Inherited freckles

Punnett square eye colour

	Dad		B = dominant brown eyes gene
	B	b	
Mom B	BB	Bb	b = recessive blue eyes gene
b	Bb	bb	1 in 4 have blue eyes

Species: Similar but Different

It has been found that about 99% of our genes are the same as our 'cousin' the chimpanzee. Not surprising when you think how similar we are, we evolved (developed gradually) from common ancestry. The **same species can breed** and produce fertile offspring. The 1% difference is enough for us not to be able to breed with chimpanzees. Horses and donkeys are very similar but are different species, if they breed they produce a mule which is infertile (cannot reproduce).

We're 99% chimpanzee!

Who Worked it all Out?

Rosalind Franklin

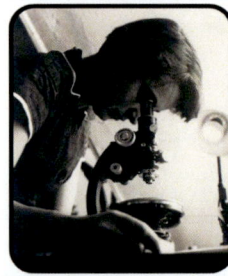

Many scientists contributed, but four names stand out. Two of them, Rosalind Franklin and Maurice Wilkins used X-rays fired at DNA. The scattering of the X-rays formed patterns (a famous image called photo 51) that they were able to use to work out what the DNA molecule might look like. James Watson and Francis Crick built on this work and used a model to come up with the 'double helix' structure that we now know to be correct. All but Rosalind received the Nobel Prize, she having died of cancer.

WHAT?

When a male identical twin has offspring with a female identical twin their kids are genetic brother or sister but technically cousins! In the future we may be able to cure diseases by replacing bad genes with good, this is called gene therapy. Some inherited characteristics are determined by many genes not just two!

Questions on Genetics and Inheritance

Comprehension

1. In biology what do we mean by inheritance?
2. What are our characteristics influenced by?
3. How many genes are there for each characteristic?
4. What do chromosomes look like?
5. Which chromosomes determine your sex?
6. Which sex chromosome do women carry?
7. Why is the population half male and half female?
8. Where is the gene found that determines the sex is male?
9. What percentage of our genes do we share with the chimpanzee?
10. What does evolved mean?
11. What can the same species do?
12. Are horses and donkeys the same species?
13. What happens if they breed?
14. What did Rosalind Franklin and Maurice Wilkins 'fire' at DNA?
15. What did the scattering of the X-rays form, enabling them to work out what the DNA molecule might look like?
16. From this work what did James Watson and Francis Crick come up with?

Additional tasks

1.   Match and memorise the words below.

Inheritance	sections of the chromosome that carry information for how we grow
Chromosome	a weaker gene that only produces the characteristic if combined with another recessive gene
Genes	the passing of genetic characteristics from parent to offspring
DNA	a stronger gene that produces a characteristic
Dominant gene	a molecule that makes up chromosomes, has a double helix shape
Recessive gene	carry the genetic information

2.   Complete the gap filling exercise using the words in bold below;

offspring, dominant, characteristic, looks, recessive, recessive, inherit, blue eye, punnett, freckles

Our characteristics are the _____ and attributes that we _____ from our parents. Things like eye colour, hair colour and _____. If the stronger gene called the _____ gene combines with another gene of that characteristic then we see that _____ in the _____. The weaker gene is called the _____ gene. We only see that characteristic if it combines with another _____ gene. For example, the recessive blue eye gene only produces blue eyes if it combines with another recessive _____ _____ gene, one from each parent. A _____ square shows the possible combinations.

3 a.   Complete the **punnett squares 1 to 4** below to show the possible outcomes for the offspring from moms and dads with the recessive and dominant gene combinations below (like opposite).
   b.   Write down how many offspring 'out of four' have blue eyes for each punnett square 1 to 4. below.

B = dominant brown eyes gene   b = recessive blue eyes gene

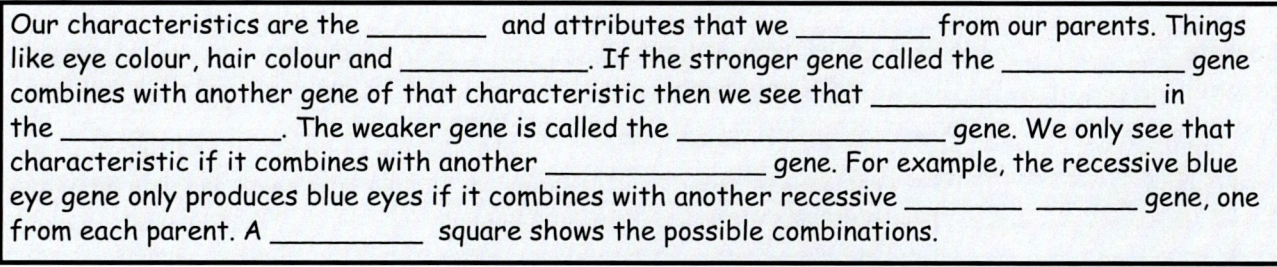

4.   Put the following in order of size;

ORGAN, NUCLEUS, MOLECULE, CELL, CHROMOSOME, TISSUE, DNA

Adaptation

Adaptations help a species to survive in its **habitat** (where organisms or communities of organisms live). If an organism (plant, animal or single cell life) is not well adapted to its environment it may not survive, for example, without long necks giraffes wouldn't be able to reach leaves high in the treetops. Adaptations usually take thousands or even millions of years, but can happen more quickly in organisms like bacteria. Superbugs, a type of bacteria, have adapted to become resistant to antibiotics and are no longer killed by most kinds of antibiotics. This adaptation is causing humans problems.

Classic Adaptation Examples

Cacti are adapted for life in the desert. They have a thick stem so that they can store a lot of water and a water proof outer layer to reduce water loss. The leaves have gone and become spines instead, this again reduces water loss (water is normally lost through leaves) and reduces the chances of being eaten. Shallow roots help absorb moisture from the surface when it is available and the roots spread widely to collect water from a larger area.

Flowering plants have adapted to increase their chance of pollination by producing nectar (sweet liquid), having bright colours or imitating the look of certain insects to attract a 'mate' over other plants and hopefully get more pollen.

The Venus fly trap lives in areas where the soil is very poor. When insects enter their leaves, hairs detect movement and the leaves snap shut. Trapped insects are digested to supplement the nutrients needed for growth.

Sharks have a specially adapted fin called a caudal fin (the one at the back) that propels the shark with great speed. Their shape is very streamlined so they move through the water with little resistance. Their skeletons are made from cartilage (a firm tissue) which is very flexible. They have an amazing sense of smell and sharp teeth.

Polar bears have black skin to help absorb heat from the sun's rays and a thick layer of fat to help insulate and store energy reserves. Their round shape also helps reduce heat loss. They have big feet to spread their weight and stop them sinking into the snow and a white coat for camouflage. They are brilliant swimmers, great for hunting and moving around.

Camels can store a large amount of fat in their humps for energy and can drink 80 litres of water in one go! They sweat very little below 50°C to reduce water loss and can withstand large changes in body temperature.

Tarantulas can detect tiny vibrations in the ground to catch their prey

WHAT?

In winter, an Alaskan Wood Frog's body actually freezes and its heart stops beating to allow it to survive down to -80°C below zero! Kangaroo rats have adapted to survive desert conditions by getting all the water they need from their food. Antarctic fish have antifreeze proteins in their blood. Okapi (look like a blend between a zebra and a giraffe) can use infrasound (low pitched sound) to communicate so their predators can't hear them!

Okapi use a kind of sound that their predators can't hear. Shhhhhh!

Questions on Adaptation

Comprehension

1. What do adaptations do?
2. What may happen if an organism is not well adapted to its environment?
3. How long do adaptations normally take?
4. What does the waterproof outer layer of a cactus do?
5. What has happened to the leaves of a cactus?
6. What is the sweet liquid that plants produce called?
7. What tells a Venus fly trap to snap shut?
8. What happens to the insects that are trapped?
9. How does the specially adapted Caudal fin help a shark?
10. Why is a shark's streamlined shape so useful?
11. What is a shark's skeleton made from?
12. What colour is a polar bear's skin and how does this help?
13. What is the advantage of a polar bear's big feet?
14. Why is a polar bear's white coat useful?
15. How much water can a camel drink in one go?
16. Why is it an advantage for the camel to sweat very little below 50°C?

Additional tasks

1. Draw / invent an animal that has the characteristics to live and thrive in one or more of the habitats below.

- The sea
- A jungle
- A desert
- Antarctica (South Pole)
- Cold mountain climate
- A forest

2. Complete the adaptations crossword below.

3. Explain how you think the following adaptations help the species to survive.

- Dogs have developed an excellent sense of smell
- Springbok (small deer like animals) jump in the air to make themselves look bigger
- Some non-venomous snakes have very bright colours
- The bee orchid flower looks like a female bee
- Cheetahs have a long spine, long legs, light skeleton and large nostrils
- Mountain goats have rough pads on their hooves, their hooves spread widely and have very strong hind (back) legs for jumping

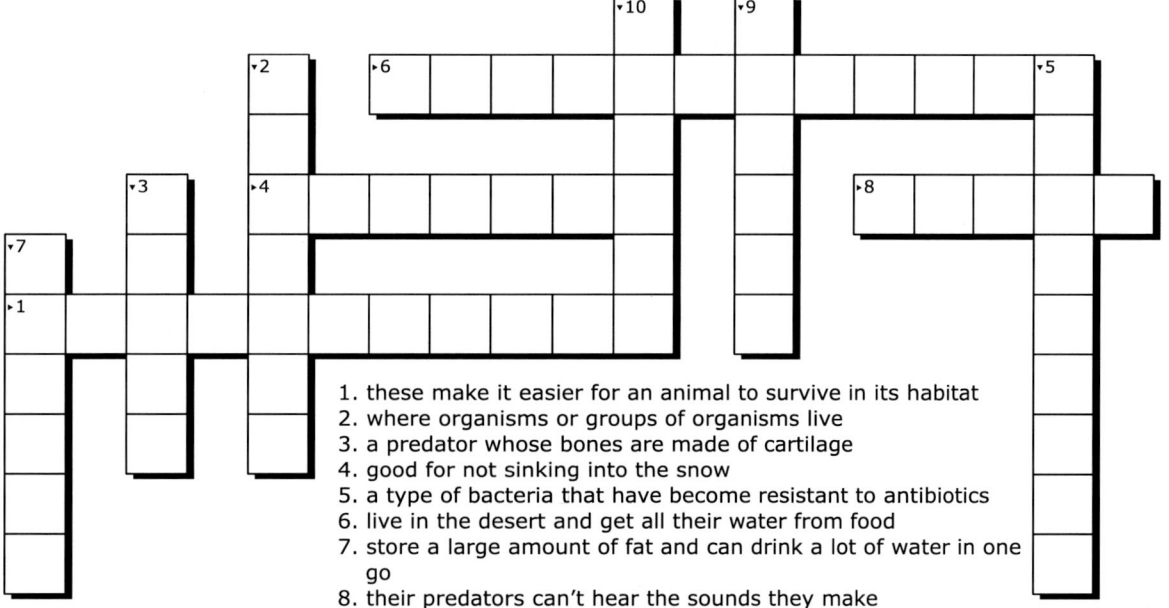

1. these make it easier for an animal to survive in its habitat
2. where organisms or groups of organisms live
3. a predator whose bones are made of cartilage
4. good for not sinking into the snow
5. a type of bacteria that have become resistant to antibiotics
6. live in the desert and get all their water from food
7. store a large amount of fat and can drink a lot of water in one go
8. their predators can't hear the sounds they make
9. the male part of a flowering plant
10. roots spread wide to collect water

Evolution and Natural Selection

To evolve means to change gradually over time. Species evolve over time because of mutations (changes) in genes that happen by accident (**naturally**) or because of damage due to environmental conditions such as exposure to harmful **radiation** (like gamma rays, high energy 'light' from radioactive sources). These mutations lead to new traits (characteristics) like having a longer neck to reach more food (giraffe), having camouflage to make you a better hunter (polar bear), having a better sense of smell to detect prey further away (shark), having a trap to catch insects (Venus fly trap) or smelling sweet to attract more insects (flowering plants).

Natural Selection

Offspring with traits that mean they are better adapted to their environment or have an advantage for finding food tend to be more likely to survive. Over long periods of time, these traits become more common in the population and are 'naturally selected', the less useful characteristics become less common and the population slowly changes.

It is called *'survival of the fittest'* for those best adapted to survive.

The tallest survive!

Sometimes this means that within a population of species, the less well adapted cannot compete and eventually die out. This is a normal process and leads to the extinction of a species.

Charles Darwin

These ideas were first presented by Charles Darwin (1809-1892). He wrote a book called 'The Origin of Species' where he presented the idea of evolution by natural selection. He travelled the world and studied many species, famously on the Galapagos Islands. He observed variation in species that could be explained by his idea.

Charles Darwin

It's Happening Now!

Farmers have been using insecticides ('icide' means to kill, insecticides are chemicals that kill insects) for many years now and some insects have become resistant. Some insects don't die, their difference from the other insects helps them to survive. Their bodies are able to break down the chemicals so that they cause them no harm. The population of these insects then grows. MRSA (or superbug) is a bacteria that has evolved to be resistant to antibiotics. It can now be difficult to treat and scientists think that it has been made worse by the overuse of antibiotics, drugs that kill bacterial infections.

Insecticide

WHAT?

'Modern' humans have been around for about 200,000 years and we've survived because we've evolved big brains! Dolphins evolved from mammals but sharks evolved from fish. Goose bumps is a left over evolutionary trait to help keep us warm by trapping a bigger layer of air, it doesn't work for us because we don't have enough hair anymore. Great White sharks have evolved to replace their old teeth with up to 19 new teeth per week or nearly 30,000 new teeth over a lifetime, they're sharp!

Antibiotics, don't overuse them!

Questions on Evolution and Natural Selection

Comprehension

1. What does evolve mean?
2. What are the two causes of mutations in genes mentioned in the text?
3. What do these mutations lead to?
4. How does having traits adapted for the environment or finding food affect an animal's chance of survival?
5. What happens to these traits in the population over time?
6. What two words do we use to describe this?
7. What do we call those that survive because they are better adapted?
8. What happens to species that are less well adapted to survive?
9. Who is credited with first presenting the ideas behind evolution?
10. Where did Charles Darwin famously study many species?
11. What is an insecticide?
12. What can some insects' bodies do to the insecticide chemicals?
13. What happens to the population of these insects?
14. What is another name for MRSA?
15. What have MRSA bacteria evolved to be resistant to?
16. What has made this worse?

Additional tasks

1. Match and memorise the meanings of the terms below.

Mutate	single celled organisms
Evolve	the characteristic of an animal, for example thick fur
Traits	chemicals that kill insects
Insecticides	to change from what you were
Bacteria	animals with the best adaptations for survival
Survival of the fittest	to change over time

2. Complete the sentences choosing from the words in bold describing what trait each animal has evolved over time to help them survive.

smell, speeds, upright, sharp, brains, hearing, sensitive, long, teeth, nectar, wolf, bipedalism, 'fly', detect, streamlined

- **Sharks** have evolved to constantly replace their _____ over a lifetime. This ensures they are able to maintain many rows of _____ teeth.
- **Humans** have evolved big _____ enabling them to solve problems and also evolved to walk _____ on two legs called _____.
- **Dogs** have evolved excellent _____ , sharp teeth and an exceptional sense of _____ to help them hunt. All from their ancestor, the _____.
- **Tarantulas** have evolved to be _____ to small vibrations in the ground to _____ prey.
- **Humming birds** have evolved _____ beaks so that they can reach _____ inside flowers.
- **Penguins** have evolved wings that allow them to '_____' underwater at high _____ to catch fish and are beautifully _____ to reduce water resistance.

3. Write true or false next to the statements about evolution below.

Every one now believes the theory of evolution (_____)	Evolving is a slow process 'normally' (_____)
Darwin was the only one to come up with the theory (_____)	Evolution has stopped now (_____)
The Goblin shark has barely evolved over millions of years (_____)	Mutations drive evolution (_____)
Some humans that live at high altitude have evolved to have higher blood oxygen content (_____)	
We are still learning about evolution (_____)	If species don't evolve they risk extinction (_____)

Biodiversity and Gene Banks

The desert food web shows the food chains of a diverse range of plants and animals. **Diverse** means there are **many different types**. If in this food web an insecticide is used to kill all of the grasshoppers, there would be no food for the lizard which may die out in this habitat. In turn, this would mean less food for the owl, rattle snake and tarantula. Or if the mesquite trees die of disease, the kangaroo rat may not survive and this in turn means less food for the tarantula and owl.

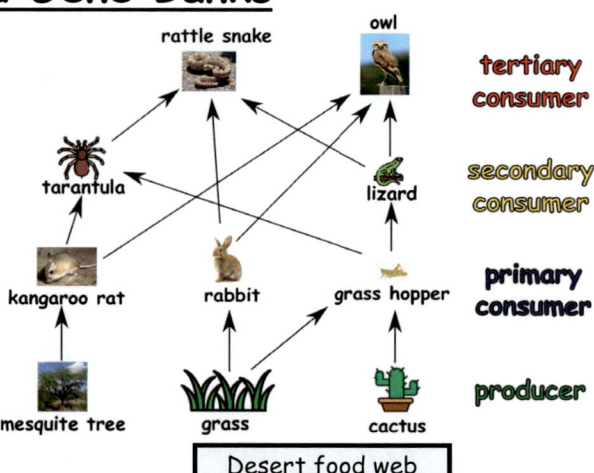

Desert food web

Importance of Biodiversity

Biodiversity is essential for maintaining healthy populations in ecosystems.

Less biodiversity means that **ecosystems** are **less able to cope with change** from year to year. Species are **more likely** to die out and become **extinct**. In a diverse ecosystem, organisms can survive on other sources of food if there is a bad year, such as extreme weather (drought say), disease, over-predation or human activity. The grasshopper can eat more cactus if there is very little grass in a particular year. Organisms in ecosystems are dependent on each other. This is called **interdependence.**

If we invented a way to make honey without bees and allowed bee numbers to drop, the human food supply would be put in danger. Honey bees pollinate much of the fruit plants, vegetables and crops that we eat. This ensures seeds are produced for further planting and fruits form on the plants for us to eat. Without them **much of the food we eat** would **not be available**. They also pollinate wild flowers and plants which enable them to reproduce, which in turn provides a habitat for insects, which in turn feed birds and other animals. Organisms **depend** on each other.

Introduction of **non-native** species can **disrupt biodiversity**. Cane toads (non-native) were introduced to Australia to control a cane beetle pest. Native predators, like some lizards, are not adapted to their poisonous glands and their numbers have declined. Reduction in prey for other native animals that depend on the same diet (insects) as the toads, has also put pressure on these native species, as the cane toad population rises (now estimated at 200 million) and the area they inhabit increases.

The cane toad was introduced to Australia

Gene Banks

Even by creating protected areas and having captive breeding programs (breeding endangered animals, mainly in zoos), species can still become extinct. Gene banks are a way to store genetic material of different species for the future. They can be used for research or to try and reproduce 'lost' species. The type of material stored includes:

- Seeds and pollen
- Sperm, eggs and embryos
- Blood
- Tissue

Cryobank, seeds stored at −196°C in liquid nitrogen

> **WHAT?**
> Scientists are worried that species of plants and animals are being lost before we can learn about them and their potential benefits for human medicine and the planet.

Questions on Biodiversity and Gene Banks

Comprehension

1. What does the desert food web show?
2. What does diverse mean?
3. What might happen if insecticide is used to kill the grasshoppers?
4. What is biodiversity essential for?
5. What does less biodiversity in an ecosystem mean for the various species in it?
6. What can organisms do if there is a bad year in a diverse ecosystem?
7. What would be put in danger if we allowed the number of honey bees to decrease?
8. Why is this?
9. What can the introduction of non-native species do?
10. Why were Cane toads introduced to Australia?
11. Why did the number of some non-native predators decline (like lizards)?
12. What has put pressure on other native animals?
13. What still happens even with protected areas and captive breeding programs?
14. What are gene banks a way of doing?
15. What can the genetic material be used for?

Additional tasks

1. Use these three food chains; **leaves, rabbit, fox; corn, rat, snake; grass, vole, ferret** and a **wolf** and **eagle** as the tertiary consumers, to fill the boxes below and draw arrows between who eats what.

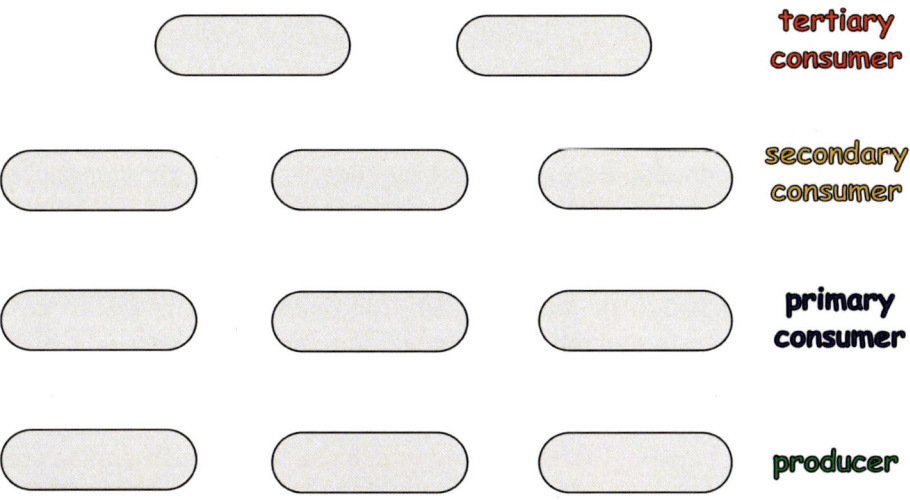

tertiary consumer

secondary consumer

primary consumer

producer

2. Here are some statements about captive breeding programs, put them under the title _**Pros**_ (advantages) or _**Cons**_ (disadvantages).

- Captive breeding programs are not cheap.
- We learn a lot about the animals in captive breeding programs.
- Many people have jobs in breeding programs.
- Animals are often not introduced back into the wild and this should be the aim.
- Reintroduced species often don't survive.
- It means we can still see endangered animals without having to enter their habitat.
- Captive breeding programs have limited success.
- Some endangered animals may still have benefits to humankind that we still don't know about.
- Some habitats are reopening to wild animals, if we don't have captive breeding programs we may not be able to reintroduce.
- It's important for maintaining biodiversity.

3. Write down **your opinion** as to whether captive breeding programs are useful or a waste of time and money.

Predator, Prey and Populations

A predator is an animal that catches and kills another animal for food. The prey is the animal that gets eaten. A cat (predator) and mouse (prey) are good examples.

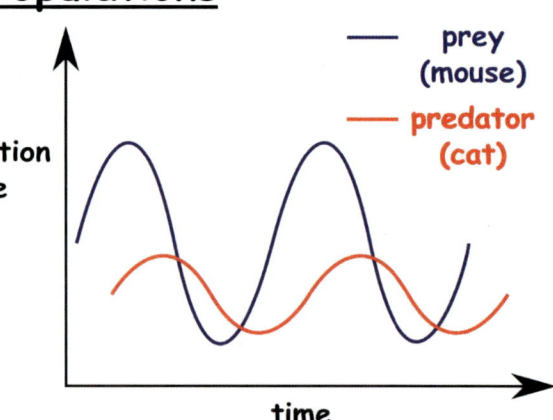

prey (mouse)

predator (cat)

population size

time

Imagine a healthy population of cats and mice living on an island in the middle of nowhere. What would happen? The cats eat the mice of course. However, as this happens there is less food available for the cats, they don't breed as much so the cat population starts to decrease. As the cat population starts to decrease there are less cats to catch and eat the mice. The mice population recovers and begins to rise. As the population of the mice increases again, there is more food for the cats to catch and eat, their population starts to recover and rise again. As the population of the cats begins to increase again, more mice are caught and eaten so their population begins to fall again. This happens over and over again in a cycle.

Predator prey graphs show the change in population over time. Only considering one predator and one prey is simple to follow. However, most predators eat more than one prey. Also the **food available** for the **prey population** can be affected by the environmental conditions such as weather, so their numbers can also be influenced by factors other than predators.

Populations and Competition

Competition from other predators that occupy the same habitat can affect both the population of predator and prey. If, for example, lions try to enter the territory of a hyena's den, the hyenas will viciously defend their territory, they don't want the lions to be able to hunt where they do and steal their **food** and **space**. Animals of the same species will also compete for territory, not only for food, but also for **breeding rights**. Where water is scarce this is also competed for.

The famous 'Darwin's finches' on the Galapagos islands in the pacific, are a varied group of 14 species of small birds that have different sized beaks. On islands where more of the species have medium sized beaks, the population of these species can struggle. They compete for the same sized seeds. On these **same islands** species of birds with larger and smaller sized beaks do better. The birds with medium sized beaks have a different diet, so there is less competition and more food is available for the smaller and larger beaked birds.

Darwin's finches

1. Geospiza magnirostris.
2. Geospiza fortis.
3. Geospiza parvula.
4. Certhidea olivacea.

Introduction of non-native species can reduce populations with unforeseen consequences. **Grey squirrels** (North American), have taken over almost all the habitat in England because they are bigger, stronger and compete for food better than the smaller native red squirrel.

Red and grey squirrels

WHAT?

Perhaps the most successful mammal land hunter is the African wild dog with successful kill percentages of around 85% which compares to about 25% for lions. The beautiful Tasmanian Tiger became extinct around 1920 due to human encroachment, over hunting and the introduction of non-native species and disease.

Questions on Predator, Prey and Populations

Comprehension

1. What is a predator?

2. What is a good example of a predator and a prey?

3. What happens to the population of mice as the cats eat them?

4. Why does this cause the cat population to decrease?

5. What causes the mice population to begin to rise again?

6. Why over time does this allow the cat population to increase again?

7. What do predator prey graphs show?

8. When are they simple to follow?

9. Apart from predators, what else can affect the number of prey?

10. Why don't hyenas want lions in their territory?

11. Why will animals of the same species also compete for territory?

12. Especially if scarce, what else can be competed for?

13. What are the famous 'Darwin's finches' on the Galapagos islands?

14. Why does the population of birds with medium sized beaks struggle when there are more birds with medium sized beaks?

15. Why do populations of birds with shorter and longer beaks do better on the **same** island?

Additional tasks

1. Plot the number of predator and prey on the graph below and draw in as smooth a curve as you can. Label both lines.

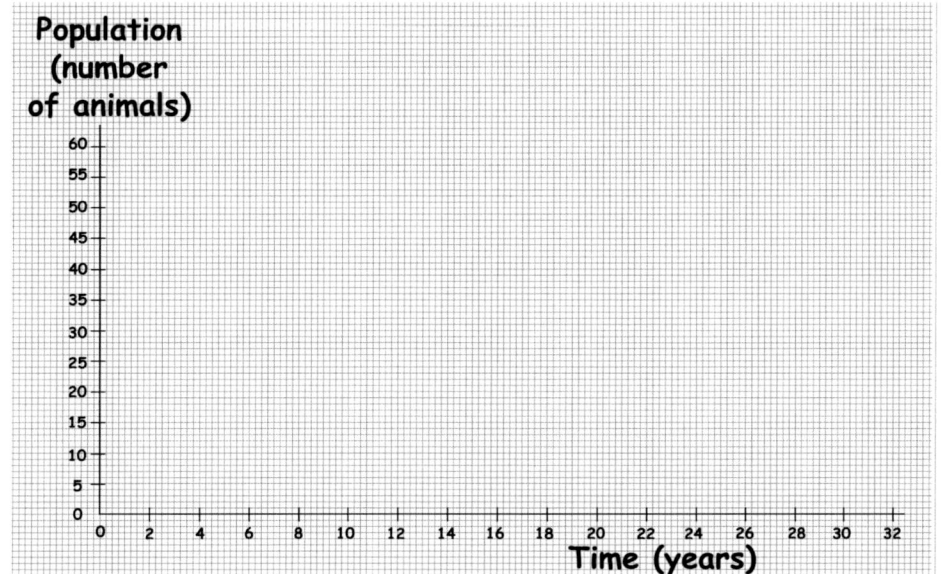

Predator number	Prey number	Time (years)
5	20	4
10	40	8
20	60	12
23	20	16
20	10	20
10	20	24
5	40	28
10	60	32

2. How long does it take the predator numbers to go from a **maximum** to a **minimum** value (or vice versa)?

3. Many factors limit how big a population can become. Human population is heading towards 8 billion. It can't grow forever otherwise we wouldn't be able to grow enough food for everyone and have enough space for housing.

Below are some limiting factors that affect the size of a population.

NUTRIENTS IN SOIL	PREDATORS
FOOD	LIGHT TO GROW
PREY	SPACE
DISEASE	OXYGEN
WAR	WEATHER OR CLIMATE

Write about how you think these factors can affect the size of a population of **any** species, e.g. **not many nutrients in the soil means not many tomatoes on my tomato plant!**

Pyramids of Numbers and Toxins in Food Chains

Toxins are poisonous chemicals that may enter an organism. They have four routes into an organism. Through the skin (absorption), breathed in (inhalation), injected or most importantly with food chains eaten (ingested). Examples of toxins can include **pesticides**, used for killing pests like insects and weeds that can damage crops. **Mercury** and **lead** which are toxic metals. All can be passed up the food chain.

Pyramids of Numbers

These show us the size of a population at each level in a food chain. Each level in a food chain is called a **trophic level**. On a pyramid of numbers it is drawn in proportion to the size of the population. They often look like pyramids because the numbers usually start off big and get smaller.

Pyramid of numbers

5 hawks

100 sparrows

1,000 caterpillars

2,000 cabbages

10 ladybirds

2,000 greenfly

1 bush

However, one bush can feed thousands of greenfly (tiny insect pests that feed on plants) and a large number of greenfly can be food for a small number of ladybirds. Since each level only tells us the size of the population and not the size of the organism, they don't always have a pyramid shape.

Toxins Entering Food Chains

Toxins can get into food chains in many ways. Chemical fertilisers can wash off from fields and into rivers and reservoirs. Pesticides can get on insects which are then eaten by birds. Mercury can enter water ways and oceans from the burning of fossil fuels, mining and manufacturing. Soil can be contaminated by toxins released in air pollution, these can then be absorbed by plants through their roots.

Toxin Accumulation

Accumulate means to build up, toxin concentration can build up as it is transferred higher up in a food chain. Mercury in the oceans is absorbed by **phytoplankton** (tiny ocean **plants**), these are then consumed by **zooplankton** (small ocean **animals**), which are then consumed by small fish such as **herring**. These are then consumed by larger fish such as **tuna** and **shark**. The diagram below has numbers just to show how the toxins can build up. Mercury in tuna and shark though, can reach high enough levels that they are harmful for humans to eat.

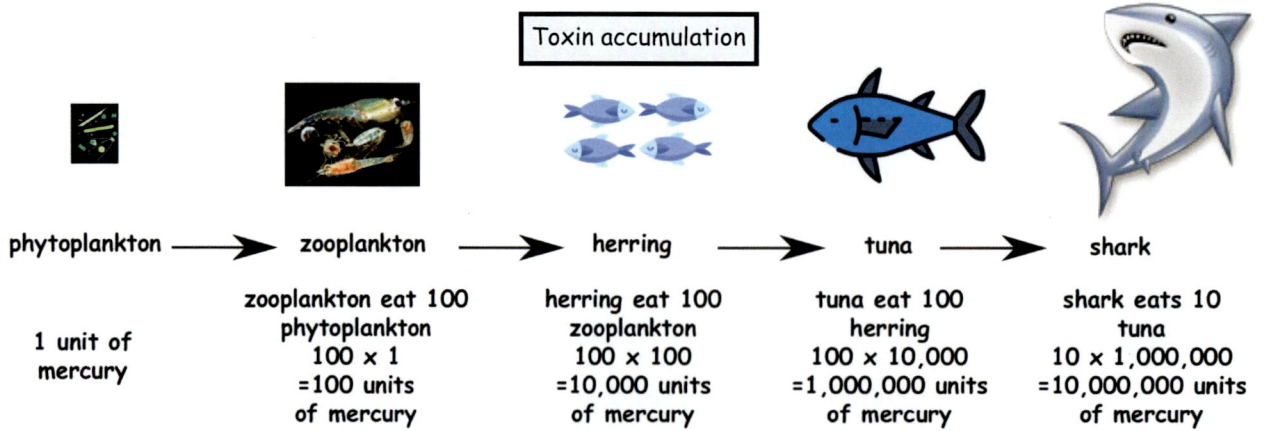

Toxin accumulation

phytoplankton →	zooplankton →	herring →	tuna →	shark
1 unit of mercury	zooplankton eat 100 phytoplankton 100 x 1 =100 units of mercury	herring eat 100 zooplankton 100 x 100 =10,000 units of mercury	tuna eat 100 herring 100 x 10,000 =1,000,000 units of mercury	shark eats 10 tuna 10 x 1,000,000 =10,000,000 units of mercury

> **WHAT?**
>
> In a spoon full of sea water there are around one million plankton, without them ocean food chains would collapse. Phytoplankton are responsible for 20% of all the photosynthesis on earth so they're mighty important producers.

Questions on Pyramids of Numbers and Toxin Accumulation

Comprehension

1. What are toxins?	8. Why do they often look like pyramids?
2. How many routes do they have into an organism?	9. How many green fly could one bush feed?
3. What does ingested mean?	10. Each trophic level tells us the size of the population but not what?
4. What are pesticides used for?	11. How can chemical fertiliser get into our water?
5. Which toxic metals can be passed up the food chain?	12. What is one of the ways that toxins can get into soils?
6. What do pyramids of numbers show us?	13. What happens to the toxin concentration as it is transferred higher up the food chain?
7. Complete the sentence. *Each level in the food chain is drawn in _____ to the size of the population.*	14. How high can the mercury levels reach in tuna and shark?

Additional tasks

1. Draw a pyramid of numbers in the boxes below for the following two food chains;

5,000 Clover leaves, **100** Snails, **10** Robins, **2** Buzzards (birds of prey)

Pyramid of numbers

1 Oak tree, **1000** Caterpillars, **50** Pigeons, **2** Kitty hawks (birds of prey)

Pyramid of numbers

2. Another way of drawing pyramids for food chains is to draw **pyramids of biomass**. This is where each trophic level is drawn to represent the **mass** of living material (biomass) rather than the number of each species.

a. Complete the table below to calculate the **total biomass** for each organism by multiplying the number of organisms by their mass.

	Caterpillar	Robin	Elderberry bush
Mass of organism (g)	3	75	5000
Number of organisms	100	2	1
Total biomass (g)			

3. Use the total mass to draw a **pyramid of biomass** for the food chain.

Elderberry bush ⟶ Caterpillar ⟶ Robin

Pyramid of biomass

Variation

There is clearly variation (differences) between different species. Pigs can't fly because they don't have wings! There is also variation **within** a species. Dogs come in all shapes and sizes but are the same species and can breed with each other. Humans too have lots of variation. The differences lead to characteristics (features) that are classed as either continuous or discontinuous.

Discontinuous means the characteristic falls into a specific category, there is nothing in between (not continuous). Human examples include **blood group**, you can be either A+, A-, B+, B-, O+, O-, AB+ or AB-. **Hair colour**, brown, black, blond, ginger etc. **Eye colour**, blue, brown, green etc. **Gender**, male or female.

Number of Year 7 pupils

A histogram

Height (cm): less than 130 | 130 to 134 | 135 to 139 | 140 to 144 | 145 to 149 | 150 to 154 | more than 154

Continuous characteristics have any value within a certain range, like **height**, **weight**, **skin colour** or **foot size**.

The table below shows data for **200 Year 7 pupils**. The students' heights are recorded and then put into the correct ranges. Also the number of students that are boys and girls is recorded.

Height (cm)	130-134	135-139	140-144	145-149	150-154
Number of pupils	10	40	100	40	10

Gender	boy	girl
Number of pupils	95	105

Continuous data is plotted on a **histogram**. A histogram plots the number of people that fall within a certain range for the characteristic. **Discontinuous data** is plotted on a **bar chart**, it shows the number of people that have that characteristic (fall into that category). The bars are separated with spaces.

Genetic and Environmental Characteristics

The genes that we get from our parents, half from mum and half from dad, give us our inherited characteristics. Our 'looks' like eye colour, hair colour, skin colour, freckles, height and others. The environment (conditions) also has an effect on our characteristics. We can sunbathe to change our skin colour. We can dye our hair. We could have tall parents but suffer from malnutrition as a child and only grow to a small height.

Number of Year 7 pupils

A bar chart

boys | girls

Gender

Asthma is thought to be influenced by both inherited factors (our genes) and the environment. This **nature versus nurture** debate has been around for a long time. Nurture can be how hard we work, practise or are encouraged by others. Claiming not to be clever or good at maths because your parents aren't is not true. We can **all read** to improve knowledge and **practise mathematics** if we wish to. However, genes do influence how easy this may be for us. Individuals that find certain tasks easier tend to do them more and become good at them, but this does not mean others cannot.

WHAT?

It is claimed that 10,000 hours of practise can make you an expert, start learning a new skill now!

Questions on Variation

Comprehension

1. What clearly exists between species?

2. Why can all dogs breed with each other?

3. What does discontinuous mean?

4. Name four human characteristics that are discontinuous.

5. What do continuous characteristics have?

6. Name four human characteristics that are continuous.

7. What does a histogram plot?

8. What sort of data is plotted on a bar chart?

9. How much of our genes come from mum and how much from dad?

10. What two factors affect our characteristics?

11. How can the environment change our skin colour?

12. What 'could' cause the child of tall parents to be small?

13. What is thought to influence asthma?

14. What debate has been around for a long time?

15. Why is it not true to say 'I'm not good at maths' or 'I'm not clever' because my parents aren't?

16. What might genes mean for certain tasks for certain individuals?

Additional tasks

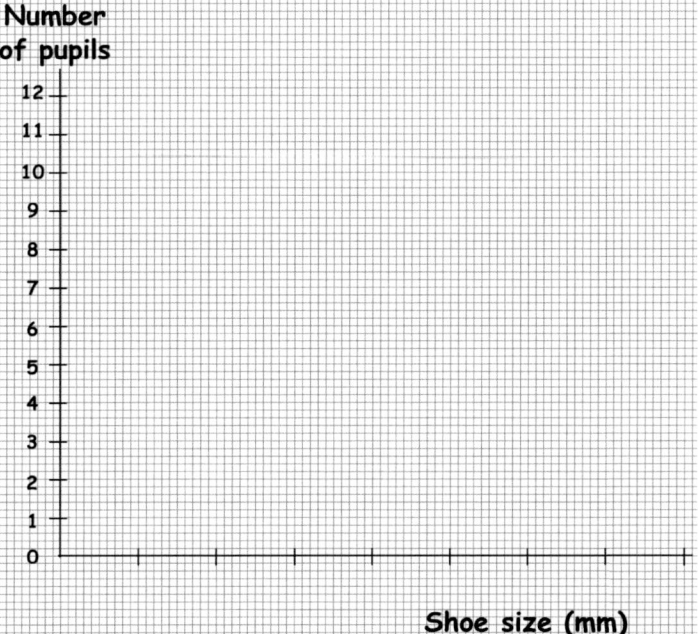

1. Draw a histogram for the data below showing the shoe size for a class of 30 year 7 pupils.

Number of pupils with that shoe size	Shoe size range (mm)
1	195-204
2	205-214
6	215-224
12	225-234
6	235-244
2	245-254
1	255-264

2. Draw a bar chart of the percentage of people with each blood type in the UK.

Percentage of people in UK	Blood type
30	A+
8	A-
8	B+
2	B-
35	O+
13	O-
2	AB+
1	AB-

CHEMISTRY

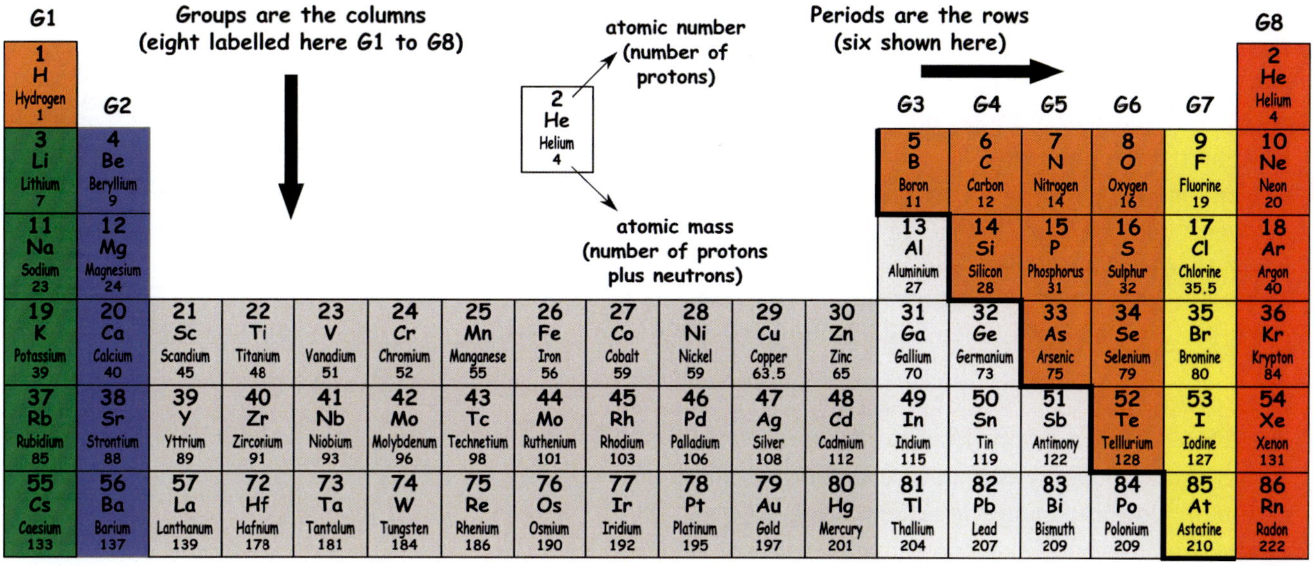

Groups are the columns
(eight labelled here G1 to G8)

atomic number
(number of
protons)

Periods are the rows
(six shown here)

2
He
Helium
4

atomic mass
(number of protons
plus neutrons)

G1																	G8
1 H Hydrogen 1	G2											G3	G4	G5	G6	G7	2 He Helium 4
3 Li Lithium 7	4 Be Beryllium 9											5 B Boron 11	6 C Carbon 12	7 N Nitrogen 14	8 O Oxygen 16	9 F Fluorine 19	10 Ne Neon 20
11 Na Sodium 23	12 Mg Magnesium 24											13 Al Aluminium 27	14 Si Silicon 28	15 P Phosphorus 31	16 S Sulphur 32	17 Cl Chlorine 35.5	18 Ar Argon 40
19 K Potassium 39	20 Ca Calcium 40	21 Sc Scandium 45	22 Ti Titanium 48	23 V Vanadium 51	24 Cr Chromium 52	25 Mn Manganese 55	26 Fe Iron 56	27 Co Cobalt 59	28 Ni Nickel 59	29 Cu Copper 63.5	30 Zn Zinc 65	31 Ga Gallium 70	32 Ge Germanium 73	33 As Arsenic 75	34 Se Selenium 79	35 Br Bromine 80	36 Kr Krypton 84
37 Rb Rubidium 85	38 Sr Strontium 88	39 Y Yttrium 89	40 Zr Zircorium 91	41 Nb Niobium 93	42 Mo Molybdenum 96	43 Tc Technetium 98	44 Mo Ruthenium 101	45 Rh Rhodium 103	46 Pd Palladium 106	47 Ag Silver 108	48 Cd Cadmium 112	49 In Indium 115	50 Sn Tin 119	51 Sb Antimony 122	52 Te Tellurium 128	53 I Iodine 127	54 Xe Xenon 131
55 Cs Caesium 133	56 Ba Barium 137	57 La Lanthanum 139	72 Hf Hafnium 178	73 Ta Tantalum 181	74 W Tungsten 184	75 Re Rhenium 186	76 Os Osmium 190	77 Ir Iridium 192	78 Pt Platinum 195	79 Au Gold 197	80 Hg Mercury 201	81 Tl Thallium 204	82 Pb Lead 207	83 Bi Bismuth 209	84 Po Polonium 209	85 At Astatine 210	86 Rn Radon 222

The Particulate Nature of Matter

Over 2400 years ago, the Greeks had the idea that all substances are made up from much smaller (minute) pieces of matter called particles. Leucippus, and his student Democritus, are thought to have first presented the idea.

These particles are too small to be seen and come in many shapes and sizes. They 'stick' together (bond) to make up all the substances we see. We now call these particles atoms, which comes from Democritus's use of the word 'atomos', which means indivisible (can't be divided or split). We now know this not to be true, the atom (which is the basic unit of matter), can be split! It is best to think of atoms as little balls that stick together and make up the every day objects that we see.

Explaining the States of Matter (Solids, Liquids and Gases)

Whether a substance is a solid, liquid or gas depends very much on the temperature of the substance. Think of water, it can be cooled to ice, or heated to a gas that we call water vapour. This affects the distance between the particles and the size of the attraction, further apart means a weaker attraction, closer together means a stronger attraction, this is key.

Solids: the particles in a solid are **close together**, this means they have **strong** forces of attraction (**bonds**) between each other. This also makes them the **most dense**, density tells us how closely packed the particles are. They have a **regular arrangement** and are **unable to move** from **their positions**, this gives a solid a **fixed shape** and **volume**. Solids **cannot flow** or be **compressed** (squashed) because there is  not enough room between the particles. Don't get confused by a sponge, it is the air gaps between you are squashing! The particles of a solid just jiggle or **vibrate** around the **same position**, just like you dancing on the same spot.

Liquids: the particles in a liquid are **further apart** than in a solid, this means the force of attraction is **medium strength** (weak **bonds**) and the particles are **able to move** from their **positions** (they still jiggle though!). They **can** move over and under each other or **flow**, meaning they **don't have** a **fixed shape**, but instead take the shape of the container  they are in e.g. a cup. They do however have a **fixed volume**. There is little space between the particles so they **cannot be compressed** either. Liquids are **usually less dense** than **solids**.

Gases: the **spacing** of particles is **far apart**, meaning the **force of attraction** is **very weak** (or even zero). The particles **whizz** around **randomly** (with no particular pattern) at high speed. They fill the shape of the container they are in, so have **no fixed shape or volume**. There is a lot of space between the particles so gases are **easily compressed**. Gases are the **least dense** state of matter.

WHAT?

There is about 7 billion billion billion, 7 000, 000, 000, 000, 000, 000, 000, 000, 000 atoms in the average human. Diamond is the hardest naturally occurring solid but scientists have made harder materials! At 'room temperature' (about 20°C) gas atoms move at around 1000mph, ouch!

Questions on the Particulate Nature of Matter

Comprehension

1. What do we call minute pieces of matter?
2. Who is first thought to have presented the idea that substances are made from particles?
3. How small are these particles?
4. What do we now call these particles?
5. What does indivisible mean?
6. Existing as a solid, liquid or gas depends very much on what?
7. What does density tell us?
8. In solids, is the force of attraction strong, medium, or weak between particles?
9. What sort of shape and volume does this give to solids?
10. In a solid the particles can't move from their positions, but what do they do in that same position?
11. How strong is the force of attraction between particles in liquids?
12. In what way can the particles in a liquid move?
13. What sort of shape do liquids take?
14. Why can't liquids be compressed?
15. How far apart are the particles in a gas and what does this mean for the force of attraction between the particles?
16. Why are gases easily compressed?

Additional tasks

1. Match the words to their meanings and memorise.

Indivisible	the gaseous (gas) form of water
Density	means with no particular pattern, the way particles in a gas move
Bond	means can't be divided or split
Water vapour	a force of attraction between particles
Volume	tells us how tightly packed particles are
Randomly	is the amount of space a substance occupies

2. Write next to the statements as to whether they are correct for a solid, liquid or a gas.

Particles are the closest together _____

Are easily compressed _____

Medium strength bonds _____

Fixed volume but not fixed shape _____

No fixed shape or volume _____

Least dense _____

Most dense _____

Usually less dense than solids _____

Particles vibrate around one position _____

Strong bonds _____

Weak or no bonds _____

Can flow _____

Atoms arranged regularly _____

3. The density of carbon dioxide as a solid, liquid and gas is given below.

Solid CO_2 (density **1560** kg/m^3)

Liquid CO_2 (density **1100** kg/m^3)

Gaseous CO_2 (density **2.0** kg/m^3)

Explain the difference in density using how the particles are arranged and the spacing between them. Draw diagrams if you wish.

4 a. Helium has a density of 0.18 kg/m^3 and air has a density of 1.3 kg/m^3. What does this mean that a helium balloon will do?

b. What do you think this tells you about why objects float?

Dalton's Atomic Model:
Atoms, Elements, Compounds and Molecules

John Dalton lived from 1766-1844. He developed the idea that matter is made from atoms that are like tiny spheres (balls) and are indivisible. He came up with some rules about how they would behave and most importantly did experiments and made observations to check. Some of his rules are as follows: atoms cannot be created or destroyed, atoms of the same elements have the same properties, different atoms (elements) have different properties and chemical changes (reactions) are due to the rearrangement of the atoms of a substance.

Elements

A pure element is made from only one type of atom. A lump of pure calcium, for example, only contains calcium atoms, pure oxygen gas has only oxygen atoms or pure carbon, like in a diamond, is only made from carbon atoms.

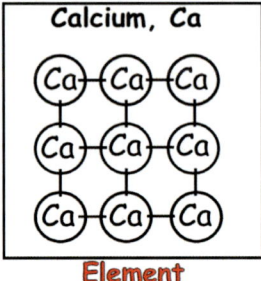

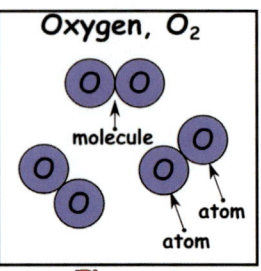

Compounds

Compounds are formed when two or more **different** atoms are bonded together. A chemical bond is when atoms are held together by an electrostatic attraction. The same force that sticks a balloon to the wall when you rub it on your clothes. Well known compounds include water (chemical formula, H_2O, below), made from hydrogen and oxygen. Carbon dioxide (chemical formula, CO_2, below), made from carbon and oxygen. Alcohol (or ethanol), made from carbon, hydrogen and oxygen. Polyethene, made from carbon and hydrogen.

Molecules

A compound like water is made up of molecules. Molecules are two or more atoms bonded together, they don't have to be different like in a compound. We can think of **molecules** as the **smallest complete unit of a substance**. The drawing above shows calcium made from calcium atoms bonded together as a solid. Next to it, is oxygen gas made from oxygen molecules. Oxygen atoms clearly exist but two oxygen atoms prefer to bond to make an oxygen molecule, so that is how they are normally found. Oxygen molecules are still an example of an element, this is because there is only one type of atom present, oxygen, it just likes to form a molecule. We draw circles to represent the atoms. The number of each circle tells us how many of each type of atom are in a molecule. Hydrogen, the most common element in the universe, likes to form a molecule, by bonding to another hydrogen atom. Helium doesn't form molecules and likes to be just an atom on its own.

> **WHAT?**
>
> The chemical name for water is dihydrogen monoxide! 'Di' means two (hydrogens) and mono means one (oxygen). Molecules of oxygen are so small we breathe in 30 000 000 000 000 000 000 000 000 (thirty thousand billion billion) molecules every breath! Helium is the second most abundant element in the universe but it is rare on earth. Without helium MRI scans for finding out (diagnosing) whether people have certain diseases will become impossible. We need to stop putting it in balloons!

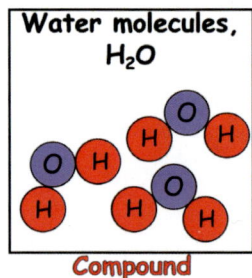

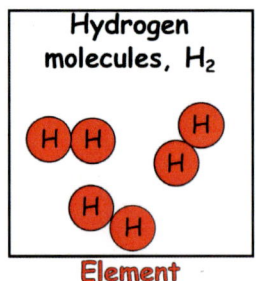

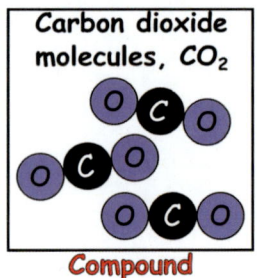

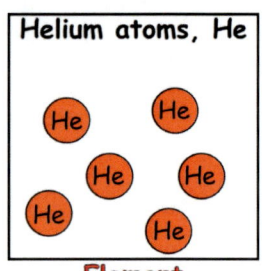

Questions on Atoms, Elements, Compounds and Molecules

Comprehension

1. What did John Dalton develop?
2. What are atoms like?
3. How did John Dalton check his rules about atoms?
4. What are chemical reactions or changes due to?
5. What is a pure element made from?
6. Which element is a pure diamond made from?
7. When are compounds formed?
8. What is a chemical bond?
9. What is the chemical formula for water?
10. What is another name for alcohol?
11. What is a molecule?
12. Why is oxygen normally found as a molecule?
13. What do we draw to represent atoms on a piece of paper?
14. What does the number of each circle tell us?
15. What is the most common element in the universe?
16. What **doesn't** helium form?
17. How is helium normally found?

Additional tasks

1. Match the words to their meanings and memorise.

John Dalton	is a molecule made from two oxygen atoms and one carbon atom
Element	a substance formed from two or more **different** atoms
Compound	a scientist who developed the idea that matter is made from atoms
Molecule	is a molecule made from two hydrogen atoms and one oxygen atom
Water	is two or more atoms bonded together, they can be the same or different atoms (the smallest complete unit of a substance)
Carbon dioxide	a substance made from only one type of atom

2. Complete the gap filling exercise, choose from the words in bold below;

    molecules, one, water, Oxygen, unit, different, same, different, carbon dioxide, compound, Helium

    A pure element will only be made from _____ type of atom. _____ is an element often used in party balloons. _____ is the element that we breathe. Oxygen and hydrogen are both elements that form _____ . Molecules are the smallest complete _____ of a substance. They are made from two or more atoms that can be _____ or the _____. A molecule like _____, H_2O is an example of a _____. Compounds are formed from two or more _____ atoms bonded together. The gas that we breathe out called _____ _____ is a compound.

3. The images below show either **an *element* made from molecules** or a **compound made from molecules.** Write underneath each image whether you think they are an element or compound.

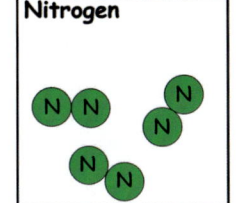
Nitrogen

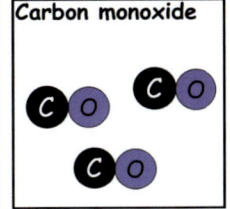
Carbon monoxide

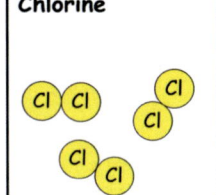
Chlorine

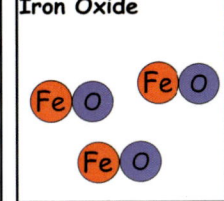
Iron Oxide

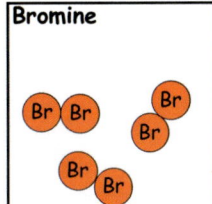
Bromine

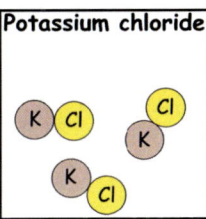
Potassium chloride

Evidence for Particles (Atoms)

Since the work of John Dalton (1803), it was thought that what caused the difference between elements; carbon, iron, oxygen etc is that they are made from different atoms. Atoms are the tiny particles that we can't see alone, but when there are lots of them, they make up the substances we can see.

A bit like dust in the air, you don't **normally** see one speck of dust, they are too small. When they fall on surfaces and build up, then you can easily see them. You have probably noticed on a sunny day when a bright beam of sunlight enters a room, you can sometimes see dust particles moving around. They seem to move in random directions with no particular pattern.

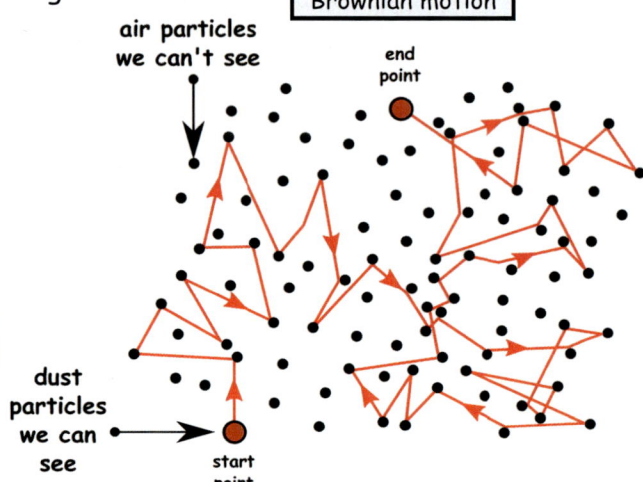

Brownian Motion

A Scottish botanist (a person who studies plant life) called Robert Brown was studying pollen grains suspended in water under a microscope in 1827. He noticed that the pollen grains seemed to move randomly. He described the motion but was unable to explain it. It is now known as **Brownian motion**.

Explanation

We know air is there because we breathe it, can feel it and even weigh it. In air, the dust particles are continually colliding with air particles that we can't see. This causes the dust particles to move erratically from their start point to their end point. It is called the **random walk**. The brilliant Albert Einstein explained this random walk using mathematics and assuming that the dust particles were colliding with **unseen** smaller particles, **air**. Most importantly his predictions matched observations. Well done Einstein!

How do we know how big they are?

Air is made from atoms and molecules. A simple way to know roughly the size of a molecule is to place a drop of oil on top of water and allow it to spread out. Having a known starting volume enables the height (diameter) of the oil molecule to be found if we assume it spreads out to a one molecule thick layer (see below). What we know about atoms comes from experiments. Many other experiments shoot small particles of matter at substances that can't be seen and observe how they bounce off, just like 'shooting' balls at something invisible and seeing if they come back or not.

WHAT?

The largest molecule ever made is still only 10 millionth of a millimetre across and can't be seen with a microscope. 10,000 of them lined up would be the thickness of a piece of paper.

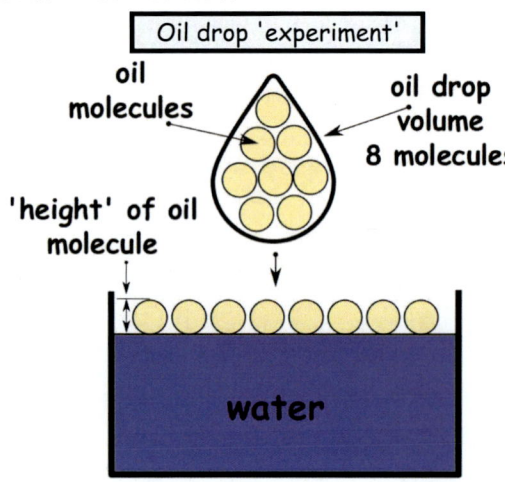

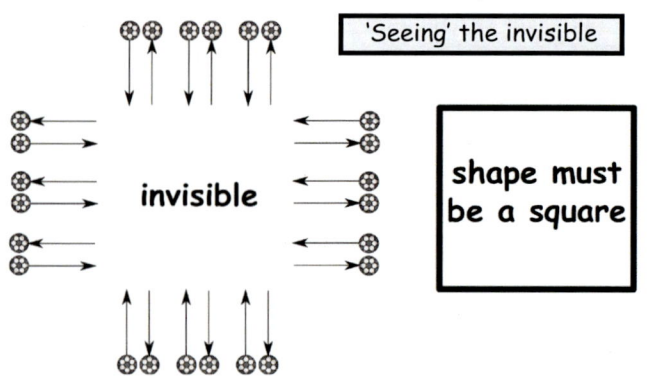

Questions on Evidence for Particles

Comprehension

1. What did scientists think caused the difference between elements?

2. Why don't you normally see a speck of dust in the air?

3. When can you sometimes see dust particles moving around in the air?

4. In what direction do the particles seem to move?

5. What was Robert Brown doing in 1827?

6. What was Robert Brown unable to do?

7. How do we know air exists?

8. What causes the dust particles to move erratically?

9. What is the name given to the particles moving erratically from their start point to end point?

10. How did Albert Einstein explain the motion?

11. What was most important about Einstein's explanation?

12. What is a simple way to know the rough size of an oil molecule?

13. What do we assume about how thick the layer of oil is?

14. What do many other experiments do?

Additional tasks

1. Sketch your own random walks below from start point to end point, for the dust particles being pushed around by the air particles. They are different every time.

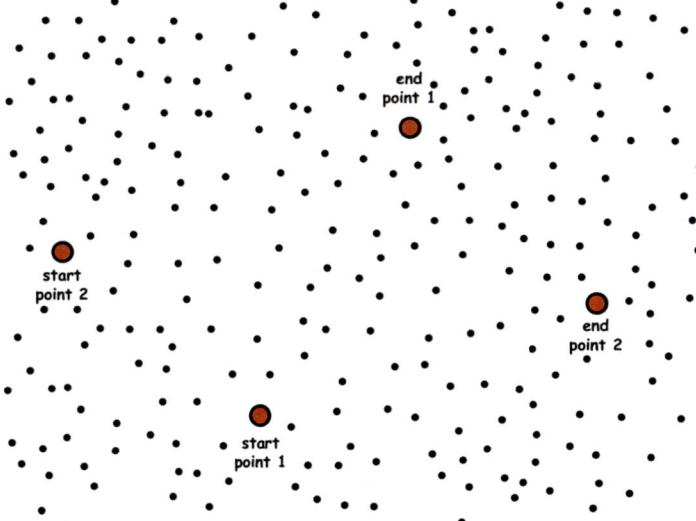

2. Draw in what you think the invisible shapes are by how the balls are bouncing off.

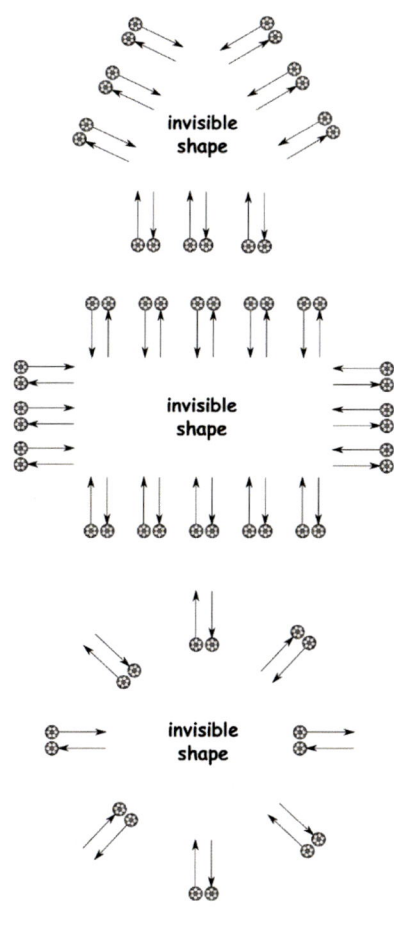

3. An atom is about **0.0000001mm** across (diameter).

Use a calculator to divide the thickness of these everyday items by the diameter of an atom to calculate how many 'atoms thick' they are. Write your answer as a number and in words.

Remember *1,000 = thousand*

1,000,000 = million

1,000,000,000 = billion

a. human hair = 0.1mm

b. piece of paper = 0.08mm

c. human skin = 2mm

d. the height of a door = 2000mm

e. house paint = 0.05mm

f. wooden shelf = 15mm

g. the length of a brick = 215mm

Chemical Symbols and Chemical Formulae

All 118 elements discovered so far have a chemical symbol. It is a code that is used instead of the full name of the element. Often it is a shortened version of the full name, like **C**, for carbon, or **He**, for helium. Others come from Latin, like **Fe** for iron, from the Latin name Ferrum, or **Pb** for lead, from the Latin name plumbum, meaning water works (water was often carried in lead pipes). Some are named after scientists like Einsteinium, Es, after Albert Einstein. All elements and their symbols can be found in the periodic table so you don't have to learn them, but it's handy to know a few common ones.

Chemical Formulae

A formula like H_2O for water, tells you the number of each atom in a molecule (the smallest complete unit of a substance).
A water molecule has **two hydrogen** atoms and **one oxygen** atom.

Carbon dioxide molecules (chemical formula, CO_2) have **one carbon** atom and **two oxygen** atoms, it's the gas we breathe out. Carbon monoxide molecules (chemical formula, CO) have **one carbon** and **one oxygen** atom, this gas is produced when fuels are burnt without enough oxygen, it's poisonous and doesn't smell, making it very dangerous in homes. Methane (chemical formula, CH_4), the gas we burn to heat our homes and cook our food, has **one carbon** and **four hydrogen** atoms. Sodium chloride, common salt, the stuff you put on your fish and chips (chemical formula, NaCl) has **one sodium** atom and **one chlorine** atom. Calcium carbonate (chemical formula, $CaCO_3$), commonly found as limestone or the harder version marble, has **one calcium** atom, **one carbon** atom and **three oxygen** atoms. Copper sulphate, a beautifully blue crystal, (chemical formula, $CuSO_4$), has **one copper** atom, **one sulphur** atom and **four** oxygen atoms. Sodium hydrogen carbonate, baking powder, (chemical formula $NaHCO_3$), has **one sodium**, **one hydrogen**, **one carbon** and **three oxygen** atoms. Glucose, (chemical formula, $C_6H_{12}O_6$) the main sugar molecule that provides us with our energy, has **six carbon** atoms, **twelve hydrogen** atoms and **six oxygen** atoms.

A chemical formula can be written for anything!

Methane molecule, CH_4

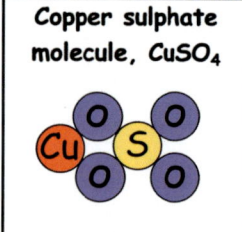

Compound

Calcium carbonate molecule, $CaCO_3$

Compound

Carbon monoxide molecule, CO

Compound

Carbon dioxide molecule, CO_2

Compound

Copper sulphate molecule, $CuSO_4$

Compound

WHAT?

The longest chemical name is for a protein, it contains 189,819 letters, we don't have room to write it! It takes over three hours to read so for short scientists call it 'Titin'. The formula is;

$C_{169723}H_{270464}N_{45688}O_{52243}S_{912}$

Chemical formulae!

Naming Compounds

This can be tricky. Compounds like methane, water and glucose are so common they are just known by their own names. Two rules that help though are as follows.

1. If a compound is made from **only two different** elements, its name ends in **–IDE**. Carbon dioxide (di meaning two), CO_2. Carbon monoxide (mono meaning one), CO. Sodium chloride, NaCl. Potassium chloride, KCl. Sodium fluoride, NaF. Iron sulfide, FeS.

2. Three or more different elements, with one of them being oxygen will mean that the name ends with **-ATE**. Calcium carbonate, $CaCO_3$. Copper sulphate, $CuSO_4$. Sodium hydrogen carbonate, $NaHCO_3$. Zinc sulphate, $ZnSO_4$.

Questions on Chemical Symbols and Chemical Formulae

Comprehension

1. How many elements have been discovered so far?
2. Often the chemical symbol is what version of the full name?
3. Others come from what language?
4. Who are some of the elements named after?
5. What is the chemical formula for water?
6. How many hydrogen and oxygen atoms does a water molecule have?
7. Why is carbon monoxide dangerous?
8. How many hydrogen and carbon atoms are there in methane?
9. In what form is calcium carbonate commonly found?
10. How many of each atom are there in baking powder?
11. What is glucose?
12. What are common compounds known by?
13. What is a compound that normally ends in –IDE made from?
14. If a compound's name ends with –ATE, what will one of the elements be?

Additional tasks

1. Match the formula to the compound and memorise.

Water	$CuSO_4$
Carbon dioxide	$CaCO_3$
Methane	H_2O
Calcium carbonate	$C_6H_{12}O_6$
Copper sulphate	CH_4
Glucose	CO_2

2. Choose from the words below to name the elements or compounds in the text box on the left hand side. Use the periodic table on pg90 to help.

Magnesium chloride, Nitrogen, Calcium oxide, Sodium carbonate, Hydrogen chloride, Iron dioxide, Magnesium carbonate, Calcium sulphate, Iron oxide, Magnesium oxide, Oxygen, Potassium sulphate, Sulphur, Silver nitrate

3. In the right hand box, write the number of each atom from the formula e.g. *Lithium sulphate,*

   Li_2SO_4, 2 X Li (lithium) atoms, 1 X S (sulphur) atom, 4 X O (oxygen) atoms.

$CaSO_4$ _____	$CaSO_4$ _____
N_2 _____	N_2 _____
Na_2CO_3 _____	Na_2CO_3 _____
HCl _____	HCl _____
$MgCl_2$ _____	$MgCl_2$ _____
FeO _____	FeO _____
FeO_2 _____	FeO_2 _____
S_8 _____	S_8 _____
$MgCO_3$ _____	$MgCO_3$ _____
CaO _____	CaO _____
MgO _____	MgO _____
O_2 _____	O_2 _____
K_2SO_4 _____	K_2SO_4 _____
$AgNO_3$ _____	$AgNO_3$ _____

Chemical Reactions: How we know they've happened

When **two chemicals react** together, **the reactants**, a **new substance** is formed, the **product(s).** Often there is more than one product in a chemical reaction. We can tell if a chemical reaction has happened by looking for:

➡ A change in colour   ➡ A change in temperature

➡ A smell being given off   ➡ Bubbles being produced

➡ A solid forming in a liquid solution (called a precipitate)

➡ Light being emitted

Glow sticks

A Change in Colour

If a chemical reaction happens, the products can be a different colour. Simply burning toast, which turns black, tells you a chemical reaction has occurred. The orange-red-brown colour on an old car or bike, tells you a chemical reaction has taken place, **rusting.**

A Change in Temperature

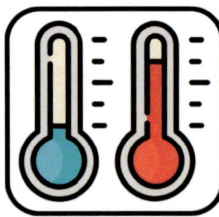

If you were to put your hand above an **unlit** Bunsen burner, you wouldn't feel anything (no chemical reaction). As soon as it is lit, a chemical reaction takes place (**combustion**) and a large amount of heat is released. This rise is temperature would burn your skin. Hand warmers for your gloves in winter have chemicals inside, that release heat when they react. Cold packs for sports injuries do the opposite, a chemical reaction causes a decrease in temperature.

A Smell Being Given Off

Many chemical reactions produce smells, some of them toxic, some harmless. Milk that has 'gone off' smells bad. This tells you that a chemical reaction has occurred due to the growth of microbes (tiny organisms / life forms), that break down the milk to produce a nasty smell. Boiled eggs smell, this is because of the **hydrogen sulphide** given off by the chemical reaction that is caused by boiling the egg.

Bubbles Being Produced / Gas Release

If you were to simply add baking powder to vinegar, you would observe that many bubbles are produced. When bubbles of gas are produced in a liquid like this we called it **effervescence.** You see the same thing when Alka Seltzer (for upset stomachs) is dropped into water. You also see **bubbles** of oxygen being produced on the **leaves** of plants in a fish tank, this is due to the chemical reaction called **photosynthesis**.

A Solid Forming in a Liquid Solution (called a precipitate)

An insoluble solid can form in a liquid, this is called a **precipitate**. Calcium carbonate (chalk), forms when carbon dioxide is bubbled through a liquid called **limewater**. The limewater goes a cloudy white colour because calcium carbonate is formed in the water (chalk in the water which is insoluble). An example you may see at home is when water is added to a Greek alcoholic drink called 'Ouzo'. A white cloudy solid immediately forms because the aniseed used to make Ouzo has chemicals in that don't dissolve in water, it appears as a solid when water is added.

Precipitate formed in Ouzo

WHAT?

The 'smelliest' molecule is called 'ethyl mercatan' (C_2H_5SH), it smells like sewers and rotting onions, it is toxic! The hottest chemical reaction is when dicyanoacetylene, C_4N_2, burns in oxygen, it reaches nearly 5000C.

Questions on Chemical Reactions

Comprehension

1.	What are the two chemicals that react together called?
2.	What sort of substance is formed?
3.	How many products are often formed?
4.	How many ways can we tell if a chemical reaction has happened?
5.	What is the name given to a solid that forms in a liquid?
6.	What is a simple example of the products of a chemical reaction being a different colour?
7.	Why wouldn't you feel anything if you put your hand above an **unlit** Bunsen burner?
8.	What do hand warmers have inside them?
9.	What does milk that has 'gone off' tell you?
10.	Why do boiled eggs smell?
11.	What do we call it when bubbles of gas are given off in a liquid?
12.	How can you tell oxygen gas is produced by plants in a fish tank?
13.	What chemical reaction is this due to?
14.	Why does limewater go cloudy when carbon dioxide is bubbled through it?
15.	What happens when water is added to Ouzo?

Additional tasks

1. Match the words to their meanings and memorise.

Precipitate	the name given to bubbles formed in a liquid
Rusting	a chemical used to test for the presence of carbon dioxide gas
Hydrogen sulphide	a commonly used word for the chemical Calcium carbonate, $CaCO_3$
Effervescence	a solid formed in a solution (liquid)
Limewater	a smelly chemical given off from boiled eggs
Chalk	a chemical reaction between iron (or steel), air and water producing orange – red - brown *rust* (chemical name iron oxide)

2. Complete the chemical reaction word search below.

PRODUCTS, ODOUR, EFFERVESCENCE, LIMEWATER, PRECIPITATE, RUSTING, HYDROGENSULPHIDE, TEMPERATURE, BUBBLES, SMELL, COLOUR, CHALK, EMISSION, BUNSENBURNER

3. Underline what tells you a chemical reaction might have happened in the statements below. *One of them is 'wrong', can you spot it and explain why?*

```
A B H B U B B L E S C D E F G H
I J Y K L M N O F P Q R S T U V
W X D C P Y Z P F M Y L B D N N
U H R H R C U S E O D O U R O F
O Z O A E Y N I R I U R N I J A
Z U G L C T K V V Q D U S Z S G
Q G E K I Y X F E Z M S E D T S
O V N A P X L J S G I U N K T C
X X S M I S I O C M M D B C S T
R E U D T E M P E R A T U R E H
U A L Z A X E S N A Q D R U D J
I O P Q T M W E C U O U N S V A
P W H S E S A C E R O V E T T Y
R L I T N F T U P L Z P R I G B
Z Y D L O U E U O Z O O Y N C C
S M E L L I R C J W S C H G K O
```

a.	Magnesium burns very brightly in air and gets very hot
b.	Add magnesium to acid it fizzes and gets warm
c.	Colourless silver nitrate solution is added to sodium bromide solution and a cream solid forms
d.	Acetic acid is added to alcohol and a noticeable aroma is smelt
e.	Copper carbonate (green) is heated and turns black
f.	An ice cube left in a beaker melts
g.	Barium hydroxide and ammonium chloride are mixed and the beaker gets too cold to hold
h.	Bubbles appear on a pond plant underwater
i.	Baking powder releases carbon dioxide when a cake is baked to make it rise

Chemical Reactions: Atoms Rearranged

We already know that a chemical reaction may have taken place when we see a change in colour, a change in temperature, bubbles being produced, a smell being given off or light emitted. We always start with **reactants** and 'go to' (make) **products**. We write this as a chemical equation (no equals sign), using arrows to show what we start with and end up with. The 'equation' below shows what happens when hydrochloric acid, HCl, reacts with the alkali sodium hydroxide, NaOH.

Reactants $\longrightarrow$ Products	HCl + NaOH $\longrightarrow$ NaCl + H$_2$O
(at the start) (at the end)	(at the start) (at the end)

The reason that this happens is, when two substances react together, **bonds** (forces that hold atoms together) can be **made** or **broken** to produce new substances.

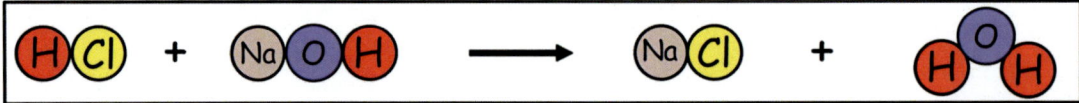

Physical Change Vs Chemical Reaction

We know that a chemical reaction has taken place as opposed to (instead of) a physical change, because a **new product is formed**. *The atoms have rearranged their positions and formed new compounds*. Compare ice (solid) melting, then the water (liquid) boiling, all of the time we still have water molecules since no chemical reaction has occurred only a **physical change**.

No new compound is formed, only the **state of matter has changed** (solid/liquid/gas). It is easy to reverse a physical change, put water in the freezer, liquid to solid, take it out again, solid to liquid. **Dry ice (solid carbon dioxide)**, can change straight from a solid to a gas. It is still a physical change, since we still only have carbon dioxide at the end, no new product. Changing from a solid straight to a gas is called **sublimation**. The reverse is also possible, carbon dioxide gas can be turned straight back into dry ice. This is called **deposition**, still a physical change, we still only have carbon dioxide molecules afterwards.

Chemical reactions can't usually be reversed (at least not easily), for example, strike a match and let the chemical reaction finish, you can't get back what you started with. Or hard boil an egg and then try to get back to what you had before, almost impossible!
A chemical reaction has happened, new bonds have been made producing a new substance, in this case a boiled egg you can eat!

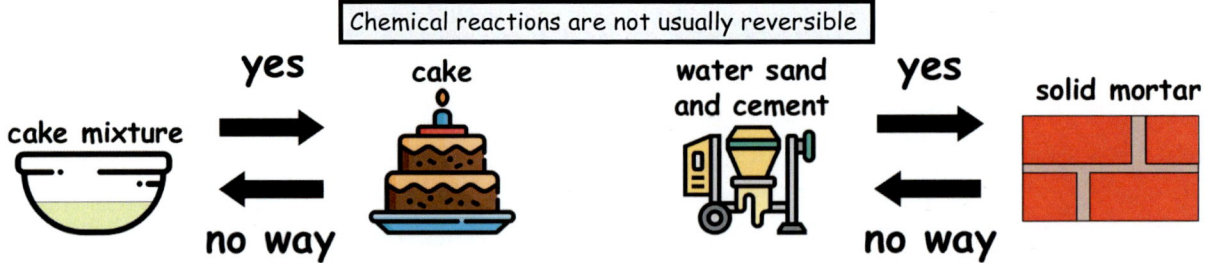

Chemical reactions are not usually reversible

yes — cake — water sand and cement — yes — solid mortar

cake mixture — no way — no way

Add water to sand and cement, a chemical reaction occurs and the mixture goes so hard we use it to hold bricks together when building houses. This is called **mortar**. Mix eggs, flour, butter and sugar (a cake mixture), bake them in the oven and you make a cake. You know a chemical reaction has taken place because you can't get back to the ingredients you started with.

Mixing is often a physical change, no new product

> **WHAT?**
> Reversible reactions do exist! Handwarmers use a liquid chemical that crystallises and releases heat. The reaction can be reversed by heating the crystals back to a liquid in hot water. Mixing sand, cement and stones is a physical change, adding water causes a chemical reaction giving us concrete.

Questions on Chemical Reactions: Atoms Rearranged

Comprehension

1. How do we already know when a chemical reaction has taken place?

2. We always start with reactants and 'go to' what?

3. What does a chemical equation show us?

4. What can happen when two substances react together?

5. What are bonds?

6. How do we know a chemical reaction has taken place instead of a physical change?

7. What can't 'usually' happen to chemical reactions?

8. What change happens if you put water in the freezer?

9. What does sublimation mean?

10. Is boiling an egg a chemical or physical change?

11. What happens when you add water to sand and cement?

12. What is in a cake mixture?

13. How do you know a chemical reaction has taken place when you bake a cake?

14. What is a an example of a reversible reaction? (WHAT? box)

Additional tasks

1. Write next to the examples below whether you think they are chemical or physical changes.

Frying an egg _____

Boiling water _____

Dropping a metal in acid _____

Mixing sand with water _____

Evaporating alcohol _____

Melting chocolate _____

A cloud making rain _____

Filtering dirty water _____

Milk going off _____

Mixing sugar and salt _____

Burning toast _____

A lit sparkler _____

Rotting wood _____

Mixing oil and water _____

Making popcorn _____

Rusting _____

2. Sketch the arrangement of the particles in a solid, liquid and gas then label the arrows with the following words (pg54 and pg130 help);

MELTING, VAPOURISING, CONDENSING, SOLIDIFYING (FREEZING), DEPOSITION, SUBLIMATION

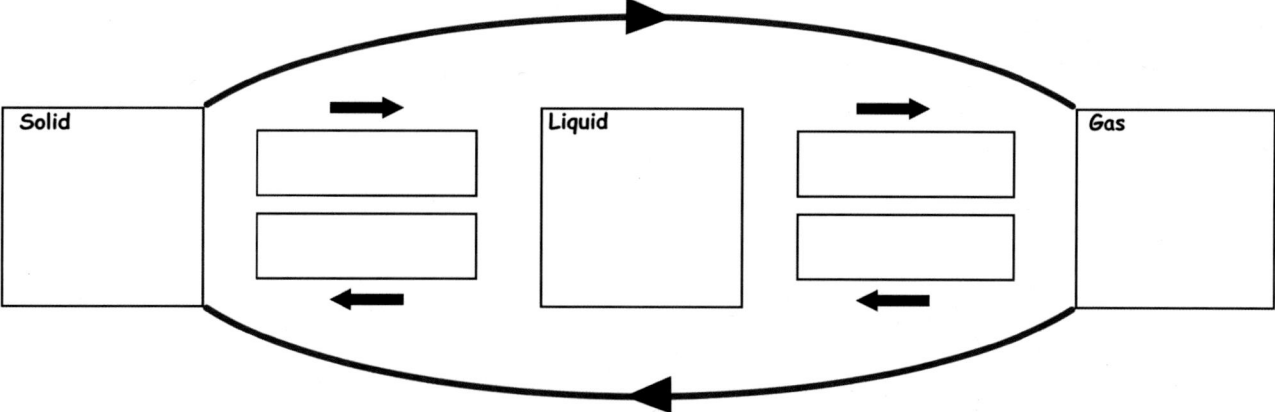

3. Write down some thoughts on whether dissolving sugar in water is a chemical or physical change. Think about whether something new is formed and if it is possible to get back to what you started with.

Conservation of Mass and Balancing Equations

Conservation of Mass

This tells us that the total mass (weighed) of the chemicals we start with, is equal to the total mass of the chemicals we end up with. **This is always true.** Magnesium reacts with oxygen to make magnesium oxide, MgO. Oxygen is found as a molecule, O_2 **not** as an atom, O. **So we can't write,** $Mg + O \longrightarrow MgO$. We have to write $Mg + O_2 \longrightarrow MgO$. **But,** this is unbalanced, now there are two oxygen atoms on the left and only one on the right, we're missing an oxygen atom! They don't **weigh** the same, **not balanced**. Putting numbers in front

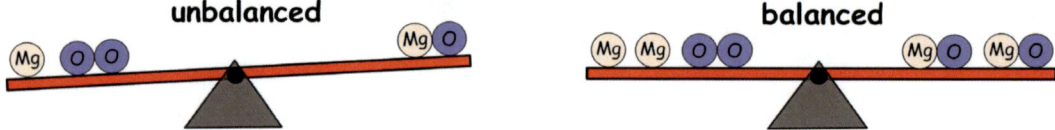

of the chemicals (to times them) enables us to balance. $2\,Mg + O_2 \longrightarrow 2\,MgO$. Two magnesium atoms react with one oxygen molecule to make two magnesium oxide molecules. This is always the case in this reaction, the equation is now balanced. **Mass conserved.**

Already Balanced (Examples)

$C + O_2 \longrightarrow CO_2$ This equation shows on the left hand side **one** carbon atom, **C** reacting with **one** oxygen molecule, O_2 (**two oxygen atoms** bonded), to produce one **carbon dioxide molecule, CO_2**, on the right hand side. The number of atoms before and after the reaction is the same. **Mass conserved.**

$CO_2 + H_2O \longrightarrow H_2CO_3$ This equation shows **carbon dioxide, CO_2,** reacting **with water, H_2O,** to make **carbonic acid, H_2CO_3**. Counting we see **three** oxygen atoms, 'O's on the left and **three** on the right. We see **two** hydrogen atoms, 'H's, on the left and the right and **one** carbon on the left and right. **Mass conserved.**

Balancing with Numbers (Examples)

$H_2 + O_2 \longrightarrow H_2O$ This equation shows, on the left hand side a **hydrogen molecule** (**two hydrogen atoms** bonded, H_2), and an **oxygen molecule, O_2** reacting to make **water, H_2O**. There is only **one oxygen** atom on the right hand side and **two oxygen** atoms on the left hand side, so it's not balanced. We can put numbers in front of the molecules to show that there is more than one of them to balance the equation.

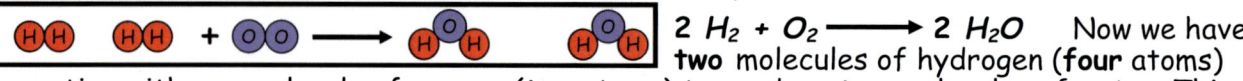

$2\,H_2 + O_2 \longrightarrow 2\,H_2O$ Now we have **two** molecules of hydrogen (**four** atoms) reacting with **one** molecule of oxygen (**two** atoms) to produce **two** molecules of water. This means we now have the same number of atoms on both sides. **Four** hydrogen and **two** oxygen, balanced. **Mass conserved.**

$N_2 + H_2 \longrightarrow NH_3$ This equation shows **nitrogen, N_2** reacting with **hydrogen, H_2** to produce an **ammonia molecule, NH_3**. It is not balanced because there are **three** hydrogens on the right hand side and only **two** on the left. Also **one** nitrogen on the right hand side and **two** on the left. We can put numbers in front to balance the equation.

$N_2 + 3\,H_2 \longrightarrow 2\,NH_3$ Now we have **six** hydrogen atoms on the left hand side and **six** hydrogen atoms on the right hand side and **two** nitrogen atoms on the left hand side and **two** on the right hand side, balanced. **Mass conserved.**

$PbO + C \longrightarrow Pb + CO_2$ This equation shows lead oxide reacting with carbon to produce **lead metal, Pb** and **carbon dioxide, CO_2**. It is not balanced because there are **two** oxygen atoms on the right hand side and **only one** on the left.

$2\,PbO + C \longrightarrow 2\,Pb + CO_2$ Now we have **two lead atoms** on the **left** and **right** hand side and **two oxygen atoms** on the left and right hand side. We still have **one carbon** on the **left** hand side **and one** on the **right** hand side, balanced. **Mass Conserved.**

WHAT?

There are no more atoms today than when the universe began in the 'big bang' 13.8 billion years ago. Mass conserved! The atoms still exist and just rearrange themselves in chemical reactions.

Questions on Conservation of Mass and Balancing Equations

Comprehension

1. What does conservation of mass tell us?
2. How often is conservation of mass true?
3. Why can't we write Mg + O ?
4. When one carbon atom reacts with one oxygen molecule, what is produced?
5. How do the number of atoms before and after always compare?
6. What is the product of reacting carbon dioxide with water?
7. When hydrogen reacts with oxygen, what molecule is produced?
8. What does putting numbers in front of the molecules show?
9. How many atoms are there in two molecules of hydrogen?
10. The number '2' in front of H_2 and the '2' in front of H_2O means how many atoms of hydrogen are on both sides of the equation?
11. What does the reaction between nitrogen and hydrogen produce?
12. Why is the first equation for nitrogen plus hydrogen not balanced?
13. Once balanced how many hydrogen and nitrogen atoms are there on the left and right hand side of the equation?
14. When lead oxide reacts with carbon what are the products?

Additional tasks

1. Balance the equations below, to help there is a space if a number is needed.

a.	___K +	F_2	⟶	___KF
b.	___Na +	Cl_2	⟶	___NaCl
c.	___Ca +	O_2	⟶	___CaO
d.	S_8 +	___O_2	⟶	___SO_2
e.	___Al +	___Br_2	⟶	___$AlBr_3$
f.	Mg +	___HCl	⟶	$MgCl_2$ + H_2
g.	CH_4 +	___O_2	⟶	___H_2O + CO_2
h.	___Al +	___FeO	⟶	Al_2O_3 + ___Fe

2. Draw diagrams like the ones opposite to show the atoms and molecules for the reactions below, e.g.

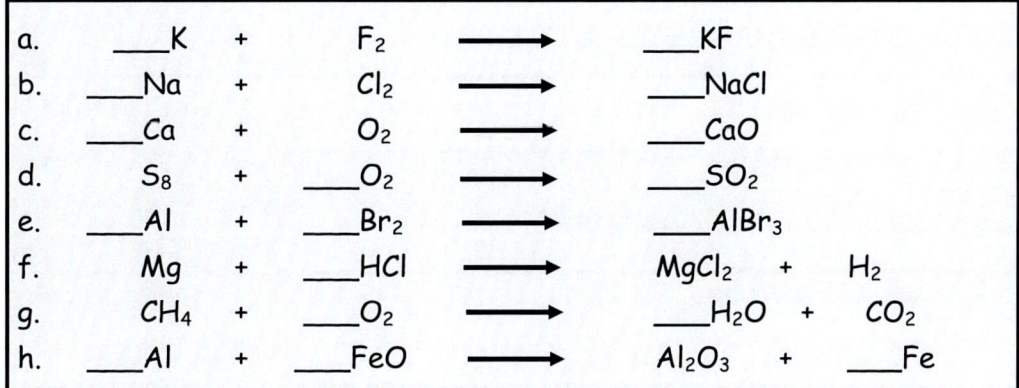

$$2 K + F_2 \longrightarrow 2 KF$$

A. $2 C + O_2 \longrightarrow 2 CO$	
B. $2 Cu + O_2 \longrightarrow 2 CuO$	
C. $2 HCl + 2 K \longrightarrow 2 KCl + H_2$	
D. $2 Mg + O_2 \longrightarrow 2 MgO$	
E. $2 Ca + O_2 \longrightarrow 2 CaO$	
F. $CaCO_3$ (pg60) $\longrightarrow CaO + CO_2$	

3. Acid in a flask is placed on a balance, the balance reads 100g. Magnesium weighing 10g is added to the beaker and the mass goes up to 110g. The magnesium starts *fizzing* and the mass goes down.

a. Why do you think the mass goes down when we know mass is conserved (same before and after)?

b. What would happen to the mass if a bung was placed on top and why?

Changes of State: Solids, Liquids and Gases

When we talk of changing state, we mean turning from a solid to a liquid and then to a gas (or the other way around). To do this, energy either has to be supplied to the particles (they gain energy), or released by the particles (they lose energy). Think about water in its gaseous state (as a gas). There is a lot of it in the air but we can't see it and we nearly always think of water as a liquid. The water molecules in the air have a lot of energy, they whizz around at high speed. If we remove energy from them (cool

Condensation

them down), they don't move as quickly and start to get closer together. The gas shrinks or contracts. Since the molecules are closer together, there is a stronger force of attraction. They begin to change from being a gas into a liquid, as they 'clump' together forming weak bonds. This is what happens when we see

Ice

condensation forming on a window. If we continue to remove energy from the water molecules then they start to move even slower and the force of attraction between the particles gets even larger. Eventually the force of attraction is large enough to keep the water molecules in fixed positions, all they can do is vibrate or jiggle around one position, we have now formed a solid, ice.

Graphing the Changes: Ice to Gaseous Water

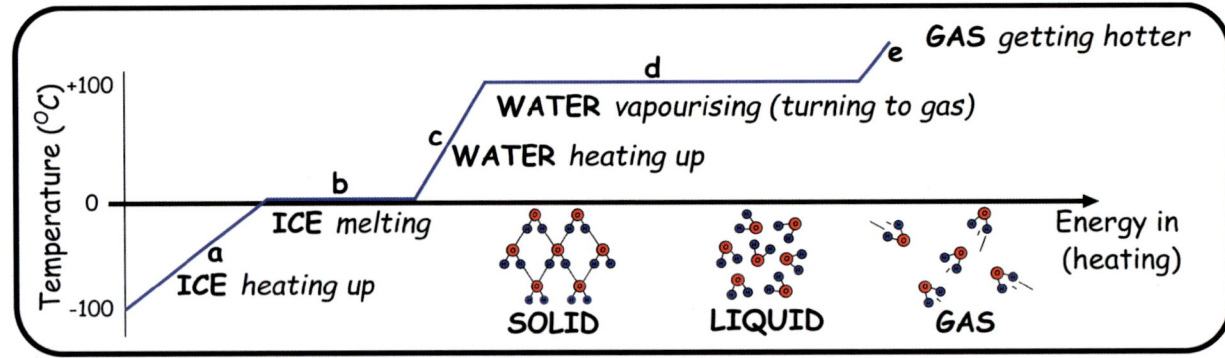

The graph starts with line 'a', ice at –100°C. It is possible, however, to cool particles down further. As the ice heats up it meets line 'b', here the ice begins to melt at 0°C and there is no change in temperature, the **'energy in'** is **breaking bonds** to change from a **solid** to a

liquid (melting). When line 'b' meets 'c', all of the ice has melted. The **water** starts to **rise in temperature**. When line 'c' meets 'd', the water is at 100°C and starts to 'boil off' (vapourise), changing from a **liquid to a gas**. There is no change in temperature and the **'energy in'** is used to **break bonds**, turning the **water** into a **gas**. At 'e' all the water is a gas (**water vapour**) and any 'energy in' now just makes the water molecules move **faster**.

Internal Energy

This is the energy that all substances have due to their particles movement (kinetic energy) and the attraction between them. What's important to know is, the **hotter** a substance, the **more internal energy** it has (particles vibrate or move faster). The further apart the particles,

> **WHAT?**
> It takes about five times as much energy to 'boil water' than it does to heat it up to boiling point (100°C). This is because bonds have to be broken when boiling water. Absolute zero (-273°C) is the lowest theoretical temperature we can reach, atoms stop moving!! Continuing to heat water molecules above 100°C produces 'super heated steam'.
> A fourth state of matter exists called a **plasma**, atoms lose electrons making positive ions. These ions and electrons whizz about just like a gas. Our sun is a plasma as is any flame on earth.

the more internal energy they have. This means that solids have the least internal energy, then liquids and gases have the most.

Questions on Changes of State

Comprehension

1. When we talk of changing state, what do we mean?
2. To do this what must happen?
3. What do we mean by gaseous state?
4. How do we nearly always think of water?
5. What happens if we remove energy from the water molecules in the air?
6. If the water molecules are closer together, what happens to the force of attraction between them?
7. What change of state begins to happen?
8. If we continue to remove energy from water molecules what happens to them?
9. What happens to the force of attraction eventually?
10. What state of matter is now formed?
11. What does line 'a' show on the graph?
12. What happened to the 'energy in' during line 'b' on the graph?
13. When line 'b' meets 'c', what has happened to all the ice?
14. What happens to the water at 100°C and what is another name for it?
15. At 'e' on the graph, what has happened to all the water?
16. Which have more internal energy, hot or cold substances?

Additional tasks

1. Label the y-axis (vertical) and the x-axis (horizontal) and the five different parts of the graph.

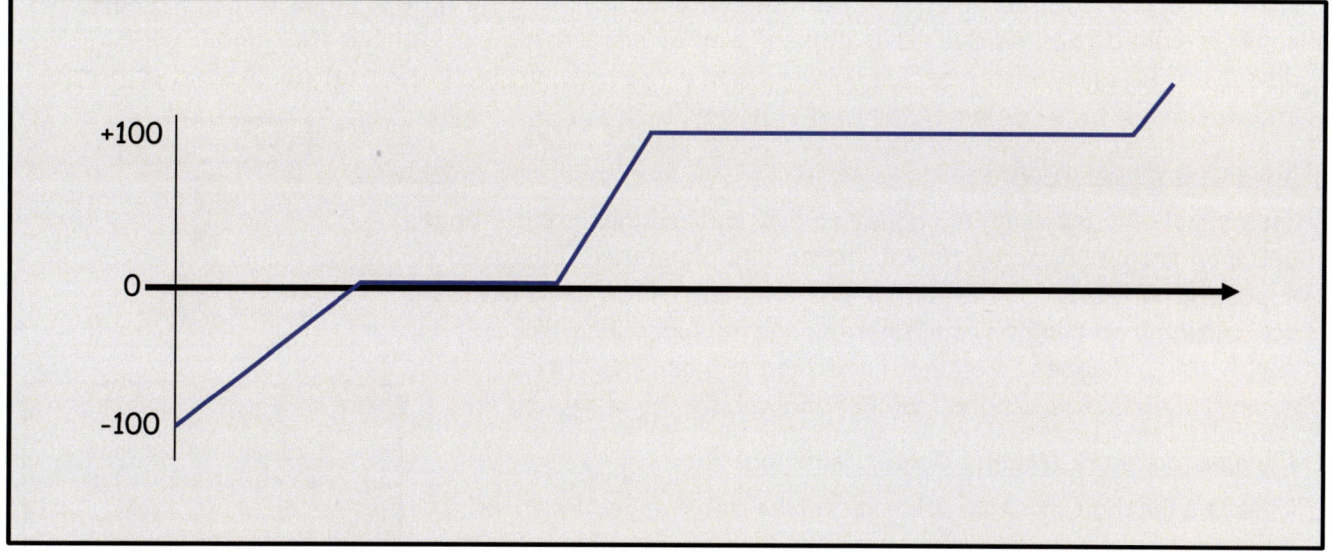

2. A chemical called salol has a melting point of 42°C. Salol is placed in a test tube with a thermometer and heated to 70°C. The temperature was then recorded every minute for 20 minutes as the **salol cooled**.

a. Plot a graph of the data with temperature (°C) on the y-axis against time (mins) on the x-axis. Connect the points to make a line.

b. Label the three parts of the line with; **SOLIDIFYING (FREEZING), LIQUID COOLING, SOLID COOLING**.

c. Which part of the graph shows no change in temperature.

Temperature of salol (°C)	70	65	60	55	51	47	45	43	42.5	42	42	42	42	40	38	36	34	32	30	29	28
Time (minutes)	0	1	2	3	4	5	6	7	8	9	10	11	12	13	14	15	16	17	18	19	20

3. Arrange the points below into two sentences to explain the *flat section* of the graph (spot the clues!).

> this releases heat energy into the salol / bonds are formed /
> This happens until all liquid has turned to solid / and stops the temperature falling. /
> and the temperature begins to fall again. / During solidification

Pure Substances, Mixtures and How to Separate them

A pure substance is made from only one type of **atom or molecule,** pure water, only H_2O, pure helium, only He, etc. Often substances are mixtures, like salty water, or air, which is a mixture of gases, mainly nitrogen and oxygen. A **mixture** is a combination of **substances** that **aren't chemically combined** or **bonded together.** When you only want part of a mixture of different substances, you need a way of separating what you don't want, from what you do. This could be simply picking out the chocolates you want from a 'Roses' box (a mixture of sweets), or allowing sand to sink to the bottom of your bucket before pouring off the water (a mixture of sand and water). We can separate a mixture of oil and water which are immiscible (immiscible means liquids that don't stay mixed) using a separating funnel. Oil floats on water, a tap at the bottom of the funnel allows the water to flow out leaving the oil behind.

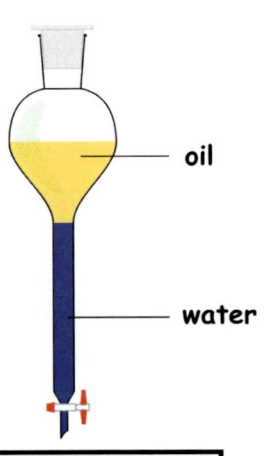

oil

water

Separating funnel

Filtering

Just like when you drain the water from cooked vegetables, rice or pasta using a colander, filtering simply allows the liquid (usually water) to pass through gaps and the solid not to. In the lab we usually use filter paper and a funnel. This allows the liquid to pass through (**the filtrate**) and the insoluble (doesn't dissolve) solid not to. The solid that gets left behind on the filter paper is called **the residue**. It is a great way of separating substances that don't dissolve (like dirty water or tea leaves from a tea pot), from those that do. A sand and water mixture can be separated this way.

Tea

Magnetic Separation

This simply means using a magnet to pick out magnetic substances like iron from non-magnetic substance like aluminium. It's used to separate pop cans for recycling. The example often used in labs is separating iron filings from a non-magnetic substance like sulphur, simply use a magnet to pick out the iron filings. The three magnetic elements are iron, nickel and cobalt.

Using magnets

iron filings

sulphur

WHAT?

A form of chromatography called electrophoresis is used to produce DNA 'fingerprints'. It can be used to identify individuals by their DNA. Great for catching criminals! Silicon 99.9999999% pure, which comes from sand is used in making computer chips.

Chromatography (Means Colour Writing)

This is a method of separating dissolved substances like the different colours that make up an ink. Place a dot of ink from a felt tip pen onto kitchen roll, add a few drops of water and you will likely see a separation of colours. We usually use filter paper dipped into water and the inks we are investigating are dotted on a line at the bottom of the paper. Some of the colours (chemicals) move **faster** and **don't** stick to the paper very well, these are carried further up. Others stick to the paper **better** and move **slower** so they don't move as far up the paper. In this way the dissolved substances can be separated to produce a **'chromatogram'**. A record which shows the separated inks. We can compare chromatograms to see if inks contain the same colours. Ink **Z** in a felt tip contains dyes **X** and **Y**. Dye **X** is banned because it is toxic, so felt tip **Z** won't be allowed to be sold in shops.

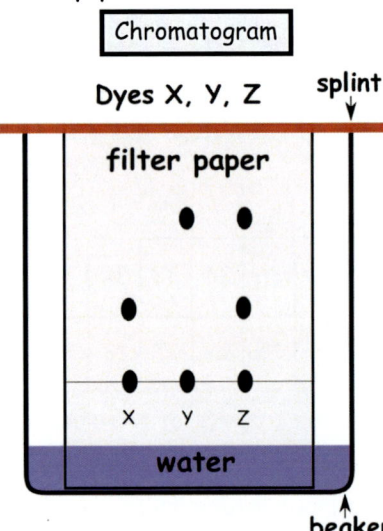

Chromatogram

Dyes X, Y, Z

splint

filter paper

X Y Z

water

beaker

Questions on Pure Substances, Mixtures and Separation

Comprehension

1. What is a pure substance made from?
2. What are two examples of mixtures?
3. In a mixture the substance aren't what?
4. How could you separate a sand and water mixture?
5. What does immiscible mean?
6. What does filtering simply allow to happen?
7. What is the insoluble solid that doesn't pass through after filtering called?
8. What does magnetic separation simply mean?
9. What are the names of the three magnetic elements?
10. What does the word chromatography mean?
11. Chromatography is a method of what?
12. When performing chromatography what happens to some of the colours (chemicals)?
13. What happens to the others?
14. When the dissolved substances are separated what is produced?
15. How can we see if inks contain the same colours?

Additional tasks

1. Match the words below to their meanings and memorise.

Mixture	describes liquids that don't stay mixed, like oil and water
Immiscible	a combination of substances that are not chemically combined (bonded)
Filtrate	the three magnetic metals
Residue	a record of the separated substances by chromatography
Iron, Nickel and Cobalt	the liquid that passes through the filter
Chromatogram	the solid left behind after filtering

2. Six new felt tips need to be tested to make sure that they don't contain any of dyes, **A, B** or **C** that are banned. Compare the chromatograms and state whether felt tip pens 1 to 6 contain any of the banned dyes.

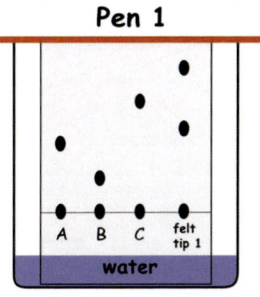
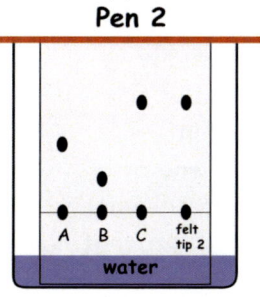
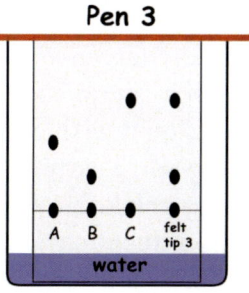
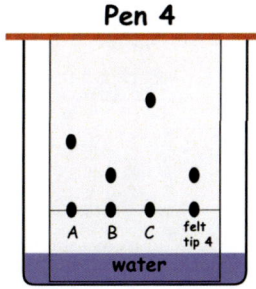
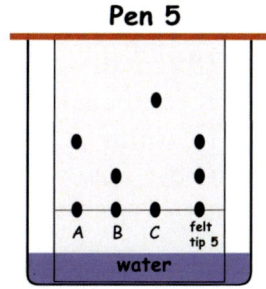
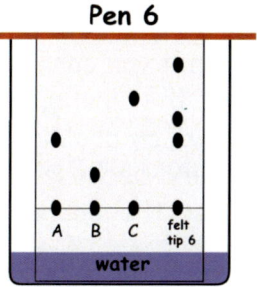

3. **Four** boys share a desk. One of the boys feels a push in his side and notices some blue/black ink on his white shirt. **Two** of the other boys have **different black** pens and **one** has a **blue** pen. It is difficult to tell if the ink is blue or black. The teacher uses a cotton bud to absorb some of the ink and says to the three boys 'I'm going to find out who did this, give me your pens'.
Explain how the teacher could use chromatography to find out which pen it was.

Evaporation and Distillation

Evaporation

Evaporation

Evaporation of a liquid like water happens because the molecules at the surface escape into the air. It can happen at any temperature when water is a liquid. The water molecules are only held together by weak forces, so some are able to 'break away' at the surface. They take away energy leaving the liquid cooler, this is why we get cool from sweating. The evaporating sweat carries away energy, leaving us cooler. Sweat, is just salty water (salt dissolved in water). You may have noticed that your skin is salty after sweating. This is because the water evaporates, leaving the salt behind. In this way we have separated a solid from a liquid. Dissolved mud can be seen left behind when puddles have evaporated. Leave the water to evaporate from a sugary drink and you will be left with the sugar. This effect happens quickly at higher temperatures and slowly at lower temperatures. You could boil the liquid but sometimes end up burning the solid you are trying to separate. It is better to evaporate just below the boiling point of water (100°C).

Salt farming

Sweating

Simple Distillation

Simple distillation is a way of separating the two different parts (components) of a **mixture,** that have different boiling points. It involves boiling a liquid and then condensing the vapour (usually water) in a condenser. Left behind is a solid or another liquid with a different boiling point. Distilling salty water (**saline water**) is a way of obtaining **drinkable (potable)** water from seawater, it's called **desalination**. It is also a way of separating out a mixture of two liquids that have different boiling points, such as a mixture of alcohol and water.

Alcohol boils at 78°C, water boils at 100°C. This means that you can heat the mixture to 78°C and 'boil off' the alcohol. The alcohol is then turned back to a liquid, by cooling it in a condenser. The water is left behind because it boils at 100°C. You have now separated the alcohol (pure) from the mixture.

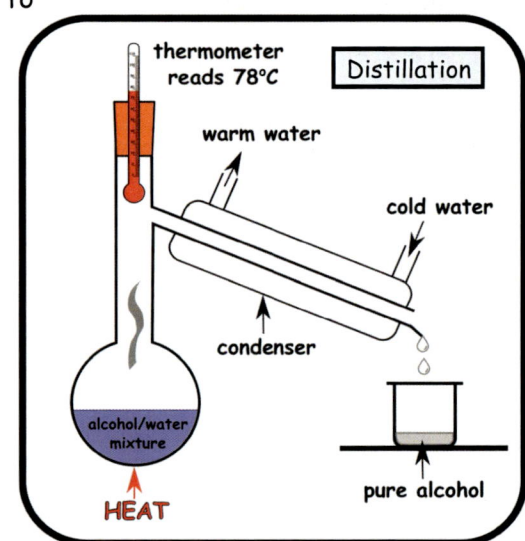

thermometer reads 78°C

Distillation

warm water

cold water

condenser

alcohol/water mixture

HEAT

pure alcohol

water   alcohol

Water and alcohol boil at different temperatures

water boils at 100°C   alcohol boils at 78°C

WHAT?

Desalination is obtaining drinking water from sea water. In Dubai they obtain 98% of their drinking water by desalination. It takes about 10 pints of sea water to make 5 pints of drinking water. In Scottish distilleries, whisky, a high strength alcoholic drink, is distilled from beer, a low strength alcoholic drink, by evaporating the alcohol from the beer and condensing it back to a liquid. Scotland sells about 5.5 billion pounds worth of whisky a year!

Questions on Evaporation and Distillation

Comprehension

1. What happens to the molecules when we evaporate a liquid like water?

2. At what temperature can evaporation take place?

3. When water molecules break away at the surface what do they take with them?

4. What does this do to the liquid left behind?

5. When you sweat and the water evaporates, what is left behind?

6. What can be seen left behind when a puddle evaporates?

7. If you let the water evaporate from a sugary drink what are you left with?

8. What can make this effect faster?

9. Why is it better to evaporate just below the boiling point?

10. Simple distillation is a way of doing what?

11. What does it involve?

12. What are we able to obtain by distilling sea water?

13. What is this process called?

14. We can use distillation to separate a mixture of liquids because they have different what?

15. You can separate a mixture of alcohol and water by boiling off the alcohol at what temperature?

Additional tasks

1. Label the apparatus below.

   Label A-F below using the following.
   Water/salt mixture, condenser, cold water in, thermometer reads 100°C, warm water out, pure water

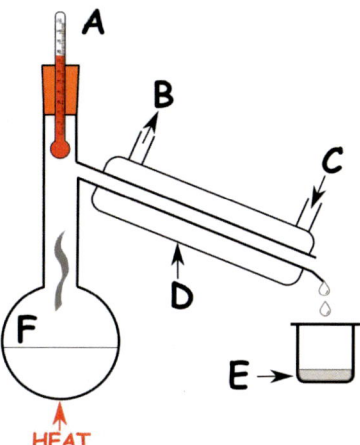

2. Label the apparatus below.

   Label A-F below using the following.
   Acetone and water mixture, condenser, cold water in, thermometer reads 65°C, warm water out, pure acetone

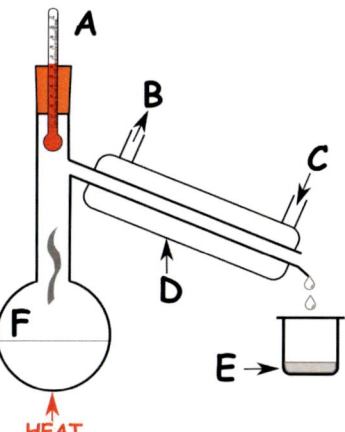

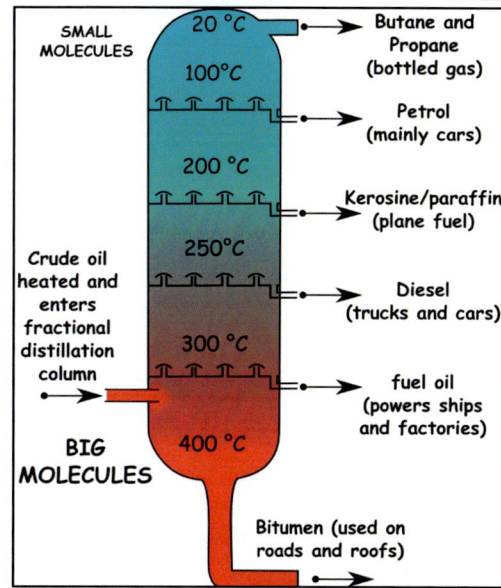

3. Crude oil is a **mixture** and can be separated into its useful parts using **fractional distillation**. Complete the gap filling exercise that begins to explain how fractional distillation works. *Most answers are in the diagram, **look carefully**.*

   Crude oil, condenses, coolest, Gases, boiling, different, diesel, points, hottest, petrol, sized, 100°C, 250°C

   The column is _____ at the bottom and _____ at the top. _____ ____ is a mixture of different _____ molecules that have different _____ points. This means they condense back to liquids at _____ temperatures. At different _____ up the column we can collect the liquid that _____ at that temperature. The _____ part of crude oil condenses at about _____. The _____ part of crude oil condenses at about _____. _____ collect at the top and are the smallest molecules.

73

Dissolving

Dissolving means when a solid becomes part of the liquid it is in. We all recognise when something dissolves because the solid appears to disappear. Take a spoonful of sugar crystals and put them into water and it is not long before you can't see them any more. They are still there of course. The sugar molecules have been surrounded by water molecules that spread out within the liquid, so you can no longer see them. The substance you are dissolving (e.g. sugar) is called the **solute**. The liquid you are dissolving into, usually water, is called the **solvent**. **Water** is often called the **'universal solvent'**, meaning it dissolves most things. Another common solvent is alcohol. The result of dissolving a solute into a solvent is called a **solution**. A substance that does not dissolve is said to be **insoluble**. An obvious example is sand, just think of the seaside, there wouldn't be a beach if sand dissolved!

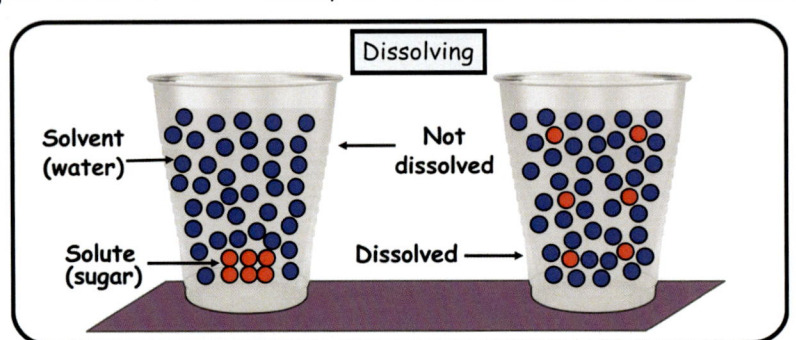

How well a substance dissolves is called its **solubility**. If you keep adding a solute like sugar to water, eventually no more can be dissolved, the solution is **saturated**. This is like when you come in from the pouring rain and someone says you are saturated. They mean you can't get any wetter!

Why do Some Substances Dissolve and Not Others?

It is simply down to forces. The solute molecules, say sugar, are held together by attractive forces. However, if the force of **attraction** between the **water molecules** and the **sugar molecules** is **stronger** than the attractive forces between the sugar molecules, the sugar will dissolve.

It is not just solids that dissolve in liquids, gases do too. Your can of pop wouldn't be very fizzy without the dissolved carbon dioxide in it. Fish wouldn't be able to breathe without the oxygen that is dissolved in water. Temperature affects how quickly substances can dissolve. Add a spoonful of sugar to ice cold water, it will dissolve slowly. Add sugar to a hot cup of tea, it will dissolve in seconds.

Gases also dissolve

Right Solvent for the Job

Water has no effect on nail polish, it is waterproof! You need to use nail polish remover to get rid of it. This is a **solvent** called **acetone**, it has a strong smell like alcohol and is great for dissolving nail polish. Acetone will also dissolve fats, you've probably noticed fats just float on water.

Nail polish

WHAT?

Fish can sometimes be seen coming to the surface 'gasping' for air, when there is not enough oxygen dissolved in the water, for them to 'breathe'. There are about 47 000 000 000 000 000 000 (47 billion billion) kilograms of salt dissolved in the world's oceans. Saliva is produced to help dissolve the food that we eat and helps our tongues to taste the food. Strong acids can dissolve metals!

Questions on Dissolving

Comprehension

1.	What does dissolving mean?
2.	What 'appears' to happen to the solid that is dissolved?
3.	What happens to the sugar molecules, once they are surrounded by the water molecules?
4.	What is the substance you are dissolving called?
5.	What name is often given to water?
6.	What is another common solvent?
7.	What does solubility tell you?
8.	What do people mean when they say you are saturated because of the rain?
9.	Why some substances dissolve and others don't, is simply down to what?
10.	What will happen if the force of attraction between the water molecules and sugar molecules is stronger than the attractive force between the sugar molecules?
11.	What else will dissolve in liquids?
12.	Which gas is dissolved in fizzy drinks?
13.	What can affect how quickly substances dissolve?
14.	Why do fish sometimes come to the surface to 'gasp' for air? (WHAT? box)
15.	What has no effect on nail polish?
16.	What solvent is nail polish remover and what else can it dissolve?

Additional tasks

1. Match the words to their meanings and memorise.

Solute	what is produced when a solute dissolves in a solvent e.g. salty water
Solvent	not able to be dissolved, e.g. chalk, sand, glass
Solution	the substance being dissolved
Soluble	when no more solute can be dissolved by the solvent
Insoluble	the liquid you are dissolving into
Saturated	able to be dissolved, e.g. sugar, salt, metal in acid

2. The table below shows how much sugar dissolves in 100ml of water and how this changes with temperature. Plot solubility (grams of sugar per 100ml of water) on the y-axis against temperature (°C) on the x-axis. Draw in a smooth curve.

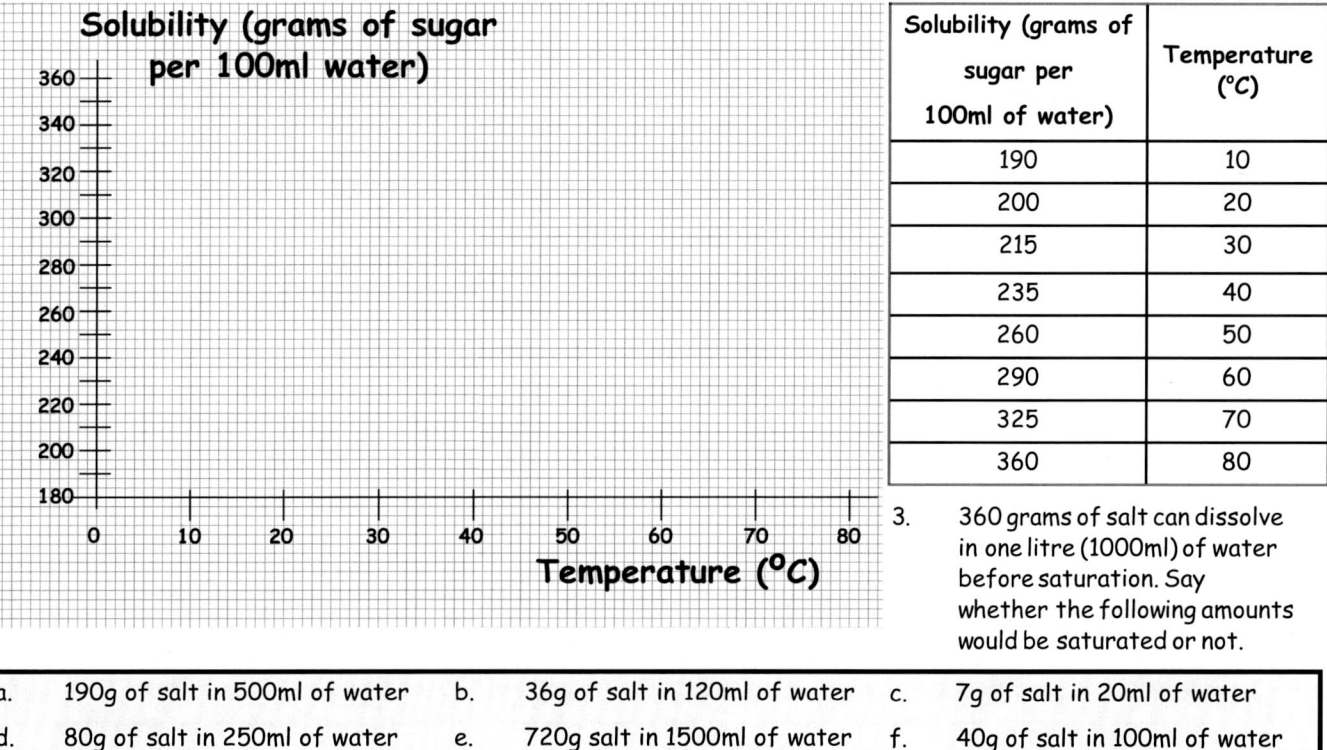

Solubility (grams of sugar per 100ml of water)	Temperature (°C)
190	10
200	20
215	30
235	40
260	50
290	60
325	70
360	80

3. 360 grams of salt can dissolve in one litre (1000ml) of water before saturation. Say whether the following amounts would be saturated or not.

a.	190g of salt in 500ml of water	b.	36g of salt in 120ml of water	c.	7g of salt in 20ml of water
d.	80g of salt in 250ml of water	e.	720g salt in 1500ml of water	f.	40g of salt in 100ml of water

Combustion

Combustion is another name for burning. If you think of a lit candle, you will have noticed that over time the candle gets smaller and smaller. This is because the wax that a candle is made from, is the fuel for the combustion to continue. The fuel is being used up.

Combustion: What is Needed?

Fire triangle

The requirements (what is needed) for combustion are three fold (need three things). A **fuel** (the material to burn), like gas, wood, oil etc. A supply of **oxygen** (this normally comes from the air) and **heat** to get the reaction started. We talk about the fire triangle because three things are needed and a triangle has three sides! Remove any one of the three, the flames go out.

A match

Complete Combustion: Burning Hydrocarbons

Fuel + Oxygen ⟶ Carbon dioxide + Water

$$CH_4 + 2 O_2 \longrightarrow CO_2 + 2 H_2O$$

Hydrocarbons are a really common fuel. The equation on the left is for burning methane gas, CH_4, from your gas cooker for example. This is **complete combustion**, the products are carbon dioxide and water. Complete combustion happens when there is plenty of oxygen available, it produces a '**clean burn**'.

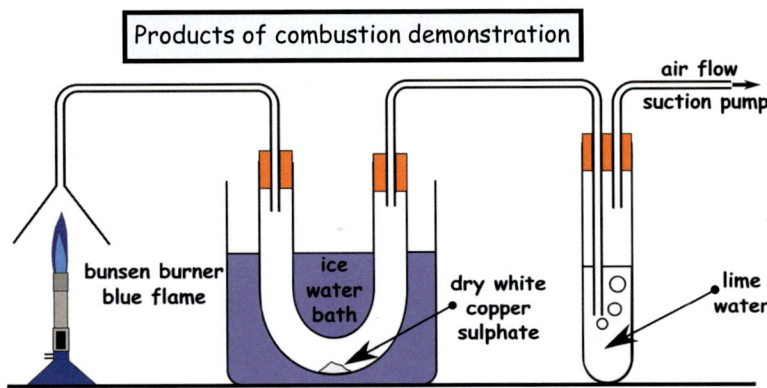

Products of combustion demonstration

bunsen burner blue flame

ice water bath

dry white copper sulphate

air flow
suction pump

lime water

Hydrocarbons are compounds made from hydrogen and carbon only. Methane, along with propane and butane (all hydrocarbons), are used widely as fuels for heating and cooking. You may have noticed, that if the gas oven is on for a long time, the windows will 'steam up'. This is because, all the water that is produced by burning methane, begins to condense on the windows. A demonstration that shows the products of combustion is shown in the diagram. The products are 'sucked through' a 'U' tube, which contains a chemical that **turns** bright **blue** with **water**. The second tube contains a liquid called **limewater**. This goes **cloudy** if **carbon dioxide** is passed through it. The limewater does go cloudy and the chemical in the 'U' tube turns blue, so we know the products are carbon dioxide and water.

Incomplete Combustion

Soot

Incomplete combustion, also called '**dirty burning**', happens when there isn't enough oxygen for complete combustion. We still get water as one of the products, but we also get **carbon monoxide** (a poisonous, odourless gas) and **carbon** or **soot**. A Bunsen burner on a yellow flame produces incomplete combustion. Put a piece of glass above this flame and it quickly turns black because of the soot produced from incomplete combustion.

Fuel (hydrocarbon) + Oxygen ⟶ Carbon monoxide + Water + Carbon (soot)

$$4 CH_4 + 5 O_2 \longrightarrow 2 CO + 8 H_2O + 2 C$$

WHAT?

You should roll around on the ground or smother the flames if your clothes catch fire. This 'starves' the fire of oxygen to put it out. A flame is a plasma which is an example of the 'fourth state of matter'. The methane gas we use to cook and heat our homes doesn't smell, a smell is added so we know if there is a leak!

Questions on Combustion

Comprehension

1.	What is another name for combustion?	8.	What are hydrocarbons made from?
2.	What are the three requirements for combustion?	9.	As well as methane what other common fuels are used for heating and cooking?
3.	Where does the oxygen normally come from?	10.	Why do the windows 'steam up' when a gas oven is on for a long time?
4.	What happens if you remove one of the requirements for combustion?	11.	In the combustion experiment what happens to the limewater and the chemical in the 'U' tube?
5.	What are hydrocarbons commonly used as?	12.	What is **incomplete** combustion also called?
6.	What are the products of burning methane, CH_4?	13.	When does incomplete combustion happen?
7.	When does complete combustion happen?	14.	What are the three products of incomplete combustion?

Additional tasks

1. Write out the word equation for complete combustion and incomplete combustion below;

Complete combustion

Incomplete combustion

2. Using the 'balanced' symbol equations opposite, write the number of carbon, hydrogen and oxygen atoms underneath the left hand side and right hand side of **both** equations.
   Remember 4 CH₄ means 4 X C, 4 carbon atoms (4 C) and 4 X H₄, 16 hydrogen atoms (16 H). They should be the same on both sides!

3. **Identical candles** are lit and then different sized (volume) beakers are placed on top. A stop watch is then used to time how long it takes before the candles go out.

a. Why do the candles go out?

b. Why do they burn longer under bigger beakers?

c. What pattern can you see in the results? What is the name for this relationship (pg152)?

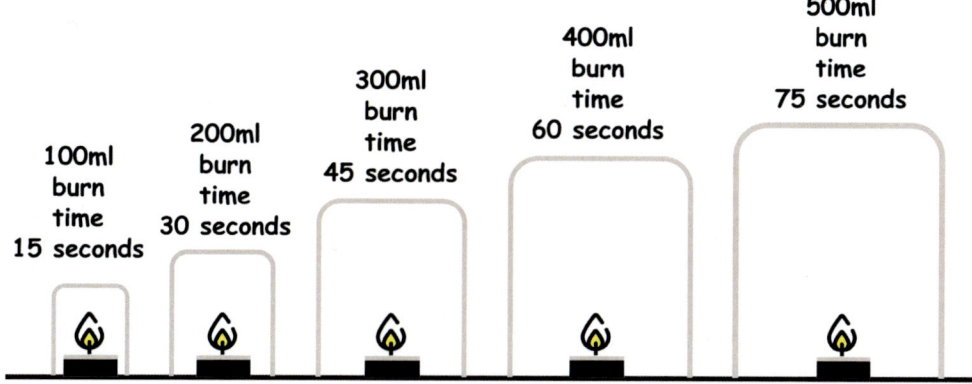

100ml burn time 15 seconds **200ml burn time 30 seconds** **300ml burn time 45 seconds** **400ml burn time 60 seconds** **500ml burn time 75 seconds**

d. If you plotted burn time (y-axis) against volume (x-axis), what would a graph of the results look like (pg152)?

e. Predict how long you think it would take for the candle to go out under a 1000ml volume beaker.

Thermal Decomposition

Thermal refers to heat, decompose means to break down into parts. Thermal decomposition is using heat to break down a compound into its parts. In the laboratory this usually means using a Bunsen burner to heat a solid like, **calcium carbonate**, CaCO₃ (also called **chalk or limestone**). Some substances show a change after heating them, others might look the same after heating. Calcium carbonate looks the same after heating, however, if you add water to it before heating no reaction is seen. Add water after it is heated and it will fizz, something new is formed called **calcium oxide**, CaO (other name 'quicklime'). Calcium oxide is used to make cement, every year **huge amounts** are made in industrial **'lime kilns'**.

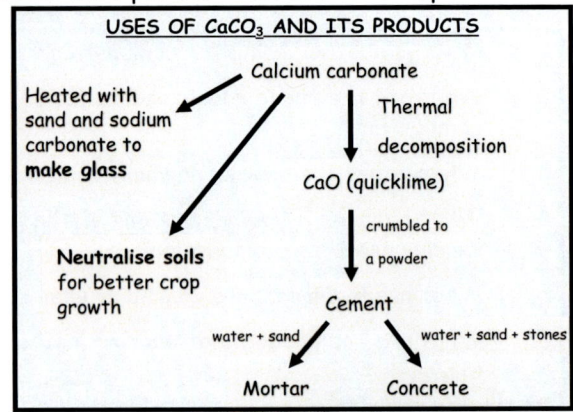

USES OF CaCO₃ AND ITS PRODUCTS

Calcium carbonate

Heated with sand and sodium carbonate to **make glass**

Thermal decomposition

CaO (quicklime)

crumbled to a powder

Neutralise soils for better crop growth

Cement

water + sand → Mortar

water + sand + stones → Concrete

Calcium oxide

Thermal Decomposition: Chemical Equation

Calcium Carbonate (heated) ⟶ Calcium oxide + Carbon dioxide

$$CaCO_3 \longrightarrow CaO + CO_2$$

Other carbonates (an element bonded to CO₃), like copper carbonate, CuCO₃, give a clear colour change when heated. This **shows** that something new has formed. **Green copper carbonate** turns into a **black powder**.

It is known that **copper oxide** is a **black powder**, so when copper carbonate is heated we know one of the products is copper oxide. At the same time a gas is given off. We can see this by connecting a delivery tube and putting the end of the tube into water. Bubbles appear from the end of the tube so we know one of the products is a gas. If this gas is allowed to bubble through a liquid called 'limewater', the limewater turns from clear to cloudy. This happens when the gas carbon dioxide is passed through limewater so we know the gas given off when copper carbonate is heated must be carbon dioxide.

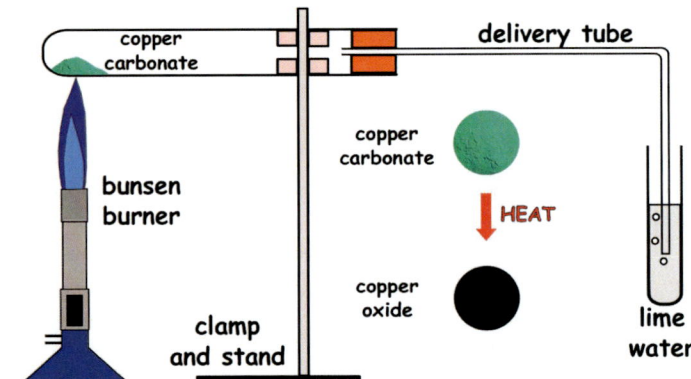

Thermal decomposition

copper carbonate

delivery tube

bunsen burner

copper carbonate

HEAT

copper oxide

clamp and stand

lime water

Thermal Decomposition: Chemical Equation

Copper Carbonate (heated) ⟶ Copper oxide + Carbon dioxide

$$CuCO_3 \longrightarrow CuO + CO_2$$

Lime kiln

Many carbonate compounds decompose in the same way as copper carbonate and calcium carbonate do. They are dug up from the ground (mined). Zinc carbonate, ZnCO₃ for example, decomposes to zinc oxide and carbon dioxide. **Zinc oxide** has lots of uses in medicine. It can also be found in sunscreens because it filters harmful UV rays. It is used widely in cosmetics (make up products) too.

WHAT?

About 10 billion cubic metres (m³) of concrete are produced each year using cement. It's enough to build about 50,000 skyscrapers!

A use of zinc oxide

Questions on Thermal Decomposition

Comprehension

1. What is heat used for in thermal decomposition?

2. What do we usually use to heat the solid in a laboratory?

3. What is another name for calcium carbonate, $CaCO_3$?

4. What happens if you add water to calcium carbonate, $CaCO_3$ before it is heated?

5. What is another name for calcium oxide, CaO?

6. Where are huge amounts of calcium oxide, CaO made every year?

7. What is formed after calcium carbonate, $CaCO_3$ is heated?

8. What does copper carbonate, $CuCO_3$ turn into after heating?

9. How do we know a gas is given off when copper carbonate, $CuCO_3$ is heated?

10. How do we know that this gas is carbon dioxide, CO_2?

11. Where do carbonates come from?

12. What does zinc carbonate, $ZnCO_3$ decompose to?

13. Where does zinc oxide, ZnO, have lots of uses?

14. What products can it be found in?

Additional tasks

1. Complete the word equations for the thermal decomposition of the carbonates below.

Calcium Carbonate	$\xrightarrow{\text{(heat)}}$ Calcium _____ + Carbon dioxide
Copper Carbonate	$\xrightarrow{\text{(heat)}}$ _____ oxide + _____ dioxide
Zinc Carbonate	$\xrightarrow{\text{(heat)}}$ Zinc _____ + _____ _____
Magnesium Carbonate	$\xrightarrow{\text{(heat)}}$ _____ _____ + Carbon dioxide
Sodium Carbonate	$\xrightarrow{\text{(heat)}}$ _____ _____ + _____ _____

2. Solve the following 12 clues.

i.	Another name for calcium carbonate	vii.	Decompose refers to?
ii.	Calcium carbonate will thermally decompose to?	viii.	Another name for calcium oxide?
iii.	Thermal refers to?	ix.	Used to heat things in a lab?
iv.	An element bonded to CO_3 is called a?	x.	Has many uses in medicine?
v.	A black powder from heating copper carbonate?	xi.	Cement, water and sand make?
vi.	This liquid turns cloudy when carbon dioxide is bubbled through?	xii.	Huge amounts of calcium oxide are made in?

3. Complete your own version of the flow chart 'Uses of $CaCO_3$' as a **mind map**. Draw pictures if you like. Other uses you can add include: as *writing chalk, in indigestion tablets, used in making steel, used in making paper, used in making paints, used in dietary supplements, used in cosmetics, used in bread making, used in animal feed and used in making many pills.*

Oxidation Reactions

Oxidation reactions are very common indeed, without them, we wouldn't be alive!

When we breathe we take oxygen into our lungs, which reacts with glucose (a sugar) in our blood. This is an oxidation reaction which releases energy for our life processes (called respiration), without this life isn't possible. Steel (which is made mainly from iron) will **rust** when exposed to oxygen forming **iron oxide**, an oxidation reaction. Once bitten an apple soon turns brown, this is another common example of oxidation. Patients are often given 'extra' oxygen from a bottle if they have suffered a heart attack or have problems breathing.

Rusting ship

Browning apple

Oxidation is the addition of oxygen during a chemical reaction. This sometimes requires heat energy to make it happen, but can also release heat energy. The product is called an **oxide**, carbon dioxide is an example of an oxide.

Copper oxide

Oxygen bottle

Oxidation Examples: Chemical Equations

Copper + Oxygen $\longrightarrow$ Copper oxide

$2\ Cu\ +\ O_2\ \longrightarrow\ 2\ CuO$ (**oxygen added**)

The above chemical equation is for copper being heated to high temperatures in air, copper oxide, a black powder is produced.

Magnesium + Oxygen $\longrightarrow$ Magnesium oxide (**oxygen added**)

$2\ Mg\ +\ O_2\ \longrightarrow\ 2\ MgO$

The above reaction releases a large amount of heat energy. Once the reaction starts, magnesium, Mg, burns very brightly in air (oxygen, O_2).

Burning magnesium

Combustion Again

Combustion (burning) is an oxidation reaction. Hydrocarbons (molecules made from hydrogen and carbon only) are very common fuels that burn producing carbon dioxide, CO_2 and water, H_2O, along with lots of heat. Another common fuel is coal, which is mostly carbon. Carbon burns producing only carbon dioxide and it is easy to see from the chemical equation, that carbon is oxidised to carbon dioxide.

Carbon + Oxygen $\longrightarrow$ Carbon dioxide (**oxygen added**)

$C\ +\ O_2\ \longrightarrow\ CO_2$

Coal is mostly carbon

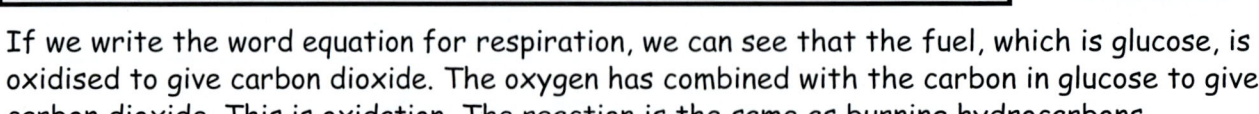

Respiration

Glucose + Oxygen $\longrightarrow$ Carbon dioxide + Water + Energy

$C_6H_{12}O_6\ +\ 6\ O_2\ \longrightarrow\ 6\ CO_2\ +\ 6\ H_2O\ +$ Energy

If we write the word equation for respiration, we can see that the fuel, which is glucose, is oxidised to give carbon dioxide. The oxygen has combined with the carbon in glucose to give carbon dioxide. This is oxidation. The reaction is the same as burning hydrocarbons.

Respiration is '**slow burning**' and happens at lower temperatures than the burning we are used to where flames are visible.

WHAT?

Coal unfortunately contains sulphur too, when burned the sulphur reacts with oxygen and water in the air. This makes sulphuric acid, H_2SO_4, or acid rain. Uh-oh!

Questions on Oxidation Reactions

Comprehension

1.	What would happen to us without oxidation reactions?	8.	What is produced when hydrocarbons are burned?
2.	What is steel mainly made from?	9.	What is coal mainly made from?
3.	Why does an apple soon turn brown once bitten?	10.	What is the product of burning carbon?
4.	What is oxidation?	11.	During respiration what is glucose oxidised to give?
5.	What is the product of oxidation called?		
6.	What is produced when copper is heated to high temperatures in air?	12.	What is respiration the same as?
		13.	Because of this, what is respiration also called?
7.	What kind of reaction is combustion?	14.	What sort of temperatures does respiration happen at?

Additional tasks

1. Complete the word equations for oxidation below.

a.	Zinc	+	Oxygen	⟶ _____
b.	Beryllium	+	_____	⟶ Beryllium oxide
c.	_____	+	Oxygen	⟶ Calcium oxide
d.	_____	+	Oxygen	⟶ Iron oxide
e.	Aluminium	+	_____	⟶ Aluminium oxide
f.	Nickel	+	Oxygen	⟶ _____
g.	_____	+	Oxygen	⟶ Sulphur dioxide
h.	Silicon	+	Oxygen	⟶ _____ dioxide
i.	_____	+	_____	⟶ Carbon dioxide

2. Unscramble the words below to do with oxidation. They all appear on the opposite page!

USNRGTI _____

ITIDAONXO _____

RONBINGW _____

XINOIIGDS _____

OYNXEG _____

RODIIOENX _____

OPICXREPDEO _____

OBOCISNMTU _____

EPIRTRNSOIA _____

ABICXDEROONID _____

URNBGNI _____

REHBEAT _____

3. Use the periodic table to help with names.

a. Write the name of the oxide below underneath its chemical formula.

Sulphur trioxide, Aluminium oxide, Iron oxide, Chromium oxide, Vanadium oxide, Di hydrogen monoxide, Barium oxide, Lithium oxide, Potassium oxide

Al_2O_3	V_2O_5	SO_3
CrO_3	Fe_2O_3	BaO_2
Li_2O	H_2O	K_2O

4. Write the number of each atom in the molecule from its formula e.g. one form of iron oxide has the formula Fe_3O_4. This means 3 X Fe (iron) atoms and 4 X O (oxygen) atoms.

Displacement Reactions and the Reactivity Series

The dictionary definition of displacement is, 'the action of moving something from its place or position'. Imagine your little brother or sister taking your favourite toy without asking. You are able to 'grab it back' because you are stronger, and once you have it back they are not able to get it off you because they are not strong enough. In chemistry we say the stronger chemical is more reactive. Look carefully at the box containing pretend chemicals '**X**', '**Y**' and '**Z**'. Chemical '**Z**' is more reactive than chemical 'Y'. 'X' and 'Y' are attracted (bonded) but 'Z' can attract 'X' more strongly than 'Y' so it is able to steal 'X' from 'Y'. We say 'Z' **displaces** 'Y'.

Chemical reaction

Z ↑ Most reactive $XY + Z \longrightarrow XZ + Y$

'Z' displaces 'Y'

Y

$XZ + Y \longrightarrow XZ + Y$

X | Least reactive   _'Y' cannot displace 'Z'_

The Classic Experiment: Displacing Salts

Reacting solutions of **magnesium sulphate**, **zinc sulphate**, **iron sulphate** and **copper sulphate** with their pure metals, enables us to see which metal is most reactive. Elements can be put in order of least reactive to most reactive, this is called the **reactivity series**. A metal higher up in the reactivity series is able to 'steal' the sulphate part of the salt leaving the less reactive **metal** behind (displaced). If magnesium metal (most reactive) is added to zinc sulphate, iron sulphate and copper sulphate, the sulphate is 'stolen' in each case leaving behind **zinc** metal, **iron** metal and **copper** metal. This is illustrated below.

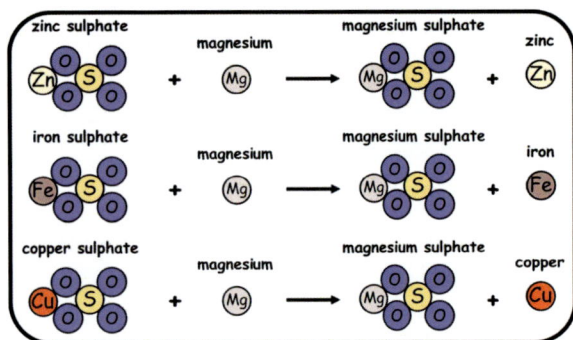

'Stealing' the toy

Reactivity series

potassium	↑ Most reactive
sodium	strong
calcium	
magnesium	
aluminium	
carbon	
zinc	
iron	
tin	
lead	
hydrogen	
copper	
silver	weak
gold	
platinum	Least reactive

You can see a chemical reaction is taking place because the metal that is left behind becomes visible. Adding magnesium to magnesium sulphate produces no reaction, because magnesium can't be more or less reactive than itself. Each metal is added to each salt solution in turn. The results are normally summarised in a results table like the one below.

Thermite reaction

Salt solution	Magnesium metal	Zinc metal	Iron metal	Copper metal
Magnesium sulphate	No reaction	No reaction	No reaction	No reaction
Zinc sulphate	**Yes,** zinc displaced	No reaction	No reaction	No reaction
Iron sulphate	**Yes,** iron displaced	**Yes,** iron displaced	No reaction	No reaction
Copper sulphate	**Yes,** copper displaced	**Yes,** copper displaced	**Yes,** copper displaced	No reaction
Number of reactions	_3_	_2_	_1_	_0_

WHAT?

The 'thermite' reaction is a displacement reaction that is so exothermic (heat releasing), it gets hot enough to weld metal together. Some explosions are just very very fast displacement reactions.

Questions on Displacement Reactions and the Reactivity Series

Comprehension

1. What is the dictionary definition of displacement?	9. What is a metal higher in the reactivity series able to do?
2. Why are you able to grab back your favourite toy from your little brother or sister?	10. Which is the most reactive metal of the four in the classic experiment?
3. In chemistry how do we describe the stronger chemical?	11. How can we see that a chemical reaction has taken place?
4. Why is 'Z' able to steal 'X' from 'Y'?	12. Why does adding magnesium to magnesium sulphate produce no reaction?
5. What do we say that 'Z' has done to 'Y'?	13. Which displacement reaction gets hot enough to weld metal together? (WHAT? box)
6. What are the names of the four salts in the classic displacement experiment?	14. What are some explosions examples of? (WHAT? box)
7. What are the salts (sulphates) reacted with?	
8. What do we call it when elements are put in order of reactivity?	

Additional tasks

1. In the empty spaces of the jumbled table below, write either, **no reaction** or **yes** followed by the **name** of the metal **displaced**. Try using the reactivity series rather than the table opposite.

Salt solution	Iron metal	Magnesium metal	Copper metal	Zinc metal
Magnesium sulphate				
Zinc sulphate				
Iron sulphate				
Copper sulphate				
Number of reactions				

2. Use the reactivity series to write **WILL** or **WILL NOT** to the following.

Potassium _____ displace platinum   Sodium _____ displace calcium

Magnesium _____ displace calcium   Carbon _____ displace aluminium

Zinc _____ displace tin   Lead _____ displace copper

Copper _____ displace carbon   Tin _____ displace silver

Silver _____ displace gold   Platinum _____ displace copper

Sodium _____ displace magnesium   Aluminium _____ displace lead

Hydrogen _____ displace zinc   Carbon _____ displace iron

3. Here is a mnemonic for remembering the reactivity series. Make a better one of your own.

Please Stop Calling Me A Careless Zebra Instead Try Learning How Copper Saves Gold Please.

Acids, Alkalis, Neutralisation and the pH Scale

Acids and alkalis can be thought of as chemical opposites. If the right amount of acid and alkali are mixed together their chemical properties cancel each other out, we call this **neutralisation**. Acids and alkalis are both corrosive, this means that they can damage your skin and attack metals.

Corrosive

Acids

Hydrochloric acid, HCl, and **sulphuric acid, H_2SO_4**, are the most commonly used acids in schools. People often think acids are dangerous, this is only true if they are concentrated or 'strong'. Acids are extremely useful and we use them all the time. Vinegar (acetic acid), is an acid we put on our chips. Citrus fruits (oranges, lemons and limes) contain citric acid which makes them sour. Vitamin C (ascorbic acid), is essential for healthy skin. Our fizzy drinks are also acidic due to the carbonic acid from dissolved carbon dioxide. Hydrochloric acid in our stomachs is essential for killing bacteria and making our enzymes (biological catalysts) work properly. Car batteries rely on very strong sulphuric acid to work. It is known that the sting from a **bee** is acidic and has something to do with the pain we experience.

Alkalis

Sodium hydroxide, NaOH, is the most commonly used alkali in schools (also called caustic soda). Like acids, alkalis are only really harmful if they are concentrated or 'strong'. Household products such as drain cleaner or bleach, however, are strong so care must be taken when using them. Sodium hydroxide is used in making soap, this leaves it alkaline. Soap helps water to penetrate dirt better and clean our skin. Washing up liquid is alkaline and is great for penetrating grease, washing powder too. Baking powder is an alkali that releases carbon dioxide when baking to make cakes rise. If you have an upset stomach, you can take an alkaline indigestion tablet to help calm your stomach. It neutralises excess (too much) acid. It is known that the sting from a **wasp** is alkaline and has something to do with the pain we experience.

Indicators and the pH scale.

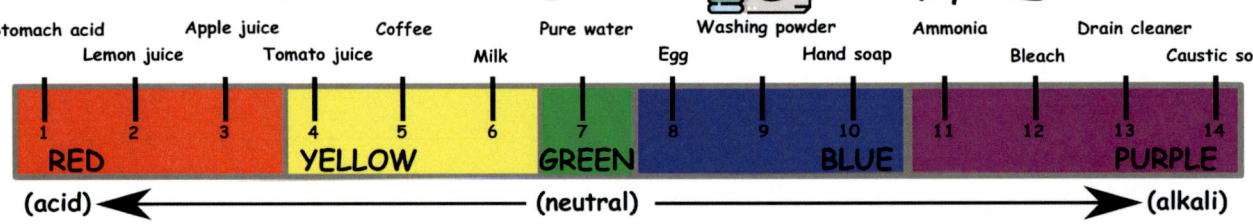

| Stomach acid | Apple juice | Coffee | Pure water | Washing powder | Ammonia | Drain cleaner |
| Lemon juice | Tomato juice | Milk | Egg | Hand soap | Bleach | Caustic soda |

1 2 3 4 5 6 7 8 9 10 11 12 13 14
RED   YELLOW   GREEN   BLUE   PURPLE

(acid) ← (neutral) → (alkali)

In chemistry we use indicators to tell us if a solution (substances dissolved in liquids), is acidic or alkaline. The pH scale is a number scale from 1 to 14 that tells us how strong an acidic or alkaline solution is. **One** on the scale is strongly acidic, **seven** is neutral (neither acidic nor alkaline), and **fourteen** is strongly alkaline. To know the pH of a solution we often use universal indicator, it is brilliant! If we add a few drops to a solution it changes to a colour that matches a number on the pH scale. If universal indicator turns more towards **yellow/red**, then what we are testing is an **acid**. If it turns more towards **blue/purple** then it is **alkaline**. If it stays **green**, it is **neutral**. Another common indicator is 'litmus'. This is usually a strip of paper that 'only' changes to red if acidic or blue if alkaline. It doesn't tell us the pH because there are no 'in-between' colours. It is less useful than the brilliant universal indicator which is actually a mixture of indicators.

> **WHAT?**
>
> Fluoroantimonic acid is the strongest acid and explodes on contact with water! It can dissolve glass. pH stands for potential of hydrogen.

Questions on Acids, Alkalis, Neutralisation and the pH Scale

Comprehension

1. How can acids and alkalis be thought of?
2. If we mix the right amount of acid and alkali what can happen?
3. What do we call this?
4. What are the two most commonly used acids in schools?
5. When is it true that acids are dangerous?
6. Why is the hydrochloric acid, HCl, in our stomachs essential?
7. What might have something to do with the pain we experience from bee stings?
8. What is the most commonly used alkali in schools?
9. How does the sodium hydroxide used in making soap leave it?
10. How do indigestion tablets help calm your stomach?
11. What might have something to do with the pain we experience from wasp stings?
12. What do we use indicators for in chemistry?
13. What is the pH scale and what does it tell us?
14. What do we often use to know the pH of a solution?
15. What colour is neutral on the pH scale?
16. Why can't litmus indicator tell us the pH?

Additional tasks

1. Complete the jumbled pH table below using the examples given on the opposite page.

pH	Example	Acid or alkali?
4		
8		
10		
6		
11		
5		
1		
12		
2		
9		
3		
14		
7		
13		

3. Design your own leaflet explaining the benefits and uses of acids and alkalis (A4 paper folded in half).

2. Complete the gap filling exercise below. Choose from the following words.

acid particles, corrosive, skin, test tubes, acidic, Sulphuric acid, soaps, concentrated, 12, Hydrochloric acid, acetic acid, sodium hydroxide, washing powders, volume, strong, neutralise, stomachs, alkaline, neutral, red, metals, blue, bleach

Acids are only dangerous if they are _____ or _____. Concentration is how many _____ _____ are in a certain _____. Acids and alkalis can be _____. This means they can damage your _____ or attack _____. The hazard symbol for corrosive has a picture of two _____ _____ in it. _____ _____, H_2SO_4 is used in car batteries. _____ _____ helps our digestive system to work properly. Another name for vinegar is _____ _____.

Alkalis like _____ _____ are commonly used in schools. _____ is alkaline and has a pH of about ____. So are _____ and _____ _____. Alkalis _____ acids so can be used to treat upset _____. pH stands for potential of hydrogen. On the pH scale, pH-1 is strongly _____, pH-14 is strongly _____ and pH-7 is _____. pH-7 is green, becoming more acidic the colour changes to yellow then _____, becoming more alkaline the colour changes to more _____ then purple.

Or design your own hazard symbol, warning of the dangers of strong acids and alkalis.

Reacting Acids and Alkalis and Acids and Metals

We know that when reacting an acid and an alkali together we can get neutralisation, the solution produced would have a pH of 7. The reaction between both acids and alkalis and acid and metals, are very common and give predictable results. In words we say that an **acid** plus an **alkali**, produces a **salt** and **water**. If we react an **acid** with a **metal**, we produce a **salt** and **hydrogen** gas. This is always true, so we can work out what the products of a reaction are going to be if we know;

1. The name of the acid	2. The name of the alkali	3. The name of the metal
e.g. hydrochloric acid, HCl	e.g. sodium hydroxide, NaOH	e.g. zinc, Zn or sodium, Na

Acid plus Alkali

Acid plus Alkali
Using hydrochloric acid, HCl
acid + alkali ⟶ salt + water
HCl + NaOH ⟶ NaCl + H₂O
Sodium chloride, NaCl produced.

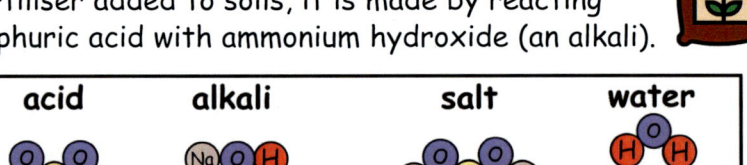

When we use **hydrochloric acid**, HCl, the salt produced is a **chloride**. When we use **sulphuric acid**, H_2SO_4, the salt we produce is called a **sulphate** (SO_4 is sulphate). To obtain the salt produced, we could evaporate off the water. Ammonium sulphate is a fertiliser added to soils, it is made by reacting sulphuric acid with ammonium hydroxide (an alkali).

Fertiliser

Acid plus Alkali
Using sulphuric acid, H_2SO_4
acid + alkali ⟶ salt + water
H_2SO_4 + 2NaOH ⟶ Na_2SO_4 + $2H_2O$
Sodium sulphate, Na_2SO_4 produced.

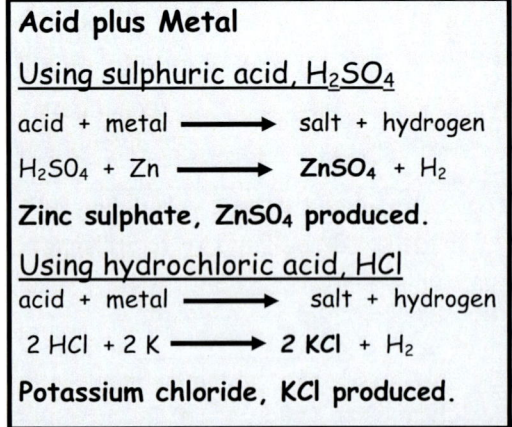

Acid plus Metal

If we react an acid and a metal together, for example, by putting some magnesium metal into hydrochloric acid, HCl, you will quickly see that bubbles of gas are produced.
We can know what the gas is by testing it. The test for **hydrogen** gas is that a '**lit splint**' (or burning stick) produces a **squeaky pop** sound, if it is brought near hydrogen gas. Add some magnesium to hydrochloric acid in a test tube, put in a lit splint and you will get a squeaky pop sound. Whatever the metal is that you react with an acid, you still get hydrogen gas and a salt produced. How quickly the reaction takes place depends on the reactivity of the metal and the strength of the acid. Acid in rain speeds up the corrosion of metal.

Acid plus Metal
Using sulphuric acid, H_2SO_4
acid + metal ⟶ salt + hydrogen
H_2SO_4 + Zn ⟶ $ZnSO_4$ + H_2
Zinc sulphate, $ZnSO_4$ produced.
Using hydrochloric acid, HCl
acid + metal ⟶ salt + hydrogen
2 HCl + 2 K ⟶ 2 KCl + H_2
Potassium chloride, KCl produced.

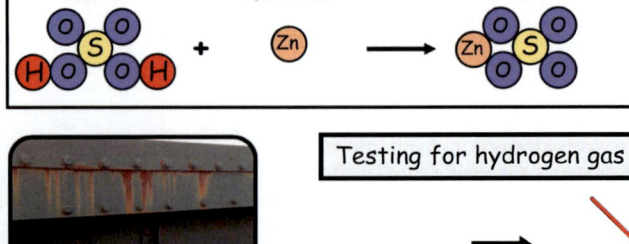

Acid Corrosion

Testing for hydrogen gas

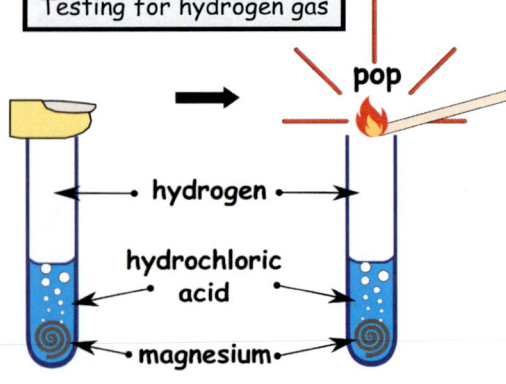

pop

hydrogen

hydrochloric acid

magnesium

WHAT?
Salt (sodium chloride) makes water freeze at a lower temperature than zero degrees. It is put on roads and paths in winter to stop ice forming, so we don't slip.

Questions on Reacting Acids and Alkalis and Acids and Metals

Comprehension

1. What can happen when you react an acid with an alkali?

2. What does an acid plus an alkali produce?

3. What is produced when an acid reacts with a metal?

4. When hydrochloric acid, HCl, is reacted with sodium hydroxide, NaOH, what is the name of the salt produced and what is its formula? (text box)

5. When sulphuric acid, H_2SO_4, is reacted with sodium hydroxide, NaOH, what is the name of the salt produced and what is its formula? (text box)

6. What is the name of the salt produced when using hydrochloric acid, HCl?

7. What is the name of the salt produced using sulphuric acid, H_2SO_4 ?

8. Which fertiliser is made by reacting sulphuric acid, H_2SO_4 with ammonium hydroxide?

9. If magnesium metal is added to hydrochloric acid, HCl, what will you quickly see?

10. What is the test for hydrogen gas?

11. How quickly a reaction takes place between an acid and metal depends upon what?

12. When sulphuric acid, H_2SO_4 is reacted with zinc metal, what is the name and formula of the salt produced?

13. When hydrochloric acid, HCl, reacts with potassium metal, what is the name and formula of the salt produced?

Additional tasks

1. Write the name of the salt produced underneath the chemical formula. Use the periodic table (pg90) to help and choose from: **Calcium sulphate, Magnesium chloride, Calcium chloride, Magnesium sulphate, Potassium chloride, Calcium sulphate, Sodium sulphate and Calcium chloride**

$$H_2SO_4 + Ca(OH)_2 \longrightarrow CaSO_4 + 2H_2O \qquad 2HCl + Ca(OH)_2 \longrightarrow CaCl_2 + 2H_2O$$

$$2HCl + Mg \longrightarrow MgCl_2 + H_2 \qquad H_2SO_4 + Mg \longrightarrow MgSO_4 + H_2$$

$$2HCl + Ca \longrightarrow CaCl_2 + H_2 \qquad 2HCl + 2K \longrightarrow 2KCl + H_2$$

$$H_2SO_4 + Ca \longrightarrow CaSO_4 + H_2 \qquad H_2SO_4 + 2Na \longrightarrow Na_2SO_4 + H_2$$

2. Ammonium sulphate (a fertiliser) is made by adding sulphuric acid (an acid) to ammonium hydroxide solution (an alkali). The steps are shown below.

a. What colour would the ammonium hydroxide solution and universal indicator be to begin with? (pg84)

b. When enough acid is added to neutralise the ammonium hydroxide what colour would you expect? (pg84)

c. After neutralisation, apart from ammonium sulphate what else is produced?

d. Why is the Bunsen burner used to heat the solution?

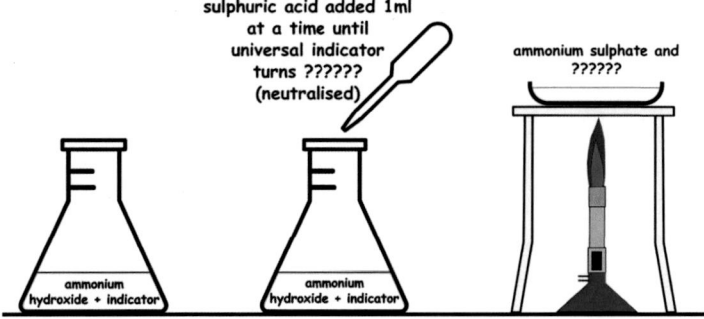

sulphuric acid added 1ml at a time until universal indicator turns ?????? (neutralised)

ammonium sulphate and ??????

ammonium hydroxide + indicator

ammonium hydroxide + indicator

3. Ammonium sulphate is a good fertiliser for grass (lawns). Explain how you could you test how effective it is? Think about;

- What would you measure?

- What would you keep the same / control?

- How would you make it reliable (repeats?)

Exothermic and Endothermic Chemical Reactions

Whenever a chemical reaction takes place, heat is either emitted (given out) or absorbed (taken in). If the reactants **release heat** during the reaction (become **hotter** than the surroundings), it is called an **exothermic reaction**. We measure an **increase** in **temperature**. This could be a few degrees, hundreds of degrees, or even thousands of degrees, like an explosion. If the **reactants absorb heat** energy to make the reaction happen (become **colder** than the surroundings), it is called an **endothermic reaction**. We measure a decrease in temperature.

Explosion

WHAT?

Add a little washing powder to water and you produce an exothermic reaction!

Rearranging Atoms

Chemical reactions occur when the atoms in the reacting substances rearrange themselves. Chemical bonds are broken and made during a reaction. When chemical bonds are formed, heat energy is released. When chemical bonds are broken heat energy is absorbed. If **more** energy is **released** in bond making, than breaking, the reaction is **exothermic**. If **more** energy is **absorbed** in bond breaking than making the reaction is **endothermic**.

Confusion sometimes occurs when thinking about endothermic reactions. This is because heat energy is absorbed, but the temperature drops. What's key to remember is that the heat energy is coming from the reacting chemicals themselves, the heat energy that was present becomes chemical energy of the products, so the result is colder than the surroundings.

EXO hotter than surroundings

ENDO cooler than surroundings

Energy level diagrams

'ENDOTHERMIC'

Chemical Energy

after

before

Reaction happening

'EXOTHERMIC'

Chemical Energy

before

after

Reaction happening

Energy Level Diagrams

These are just a way of showing that in endothermic reactions, afterwards the products have **more** chemical energy. In exothermic reactions the products have **less** chemical energy.

Endothermic Reactions: Endothermic reactions are 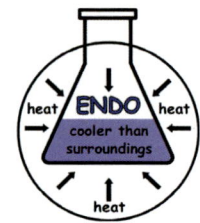 less common in nature. **Thermal decomposition,** which is using heat to break down chemicals is a good example of an endothermic reaction. Dissolving some salts in water is another. Here, **more heat energy** is needed to break the attractions (bonds) holding the salt particles together, **less heat energy** is released when they form new attractions dissolved in the water, so it's endothermic. Salts like ammonium chloride use this principle in 'cold' packs.

Cold pack

Exothermic Reactions: Exothermic reactions are much more common. Burning or combustion is the most obvious exothermic reaction. An explosion is also an exothermic reaction. **Neutralisation reactions**, when an acid reacts with an alkali are exothermic. All reactions between an acid and a metal are exothermic. Drop some magnesium ribbon in a test tube with acid, it feels warm quickly. Displacement reactions, when a more reactive element takes the place of a less reactive element, are exothermic. Respiration, the chemical reaction of releasing energy from our food is also exothermic.

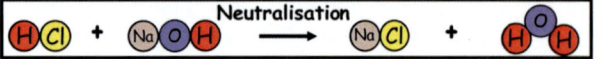
Neutralisation

HCl + Mg

Sparkler

Questions on Exothermic and Endothermic Chemical Reactions

Comprehension

1. What happens whenever a chemical reaction takes place?

2. When the reactants release heat (get warm or hot), what is this reaction called?

3. What will you see, if you measure the temperature before and after an exothermic reaction?

4. When the reactants absorbs heat (get colder), what is this reaction called?

5. What will you see if you measure the temperature before and after an endothermic reaction?

6. What happens to chemical bonds during a chemical reaction?

7. What happens when chemical bonds are formed?

8. What happens when chemical bonds are broken?

9. What happens to the 'heat energy' during an endothermic reaction?

10. What do energy level diagrams show?

11. Why is dissolving some salts in water endothermic?

12. What is an 'obvious' exothermic reaction?

13. What is neutralisation and is it exothermic or endothermic?

14. What is the chemical reaction of releasing energy from our food called?

Additional tasks

1. Complete the third column of the table by writing whether the chemical reaction is **endothermic** or **exothermic**.

Starting temperature of reactants (^{o}C)	Final temperature of products (^{o}C)	Endothermic / Exothermic ?
20	30	
25	6	
-10	15	
22	65	
16	5	
18	-6	

2. If we take away the **energy released** in **making** bonds from the **energy absorbed** in **breaking** bonds we can work out if a reaction is endothermic or exothermic.

a. Minus the **energy released** from the **energy absorbed** (the energy difference) and complete the last two columns of the table. Try **without** a calculator!

Chemical Reaction	Energy absorbed breaking bonds (KJ/mole)	Energy released making bonds (KJ/mole)	Energy difference	Exothermic/ Endothermic
$C + O_2 \longrightarrow CO_2$	1200	1600		
$H_2 + Cl_2 \longrightarrow 2HCl$	678	862		
$2HBr \longrightarrow H_2 + Br_2$	732	629		
$2H_2 + O_2 \longrightarrow 2H_2O$	1368	1852		
$2H_2O \longrightarrow 2H_2 + O_2$	1840	1371		
$CaCO_3 \longrightarrow CaO + CO_2$	178	0		
$C + 2H_2O \longrightarrow CO_2 + 2H_2$	394	484		
$CH_4 + Cl_2 \longrightarrow CH_3Cl + HCl$	654	763		

3. a. What do you notice about the energy difference for an exothermic reaction?

   b. Complete these two sentences.

Exothermic reactions have a **negative** energy difference, the _____s have less chemical energy. Energy is released. Endothermic reactions have a **positive** energy difference, the _____s have more chemical energy. Energy is absorbed.

Periodic Table of Elements: What it tells us and how it Works

In the 1800's, scientists were discovering lots of new elements. They began by putting them in order of weight and looking for patterns in the way they react. **Dimitri Mendeleev** had great success with this method. He began putting elements in order of their mass in rows (now called periods). He arranged the rows on top of each other, so that elements with similar properties formed columns (now called groups). Patterns became clear and Mendeleev was so convinced of his method, he left gaps for elements that he predicted should exist. The gaps were filled later, as more elements were discovered. He is regarded as the father of the periodic table. There are now 118 known elements (not all shown below).

Groups are the columns (eight labelled here G1 to G8)
atomic number (number of protons)
Periods are the rows (six shown here)

atomic mass (number of protons plus neutrons)

G1	G2											G3	G4	G5	G6	G7	G8
1 H Hydrogen 1																	2 He Helium 4
3 Li Lithium 7	4 Be Beryllium 9											5 B Boron 11	6 C Carbon 12	7 N Nitrogen 14	8 O Oxygen 16	9 F Fluorine 19	10 Ne Neon 20
11 Na Sodium 23	12 Mg Magnesium 24											13 Al Aluminium 27	14 Si Silicon 28	15 P Phosphorus 31	16 S Sulphur 32	17 Cl Chlorine 35.5	18 Ar Argon 40
19 K Potassium 39	20 Ca Calcium 40	21 Sc Scandium 45	22 Ti Titanium 48	23 V Vanadium 51	24 Cr Chromium 52	25 Mn Manganese 55	26 Fe Iron 56	27 Co Cobalt 59	28 Ni Nickel 59	29 Cu Copper 63.5	30 Zn Zinc 65	31 Ga Gallium 70	32 Ge Germanium 73	33 As Arsenic 75	34 Se Selenium 79	35 Br Bromine 80	36 Kr Krypton 84
37 Rb Rubidium 85	38 Sr Strontium 88	39 Y Yttrium 89	40 Zr Zirconium 91	41 Nb Niobium 93	42 Mo Molybdenum 96	43 Tc Technetium 98	44 Ru Ruthenium 101	45 Rh Rhodium 103	46 Pd Palladium 106	47 Ag Silver 108	48 Cd Cadmium 112	49 In Indium 115	50 Sn Tin 119	51 Sb Antimony 122	52 Te Tellurium 128	53 I Iodine 127	54 Xe Xenon 131
55 Cs Caesium 133	56 Ba Barium 137	57 La Lanthanum 139	72 Hf Hafnium 178	73 Ta Tantalum 181	74 W Tungsten 184	75 Re Rhenium 186	76 Os Osmium 190	77 Ir Iridium 192	78 Pt Platinum 195	79 Au Gold 197	80 Hg Mercury 201	81 Tl Thallium 204	82 Pb Lead 207	83 Bi Bismuth 209	84 Po Polonium 209	85 At Astatine 210	86 Rn Radon 222

(central key box: 2 He Helium 4)

Elements and Atoms

Each element in the periodic table is made from a different kind of atom. The atom is the smallest piece of matter that has the same properties as the chemical element. Atoms themselves are made up of three even tinier particles (pieces of matter), which aren't 'normally' found on their own. They are normally found as part of the atom.

Lithium atom

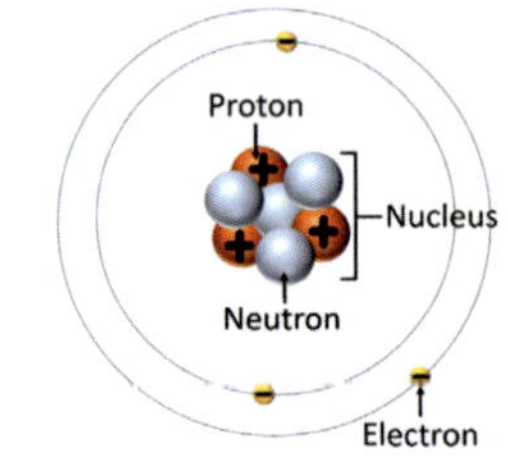

The proton which is positively charged (has a charge of +1), the neutron which has no charge (neutral) and the electron which is negatively charged (has a charge of -1). The number at the top of each 'square' in the periodic table is the number of protons in the atom, it is called the **atomic number**. This is the same as the number of electrons. The number at the bottom is the **atomic mass**, it is how 'heavy' an atom is. Atomic mass is the number of protons added to the number of neutrons. Going left to right along a period (row), each element has one more proton and gets slightly bigger.

particle	charge	mass (relative)
proton	+1	1
neutron	0	1
electron	-1	1/2000

Since atoms have the same number of protons (positive charges) as electrons (negative charges), their charges cancel, meaning the atom is neutral. Carbon, for example has six protons and six electrons meaning, +1+1+1+1+1+1-1-1-1-1-1-1=0, no charge, neutral. Hydrogen has only one proton and one electron, +1-1=0, no charge, neutral. Electrons are arranged in layers (or shells) around the protons and neutrons at the centre (**nucleus**) of

WHAT?

Atoms are so small that no one has ever 'seen' one with visible light! We know they exist from experiments. The atom is mostly empty space like the solar system.

the atom, like the layers of an onion. Scientists worked out rules to tell them how many electrons fit in each layer. It is the number electrons in the outer layer of an atom that decide how one element (certain kind of atom) will react with another element. This is how chemistry works.

Questions on The Periodic Table of Elements

Comprehension

1. When scientists began discovering lots of new elements what did they put them in order of?

2. Who had great success with this method?

3. How did he arrange the rows?

4. What did Dimitri Mendeleev leave in his table, for elements he predicted should exist?

5. Each element in the periodic table is made from a different what?

6. Complete the sentence ; the atom is the smallest…

7. How many particles are atoms made from and where aren't they normally found?

8. What is the name of the three particles that the atom is made from?

9. What does the number at the top of each 'square' in the periodic table tell you and what is it called?

10. Why do the charges of an atom cancel out?

11. What does this mean that the atom is?

12. How are the electrons arranged in an atom?

13. What decides how one element reacts with another element?

14. What is the atomic number of chlorine?

Additional tasks

1. Use the periodic table to complete the number of protons, number of electrons and number of neutrons for each element. The first one is done for you.

Element	Number of protons	Number of electrons	Number of neutrons
Boron - 11	5	5	11 - 5 = 6
Carbon - 12			
Magnesium - 24			
Fluorine - 19			
Potassium - 39			
Lithium - 7			
Iron - 56			
Gallium - 70			

2. Unscramble these **amazing elements** from their description. Use the periodic table pg90 to help.

Precious, malleable metal - **GODL**

Liquid metal at room temperature - **ERRMYCU**

Important for strong bones - **ALUCMCI**

Keeps our swimming pools clean - **HLNCIREO**

Gas that makes up 78% of air - **ITNNEORG**

Gas that makes up 21% of air - **OYNXEG**

Heaviest naturally occurring element - **RAUUMNI** (begins with U, on last column of wordsearch)

A magnetic metal - **CBTOLA**

Most reactive metal in group 1 - **CASMEUI**

Use in computer chips - **ILOSNIC**

A radioactive gas in group 8 - **RANDO**

Important in a healthy diet - **ELUSINME**

Most commonly used radioactive element in medical imaging - **EHUTIEMCTN**

A gas that gives us pretty lights - **NENO**

3. Use the periodic table to identify elements a. to i. below.

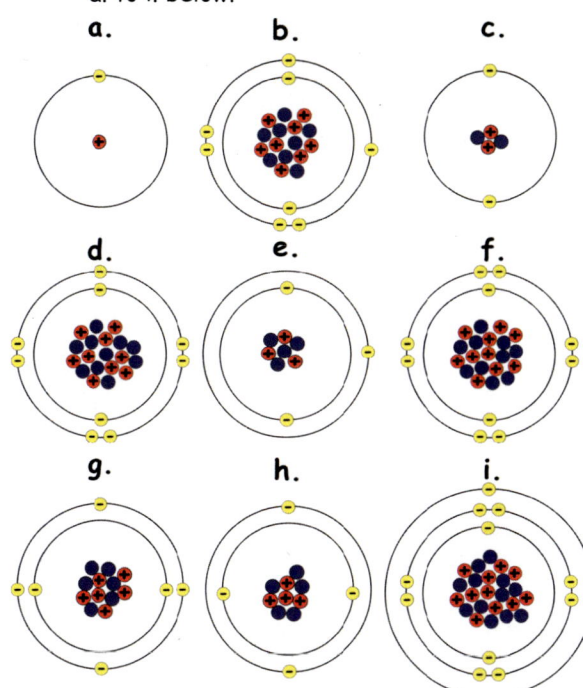

Properties of Metals and Non-metals

A stepped black line (thick), starting under boron and continuing under silicon, arsenic, tellurium and astatine separates the metallic elements (metals) from the non-metals. Metals lie to the left of this line (grey blue green) and non-metals to the right of this line.

Groups are the columns (eight labelled here G1 to G8)

Periods are the rows (six shown here)

atomic number (number of protons)

| 2 He Helium 4 | atomic mass (number of protons plus neutrons) |

G1	G2											G3	G4	G5	G6	G7	G8
1 H Hydrogen 1																	2 He Helium 4
3 Li Lithium 7	4 Be Beryllium 9											5 B Boron 11	6 C Carbon 12	7 N Nitrogen 14	8 O Oxygen 16	9 F Fluorine 19	10 Ne Neon 20
11 Na Sodium 23	12 Mg Magnesium 24											13 Al Aluminium 27	14 Si Silicon 28	15 P Phosphorus 31	16 S Sulphur 32	17 Cl Chlorine 35.5	18 Ar Argon 40
19 K Potassium 39	20 Ca Calcium 40	21 Sc Scandium 45	22 Ti Titanium 48	23 V Vanadium 51	24 Cr Chromium 52	25 Mn Manganese 55	26 Fe Iron 56	27 Co Cobalt 59	28 Ni Nickel 59	29 Cu Copper 63.5	30 Zn Zinc 65	31 Ga Gallium 70	32 Ge Germanium 73	33 As Arsenic 75	34 Se Selenium 79	35 Br Bromine 80	36 Kr Krypton 84
37 Rb Rubidium 85	38 Sr Strontium 88	39 Y Yttrium 89	40 Zr Zirconium 91	41 Nb Niobium 93	42 Mo Molybdenum 96	43 Tc Technetium 98	44 Ru Ruthenium 101	45 Rh Rhodium 103	46 Pd Palladium 106	47 Ag Silver 108	48 Cd Cadmium 112	49 In Indium 115	50 Sn Tin 119	51 Sb Antimony 122	52 Te Tellurium 128	53 I Iodine 127	54 Xe Xenon 131
55 Cs Caesium 133	56 Ba Barium 137	57 La Lanthanum 139	72 Hf Hafnium 178	73 Ta Tantalum 181	74 W Tungsten 184	75 Re Rhenium 186	76 Os Osmium 190	77 Ir Iridium 192	78 Pt Platinum 195	79 Au Gold 197	80 Hg Mercury 201	81 Tl Thallium 204	82 Pb Lead 207	83 Bi Bismuth 209	84 Po Polonium 209	85 At Astatine 210	86 Rn Radon 222

Metals

Metals have familiar properties, like being **good at conducting**, which means they allow electricity and heat to pass through them easily. They are often **strong** and **shiny**. They can make a nice ringing sound when you hit them, this is called being **sonorous**. You often need very **high temperatures to melt** metals and even higher to boil them. Yes boil, once melted liquid metal can be boiled. They are heavy for their size meaning they are **dense**.

strong

Three of the metals are magnetic, namely, **iron, nickel** and **cobalt**. Steel, which is made mainly from iron, is used to make loads of stuff, so much of the metal around us is magnetic.

We can pull many metals into long thin wires, this is called being **ductile**. This makes them great for 'wiring' appliances. **Copper** is particularly good at this, which is why the **cables** that connect to our electrical appliances are made from copper surrounded by plastic.

shiny A useful property of some metals, particularly gold, is their ability to be hammered into thin sheets or other shapes without breaking, this is called being **malleable**. Gold can be made into gold leaf, extremely thin gold to cover items such as ornaments and paintings because of its attractive colour.

Metals can be mixed to make **alloys** (a mixture of metals) with useful properties. You might, for example, mix a strong heavy metal, with a light, but weak one. Hopefully the result will be a light but strong metal.

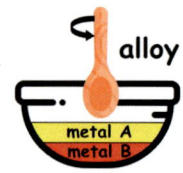
alloy
metal A
metal B

Non-metals

They have almost the opposite properties to metals. They are **bad at conducting electricity** and **heat** which means they are **good** at being **insulators**. They are not normally strong. They melt easily and **often** exist as **gases at room temperature** (about 20°C). This means they have already boiled! Many have boiling temperatures that are minus. They are not heavy for their size so are **not dense**. They are definitely **not magnetic**. They are also **dull** (not shiny), because they don't reflect light well like metals.

weak

gas 20°C

WHAT?

The elements in the middle section of the table in dark grey, are called the transition metals, because they are 'in between' group 2 and group 3.

Questions on Properties of Metals and Non-Metals

Comprehension

1. What separates the metals from the non-metals on the periodic table?

2. What are metals good at?

3. What does this mean?

4. What does sonorous mean?

5. What do we mean by being dense?

6. What are the names of the three magnetic metals?

7. Why is much of the metal 'around us' magnetic?

8. What is the property of being able to pull metal into wires called?

9. Which metal is particularly ductile?

10. What does being malleable mean?

11. What is a mixture of metals called?

12. Why might you mix a strong, heavy metal, with a light, weak one?

13. Non-metals are bad at conducting electricity and heat which means they are good at what?

14. In what form do non-metals often exist at room temperature?

15. Why are non-metals dull?

Additional tasks

1. Write the following properties in the metals or non-metals column of the table below.

   malleable, good conductors, not sonorous, bad conductors, strong, high melting points, ductile, not strong, not ductile, not malleable, sonorous, low melting points

Metals	Non-metals

2. Solve the jumbled words that describe the properties of metals.

ONUSORSO	HYINS
UCLDETI	DEENS
ALSLYO	BDA NURIOASSTL
GODO ODRCOCSNTU	ALLMBEELA
SRGTNO	AGIMTECN
IGHH GMLENTI PINTSO	EHAVY

3 a. Shade or colour in a different colour the metals and non-metals. Write a key for the colour or shade you have used. **Remember, although hydrogen is in G1 (group 1) it's not a metal!**

b. Choose two metals and two non-metals and write about any uses you know for them. Do more if you can.

1 H Hydrogen 1																	2 He Helium 4
3 Li Lithium 7	4 Be Beryllium 9											5 B Boron 11	6 C Carbon 12	7 N Nitrogen 14	8 O Oxygen 16	9 F Fluorine 19	10 Ne Neon 20
11 Na Sodium 23	12 Mg Magnesium 24											13 Al Aluminium 27	14 Si Silicon 28	15 P Phosphorus 31	16 S Sulphur 32	17 Cl Chlorine 35.5	18 Ar Argon 40
19 K Potassium 39	20 Ca Calcium 40	21 Sc Scandium 45	22 Ti Titanium 48	23 V Vanadium 51	24 Cr Chromium 52	25 Mn Manganese 55	26 Fe Iron 56	27 Co Cobalt 59	28 Ni Nickel 59	29 Cu Copper 63.5	30 Zn Zinc 65	31 Ga Gallium 70	32 Ge Germanium 73	33 As Arsenic 75	34 Se Selenium 79	35 Br Bromine 80	36 Kr Krypton 84
37 Rb Rubidium 85	38 Sr Strontium 88	39 Y Yttrium 89	40 Zr Zirconium 91	41 Nb Nobium 93	42 Mo Molybdenum 96	43 Tc Technetium 98	44 Mo Ruthenium 101	45 Rh Rhodium 103	46 Pd Palladium 106	47 Ag Silver 108	48 Cd Cadmium 112	49 In Indium 115	50 Sn Tin 119	51 Sb Antimony 122	52 Te Tellurium 128	53 I Iodine 127	54 Xe Xenon 131
55 Cs Cesium 133	56 Ba Barium 137	57 La Lanthanum 139	72 Hf Hafnium 178	73 Ta Tantalum 181	74 W Tungsten 184	75 Re Rhenium 186	76 Os Osmium 190	77 Ir Iridium 192	78 Pt Platinum 195	79 Au Gold 197	80 Hg Mercury 201	81 Tl Thallium 204	82 Pb Lead 207	83 Bi Bismuth 209	84 Po Polonium 209	85 At Astatine 210	86 Rn Radon 222

Properties of G1, G2, G7 and G8

Groups are the columns (eight labelled here G1 to G8)

Periods are the rows (six shown here)

atomic number (number of protons)

atomic mass (number of protons plus neutrons)

G1	G2											G3	G4	G5	G6	G7	G8
1 H Hydrogen 1																	2 He Helium 4
3 Li Lithium 7	4 Be Beryllium 9											5 B Boron 11	6 C Carbon 12	7 N Nitrogen 14	8 O Oxygen 16	9 F Fluorine 19	10 Ne Neon 20
11 Na Sodium 23	12 Mg Magnesium 24											13 Al Aluminium 27	14 Si Silicon 28	15 P Phosphorus 31	16 S Sulphur 32	17 Cl Chlorine 35.5	18 Ar Argon 40
19 K Potassium 39	20 Ca Calcium 40	21 Sc Scandium 45	22 Ti Titanium 48	23 V Vanadium 51	24 Cr Chromium 52	25 Mn Manganese 55	26 Fe Iron 56	27 Co Cobalt 59	28 Ni Nickel 59	29 Cu Copper 63.5	30 Zn Zinc 65	31 Ga Gallium 70	32 Ge Germanium 73	33 As Arsenic 75	34 Se Selenium 79	35 Br Bromine 80	36 Kr Krypton 84
37 Rb Rubidium 85	38 Sr Strontium 88	39 Y Yttrium 89	40 Zr Zirconium 91	41 Nb Niobium 93	42 Mo Molybdenum 96	43 Tc Technetium 98	44 Mo Ruthenium 101	45 Rh Rhodium 103	46 Pd Palladium 106	47 Ag Silver 108	48 Cd Cadmium 112	49 In Indium 115	50 Sn Tin 119	51 Sb Antimony 122	52 Te Tellurium 128	53 I Iodine 127	54 Xe Xenon 131
55 Cs Caesium 133	56 Ba Barium 137	57 La Lanthanum 139	72 Hf Hafnium 178	73 Ta Tantalum 181	74 W Tungsten 184	75 Re Rhenium 186	76 Os Osmium 190	77 Ir Iridium 192	78 Pt Platinum 195	79 Au Gold 197	80 Hg Mercury 201	81 Tl Thallium 204	82 Pb Lead 207	83 Bi Bismuth 209	84 Po Polonium 209	85 At Astatine 210	86 Rn Radon 222

(atomic number example: 2 He Helium 4)

Group 1 These are called the *alkali metals*. One of the ways to investigate their reactivity is to **drop them into water**. Lithium, sodium and potassium aren't very dense (heavy for their size) and float on water. They react quickly with water, producing an alkaline solution and hydrogen gas. They get **more reactive** as you move **down the group**, reacting faster and faster with water. Potassium produces its own flame by getting so hot it sets the hydrogen gas alight.

Lithium

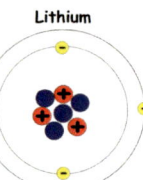

They are **quite soft** metals, so soft they can be cut with a knife. They get softer as you move down the group towards caesium. Lithium, sodium and potassium float on water, but **density increases** as you **move down** the group and when you reach rubidium it sinks. This is because it is more dense than water. Group 1 elements **melt** (turn from solid to liquid) **more easily** as you **move down the group**. Lithium melts at 180°C, whilst potassium melts at 63°C. Their **boiling points** also **decrease** as you **move down the group**. They all have **one electron** in their **outer shell**, which is why they react in a similar way.

Beryllium

Group 2 These are called the *alkali earth metals*, they react less quickly with water, but still produce an alkaline solution and hydrogen gas. They also react faster as you move down the group. Like group 1, they melt more easily **(melting point decreases)** as you move down the group towards barium. Their **boiling points** also **decrease** as you move down the group. They get heavier for their size too, moving down the group **(density increases)**. They all have **two electrons** in their **outer shell** which is why they react in a similar way.

Fluorine

Group 7 These are called the *halogens*. **Fluorine** and **chlorine** are **gases** at room temperature (20°C), whilst **bromine** is a **liquid** and **iodine** is a **solid**. This tells us that their **melting** and **boiling points increase** down the group. Most famous of the halogens is probably chlorine. It is used to make our water safe to drink and is the smell of the swimming baths. It is also used to make bleach. All of this is because it is brilliant at killing bacteria. Halogens behave in the opposite way to group 1 and 2. They get **less reactive** as you move down the group. All have **seven electrons** in their **outer shell** which is why they all react in similar ways.

Group 8 These are called the *noble gases*. They don't like reacting with anything, like the nobility! All but helium have **eight electrons** in their outer shell, **this means it is full**. This is why they are very unreactive. They can be made to conduct electricity though giving us pretty 'neon' lights.

Neon

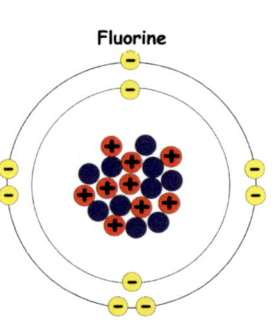

> **WHAT?**
>
> Caesium from group 1 explodes if dropped into water, watch out! Fluorine is one of the most reactive elements and fluorine gas is deadly. Sodium fluoride though, a compound of fluorine, is in tooth paste and strengthens our teeth.

Questions on Properties of G1, G2, G7 and G8

Comprehension

1.	What are the Group 1 (G1) elements called?	9.	What happens to their melting point as you move down the group?
2.	What is one of the ways to investigate their reactivity?	10.	Why do Group 2 elements react in a similar way?
3.	What do the alkali metals produce when they react with water?	11.	What are the Group 7 elements called?
4.	What happens to the reactivity as you move down Group 1?	12.	What state of matter are fluorine, chlorine, bromine and iodine at room temperature (20°C)?
5.	Why does rubidium sink when dropped into water?	13.	What happens to the reactivity as you move down Group 7?
6.	Why do Group 1 elements react in a similar way?	14.	Why do Group 7 elements behave in a similar way?
7.	What are Group 2 (G2) elements called?	15.	What are the Group 8 elements called?
8.	What do they produce when reacted with water?	16.	Why are they very unreactive?

Additional tasks

1. Match the terms to their descriptions below.

Groups	(the alkali earth metals), have two electrons in their outer shell
Group 1	(the halogens), have seven electrons in their outer shell
Group 2	(the noble gases), have full or eight electrons in their outer shell
Group 7	(the alkali metals), have one electron in their outer shell
Group 8	these are the columns in the periodic table and tell you the number of electrons in the outer shell. Elements in the same group behave similarly.

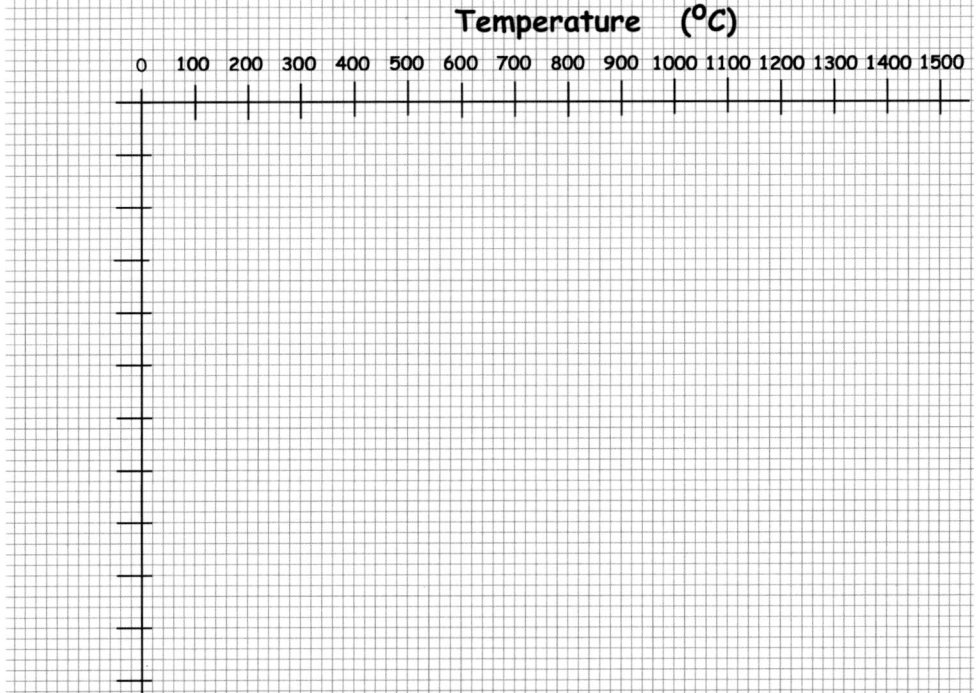

Temperature (°C)

0 100 200 300 400 500 600 700 800 900 1000 1100 1200 1300 1400 1500

2. The melting and boiling points of lithium, sodium, potassium, rubidium and caesium are listed below. Plot a bar chart of the results **side by side** for each element and draw a key.

	Melting Point (°C)	Boiling Point (°C)
Li	180	1342
Na	98	883
K	63	759
Rb	30	688
Cs	28	671

3 a. How is **this** pattern different to the group 7 elements?

b. What other pattern in behaviour of the group 7 elements is the opposite?

Metal and Non-metal Oxides

Acid rain damage

Non-Metal Oxides

When elements react with oxygen, they form oxides. Sometimes the compound formed has two oxygen atoms like carbon dioxide, CO_2, or sulphur dioxide, SO_2, or Nitrogen dioxide, NO_2. If the compound formed has only one oxygen atom, then its name will be monoxide (mono means one). Examples are carbon monoxide, CO, sulphur monoxide, SO, and nitrogen monoxide, NO, all have one oxygen atom.

Carbon, sulphur and nitrogen are **non-metals**. **Carbon dioxide, sulphur dioxide and nitrogen dioxide** will all **dissolve** in water to produce an **acidic solution**. Nearly all non-metal oxides that dissolve in water produce acidic solutions, pH less than 7.

Sulphur dioxide and nitrogen dioxide released from burning fossil fuels, dissolve in water to produce acid rain. Forests can be damaged and the wildlife that relies on them suffer. Acid reacts with limestone ($CaCO_3$) and weathers buildings made from it much more quickly. The buildings look like they've been eaten away!

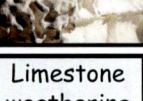
Acid rain

Carbonic Acid

The carbon dioxide that is put into our drinks to make them fizzy, also ends up making them acidic!

Carbon dioxide + Water ⟶ Carbonic acid

$$CO_2 + H_2O \longrightarrow H_2CO_3$$

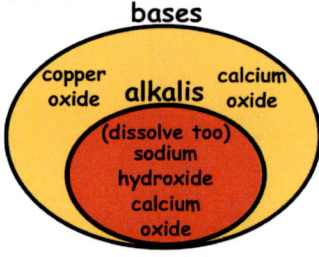
Limestone weathering

Metal Oxides

Metal oxides (a metal bonded to oxygen) that dissolve in water, for example, calcium oxide, CaO, produce alkaline solutions. This means that they have a pH greater than 7 and will neutralise acids. Many metal oxides don't dissolve in water, such as magnesium oxide, MgO, copper oxide, CuO or zinc oxide, ZnO. However they will neutralise acids. They are called bases. **All metal oxides are bases.** They are **chemical opposites** to **acids**, they react with acids to produce a salt and water. **Bases that do dissolve are called alkalis.**

Acid plus base reactions

Acid	+	Base (oxide)	⟶	Salt	+	Water
Sulphuric acid	+	Copper oxide	⟶	Copper sulphate	+	Water
H_2SO_4	+	CuO	⟶	$CuSO_4$	+	H_2O

bases

copper oxide **alkalis** calcium oxide

(dissolve too) sodium hydroxide calcium oxide

Other Bases (carbonates)

Acid plus base reactions

Acid	+	Base (carbonate)	⟶	Salt	+	Water	+	Carbon dioxide
Hydrochloric acid	+	Calcium carbonate	⟶	Calcium chloride	+	Water	+	Carbon dioxide
2 HCl	+	$CaCO_3$	⟶	$CaCl_2$	+	H_2O	+	CO_2

Carbonates, compounds that contain CO_3, are also bases. Some do dissolve in water and are therefore alkalis too. Calcium carbonate (limestone or chalk), $CaCO_3$, is probably the most well known carbonate base (acid opposite). It is often an ingredient in indigestion tablets, because it can neutralise acids. As well as producing salt and water when reacted with acid, carbonates also produce carbon dioxide gas, CO_2. Add acid to a rock and if it contains $CaCO_3$ it fizzes, **limestone**, **chalk** and **marble** all fizz. Sandstone for example doesn't.

WHAT?

Sulphur dioxide, a non-metal oxide is used as a preservative in all sorts of food, from dried fruit, vegetables, meats, soft drinks and wine. Calcium oxide, a metal oxide, is used to make cement.

Questions on Metals and Non-metal Oxides

Comprehension

1. When elements react with oxygen what do they form?

2. If the compound formed has two oxygen atoms, what will the **second part** of its name be?

3. What are the names of the three example monoxides?

4. What kind of elements are carbon, sulphur and nitrogen?

5. What will nearly all of their oxides do in water?

6. Which two compounds released from burning fossil fuels are responsible for acid rain?

7. What type of chemical are all metal oxides?

8. What are the products of the reaction between an acid and a metal oxide (base)?

9. What is the difference between alkalis and bases?

10. What other compounds are bases?

11. If a carbonate base reacts with an acid what gas is produced?

12. What is the formula for calcium carbonate?

13. What is calcium carbonate often used in and why?

Additional tasks

1. Use the difference between an **alkali** and **base** to put the following in the correct column.

   Sodium oxide (soluble in water), Iron oxide (insoluble in water), Copper oxide (insoluble in water), Potassium oxide (soluble in water), Lithium oxide (soluble in water), Tin oxide (insoluble in water)

Alkali	Base

2. Use the pattern on the page opposite **and** page 86 to predict the name of the compound produced when reacting the metal oxides and carbonates below, with sulphuric and hydrochloric acid.

a.   Sulphuric acid + Zinc oxide ⟶ _____ + Water

b.   Sulphuric acid + Magnesium oxide ⟶ _____ + Water

c.   Sulphuric acid + Calcium oxide ⟶ _____ + Water

d.   Hydrochloric acid + Zinc oxide ⟶ _____ + Water

e.   Hydrochloric acid + Magnesium oxide ⟶ _____ + Water

f.   Hydrochloric acid + Copper oxide ⟶ _____ + Water

g.   Hydrochloric acid + Zinc carbonate ⟶ _____ + Water + _____

h.   Hydrochloric acid + Magnesium carbonate ⟶ _____ + Water + _____

i.   Hydrochloric acid + Sodium carbonate ⟶ _____ + Water + _____

j.   Sulphuric acid + Zinc carbonate ⟶ _____ + Water + _____

k.   Sulphuric acid + Magnesium carbonate ⟶ _____ + Water + _____

l.   Sulphuric acid + Calcium carbonate ⟶ _____ + Water + _____

3. Write out four equations of your own. Two for the reaction between **lithium oxide** and **lithium carbonate** with **sulphuric acid** and two for the reaction of **potassium oxide** and **potassium carbonate** with **hydrochloric acid**.

Using Carbon to Obtain Metal from Ores

Ores are rocks from the ground that contain **enough useful material** (usually metal) to make them **worth digging up**. Once the ore has been obtained, the useful metal has to be extracted using chemical methods. One way is to use **electrolysis,** this uses an **electric current** to extract the metal from a molten (liquid) state, it is a **very expensive** process.

Carbon and the Reactivity Series

Elements **higher up** in the reactivity series are able to 'push out' and take the place of (**displace**), elements **lower down** in the **series**. If magnesium metal, for example, reacts with copper sulphate, the magnesium is able to displace the copper from copper sulphate, copper metal is left behind (see pg82 for recap). The reactivity series, means that we can predict the outcome of reacting metals with other metal compounds.

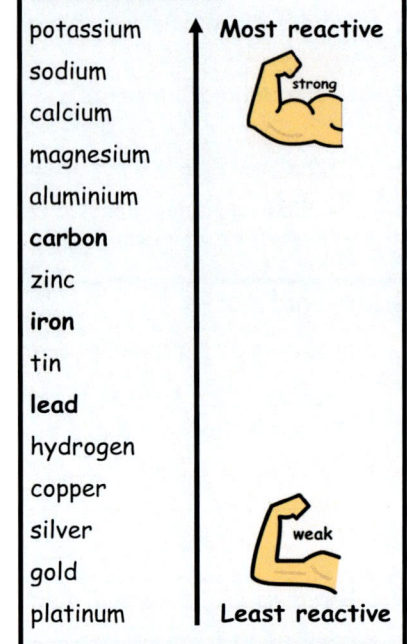

Reactivity series	
potassium	Most reactive
sodium	
calcium	
magnesium	
aluminium	
carbon	
zinc	
iron	
tin	
lead	
hydrogen	
copper	
silver	weak
gold	
platinum	Least reactive

Carbon's position in the reactivity series is between zinc and aluminium. There is a lot of carbon available from coal, so it is cheap. It can be used to extract metals from their ores if they are lower down in the reactivity series. Metals extracted this way include zinc, iron, tin, lead and copper. Ores of these metals contain oxides, the metal bonded to oxygen. Adding carbon to the ores and heating, means carbon is able to displace the metal from its oxide leaving behind the metal we want. The word equation for this reaction is shown above.

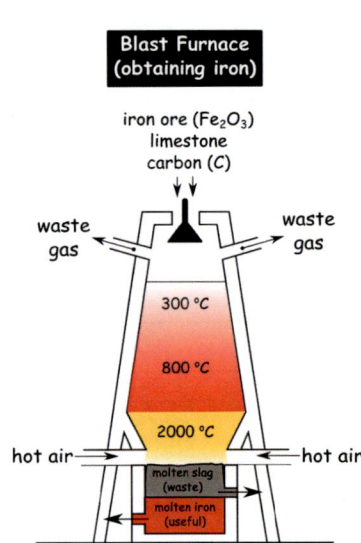

Blast Furnace (obtaining iron)

iron ore (Fe_2O_3)
limestone
carbon (C)

waste gas — waste gas

300 °C
800 °C
2000 °C

hot air — hot air
molten slag (waste)
molten iron (useful)

$$\text{Metal oxide} + \text{Carbon} \xrightarrow{\text{heat}} \text{Metal} + \text{Carbon dioxide}$$
(from ore)   (metal extracted)

Obtaining Iron using Carbon

   Uses of iron

Two widely used metals can be obtained from their ores using carbon. **Hematite** is an iron ore that contains **iron oxide**. The iron can be obtained by using carbon to displace the iron from iron oxide, to leave behind what we want, iron metal. This is done using lots of heat in **giant blast furnaces**. Iron is used to make steel so it is an extremely useful metal. Steel is

Iron oxide + Carbon ⟶ Iron + Carbon dioxide

$$2\,Fe_2O_3 + 3\,C \longrightarrow 4\,Fe + 3\,CO_2$$

Carbon displaces iron from iron oxide.

used to make cars, ships, bikes, buildings, railways, pylons, domestic appliances, nails, screws, pipes…

  Uses of lead

Obtaining Lead Using Carbon

We can also obtain lead from lead oxide found in ores using carbon. A mixture of carbon and lead oxide are heated, this causes carbon to displace the lead from lead oxide, lead metal is left behind. Lead is widely used in car batteries and glass making.

Lead oxide + Carbon ⟶ Lead + Carbon dioxide

$$2\,PbO + C \longrightarrow 2\,Pb + CO_2$$

Carbon displaces lead from lead oxide.

WHAT?

Aluminium, a very useful metal, can't be extracted from its ore with carbon. It's higher in the reactivity series, so loads of electricity has to be used. It takes over 10 times the amount of energy to extract aluminium compared to iron.

Questions on Using Carbon to Obtain Metal from Ores

Comprehension

1. What are ores?
2. How are useful metals extracted from ores?
3. What does electrolysis do?
4. What are elements higher up in the reactivity series able to do?
5. What is magnesium metal able to do to copper sulphate?
6. What does the reactivity series mean we can do?
7. Where is carbon in the reactivity series?
8. Why is carbon cheap?
9. What can carbon be used for?
10. Which metals are extracted using carbon?
11. How is carbon used to extract the metal from its ore?
12. What is the name of an iron ore?
13. How is iron obtained from iron oxide?
14. How is lead obtained from lead oxide?
15. Give two uses of lead.

Additional tasks

1. Label the blast furnace below.

Blast Furnace (obtaining iron)

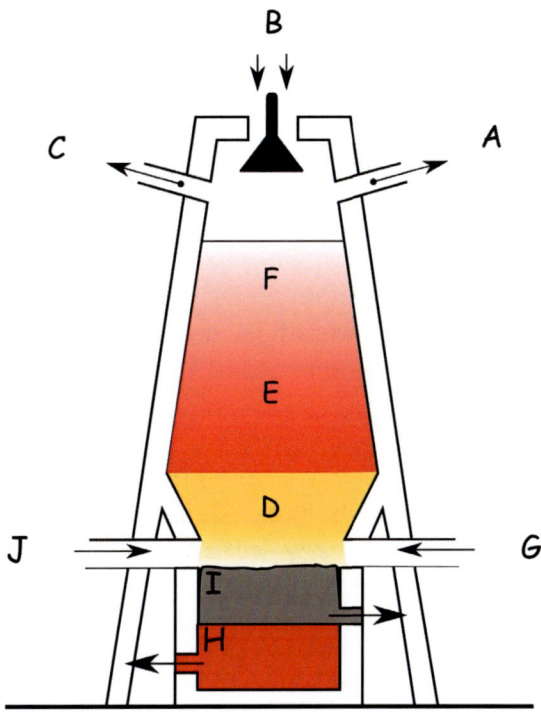

2. Use the periodic table to help (pg 90). Unscramble the names of the **metals** from their ores.

Acanthite an ore used for the production of **SLRIEV**

Bauxite an ore used for the production of **LUUAIIMMN**

Chalcocite an ore used for the production of **CPROEP**

Chromite an ore used for the production of **HRUCIMMO**

Cinnabar an ore used for the production of **ERRMYCU**

Cobaltite an ore used for the product **BLATCO**

Galena an ore used for the production of **ELDA**

Hematite an ore used for the production of **RNOI**

Malachite an ore used for the production of **CPROEP**

Scheelite an ore used for the production of **UNETTSNG**

Sperrylite an ore used for the production of **LAUPNIMT**

Sphalerite an ore used for the production of **CZNI**

Pentlandite an ore used for the production of **NCLIEK**

Rutile an ore used for the production of **ITUTINMA**

3. Other metals that can be extracted using carbon include zinc, tin and copper. This is because they are below carbon in the reactivity series.

   Copper is used to make wires that carry electricity. It is also used to make water pipes and pots and pans.

   Zinc is used to galvanize steel (coat it with zinc to stop it rusting). It is used in making brass for fittings such as door handles, taps and electric plug pins. It is also used in making batteries.

   Tin's famous use is the 'tin can'.

   Write about how our lives are made better through the use of these metals.

Polymers (Plastics), Ceramics and Composites

Polymers

Polymers or plastics are **synthetic materials** (man-made from chemicals). They are made by joining molecules together in a chain (like a daisy chain). The molecules that link together are called **monomers**. A well known polymer is **polyethene**, it is made from thousands of **ethene** molecules joined together ('poly' means many). **Polymers** have loads of brilliant uses.

Polyethene bottles

PVC windows

PTFE is used on non-stick pans. It makes it possible to fry an egg without it getting stuck to the pan. It is also used in lubricants (friction reducers), like the sprays used to 'oil' your bicycle chain. **PVC (polyvinyl chloride),** is used to make windows, 'plastic pipes' for plumbing systems (pipes for water and heating) and wire insulation. It is also used in making fabrics, so can be used to make shoes and clothes. It is water resistant and resistant to chemicals.

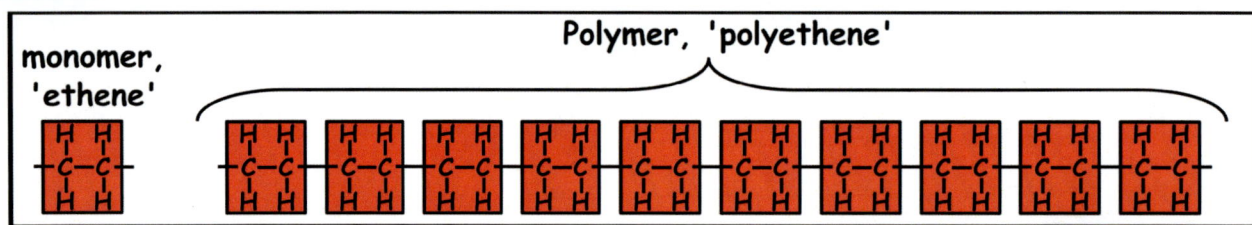

monomer, 'ethene'

Polymer, 'polyethene'

Composites

Composite means made of several parts or components. A composite material is made from two or more different materials. A simple example is **sand and cement**. On their own they are not particularly useful, but mix sand and cement with a little water, you make **mortar**, this is the stuff in-between bricks that holds buildings together. Add **sand, cement** (a little water) and mix in **stones**, you will make **concrete**. It is

Concrete

Carbon fibre bike

the most widely used building material in the world, concrete is a composite material. Other composites include **carbon fibre** made from **strands of carbon** and **plastic resin**. It's very strong and light. It is used in making bicycles, cars and is replacing aluminium in aeroplanes. **MDF (medium density fibreboard)** is very widely used in all-sorts of furniture manufacture, it is essentially **sawdust** and **glue** compressed together.

Ceramics

When we see the word **ceramics** we often think of '**pottery**' (plates and cups) and this is true. Ceramics are made by **baking** a starting material like **clay** in an **oven**. Ceramics are **hard, tough** and **durable**, but also **brittle** (break easily). They are **very water resistant** and can withstand high temperatures. Toilets and sinks are made from ceramics coated with a shiny glaze.

Ceramic toilet

Plates and cups are ceramics made from kiln baked clay, they are brittle, hard, long lasting, very water resistant and able to withstand high temperatures.

Bricks used to build houses are **ceramics**, they are hard and very strong under compression (can withstand being squashed very hard). Hit a brick with a hammer though and it will likely crack, they're brittle. **Ceramics are brilliant insulators**, you can see ceramic disks on electricity pylons stopping the power lines touching the metal.

Ceramic mugs

WHAT?

Concrete is really strong in compression (when being squashed) but really weak in tension (when being pulled), so a lot of concrete is 'reinforced' with steel.

Questions on Polymers (Plastics), Ceramics and Composites

Comprehension

1. What are polymers or plastics?
2. How are they made?
3. What are the molecules that link together to make a polymer called?
4. What is polythene made from?
5. Why can PVC be used to make shoes and clothes?
6. What does composite mean?
7. What do you make if you mix sand, cement stones and water?
8. Why is carbon fibre used in making bikes and cars?
9. What does MDF stand for?
10. What is MDF widely used for?
11. What do we think of when we see the word ceramic?
12. What useful properties do ceramics have?
13. What are ceramics used to make?
14. Why are our houses 'made from' ceramics?
15. What property makes ceramics useful on electricity pylons?

Additional tasks

1. Memorise the materials and their uses below.

PVC (polyvinyl chloride), used to make windows (frames) and many building applications. Used to make clothes and bottles, very versatile (many uses).

PTFE (polytetrafluoroethylene), a brilliant insulator and lubricant. Used in loads of applications, non-stick pans, lubricant sprays, as an insulator in electronic circuits, Gore-Tex materials, bullet coatings to reduce friction, plumbing tape, computer mice to reduce friction ....

Concrete, a composite of sand, cement and stones, the most widely used building material in the world.

Carbon fibre, a composite of carbon and plastic resin, light and strong, used widely in bicycle, car and aeroplane manufacture.

Ceramics, hard, durable, brilliant insulators but brittle materials. Made by baking a material like clay in an oven. Great for toilets, sinks and crockery.

2. Write the materials below into the correct column in the table.

NYLON, CHIPBOARD, HOUSE BRICK, BATHROOM SINK, PLAYDOUGH, PTFE, FALSE TEETH, POLYSTYRENE, REINFORCED GLASS, TILES, FIBRE-GLASS, RUBBER, PAPIER-MACHE, A SAUCER, SILK

Polymer	Composite	Ceramic

3. Your teacher sets a challenge to find the strongest concrete mix (**sand, stones, cement** and **water**). The mix is put in a tube and allowed to set before being tested for how much weight it can withstand before breaking. Write about how you could do this experiment, think about;

- What you would change?
- How many variables would you change at once?
- Would you repeat and why?
- What graph could you plot?

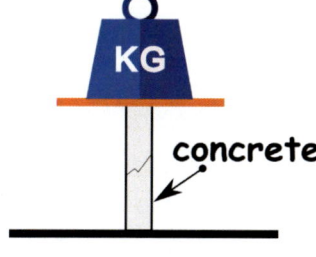

4. The above test is under **compression**. How else could you test the strength of the concrete (clue pg152)?

Composition and Structure of the Earth

The earth is a ball shaped (spherical) planet made mostly of rock. Rocks are solid minerals (chemical compounds that occur naturally). **Calcium carbonate**, $CaCO_3$, is an example and can be found on earth in a **hard form** called **marble**.

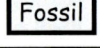

Fossil

Onion Earth: The Layers

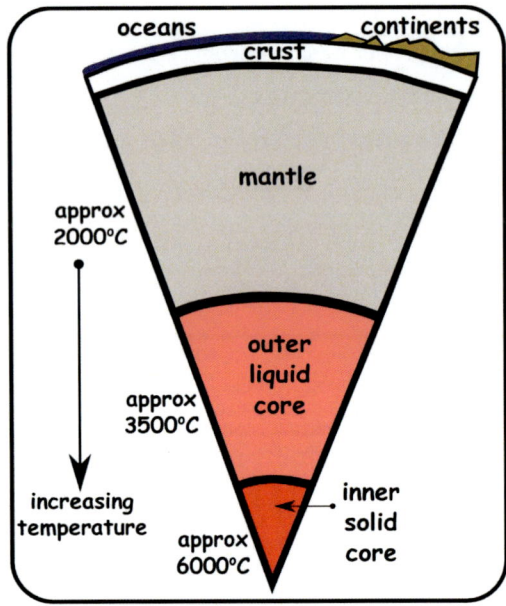
oceans   continents
crust
mantle
approx 2000°C
outer liquid core
approx 3500°C
increasing temperature
approx 6000°C
inner solid core

The earth really is layered like **an onion**. There are four distinct layers. Starting from the surface of the earth (what we stand on) is the **crust**. Heading in towards the centre, next comes the **mantle**, after that the **outer core** and finally the **inner core**.

The **crust** is solid and about 25 miles thick under the land (the continents) and about 4 miles thick under the oceans. The **mantle** underneath is about 1800 miles thick and is **almost** completely solid. The **outer core** is molten (liquid) rock and about 1400 miles thick. Finally the solid **inner core** is about 760 miles thick.

This means that the thickness (radius) of the earth is 'about' 4000 miles or 6400 km.

The density (how heavy something is for its size) of the layers **increases** as you head inwards. Picking up a **coke can sized** piece of **crust** would 'weigh' about

800g, for the **mantle**, this is about **1300g** (1.3kg), for the **outer core** about **3300g** (3.3kg) and for the **inner core** about **4200g** (4.2kg). The inner and outer cores are **made mainly** from the metals **nickel** and **iron**. Most of what we know about the earth's interior comes from studying **seismic** waves. These are the waves produced by **earthquakes**. Scientists study where and what kinds

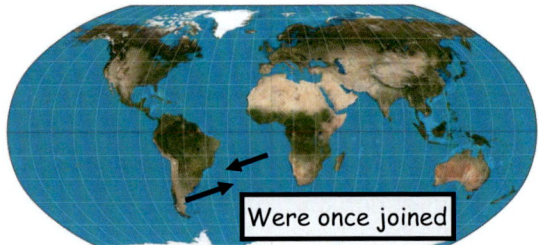
Were once joined

(there are two main types) of wave arrive at different locations on earth. They use seismometers which detect vibrations on the earth's surface.

Jigsaw Earth: Plate Tectonics

Smash a plate and it breaks into pieces (smaller plates!). Imagine the pieces now sitting on top of treacle in a bowl and the treacle is heated from below. As the treacle begins to move, the plates on top will also move. This is the theory that scientists have developed to explain why the earth looks like it does today, it is called **plate tectonics**.

Seismometer

Scientists have evidence that millions of years ago the earth was **one big continent** (land mass) called **Pangaea** (like one plate). This continent split apart, like a broken plate. The land masses (crust) moved apart from each other and sometimes collided. Collisions caused mountain ranges, like the **Himalayas**. Push your finger tips together from each hand and see how they rise up. Plates can also slip past each other causing earthquakes. Two easily understood pieces of evidence for this theory is:

1.   The continents seem to fit together like a jigsaw.

2.   Fossils (imprints in rocks) of the **same** animals, are found on different continents thousands of miles apart (South America and Africa). How could these creatures have swam so far? This is evidence they were once joined.

> **WHAT?**
>
> Alfred Wegener (1912) was the scientist who first proposed the idea that all the land was once one big super continent called Pangaea. Pangaea means 'all lands'.
>
> Earth is 4500 million years old.

Questions on Composition and Structure of the Earth

Comprehension

1. What is the earth?
2. What is a mineral?
3. How many distinct layers is the earth made from?
4. What are the names of the layers?
5. Which of the layers is the thickest?
6. About how thick is the earth? (Its radius)
7. What happens to the density of the layers as you head towards the centre?
8. What metals are the inner and outer core mainly made from?
9. Where does most of our knowledge of the earth's interior come from?
10. Imagine broken pieces of plate sitting on treacle, what happens to the plates if the treacle is heated?
11. What is this theory called?
12. Scientists have evidence that the earth was what, millions of years ago? What is its name?
13. What happened to this continent?
14. What can be caused by land masses colliding?
15. What are the two easily understood pieces of evidence for plate tectonic theory?

Additional tasks

1. Label A-F below **and** add the approximate temperatures of the mantle, outer core and inner core.

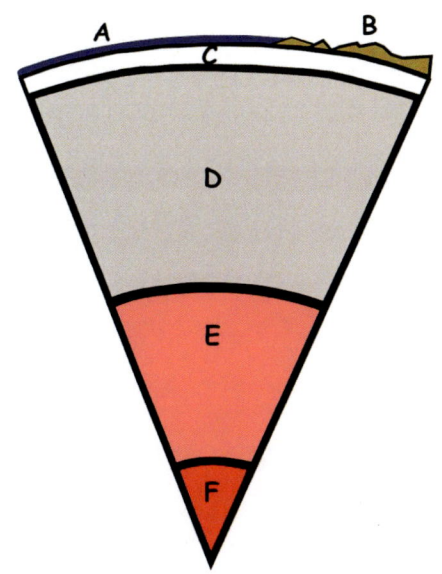

2. Complete the table by writing the name of the layer from its thickness.

Layer	Thickness (miles)
	4
	1400
	25
	760
	1800

3. In terms of **elements** the **composition** of the **mantle** is approximately **45% oxygen**, **22% silicon**, **23% magnesium** and **10% other** (includes iron, aluminium, calcium, sodium and potassium). Draw a pie chart of the composition below. Colour in or shade to make a key.

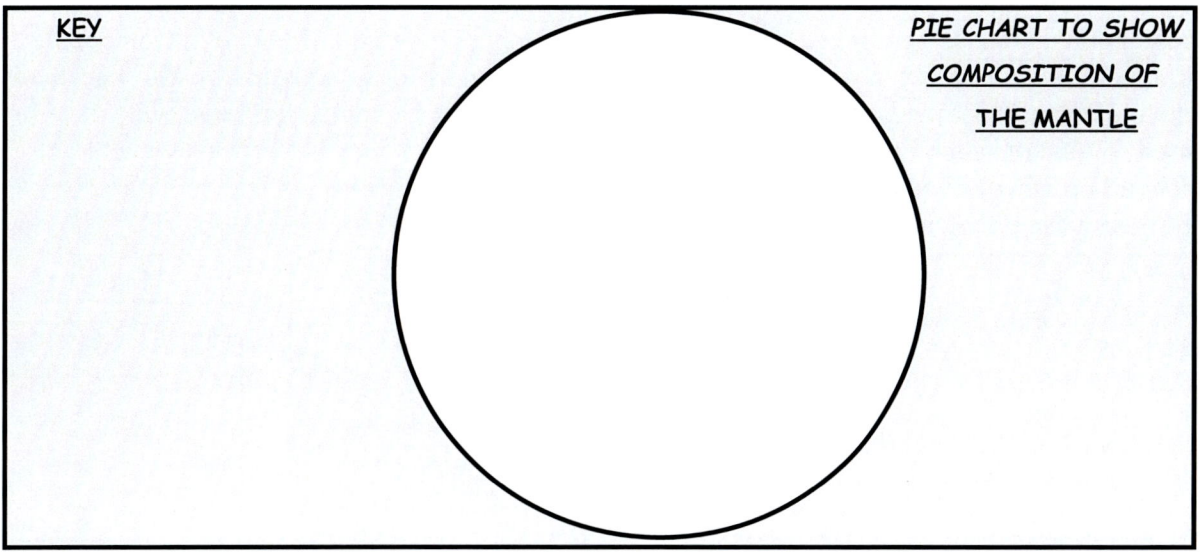

KEY

PIE CHART TO SHOW COMPOSITION OF THE MANTLE

The Rock Cycle

There are three different types of rock, **sedimentary, metamorphic** and **igneous**. The rock cycle describes how these three types of rock are formed and change over time. Over millions of years they are transformed from one kind of rock to another, before beginning the cycle again.

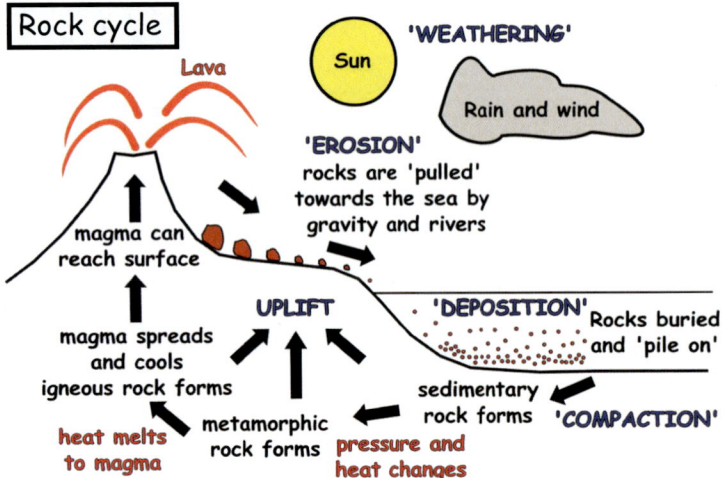

The huge amount of heat inside the earth makes the rock cycle happen. This can make solid rock melt to a liquid below the ground. We call this **magma**. Magma can get so hot, that pressure builds and the liquid rock can break through to the surface of the earth at weak points. This sometimes gives us an erupting volcano. Once the magma has reached the earth's surface, we call it **lava**. This lava can flow and spread. It cools to form solid rock. Rock formed this way is called **extrusive rock**. It is made of **smaller** crystals because it **cools quickly**. **Basalt** is an example. Magma and rock can be forced to the **surface slowly** over time, by **heat and pressure** from below earth's surface, this is called **uplift**. As the magma **cools slowly beneath** the surface, rocks with **larger** crystals are formed. This is called **intrusive rock**. An example is **granite**. Uplift can also happen when continental plates collide and form mountain ranges, like pushing our finger tips together again (pg 102).

The Cycle

Rocks at the earth's surface are **weathered** (the **breaking down** and **dissolving** of rocks). **Erosion**, which is the carrying away of the rocks by water, wind and gravity means the rocks get transported to the oceans. This is the rocks 'rolling' down hills and mountains and being carried by rivers. In the oceans they are **deposited** as sediment (small pieces that sink to the bottom). This sediment slowly **compacts**

Marble

as layers 'pile on top' of each other. This forms **sedimentary rock**, for example **sandstone**. Many churches are made from this material. Over time, this sedimentary rock can be **changed by heat and pressure** to form harder, **metamorphic rock**. An example is **marble**. **Metamorphosis** means to **change**, heat and pressure change sedimentary to metamorphic rock. Finally, again over time, metamorphic rock can be melted by heat inside the earth to produce magma. Once the magma cools and solidifies (turns to solid), **igneous rock** is formed. This can reach the surface through volcanic eruption forming extrusive rock, or be forced up slowly over time forming intrusive rock. **Pumice stone** we use to clean our skin is another example of an igneous rock.

WHAT?

Mount Nanga Parbat in the Himalayas is rising by 7mm per year! Geologists (scientists who study earth processes) estimate that each stage of the rock cycle takes around 20 million years. The hardest rock known to man is diamond, it is a compressed form of carbon and takes about 2 billion years to form!

Sandstone

Granite

Questions on the Rock Cycle

Comprehension

1. How many different types of rock are there?
2. What does the rock cycle describe?
3. What makes the rock cycle happen?
4. What is liquid rock under the ground called?
5. What do we call liquid rock above the ground?
6. Why is extrusive rock made from smaller crystals?
7. When magma cools slowly, what happens to the size of the crystals formed and what is this rock called?
8. What does weathered mean?
9. How do rocks get transported to the oceans?
10. How is sedimentary rock formed? Give an example of sedimentary rock?
11. What does heat and pressure do to sedimentary rock?
12. What does metamorphosis mean?
13. How is igneous rock formed?
14. What is the name of the igneous rock we use to clean our skin?

Additional tasks

1. Label the blanks below using the words opposite.

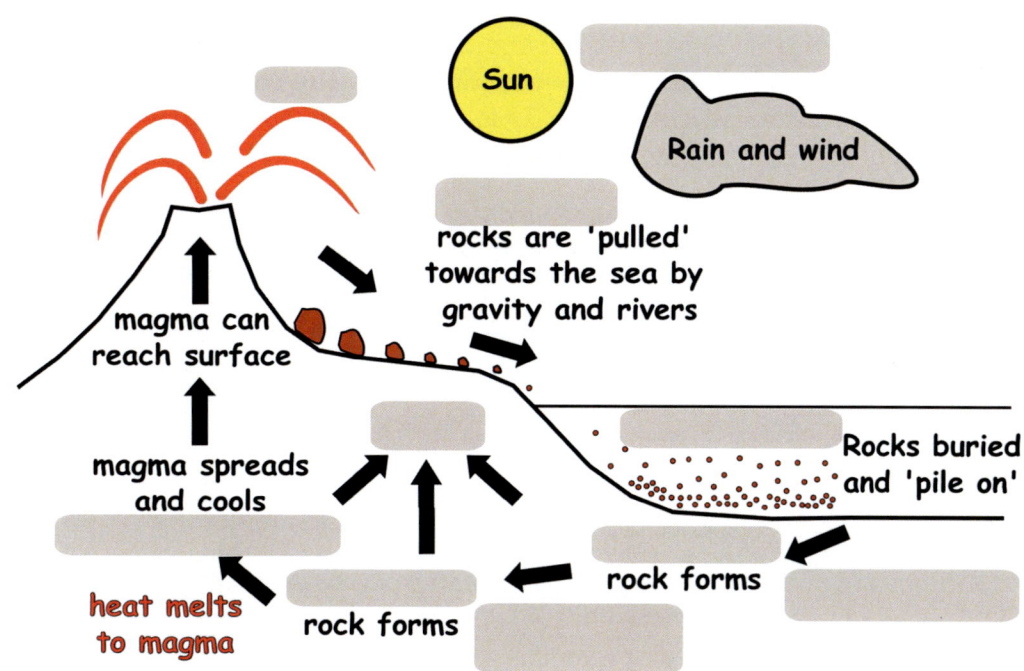

2. Solve the jumbled terms from their definitions.

a. Breaking down and dissolving of rock **ETNWIEGARH**
b. Molten rock at the surface **LAAV**
c. The name for rocks being forced to the surface from underground **ULTPFI**
d. An intrusive igneous rock **RATGENI**
e. An extrusive igneous rock **BSTALA**
f. The moving of rocks by water, wind and gravity **ROOENSI**
g. The settling of sediment layers on top of each other **EOODIINPTS**
h. An example of a sedimentary rock **ANNSOSEDT**
i. Molten rock beneath the surface **MAAGM**
j. An example of a metamorphic rock **MREALB**

3. Fossils of long dead sea animals can be found on Mount Everest.

a. How does this provide evidence for **uplift?**

b. Scientists can now use satellites to measure uplift accurately. **Nanga Parbat** in the Himalayas is rising by 7mm per year.

i. How long would it take the mountain to rise the height of a desk (about 80cm = 800mm).

ii. When Nanga Parbat does stop rising what will cause it to shrink in size again?

Earth's Limited Resources and Our Responsibilities

All living things on earth are carbon based life forms. Carbon is able to bond with lots of other molecules. It is an essential component of fats, proteins and carbohydrates. It makes up nearly 20% (1/5th) of our body mass.

The carbon cycle shows us how **carbon dioxide** is **released** or **removed** from the atmosphere by plants and animals. Look carefully at the carbon cycle. You can see that less trees capturing carbon dioxide, CO_2, and more 'human activity' releasing it, means more of the carbon in the carbon cycle ends up as carbon dioxide in the atmosphere. Fossil fuels (coal, oil and natural gas) take millions of years to form. Burning fossil fuels along with deforestation and the increase in population, is one of the biggest challenges humans face.

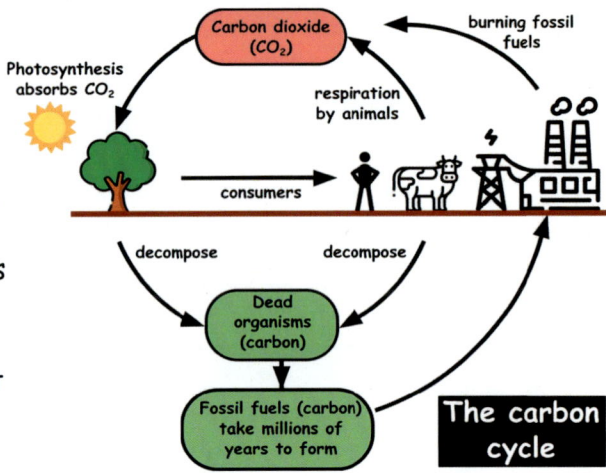

Limited Resources

As well as contributing to dangerous changes in our climate, the way we use the earth's limited resources is wasteful. By burning products from oil (such as petrol), we are wasting a resource which isn't easily obtained any other way. **Oil** is the raw material for plastics that are used in almost every aspect of life. It is also used in making drugs, cosmetics, perfumes, lubricating oils, waxes, tarmac for roads, paints…, the list goes on.

Since oil is so useful we need to think carefully about how we use it. Many governments plan to stop allowing petrol cars to be made in the near future.

Plastics are really important to use wisely. They are extremely useful but if not used responsibly are being wasted, ending up in landfill and not being recycled. **Too much plastic** is being **thrown away** irresponsibly and ending up in our **seas**, harming wildlife. Plastics can take hundreds of years to break down, they are not **biodegradable**. Most plastics however are now recyclable, so once they have finished being useful, should be put in the recycling bins to be processed for use again.

Other Resources: Metals

Metals like **lithium** and **cobalt** are used in batteries to power anything from a tablet to an electric car. Demand for elements used in batteries has grown hugely. There is not an endless supply. Most of the world's cobalt, for example, comes from Africa. Most of the world's lithium comes from South America. In the future we will have to recycle these metals from batteries because they are a valuable and limited resource.

Water

In many parts of the world there is not enough clean water. Often communities only have access to a well. Wells can run dry, and the water become polluted by human waste (caused by toilets being holes in the ground) and chemicals from farming. Chemicals can seep into the water underground. This is a real problem for millions around the world. Consuming more water than is replaced by rainfall causes drought. Most of the water we drink is taken from rivers and lakes. It is then 'cleaned' to make it drinkable (potable). This requires energy, so being wasteful with our water use is also a waste of energy. Supply can be put at risk due to the overpopulation of areas, global warming and increased use from farming. We all need to conserve and use our water wisely.

WHAT?

There is about 1,260,000,000,000,000,000,000 litres of water on earth, 1,260 billion billion litres! The world uses 300 million tons of plastic every year, recycle please.

Questions on Earth's Limited Resources

Comprehension

1. What sort of life forms are all living things on earth?

2. What does the carbon cycle show?

3. How long does it take the fossil fuels to form?

4. As well as contributing to climate change, what else is wrong with the way we use earth's resources?

5. What is the raw material for plastics?

6. What else can oil be used for?

7. Where is too much plastic ending up?

8. Which two metals are used in batteries to power anything from a tablet to an electric car?

9. Where does most of the world's cobalt and lithium come from?

10. What isn't there enough of in many parts of the world?

11. How can wells become polluted?

12. What happens if more water is consumed than replaced by rainfall?

13. What is another word for drinkable water?

14. What can put our supply of water at risk?

Additional tasks

1. Label the **carbon cycle** using the diagram opposite to help.

2. Find the words relating to earth's limited resources in the word search below.

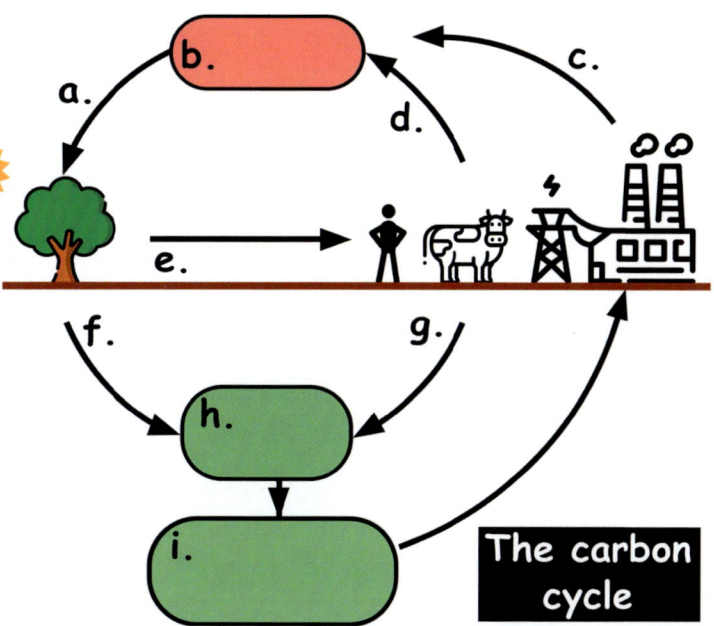

The carbon cycle

CARBONCYCLE	CARBONDIOXIDE
PHOTOSYNTHESIS	POTABLE
FOSSILFUELS	POPULATION
DEFORESTATION	RESOURCES
PLASTIC	BIODEGRADEABLE
LITHIUM	COBALT
WASTEFUL	BATTERIES

```
D  E  F  O  R  E  S  T  A  T  I  O  N  E
A  B  C  D  E  F  G  H  L  I  J  K  L  C
L  M  N  O  P  O  T  A  B  L  E  B  P  A
P  Q  R  S  T  U  B  M  V  W  A  C  H  R
X  Y  R  E  S  O  U  R  C  E  S  A  O  B
Z  P  T  A  C  I  L  E  D  L  B  R  T  O
K  O  C  Y  H  N  V  A  E  J  B  B  O  N
Z  P  L  T  F  T  R  U  W  U  A  O  S  D
V  U  I  R  M  G  F  V  A  A  T  N  Y  I
W  L  G  V  E  L  X  R  S  K  T  C  N  O
W  A  C  D  I  B  H  I  T  S  E  Y  T  X
J  T  O  S  P  N  V  O  E  S  R  C  H  I
G  I  S  F  K  F  S  H  F  G  I  L  E  D
B  O  V  A  C  D  N  Y  U  A  E  E  S  E
F  N  F  K  W  U  Q  P  L  A  S  T  I  C
H  J  A  F  V  L  N  A  H  C  Q  G  S  Y
```

3. Design a leaflet (A4 paper folded in half) informing people about earth's limited resources and how to use them wisely.
(pg108 What to do? may help)

Think about:

- Recycling
- Being less wasteful
- Burning less fossil fuels
- Deforestation
- Population size. What can be done?
- Richer countries helping poorer countries with clean water and sanitation (google what Bill Gates has done)

The Earth's Atmosphere and Climate Change

Our atmosphere (the gases that surround our planet) is made up of two main gases, **nitrogen 78%** and **oxygen 21%**. Other gases are present in small amounts such as carbon dioxide, CO_2 and methane, CH_4.

Our climate (the usual weather conditions), has begun to change rapidly over the past 200 or so years. The **population has risen** from around **1 billion** in the year 1800 to **7 billion** in the year 2000. **All of these people need energy** to heat and light their homes, energy to cook, energy to power their vehicles and if they're lucky, energy to power the plane to take them on holiday.

A lot of this energy, even electricity, still comes from **burning** coal, oil or natural gas, the fossil fuels. Carbon in these fuels, that was once trapped in the form of coal, oil or natural gas, is then released into the atmosphere as carbon dioxide, CO_2.

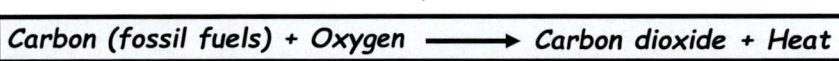

Carbon (fossil fuels) + Oxygen ⟶ Carbon dioxide + Heat

Carbon dioxide is a 'greenhouse gas'. This means that it is good at trapping heat (like a greenhouse does) in the earth's atmosphere. This is heat that would normally escape into outer space if the carbon dioxide 'blanket' wasn't there. This means the earth is heating up faster than it would 'normally', because of man-kind's actions.

Another 'greenhouse gas' is **methane**. A lot of which comes from all the cattle that we farm for meat and milk. Their flatulence (which we amusingly call farting) releases large amounts of methane. This has increased due to the rise in population and more of that population wanting to eat meat. It is a big problem.

Methane

Greenhouse Effect Problems

Although without the greenhouse effect earth would be too cold for us to live on, our consumption of fossil fuels has produced enough carbon dioxide for the earth to be heating up too fast. The **'extra' heat** causes more **evaporation** of sea and land water. This causes **drought** in some parts of the world, which can lead to famine. In other parts of the world it causes **floods** since the **extra water** in the atmosphere falls as **rain**. Other problems include **rising sea levels** from melting ice sheets and glaciers. Loss of habitable (liveable) land. **Extreme weather** such as heat waves, bush fires and storms, are also becoming much more frequent (happening more often).

Heat wave

What to Do?

There are lots of things that can be done to slow climate change, some are simple and we can do them straight away, others require governments to get involved. Examples include using more energy efficient appliances, using less energy where possible (turning appliances off), insulating our homes better, not making unnecessary journeys, switching to electric vehicles, stopping deforestation (trees absorb carbon dioxide), plant more trees, become vegetarian, generate more electricity renewably using wind, solar and tidal or simply consume less!

Heat that would escape into space is trapped

WHAT?

Climate change and loss of habitat has increased extinction rates to around 1000 species per year.

Questions on The Earth's Atmosphere and Climate Change

Comprehension

1. What is our atmosphere?
2. What are the two main gases in earth's atmosphere and what are their percentages?
3. How much has the population risen since the year 1800?
4. Where does a lot of our energy (even electricity) still come from?
5. What is a greenhouse gas good at?
6. What would happen to the heat without our carbon dioxide blanket?
7. Where does a lot of methane in the atmosphere come from?
8. Why has the amount of methane in the atmosphere increased?
9. What has the extra heat done to land and sea water?
10. What does this cause in some parts of the world?
11. What does it do in other parts of the world?
12. What's happening to the frequency of extreme weather?
13. What sort of vehicle could we switch to that would help?
14. Generating electricity through which methods would also help?

Additional tasks

1. Use the data in the table to plot the average global air temperature (°C) against year.

Year	1880	1900	1920	1940	1960	1980	2000	2020
Average global air temp (°C)	13.65	13.74	13.83	14.07	13.95	14.18	14.20	14.50

2 a. What is the 'general trend' (pattern) for the data in the table.

b. What happens between 1940 and 1980?

c. What sort of 'extra' data would make any trend clearer? (Think about range and frequency)

3. Complete the gap filling exercise on global warming. Choose from the words in bold below.

warmer, Water, carbon dioxide, fossil fuels, animal, rotting, light, greenhouse, methane, re-emitted, heat energy, gases, surface, back, extra

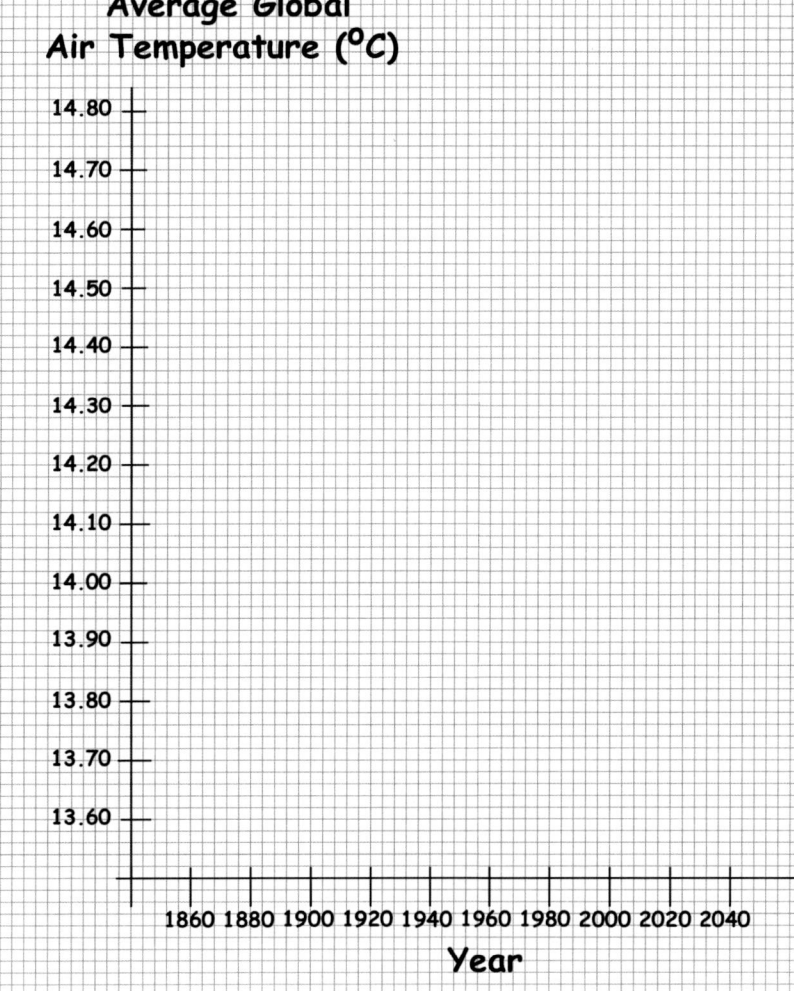

The two main _____ gases are _____ _____ and _____. Carbon dioxide comes mainly from burning _____. _____. Methane comes mainly from _____ farming and _____ vegetation. _____ in the atmosphere also helps trap heat that would escape into space. The _____ energy from the sun is absorbed by earth's _____ heating it. This energy is _____back towards space. Instead of escaping, this _____ _____ is absorbed by greenhouse _____ which re-emit some of the heat _____towards earth. The _____ greenhouse gases from human activity mean that the earth is getting _____ too fast.

Reaction Rates and Catalysts

When we talk about rates we mean how quickly something happens in time, speed is a rate. It is the distance an object travels in a given time, like how many miles an object travels in one hour (mph). In chemistry, reaction rates can be measured by how quickly products are formed, such as the volume of gas produced in a given time. The unit could be cm^3 per second. It can also be measured by how quickly reactants are used up, such as, how quickly the mass of a metal reacting with an acid decreases over time.

Decrease in mass method

mass decrease measured over time

gas given off

magnesium

acid

16.4 g

Volume of gas method

gas syringe

volume of gas measured over time

gas given off

acid

magnesium

Collision Theory

This simply tells us that for a chemical **reaction** to **occur**, the **particles** (atoms or molecules) **must collide** (bump into each other). **More collisions per second** means a **faster reaction, fewer collisions per second** means a **slower reaction.** The particles must **hit each** other **hard enough** though, for a reaction to happen (a successful collision), a bit like cracking an egg. If you tap it gently then nothing happens, but hit it hard enough, it will definitely crack.

Speeding Up Reactions

This is done by getting the reacting particles to bump into each other more often. Having **more particles** in a **given volume**, called **increasing** the **concentration**, makes a collision more likely to happen and speeds up the reaction.

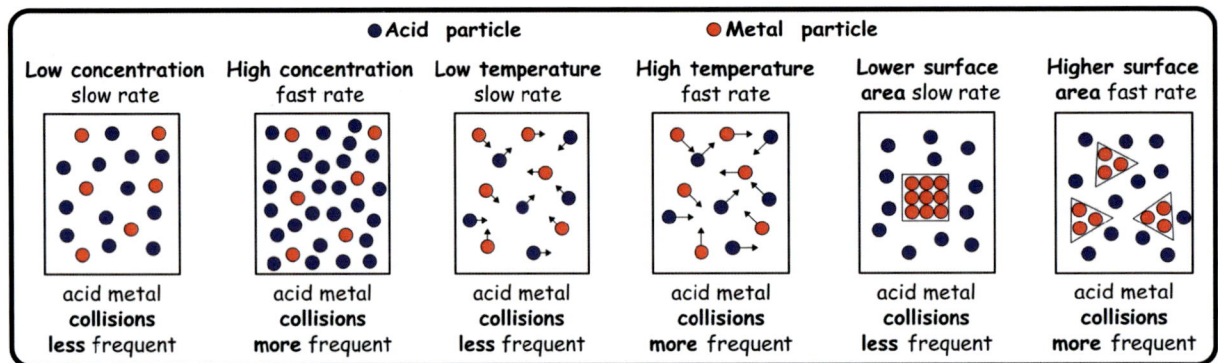

● Acid particle   ● Metal particle

Low concentration slow rate	High concentration fast rate	Low temperature slow rate	High temperature fast rate	Lower surface area slow rate	Higher surface area fast rate
acid metal **collisions** **less** frequent	acid metal **collisions** **more** frequent	acid metal **collisions** **less** frequent	acid metal **collisions** **more** frequent	acid metal **collisions** **less** frequent	acid metal **collisions** **more** frequent

Making the particles **move faster**, called increasing the **temperature**, means more collisions per second and speeds up the reaction. Making the **'target'** bigger, called **increasing** the **surface area**, makes a collision more likely and speeds up the reaction.

Catalysts

Catalysts are chemicals that you can add to a reaction to speed it up. They are great, not only do they speed up a chemical reaction (that you may want), they don't get used up or changed in anyway. This means that you can use them again and again. This means making some industrial (large scale) chemicals much cheaper to produce. Think about cracking an egg again, but this time it has a helmet on. You can still crack it, but it is more difficult, it takes more energy. Catalysts **reduce** the **energy** that two reacting particles must hit each other with, for a reaction to occur. This means many more particles present **can** react. Adding a catalyst is like taking the helmet off the egg, it is much easier to crack now and needs less energy.

no catalyst   catalyst

> **WHAT?**
>
> Enzymes called protease and lipase are added to washing powders, protease helps break down proteins and lipase helps break down fats to remove stains.

Enzymes are catalysts that speed up biological reactions.

Questions on Reaction Rates and Catalysts

Comprehension

1. What do we mean, when we talk about rates?
2. Measuring how quickly which product is formed, can measure the rate of a reaction?
3. What could be the unit of how quickly this product is formed?
4. How else can a reaction rate be measured?
5. What does collision theory tell us?
6. What does more collisions per second mean?
7. How must particles hit each other for a reaction to happen (a successful collision)?
8. What does increasing the concentration mean?
9. If the particles move faster, what must have increased?
10. What's another way of saying increasing the surface area?
11. What does this do to the likelihood of a collision?
12. What are catalysts?
13. Why can you use catalysts again and again?
14. What do catalysts do to the energy that particles must hit each other with for a reaction to occur?
15. What is an enzyme?

Additional tasks

1. Match the terms and facts below and memorise.

Concentration	particles have less energy and move slower, collisions are less frequent (often)
High temperature	smaller area to hit and collisions are less likely
Low temperature	the amount of particles in a given volume
Low surface area	chemicals that speed up reactions without being used up
High surface area	particles have more energy and move faster, collisions are more frequent (often)
Catalysts	bigger area to hit and collisions are more likely

2. The table contains data for the amount of hydrogen gas released every 10 seconds when the **same** amount of magnesium is reacted with **two different** concentrations of hydrochloric acid **A** and **B**.

a. Plot both sets of data on the graph.

Time (seconds)	0	10	20	30	40	50	60	70	80	90	100
A. Volume of H_2 (ml)	0	10	20	30	38	45	50	53	54.5	55	55
B. Volume of H_2 (ml)	0	14	28	40	48	53	55	55	55	55	55

b. How long does the reaction take to finish for **A** and for **B**?

c. Label one of the lines as **higher concentration** and the other as **lower concentration**.

d. How do we know from the **data** that the same amount of magnesium was used?

3. Put the following chemical reactions in order from **slowest** to **fastest**. One of them is deliberately 'wrong' can you spot which one and explain why?

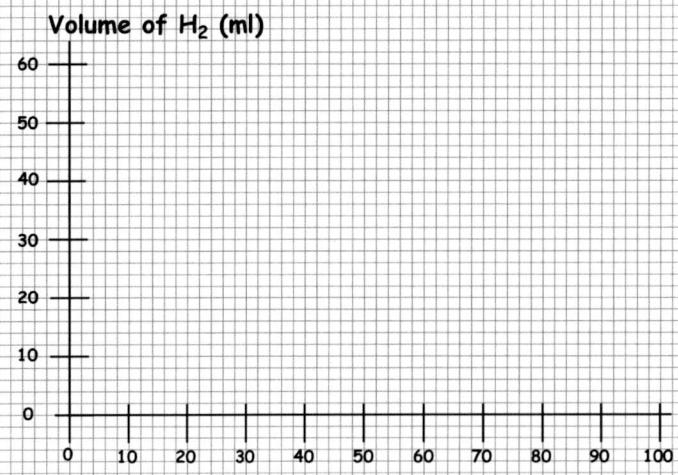

RUSTING, A BROWNING APPLE, SPARKLER, BAKING A CAKE, EXPLOSION, ROTTING FOOD, CONCRETE SETTING, BURNING TOAST, A FIREWORK ROCKET, A MATCH, ICECREAM MELTING

PHYSICS

lift from wings

air
resistance

thrust from
engines

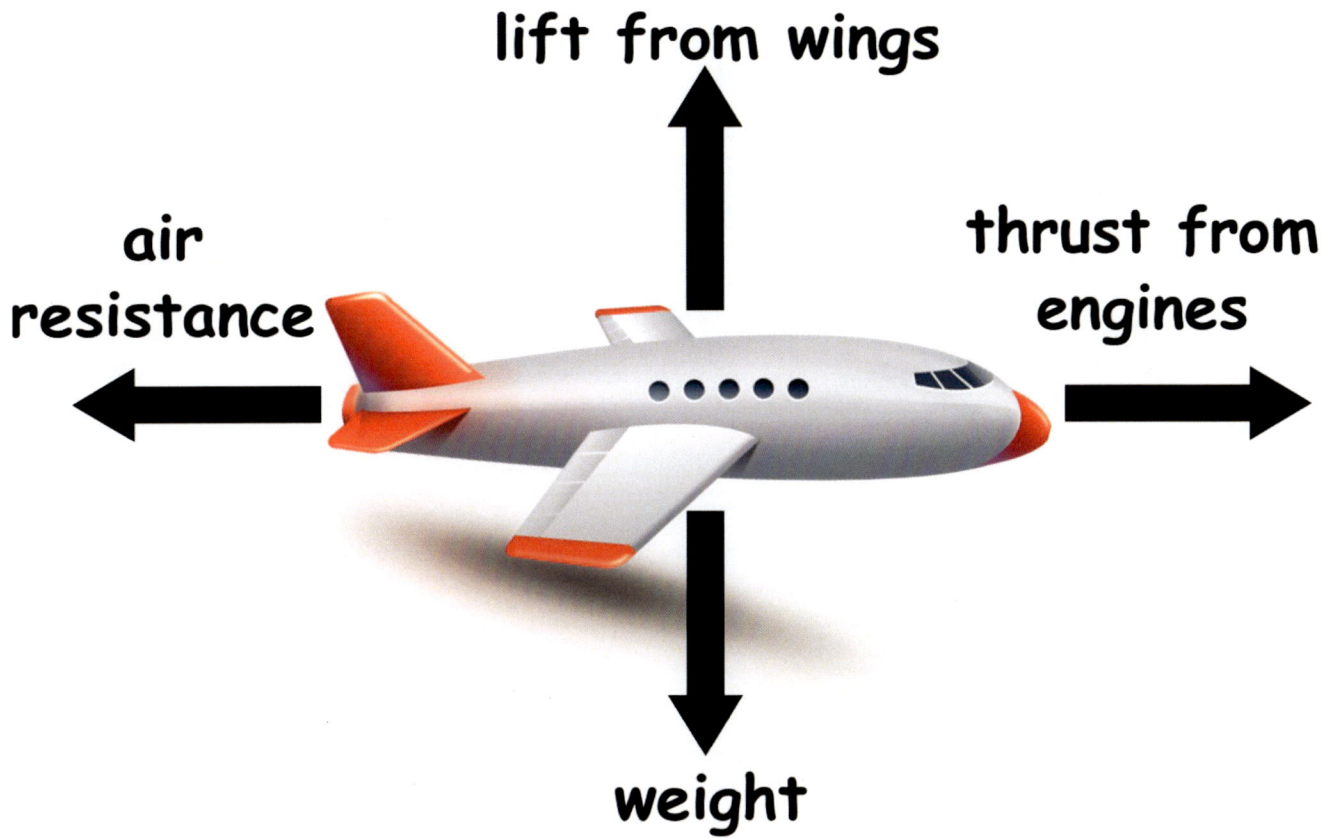

weight

Cost of Electricity and Power Ratings

Unfortunately we do have to pay for our electricity. The amount of electrical energy that an electrical appliance uses depends on its power rating and the amount of time that it is switched on. Power rating labels can normally be found as a sticker somewhere on the appliance. In the UK, the labels tells us, that by supplying the appliance with 230V (plugging into the mains) how much energy is consumed per second in watts, W. The watt is the unit of power. It tells us the amount of energy in joules consumed per second. So 5 watts is 5 joules per second, 250 watts is 250 joules per second, 1000 watts (one kilowatt, kW, kilo meaning thousand) is 1000 joules per second, 2200 watts (2.2 kW) is 2200 joules per second etc.

Power rating labels

Russell Hobs Kettle

Model number : 13882

Rating : 230V 50Hz, 2800W

Samsung LED TV

Model number : UE50

Rating : 230V 50Hz, 100W

Divide by 1000 to convert watts to kW.

Kettles have a high power rating (2800W) but we don't have them switched on for long. A TV has a low power rating (100W) but we do have them switched on for long periods of time. To calculate the **energy consumed** we have to multiply the power rating by the time the appliance is switched on for, this is because multiplying power by time gives energy.

$$\text{energy} = \text{power} \times \text{time}$$
$$\text{(kWh)} = \text{(kW)} \times \text{(hrs)}$$

The unusual unit of energy we use, instead of the joule, is the **kilowatt-hour (kWh)**. This is because using joules would mean very big values (millions because 1kWh = 3.6 million joules).

Calculating Energy used in Kilowatt-hours (kWh)

TV switched on for 5hrs	**Kettle switched on for 30 mins**
energy = power × time	energy = power × time
(kWh) = (100÷1000) kW × 5 hrs	(kWh) = (2800÷1000) kW × (30÷60) hrs
kWh = 0.1 kW × 5 hrs	kWh = 2.8 kW × 1/2 hr
= 0.5 kWh	= 1.4 kWh

Calculating your Electricity Bill

Households receive a bill every 3 months (quarterly). The electricity companies calculate how much energy, in kilowatt-hours are used over that time, for the bill shown it is;

8400-6200 = 2200 kWh.

Electricity Bill

Electricity bill (a company)

Date	15 Feb	15 May	Kilowatt hours used (kWh)
Quarterly meter reading (3 months)	6200	8400	2200
Electricity charges Standard tariff@	14 pence per kWh		
	2200 @	14 p each	*Total charges* £308.00

They then charge you for every kilowatt hour of energy you have used. The company shown above charge 14 pence for every kilowatt hour of energy used so the bill would be;
14 pence x 2200 kWh used = 30800 pence or **£308.00**. The meter readings are taken from the electricity meter in the house, this is now usually done remotely if you have a smart meter.

Electricity meters

WHAT?

The average household electricity bill is about £1000 per year. This is about 15,000,000,000J which is why we use kWh! The most energy hungry appliances are the washer and dryer so don't put clothes in the washing basket after wearing them once!

Questions on Cost of Electricity and Power Ratings

Comprehension

1. What does the amount of energy an electrical appliance uses depend upon?

2. Power ratings are normally found as what on an electrical appliance?

3. What voltage is mains electricity supply in the UK?

4. What is the unit of power?

5. How many watts are there in 1kW?

6. How do you convert watts into kilowatts?

7. How do we calculate the energy consumed by an appliance?

8. What is the unusual unit of energy that we use when calculating the energy used by an electrical appliance?

9. Why don't we use the joule?

10. How many kWh would the kettle shown opposite use, if it was switched on for 1 hour?

11. How much does one kWh cost on the electricity bill shown?

12. Where are the meter readings taken from for an electricity bill?

13. How much is the average household electricity bill? (WHAT? box)

14. What are two of the energy hungry appliances in the house?

Additional tasks

1. Convert the following times into hours and write them as a decimal and as a mixed fraction.

| A. 30 minutes | B. 80 minutes | C. 600 minutes | D. 10 minutes | E. 120 minutes |
| F. 90 minutes | G. 15 minutes | H. 200 minutes | I. 20 minutes | J. 160 minutes |

2. Convert the following power values from watts to kilowatts.

| A. 100 watts | B. 1500 watts | C. 200 watts | D. 10,000 watts | E. 6000 watts |
| F. 1000 watts | G. 500 watts | H. 800 watts | I. 2,500 watts | J. 5,500 watts |

3. Complete the energy column by calculating how much energy in kWh each appliance uses.

Appliance	Energy (kWh)	Power (kW)	Time (hours)
Kettle		2.0	1.5
Shower		9.0	0.5
Iron		5.0	2.0
Xbox 1		0.11	10.0
Toaster		1.8	0.5
Sandwich maker		1.0	0.25
Washing machine		4.0	1.5
Vacuum cleaner		0.9	1.0
Tumble dryer		2.2	0.5

Electricity bill

Date	15 May	15 August	Kilowatt hours used (kWh)
Quarterly meter reading (3 months)	8400	10,000	
Electricity charges Standard tariff@	20 pence per kWh		Total charges
		@ 20 p each	

4. Complete the electricity bill above by calculating how many kWh are used for the time period (quarter) and using the cost per kWh calculate the total charges (see opposite bill for help).

5. Arrange the following devices in order of which you think is the highest power rating (six) to the lowest power rating (one). Check your answers by **unscrambling** the name of the device to see what number is left.

e.g. Nintendo Wii   ITWINWDONOENTI

Hair dryer	SAIEHYXDRRRI
PS3 console	TSCLEPOHNRE3SEO
LED torch	DCLEROONHTE
Laptop Computer	PATLTOWPO
Hover mower	OEFEHWIVMRVORE
Trimmer for lawns	FUORIUETRMM

6. Which of the below are quarterly time periods? Like for a utility bill.

i) 1st May to 20th July

ii) 28th Feb to 18th May

iii) 10 December to 10th March

iv) 16th June to 16th August

v) 15th May to 15th September

vi) 28th April to 28th July

Energy Stores

Energy is measured in **joules**, it is all around us and is 'stored' in eight different ways. It can flow (transfer) from one store to another. The eight different **energy stores** are described below, most of them we know well, even if we don't realise.

<u>Chemical Potential Energy</u> Chemical bonds have the potential (the ability) to transfer energy through chemical reactions. This is chemical energy. The petrol we put in our cars, the gas we burn, the food we eat and the batteries that power our devices all store chemical energy. When we recharge a battery we use an electric current to reverse the chemical reaction that provided the energy to power our device.

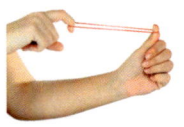

<u>Gravitational Potential Energy</u> An object raised above the ground has gravitational potential energy (GPE for short). The higher and heavier an object is the more GPE it has.

gravity

<u>Elastic Potential Energy</u> Stretched (or squashed) objects store elastic potential energy, an elastic band is the obvious example, stretched of course! All objects can stretch, squash or bend a little to store elastic potential energy. Your pencil will **bend**, a tennis ball will **squash** and slinkies **stretch** brilliantly.

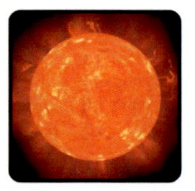

<u>Nuclear Energy</u> This is the energy that can be released from the nucleus (centre) of an atom. It can emit energy as **radiation**. A nucleus can also **split** apart called **fission** or **join** with another nucleus called **fusion,** both release large amounts of energy. If we control this energy release we can generate electricity, if we allow it to race ahead uncontrolled, we have a nuclear explosion. The sun emits its energy due to nuclear fusion.

<u>Magnetic Potential Energy</u> The north poles of two magnets repel, push them together and hold them. You have stored some magnetic energy. Let go of one and it gets pushed away decreasing the magnetic energy store. It's the same if two magnets attract each other, except they get closer together not further apart when you let go.

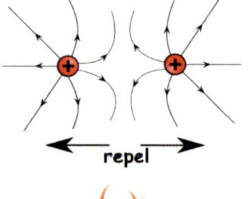

repel

<u>Electric Potential Energy</u> Positive (+) and negative (-) charges (opposites) **attract**. Two positives or two negatives (like) **repel** (push apart). Charges can store electric potential energy due to this attraction or repulsion just like magnets can. In a circuit charges are pushed through wires, this makes an electric current which can **transfer** energy.

repel

<u>Thermal Energy</u> Thermal is another word for heat. We can increase a store of thermal energy by making something hotter. This energy must come from somewhere though, this could be another store, like chemical when burning gas, or another object that is hotter.

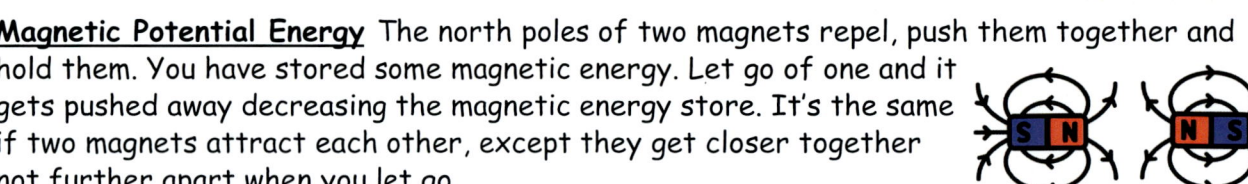

<u>Kinetic Energy</u> This is the energy an object stores due to its motion, no motion, no kinetic energy. The faster an object moves the more kinetic energy it has. Heavier objects also have more kinetic energy. Imagine a ping pong ball and a golf ball hitting you at the **same speed**. The golf ball hurts much more because it is heavier, so it has more kinetic energy.

> **WHAT?**
>
> The sun emits about 400,000,000,000,000,000,000,000,000 joules of energy every second, 400 million, billion billion! There is no more energy now than when the universe first began 13.8 billion years ago! Energy just keeps flowing from one store to another. The Joule which is the unit of energy is named after the physicist James Prescott Joule, 1818-1889.

Questions on Energy Stores

Comprehension

1. How many different ways can energy be stored?
2. What type of energy do batteries store?
3. What are we doing when we recharge a battery?
4. How does an object gain GPE?
5. What increases the GPE an object has?
6. Apart from being stretched how else can objects store elastic potential?
7. What is nuclear energy released from?
8. What happens to a nucleus during fission and fusion?
9. How can you have stored magnetic energy?
10. What do positive and negative charges do to each other?
11. How do we transfer electric potential energy?
12. What is another word for heat?
13. When does an object store kinetic energy?
14. How can the kinetic energy of an object be increased?

Additional tasks

1. Match the energy type to its description and memorise.

Chemical potential energy	the energy an object has when stretched or squashed.
Gravitational potential energy	energy stored due to the attraction or repulsion of charges.
Elastic potential energy	the energy stored in chemical bonds.
Nuclear energy	energy of motion.
Magnetic potential energy	another word for heat, due to the vibration or motion of the particles of a substance.
Electric potential energy	the energy an object has by being raised above the ground.
Thermal energy	energy stored due to the attraction or repulsion of magnets.
Kinetic energy	energy stored by the nucleus of an atom.

2. Find the following **energy stores** and **flows** in the word search below.

CHEMICAL	POSITIONCHANGE	ELASTIC
NUCLEAR	LIGHT	HEATFLOW
THERMAL	GRAVITATIONAL	RADIATION
SOUND	MAGNETIC	ELECTRIC
EMISSION	KINETIC	ELECTRICCURRENT

```
A B G C D E F G H I J K E L M N
O P R P Q R S T U L C C L V W X
Y O A M A G N E T I C H E Z T F
L S V W B H F I R G S E C A F F
J I I Y Z V I T B H R M T J T B
V T T Q K H C Y C T A I R C I A
Q I A X N E S O U N D C I Q I N
Z O T A L A Y D U F I A C O Z A
R N I E T T H E R M A L C V Q J
E C O T A F B A K K T X U O B E
Y H N U C L E A R Y I F R X I L
C A A D S O P A K A O N R V K A
Y N L P O W N W Q T N E E H M S
Y G V W W L P Y P K Z Z N T E T
P E M I S S I O N I G W T X I I
Z D U F I J J B M M W B X H T C
```

3. Below are examples of where we would find or have a lot of a particular energy store. Write down the energy store next to the example.

a. A bottle of cooking gas _____

b. Helicopter hovering high in the sky _____

c. A bow and arrow fully pulled back _____

d. A radioactive element _____

e. The strip around a fridge door to keep it shut _____

f. A lightning storm _____.

g. A speeding bullet _____

h. A sauna _____

Energy Transfers (flows)

Energy is most useful to us when it is **flowing** from one store to another (also called transferring). **Forces** are involved and bring about the transfer of energy through:

- The flow of an electric current (electricity)
- A change in position, speed or a vibration (sound)
- The progress of a chemical reaction
- The flow of heat
- Emission (giving off) of light or other electromagnetic waves, called radiation.

We draw energy transfer diagrams which use arrows to show the energy flow.

A Torch

The battery in a torch stores chemical energy. The chemicals mean there is an electric potential (also called a voltage) across the ends of the battery. When you switch on your torch, the electric potential **forces (pushes) an electric current** through the bulb. The **current flow** transfers electric potential energy to heat and light. The light also ends up as heat as it bumps into objects and is eventually absorbed. **Overall, chemical energy store decreases, thermal energy store increases.**

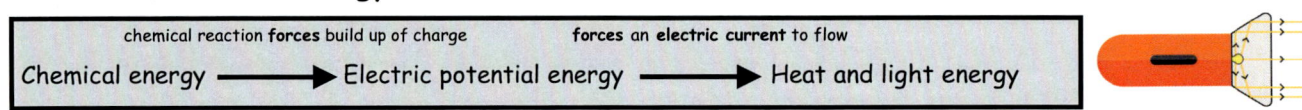

chemical reaction **forces** build up of charge	forces an **electric current** to flow
Chemical energy ⟶ Electric potential energy ⟶	Heat and light energy

A Dropped Ball

The gravitational potential energy the ball stores due to its height, decreases when it falls to the ground. The GPE is transferred to the kinetic energy store of the ball **by the force of gravity** pulling it downwards and making the ball speed up. **Overall, GPE decreases, kinetic energy increases.**

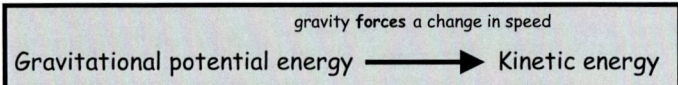

gravity **forces** a change in speed

Gravitational potential energy ⟶ Kinetic energy

gravity pulls on ball

earth

An Elastic Band Stretched then Released

If you stretch an elastic band, the chemical energy store in your food is transferred **by the force your muscles** apply to stretch the elastic band. This increases the store of elastic potential energy. On 'letting go', this energy is transferred **by the force of tension,** which causes the elastic band to speed up as it contracts (gets smaller again). This increases its kinetic energy store, decreasing the elastic potential energy store. **Overall, chemical energy store decreases, kinetic energy store increases.**

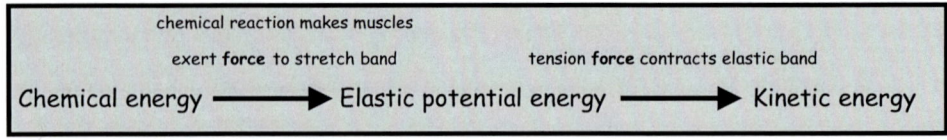

chemical reaction makes muscles exert **force** to stretch band   tension **force** contracts elastic band

Chemical energy ⟶ Elastic potential energy ⟶ Kinetic energy

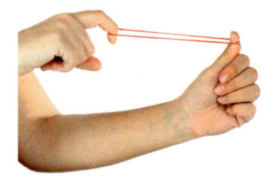

Lifting an Object Off the Ground

If you lift an object upwards, the chemical energy store in your food is transferred **by the force your muscles apply** to lift the object up. This increases the height of the object increasing its gravitational potential energy. **Overall, chemical energy store decreases, gravitational potential energy store increases.**

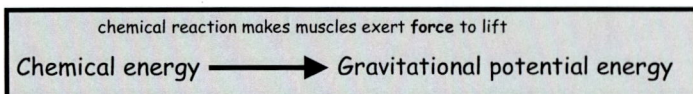

chemical reaction makes muscles exert **force** to lift

Chemical energy ⟶ Gravitational potential energy

Questions on Energy Transfers (flows)

Comprehension

1. When is energy most useful?
2. What's involved in bringing about energy transfers?
3. What does emission mean?
4. What type of energy does a battery store?
5. What happens to this energy when you switch on your torch?
6. What eventually happens to the light energy emitted by your torch?
7. Why does the ball store GPE?
8. What happens to the GPE as the ball falls?
9. How is the chemical energy store of your food transferred to elastic potential?
10. What does contract mean?
11. What type of energy increases when the elastic band is let go?
12. What type of energy decreases when the elastic band is let go?
13. What happens to the energy store of an object if you increase its height?
14. In increasing the height of an object what are chemical reactions able to do to muscles?

Additional tasks

1. Complete the table by matching the examples given below to the energy flows.

A catapult being released; A car speeding up; A falling yoyo; A solar cell powered by sunlight; A wind turbine; A rising yoyo; A car at constant speed; A tumble dryer; A kettle boiling water; A catapult being pulled back.

Examples	Energy flows
	Chemical potential to heat (explosion in engine) to kinetic energy
	Electric potential forces an electric current to flow producing heat
	GPE to kinetic
	Kinetic to GPE
	Elastic potential to Kinetic energy
	Kinetic energy to Electric potential
	Chemical potential to elastic potential
	Nuclear energy to light energy to Electric potential
	Electric potential forces an electric current to flow producing heat and kinetic energy
	Chemical potential to heat energy

2. What is wrong with these statements?

   a. When water flows down a river it has more GPE.
   b. A squashed tennis ball has less elastic potential.
   c. Pushing repelling magnets closer decreases magnetic potential energy.
   d. The sun's nuclear energy store is increasing.
   e. A hot bath has less thermal energy than a cold one.
   f. When a car slows down its kinetic energy increases.
   g. A rubbed balloon stuck to the wall has no electric potential energy.
   h. A used match has more chemical energy than an unused match

3. Write down which type of energy is **increasing** and which type is **decreasing** in the examples below.

   i. A sky diver who has just leapt from a plane.
   ii. A ball kicked up in the air.
   iii. A burning candle.
   iv. A battery powered set of LED lights.
   v. A person slowing down as they land on a trampoline (see below).

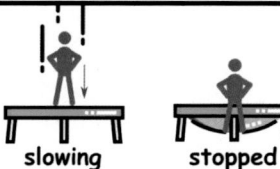

slowing   stopped

Energy Transfers (Continued)

A Growing Plant: Photosynthesis

Light energy that was emitted by the sun through nuclear reactions, is absorbed by the leaves of plants. The light energy **forces** new chemicals to be made so the chemical energy store of the plant increases. **Overall, nuclear energy store decreases, chemical energy store increases.**

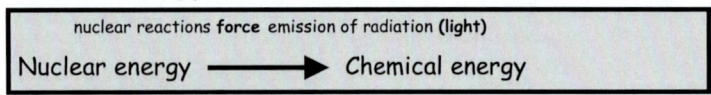

nuclear reactions **force** emission of radiation **(light)**

Nuclear energy ⟶ Chemical energy

A Bicycle Speeding Up

The chemical energy store of your food, is transferred **by the force your muscles** apply to pedal the bike. This increases the kinetic energy store of

speeding up

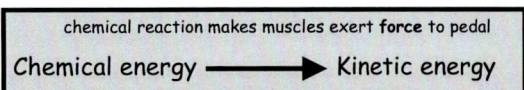

chemical reaction makes muscles exert **force** to pedal

Chemical energy ⟶ Kinetic energy

the bike, it speeds up. **Overall, chemical energy store decreases, kinetic energy store increases.**

A Bicycle Pedalled at a Constant Speed

The chemical energy store of your food is transferred **by the force your muscles** apply to pedal the bike. The tyres and moving parts get a bit warmer because of friction (surfaces rubbing together producing heat). You also have to push the air 'out of the way',

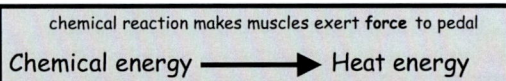

chemical reaction makes muscles exert **force** to pedal

Chemical energy ⟶ Heat energy

heating it up a tiny bit. You don't go any faster so there is no increase in kinetic energy store.

Overall, chemical energy store decreases, thermal energy store increases.

steady speed

A Bullet Fired From a Gun

The chemical energy store in the bullet is transferred to thermal energy store (a hot explosion) in the gun. The thermal energy store (hot gases expanding) **forces** the bullet from the gun, decreasing the thermal energy store and increasing the kinetic energy store of the bullet as it leaves at high speed. **Overall, chemical energy store decreases, kinetic energy store increases.**

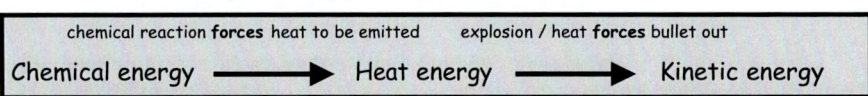

chemical reaction **forces** heat to be emitted   explosion / heat **forces** bullet out

Chemical energy ⟶ Heat energy ⟶ Kinetic energy

A Screaming Child

The chemical energy store in our food is transferred **by the force your muscles apply** to vibrate your voice box (larynx) .This vibration we call a sound wave, it

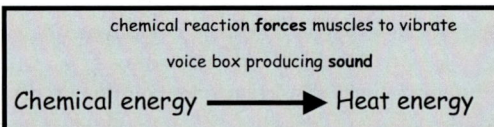

chemical reaction **forces** muscles to vibrate

voice box producing **sound**

Chemical energy ⟶ Heat energy

transfers the energy of the vibrations through the air. Eventually the energy of the vibrations just ends up being absorbed as thermal energy by

heating the stuff it bumps into a tiny bit. **Overall chemical energy store decreases, thermal energy store increases.**

WHAT?

In **one hour** enough energy from the sun (mainly sunlight), reaches the earth to supply the whole world with the energy it needs for a **whole year!** Almost all of our energy comes from the sun. Plants use it to grow which supports animal life. The energy in fossil fuels originally came from the sun. It makes the wind blow, powers the water cycle and we can use it to generate electricity.

Questions on Energy Transfers (Continued)

Comprehension

1. Through what process is light emitted by the sun?
2. What does the light energy force a plant to do?
3. What energy store increases for a bicycle speeding up?
4. What energy store decreases for a bicycle speeding up **or** moving at a constant speed?
5. What happens to the tyres and moving parts when pedalling a bike?
6. What do you have to do to the air when riding a bicycle?
7. When you pedal a bicycle at constant speed why isn't your kinetic energy increasing?
8. What sort of energy does a bullet store?
9. How is the bullet forced from the gun?
10. What does this do to the thermal energy?
11. What's another name for the voice box?
12. What do we call the vibration produced by the voice box?
13. What eventually happens to the energy of the vibrations of a sound wave?
14. How much energy reaches the earth from the sun in one hour? (WHAT? box)

Additional tasks

1. Solve the clues to do with energy below.

1. If the kinetic energy of an object is increasing it must be? S _ _ _ _ _ _ _ U _
2. Objects have to push air out of the way when they move, this is called? A _ _ R _ _ _ _ _ _ _ _
3. Earth gets most of its energy from the? S _ _
4. The chemical energy of a battery decreases through the flow of an? E _ _ _ _ _ _ C _ _ _ _ _ _

2. Draw energy transfer diagrams (the same as pages 118/120) to show the **overall** energy flow for;

i. a car slowing down (remember the brakes get hot!)

ii. a smart phone (the same as a torch?).

iii. released after being pulled back on a swing

iv. squashing a bed spring

*v. a bullet fired straight up **after** leaving a gun*

vi. a car at constant speed

3. For fun and to get some idea of what you can do with a certain amount of energy, guess which numbers match to the energy use. Answers opposite.

10,000,000,000J	500,000J	2,500,000J	1J	240,000J
120J	8,800,000J	3,000,000J	100,000,000J	1800J

1. Boil a kettle	2. Lift an apple from the floor to the table
3. An LED torch switched on for 10 minutes	4. Drive 100 miles in an electric car
5. Have a five minute shower	6. Get one person to the moon
7. Hair dry your hair (2 minutes)	8. Climb Mount Everest
9. Two minute phone call (smart phone)	10. Swim a mile

ANSWERS 6.10,000,000,000 J 1.500,000J 5.2,500,000J 2.1J 7.240,000J 9.120J 8.8,800,000J 10.3,000,000J 4.100,000,000J 3.1800J

Conservation of Energy

Energy cannot be created or destroyed, it can only flow from one store to another. All this means is that the total energy **before** a transfer is the **same** as **afterwards**. Another way of thinking of this is that you don't get something for nothing. You can't have more energy than you started with, otherwise you would be creating energy and you can't. **The light bulb example below shows what this means.**

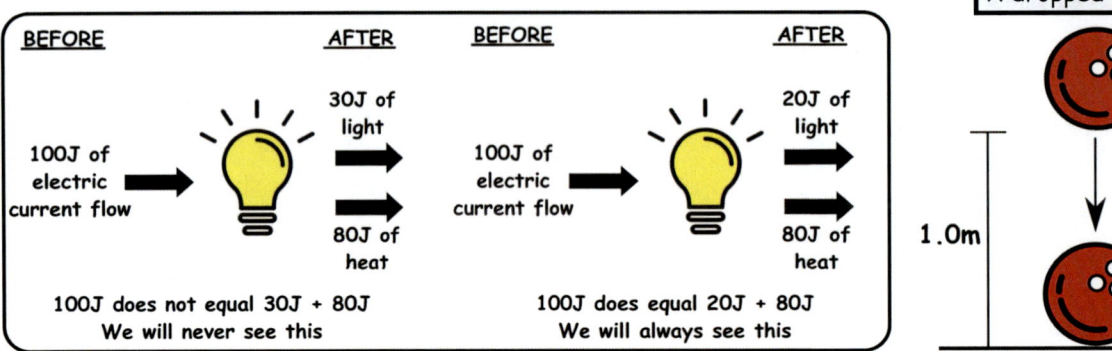

This is always true no matter what example you think of. It enables us to explain anything to do with energy, like why a ball reaches a certain speed after falling a certain distance. How much fuel a space craft needs to reach the moon. Why a pendulum swings back and forth. Examples make this easier to see.

Examples

A bowling ball that weighs 10N (1kg) and is 1 metre above the ground has 10J of GPE. Drop it and the 10J of GPE will transform into 10J of KE just before it hits the ground. **No more, no less.**

Hot tea and iced tea are mixed together, the hot tea loses 30,000J of heat and the iced tea gains 30,000J of heat. **No more, no less.**

Increase the length of an average elastic band by 10cm and the 0.25J of chemical energy from your food ends up as 0.25J of elastic potential energy in the stretched elastic band. **No more, no less.**

A wrecking ball (like a pendulum) pulled back to demolish a building has 25,000J of GPE. On release this 25,000J of GPE transforms into 25,000J of KE as the ball swings back. **No more, no less.**

> **WHAT?**
>
> If there was no air resistance or friction a pendulum would swing forever! Energy conserved!

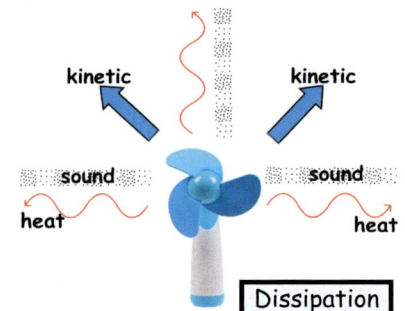

Dissipation

Dissipation

This simply means energy 'spreading out' and becoming less useful (it's still there though). Examples help us to understand. An '**AA**' battery has about 12,000J of stored chemical energy, this is really useful because I can do lots of things with it. If I put it in my hand held fan, it will transfer this 12,000J into mostly kinetic energy of the air, some heat and sound. Once I've enjoyed the cooling effect of the air rushing over my face, the kinetic energy of the air particles is just spread out amongst billions and billions of other air particles in the room (making them a tiny bit warmer). The heat, caused by friction in the motor and the electric current in the wires, gets absorbed by anything cooler in the room so it's not even noticeable. The sound just bounces around and gets absorbed as it bumps into stuff, again ending as heat, not even noticeable. There is now 12,000J more energy in the room but you can't do anything with it, like power a fan! **It has dissipated.** A **Newton's cradle** eventually stops because the energy is dissipated as heat and sound as the

Newton's cradle balls hit each other.

122

Questions on Conservation of Energy

Comprehension

<table>
<tr><td>

1. What can't happen to energy?
2. Complete the sentence about conservation of energy, "All this means is..."?
3. What is another way of thinking of this?
4. If 100J of energy flows into a bulb, how much energy must flow out?
5. How often is this true?
6. What does this enable us to do?
7. What could we calculate about a space craft?
8. What does 1kg weigh?
9. What happens to the 10J of GPE when the bowling ball is dropped?

</td><td>

10. If you increase the length of an average elastic band by 10cm how much energy does it store?
11. What does dissipation mean?
12. Roughly how much energy does an 'AA' battery store?
13. Why is this energy really useful?
14. If I put the battery into a handheld fan and turn it on what will most of the energy be transferred into?
15. What causes the heat emitted by the fan?
16. Why does a Newton's cradle eventually stop?

</td></tr>
</table>

Additional tasks

1. Write down **possible** or **not possible** next to the energy changes in the table using conservation of energy.

Energy changes	Possible / Not possible ?
A light bulb, 100J of electric current flow changes into 30J heat and 71J of light	
Stretching an elastic band, 0.25J of chemical energy changes into 0.25J of elastic potential	
Lifting a ball, 10J of chemical energy changes into 8J of GPE for the ball	
A falling bouncy ball, 2J of GPE changes to 1.9J of KE and 0.1J of heat	
A bouncy ball hitting the ground, 1.9J of KE changes into 1.9J of elastic potential	
A growing plant, 1000J of light energy changes into 800J of chemical and 100J of heat	
Mixing hot and cold drinks, the hot drink loses 20,000J, cold drink gains 18,000J	
Pushing two repelling magnets together, 0.05J of chemical energy changes to 0.05J magnetic potential energy	

2. Although energy is always conserved in an energy transfer, not all of the energy transferred ends up in the form we want. Energy that ends up in the form we don't want is called **wasted**. In the light bulb example opposite the 80 joules of heat is wasted because we want light from a light bulb. Identify the **useful (wanted)** and **wasted (unwanted) energy** in the examples below.

<table>
<tr><td>

a. A hand held fan for cooling you down
b. A remote controlled toy car powered by an electric motor
c. Sliding down a slide at the park
d. A wind turbine
e. A candle

</td><td>

f. Watching TV
g. An electronic keyboard
h. A lift in a building powered by an electric motor
i. A loudspeaker
j. A smart phone

</td></tr>
</table>

3. Complete the gap fill on wasted energy, use the following words in bold; **heat, useful, spread, wasted, wasted, friction, dissipated**

Often _____ energy, the energy we don't want, ends up being transformed into _____ energy. This heat energy becomes less and less _____, we say the energy has _____. It is now so _____ out we can't do anything useful with it. Energy is most often _____ as heat due to the flow of an electric current or because moving parts rub together and generate heat through _____.

Work and Energy

Doing house work or even writing out your homework requires energy from you. The **work done** by you is **equal to** the **energy transferred**. To calculate how much work has been done, we have to know the force applied (in newtons) and the distance it was applied for (in metres). We then multiply the two together to calculate the work done (which is equal to the energy transferred). It makes sense that the further you move something, the more energy is required and the more force you apply the more energy is required. We measure work and hence energy, in joules. Lift an apple weighing about 1 N the height of a table about 1 metre and you've done one joule of work (1Nx1m= 1J). Do it 100 times, 100J of work.

> Work done (joules) = Force (newtons) X Distance moved (metres)

Examples

Writing your homework

Force to make pen move = 0.1N   Distance moved = 2m

Work done (J) = force to make pen move (N) x distance moved (m)

Work done (J) = 0.1 x 2 = 0.2J

Tidying up your room

Force to lift clothes off floor = 4N   Height of drawer (distance) = 0.5m

Work done (J) = force to lift clothes off floor (N) x height of drawer (m)

Work done (J) = 4 x 0.5 = 2J

Where did the Energy Go? (Working Against)

Often you are working against another force that is trying to stop what you are doing. When you push your pen along the paper, **work** is done against **friction**. The work (energy) you are putting into moving your pen just ends up as heat. When you lift your clothes off the floor you have to **work** against **gravity** pulling them down. The work you do (energy put in) increases the gravitational potential energy of your clothes. They could fall back to the ground.

WHAT?

To get the average car from zero to 100 mph would take around 1,500,000 joules (1.5 million joules) of work! Power is how quickly work is done so a more powerful car would get to 100mph quicker.

Confusion Alert: imagine pushing a chair across the floor, it briefly goes from not moving to moving steadily. It speeds up, so **some** of the work you did to get it moving **increased** the kinetic energy of the chair. Once moving steadily though, there is **no change in kinetic energy**, only work against friction, the chair and the floor just get a little warmer (just like rubbing your hands together).

Let's Pretend we can Get Rid of Friction 'Completely' and Pretend there is no Air Resistance

Pushing a chair on zero friction ice

You're at our pretend **'zero friction'** ice rink with your back to the wall (so you can't slide the other way). Now you push a chair away and whilst your hands are touching and pushing the chair, the work you do increases its speed and so the kinetic energy of the chair. Once your hands **let go**, the chair moves at a constant speed, **no more work is done on it by you** and there is **no friction** or **air resistance** to slow it down **zero** friction ice and convert the kinetic energy you gave it into heat. Push it harder (more force) it speeds up more, and has more kinetic energy. The **work you have done** is **equal** to the **kinetic energy** the chair gains. Push the chair for a greater distance (move your hands further), the equation tells us that you have done more work so the chair has more kinetic energy and moves faster. Simple!

Questions on Work and Energy

Comprehension

1. What does doing housework or homework require?
2. What is the work done equal to?
3. What do we need to know to calculate work?
4. Why does this make sense?
5. If you lift **two** apples weighing **1N** each a height of **1metre** how much work is done?
6. What is the unit of work and hence energy?
7. If when doing your homework you move your pen 4m, how much work have you done?
8. Often when you do work you are working against a force, what does that force try to do?
9. When you push your pen along the paper, what are you doing work against?
10. When you lift your clothes off the floor what are you doing work against?
11. What happens to some of the work you do (energy) when starting to push a chair?
12. Once the chair is moving at a steady speed what happens to the work done on the chair?
13. When pushing the chair on 'zero friction ice' what happens to the work you do (energy transferred)?
14. If there is no friction what can't the kinetic energy transfer into?
15. What happens if you push the chair for a greater distance?
16. What does power tell us? (WHAT? box)

Additional tasks

1. Solve the jumbled words to do with work and energy.

Letters	Description	Answer
OUELJ	The unit of work	
ANSRTERFRED	When work is done, energy is always	
TREME	The unit of distance when calculating work	
CTIIORFN	What we often do work against	
ARGTIVY	Doing work against this increase GPE	
EHTA	Work against friction always transfers some energy to..	
IKETICN	If there is no friction or air resistance the work we do in pushing an object is equal to the .... energy gained	
TWENNO	The unit of force	

2. Calculate the work done (force x distance) in the following examples.

   a. Sweeping the patio a force of 10N is applied over 15m.
   b. Pushing a car, a force of 800N is applied for 12m.
   c. Climbing the stairs, legs exert 600N for a height of 3m.
   d. A car's brakes apply 2000N over 12m to stop.

   | a. |
   | b. |
   | c. |
   | d. |

3. An electric motor lifts people in an elevator between floors. Calculate the useful work done (here it is GPE, an increase in height) in lifting the people (force x distance) and then the energy wasted as heat. This is the difference between useful work done and energy consumed by motor.

Energy consumed by the motor (J)	Force from motor (N)	Distance / height lift rises (m)	Useful work done (J)	Energy wasted as heat (J)
2,500	1000	2		
37,500	6000	5		
87,500	5000	14		
60,000	8000	6		

Fuels and Energy Resources

Fossil Fuel Power Stations and Non-renewables (Generating Electricity)

Most of the world's electricity is still generated by burning fossil fuels. These are **coal, oil** and **gas**, formed from layers of dead plant and animal material being compressed over millions of years. They are **non-renewable** because they will eventually **run out**. In a conventional power station the **chemical energy** store from a fossil fuel is transferred to **heat** (thermal energy store) by burning. This heat is used to make steam that moves very quickly. The **kinetic**

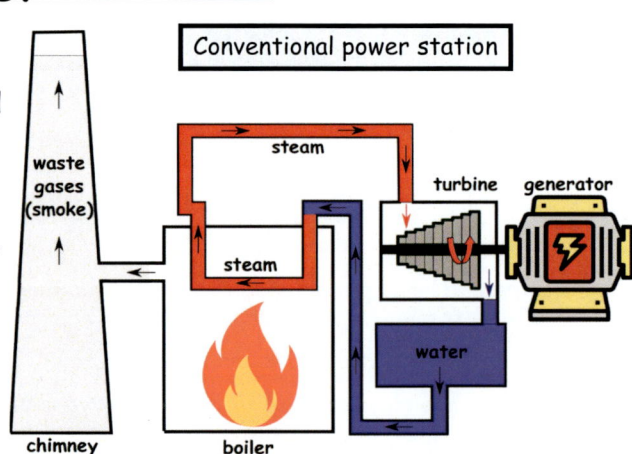

Conventional power station

energy store of the steam decreases **as it forces** a turbine (like a jet engine) to spin. The turbine is connected to a generator which produces an **electric potential**, like the ends of a battery. *Energy can **flow** from the generator as an **electric current** to our homes.* **Nuclear power** stations work in the same way except we can't burn nuclear fuel. The heat energy for a nuclear power station comes from nuclear reactions rather than chemical (combustion or burning). These take place in a nuclear reactor which then heats water to produce steam. **Nuclear fuel** also has to be dug out of the ground so it too is **non-renewable**.

Energy Transfer Diagram: Conventional Power Station

Chemical energy	→	Heat energy	→	Kinetic energy	→	Electric potential energy

Renewables

Renewable energy sources **don't run out**. They include **solar power**, panels convert the sun's energy directly into electricity, these are called photovoltaic cells. **Wind** power makes the blades of wind turbines spin,

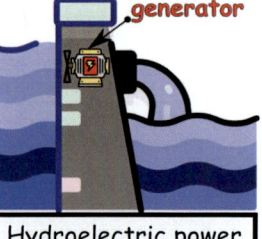
Hydroelectric power

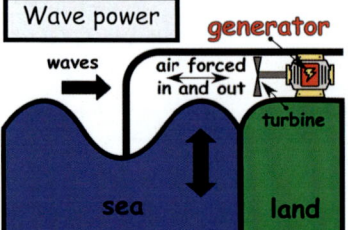
Wave power

these are connected to a generator. **Geothermal power** uses the heat from deep beneath the ground to produce steam that drives a turbine connected to a generator. **Wave power** uses the up and down motion of a wave to force air back and forth over a turbine which is connected to a generator. **Hydroelectric power** works by trapping water behind a dam and then allowing the water to flow through

Solar power

pipes which turn a turbine (like a water wheel) which is connected to a generator.

Advantages and Disadvantages (Pros and Cons)

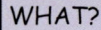
Wind power

Burning fossil fuels emits CO_2 which contributes to global warming. It also contributes to acid rain. They are a reliable energy source though and quite cheap at the moment. Wave, solar and wind are weather dependent so don't supply a reliable source all the time. The renewables don't pollute or contribute to global warming though. Geothermal depends on having accessible hot rocks under ground, not all countries have this. Nuclear produces dangerous waste which is difficult to dispose of. Hydroelectric usually requires flooding the habitat of wildlife, and relocating people.

> **WHAT?**
> China generates more electricity from hydroelectric power than any other country.

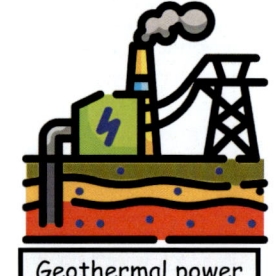
Geothermal power

Questions on Fuels and Energy Resources

Comprehension

1. How is most of the world's energy still generated?
2. What are the fossil fuels?
3. What were they formed from and how?
4. What does non-renewable mean?
5. Why does the kinetic energy of the steam decrease?
6. What does the generator produce?
7. How does the energy from the generator flow to our homes?
8. What can't we do to nuclear fuel?
9. Why is nuclear fuel also non-renewable?
10. What does a solar panel do?
11. What are the blades of a wind turbine connected to?
12. How does geothermal power work?
13. What does the up and down motion of a wave do to the air to produce electricity?
14. After trapping water behind a dam how does hydroelectric power generate electricity?
15. Why does burning fossil fuels contribute to global warming?
16. What is the problem with wave, solar and wind energy?
17. What is an advantage of renewables?
18. What is one of the problems with nuclear power?

Additional tasks

1. Solve the jumbled words below.

Letters	Description	Answer
ONBNAEWLEERNO	Energy resource that will run out	
CLUREAN EACRIONST	Nuclear power releases its energy through these	
HIANC	Country that generates most electricity from hydroelectric	
CIAD INRA	Burning fossil fuels contributes to ...	
IBNEUTR	Spins very fast like a jet engine and connected to a generator	
OTARRENEG	Transfers kinetic energy into electric potential	
IKETICN	Type of energy wind has	
BLOLAG IRAMGNW	Burning fossil fuels also contributes to ...	
BNAEWLEERO	Energy resource that won't run out	

2. Decide whether the statements below are **pros** (advantages) or **cons** (disadvantages) and match them to the renewable resources opposite .

a. sometimes birds accidentally get killed
b. there is a lot of energy washing up on our shores everyday
c. works best in hot countries
d. only practical in certain countries like Iceland
e. limited by having the right landscape to flood valleys
f. can generate on existing space like roofs
g. can be built out to sea
h. does not pollute and we live on an island so the potential is huge
i. once built they can generate electricity quickly by 'opening a tap'
j. some countries with the right landscapes can generate up to 30% of their electricity this way

3. **Biomass** is a renewable energy resource from **plant** or **animal material**. Complete the gap fill on two biomass uses.

photosynthesis, biomass, unleaded, fermented, burning, carbon dioxide, trees, global, corn, alcohol, fuel

An example of _____ is cutting down _____ and _____ them to generate electricity. The _____ _____released through burning is absorbed by the replanted trees through _____ so it is claimed not to contribute to _____ warming. Another example is growing _____ or sugar cane that can be _____ to make ethanol (_____). This alcohol can then be used as a _____ in vehicles. About 5% of _____ petrol is actually ethanol.

Simple Machines

A machine makes doing a job easier. Whatever energy you put into a machine to do a job ends up transforming into another energy store, no more and no less. A simple example of a machine is a lever. An even simpler one that often isn't thought of as a machine is a ramp or slope (technical name is an inclined plane).

Washing machine

The Ramp

To see how it works and also that we are not 'breaking' conservation of energy and getting something for nothing, let's consider an example. You need to get a lawn mower into the back of your car, it's really heavy, it weighs 1000N. Lifting it into the back of the car a height of 0.8m (80cm) requires (**Work done = 1000N X 0.8m**) 800J of work. This is too difficult so you lean a ramp on the back of the car to push it in, this requires a smaller force but for a greater distance. In fact, if the slope is 30° the **distance** to push is **twice as far** but the **force is half as much** as lifting directly. So the energy required is (**Work done = 500N X 1.6m**) 800J of work still but it is easier (requires less force).

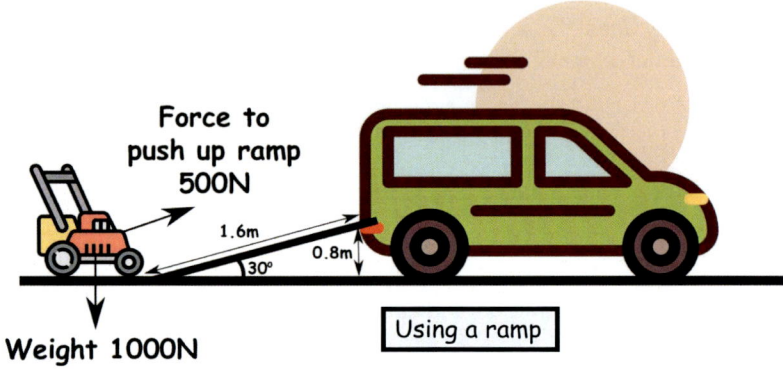

Force to push up ramp 500N

1.6m

0.8m

30°

Using a ramp

Weight 1000N

The Lever (Force Magnifier)

With a long enough lever you could lift the earth! Levers were used by ancient civilisations to help move huge stones when building structures like the pyramids. Nowadays the time you are most likely to use a lever is opening a tin of paint, removing a bottle top or taking off a bike tyre. Levers rely on the fact that the further the force is from the pivot (the point about where the turning happens), the greater the turning effect of that force. This is called the moment of the force. The short lever **magnifies** the **force by 2** (2m ÷ 1m). The lever is twice as long on one side. The Long lever **magnifies** the **force by 8** (8m ÷ 1m).

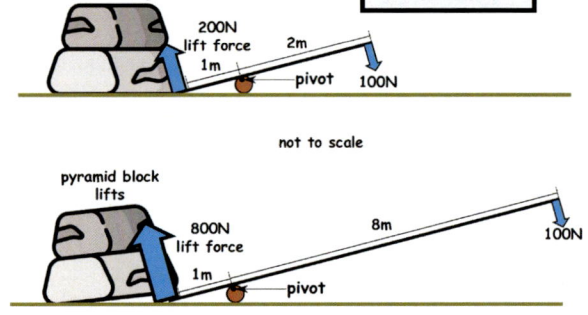

pyramid block won't budge

200N lift force

2m

1m

pivot

100N

not to scale

pyramid block lifts

800N lift force

8m

1m

pivot

100N

The lever

Pulleys

Look at the pulley on the left, there is no mechanical advantage (how much easier it is to lift something). This means to lift a 10N weight you have to pull with 10N and to lift it 1 metre you have to pull 1 metre. The picture on the right though shows two pulleys connected, look carefully and you can see that the 10N weight is supported by the two 5N forces (red) in the two ropes attached to the bottom pulley. This means a **mechanical advantage of 2** (10÷5). You only have to pull with 5N to lift a 10N weight **but** to lift it 1 metre up you have to pull 2 metres down. Conservation of energy again.

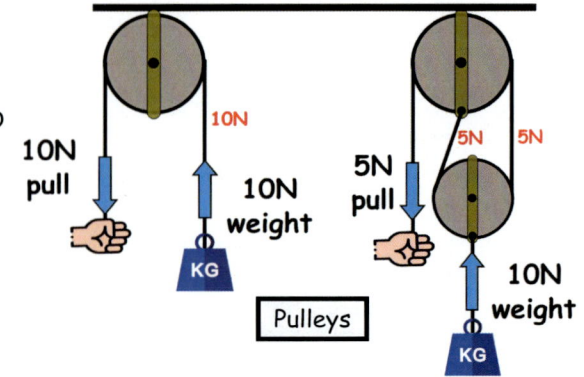

10N pull

10N

10N weight

KG

5N pull

5N   5N

10N weight

KG

Pulleys

Questions on Simple Machines

Comprehension

1. What does a machine do to a job?
2. What happens to the energy put into a machine?
3. What is the simple name for an inclined plane?
4. Why was a ramp used to get the mower into the car?
5. Although a ramp requires a smaller force what is greater when you use a ramp?
6. What would happen to the force needed to push the mower up the ramp if it was 2.4m long? (three times as far rather than twice)
7. What would the work done still be in this case?
8. What two words could be used to describe a lever?
9. What did ancient civilisations use levers for?
10. What are you most likely to use a lever for nowadays?
11. What fact do levers rely on to work?
12. What is the turning effect of a force called?
13. What is mechanical advantage?
14. Is there any mechanical advantage with the pulley on the left?

Additional tasks

1. Write down what the **lift force** is for the **force magnifiers** below and the **pull force** for **the pulleys** below. Use the examples opposite to help.

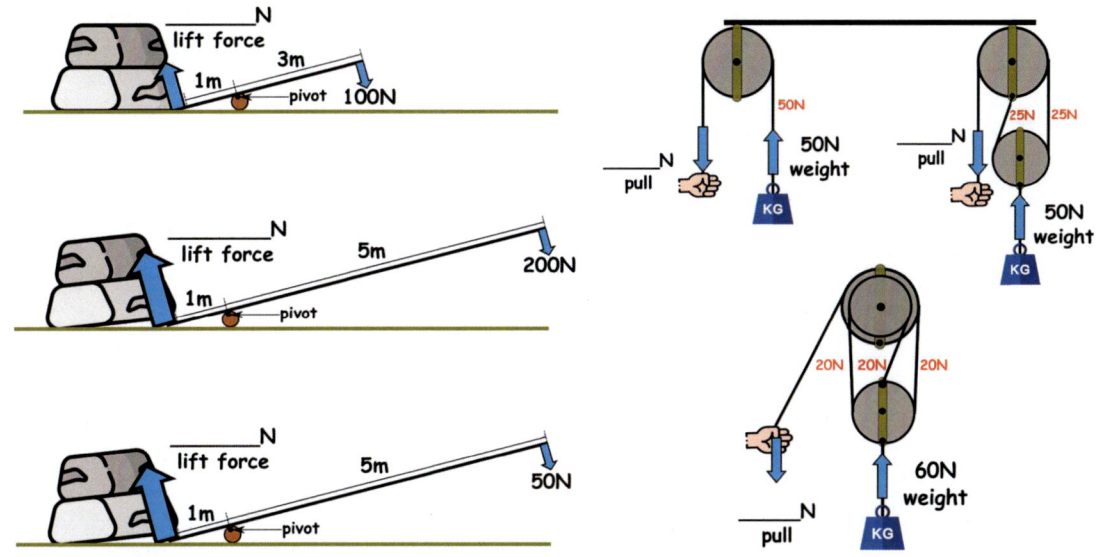

2. Unscramble these machines from their description.

Used for cleaning clothes	SIIWCMEAHHNGAN
Can be used for opening a tin of paint	LERVE
This machine makes getting around easier	ELWEH
This machine is really useful in the kitchen	IHEDHASRWS
Used to raise sails on sailing boats	PLYUEL
This machine is useful when you're hungry	INETNPROE
A machine good for splitting wood	DEWGE
This machine comes as a pair	OCRSSSIS
Good for moving heavy stuff	HERWRBWEOLA
A simple way of lifting objects	NHWCI
This machine works like a lever	SPEAD
Good for lifting heavy objects slowly	RAPM

3. Find the unscrambled machines below.

```
A  B  C  D  E  F  G  H  I  J  K  L  M  N
O  P  Q  R  S  T  U  V  W  X  Y  Z  C  W
H  P  C  Q  Z  C  G  W  R  A  M  P  O  O
S  J  C  V  K  V  P  E  H  O  X  R  N  Y
G  W  U  N  I  H  V  D  F  E  R  G  I  B
B  S  P  A  D  E  R  G  S  A  E  B  F  G
W  C  U  D  L  I  O  E  B  I  F  L  T  J
Q  I  C  C  X  W  S  L  G  L  Y  A  I  K
S  S  N  N  H  G  E  H  N  C  U  J  N  U
W  S  Y  C  N  E  Q  R  W  J  U  F  O  O
U  O  K  I  H  F  T  W  F  A  R  K  P  K
K  R  Y  W  U  J  A  R  Z  F  S  T  E·Z
S  S  S  J  E  N  I  L  D  L  L  H  N  O
B  B  W  E  P  B  M  U  P  U  L  L  E  Y
K  A  V  R  J  Z  W  B  O  N  Z  S  R  R
W  A  S  H  I  N  G  M  A  C  H  I  N  E
```

The States of Matter: Solids, Liquids and Gases

When thinking about solids, liquids and gases, water is very familiar. Water is a molecule, H_2O, and is actually shaped like a boomerang. When we draw diagrams to show how the particles are arranged we draw circles for the atoms or molecules because it is much easier. The particles in a solid have strong forces of attraction (bonds), they are packed closely together and vibrate about their 'fixed' positions. Heating a solid gives the particles more energy so they vibrate more and need more room to do this, they move apart meaning the solid expands. The particles in a liquid have weaker forces of attraction than a solid, are slightly further apart and can flow over each other. Gases have weak or no forces of attraction and are spaced far apart (see page 54).

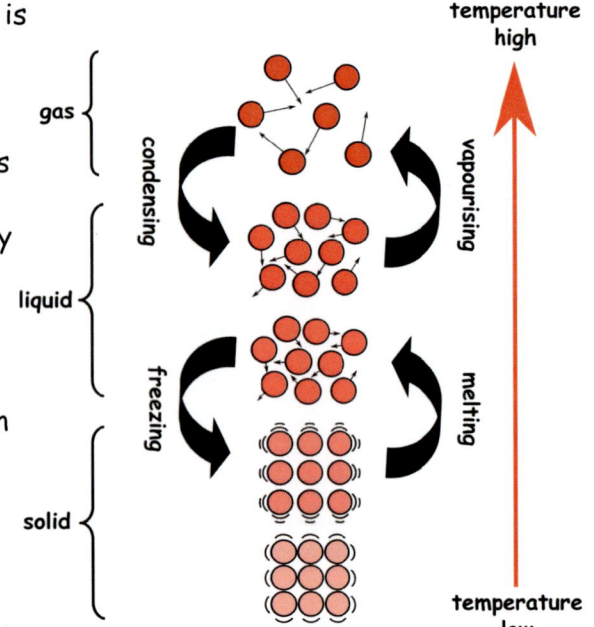

Unusual Expansion (Water's Special)

Density normally increases as matter moves from its gaseous state, to its liquid state to its solid state. This is because the particles become more tightly packed together. Water is an anomaly (it doesn't follow the pattern). As water freezes, changes from liquid to solid, it expands and becomes **less dense** than liquid water. That is why ice floats on water. Frozen water is often the cause of cracked water pipes in winter. It can cause pot holes in roads by flowing into gaps and then expanding when frozen, causing cracks to grow. Don't put a glass bottle of water in the freezer, it may crack as the ice expands.

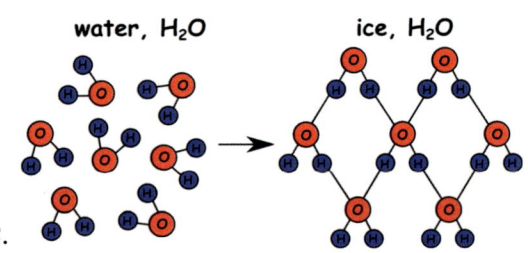

water, H_2O ice, H_2O

Usual Expansion

The usual expansion as materials get warmer explains why power lines sag more in the summer months. In hotter temperatures the metal power lines expand and lengthen. Engineers have to allow for this expansion and contraction, so that the power lines don't get too close to the ground in the summer or pull the pylons over in the winter!

Expansion joint (bridge)

Thermometers work because of the expansion of liquids as temperature rises. Most thermometers now contain a coloured alcohol which expands up a thin glass tube with a scale. The temperature is read off the scale as the liquid moves up and down. Bridges have expansion joints that look like a giant metal zip, to allow for expansion and contraction. They are often at the beginning and end of a bridge, look out for them.

Liquid expansion
5°C   70°C
alcohol

WHAT?

There is a fourth state of matter called a plasma, our sun is a plasma. A flame (fire) is part gas, part plasma. Railway tracks have gaps in them to allow for expansion to stop them buckling in the heat.

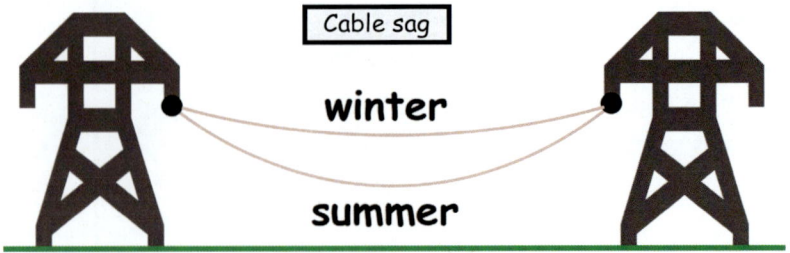

Cable sag

winter

summer

Questions on The States of Matter

Comprehension

1.	When thinking about solids, liquids and gases what is very familiar?
2.	What shape is a water molecule?
3.	What do we draw to represent the atoms or molecules?
4.	What are the forces of attraction (bonds) like in a solid?
5.	What do the particles vibrate 'about' in a solid?
6.	What happens to the particles when you heat a solid and what does this mean for the space they need?
7.	How do the forces of attraction in a liquid compare to a solid?
8.	What's the spacing of the particles like in a liquid?
9.	What's the spacing of the particles like in a gas?
10.	What normally happens to density as you move from the liquid state to the solid state?
11.	Why is this?
12.	What does anomaly mean?
13.	What happens as water changes from liquid to solid?
14.	Why does ice float on water?
15.	What can happen to power lines in the summer?
16.	How do thermometers work?
17.	What do bridges have to allow for expansion and what do they look like?

Additional tasks

1. Match and memorise the words below.

Melting	changing from a liquid to a solid
Vapourising	reduction in size of a material usually when cooled
Condensing	increase in size of a material usually when heated
Freezing	changing from a solid to a liquid
Sublimation	changing from a gas to a solid without the liquid stage, opposite to sublimation
Deposition	changing from a solid straight to a gas without the liquid stage opposite to deposition
Expansion	changing from a gas to a liquid
Contraction	changing from a liquid to a gas

2. A student wants to make their own thermometer. They fill a test tube with coloured water and put a small tube through a rubber bung and place the bung in the test tube. They mark the water level **then** place the test tube in boiling water.

a. What will happen to the water level when the test tube is placed in boiling water?

b. Why does it happen?

c. When the red water is added to the test tube it is 20°C. What will be the temperature change when it is put into the boiling water?

d. How could the student use a ruler to make a scale on the tube?

e. What would happen to the water level if the test tube was put in ice water at 0°C and why?

3. In the boxes below draw **nine** particles to show a hot and cold solid and a hot and cold liquid. Remember the particles themselves don't change size!

cold solid   hot solid

cold liquid   hot liquid

Heat Energy and Temperature

Everything has heat energy, even really cold things like ice. Heat energy exists because the particles that substances are made from move. In a solid they vibrate, in liquids and gases they can move from their position. How **quickly** particles **move** or **vibrate** we measure as the **temperature**. The particles in hotter substances move faster than in colder ones, so we measure a higher temperature.

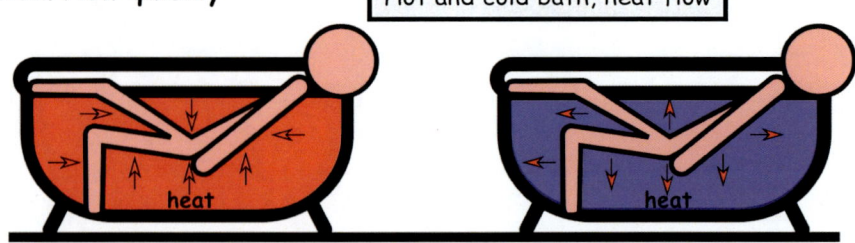
Hot and cold bath, heat flow

Heat energy always flows from a hot object to a cold one, never the other way round. Like a ball will always roll downhill, we can think of heat as rolling down from hot things to colder things.

Climb into an ice cold bath and you will heat the water up. The heat energy lost by you is equal to the heat energy gained by the water. Climb into a steaming hot bath and the water heats you up. The heat energy lost by the hot water is equal the heat energy gained by you.

Temperature

If we know the temperature of a gas we can actually work out how fast the gas particles are moving (about 1000mph at 20°C). The temperature gauge of a car tells us the engine is hotter when it's running, this means the engine's atoms are vibrating faster when the engine is hot. We normally measure temperature in degrees Celsius (°C). Using degrees Celsius is convenient because 100°C is the boiling point of water and 0°C is the freezing point of water, we are familiar with these temperatures. Most substances expand when they are heated. A thermometer made from a liquid that moves up a very thin glass tube when it gets hotter, is the usual way we think of measuring temperature. The higher the liquid moves up the tube, the hotter the temperature.

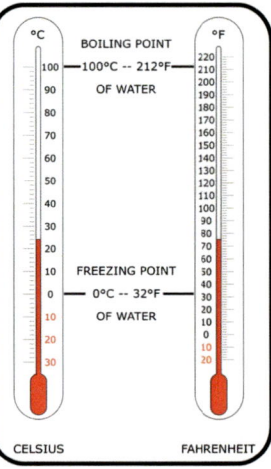
Thermometers

There are many other ways to measure temperature. Many use the principle of measuring how easily an electric current passes through

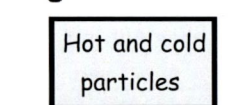
Hot and cold particles

certain circuits (the resistance). This changes with temperature. These electronic devices give a readout on a digital display as do most cars. In cars they often warn if the temperature is low enough for ice to form. Thermometer probes for measuring our body's temperature can be bought from pharmacists. Probes for measuring the temperature of cooked food are used to check if the food is cooked properly.

Food probe

Internal Energy

This is the energy that substances have due to the **vibration** (or movement) of their **particles** and the **attraction** between them. We can think of it as heat energy, because the hotter a substance is the more internal energy it has. Also the more particles that a substance is made from the more internal energy it has. If we allow a **hot** cup of tea to cool we could melt 24 ice cubes with the energy, if we allow a **warm** bath of water to cool we could melt 3500 ice cubes even though it's colder! The bath has more internal energy because there are more water molecules so the internal energy overall is greater.

WHAT?

The highest theoretical temperature that could exist is;
140,000,000,000,000,000,000,000,000,0 00,000 °C. 140 thousand billion billion billion °C. Thanks for that physicists!

Questions on Heat Energy and Temperature

Comprehension

1. What has heat energy?
2. Why does heat energy exist?
3. What does temperature tell us about the particles?
4. Which way does heat energy always move?
5. What happens to the water if you climb into an ice cold bath?
6. What happens if you climb into a hot bath?
7. If we know the temperature of a gas what can we actually work out?
8. What do we measure temperature in usually?
9. Why is degrees Celsius convenient?
10. By looking at the liquid in a thermometer, how do we know how hot it is?
11. Many methods use the principle of measuring what?
12. How do most of these devices give a readout?
13. Why are probes sometimes used for measuring the temperature of cooked food?
14. What is internal energy due to?
15. We can just think of internal energy as what?
16. Why can we melt more ice cubes with a **warm** bath of water than a **hot** cup of tea?

Additional tasks

1. Write the temperature values next to the examples in the table below, choose from;

    0°C, 37°C, 100°C, 4°C, 30,000°C, 20°C, -15°C, 6000°C, 40°C.

Examples	Temperature (°C)
Human body temperature	
Average freezer temperature	
Boiling point of water	
Average fridge temperature	
Average room temperature	
Temperature of lightning	
A hot bath	
Surface of the sun	
Freezing point of water	

2. Choose from the words below to complete the following statements.

   fast, number, gain, Probes, movement, 1000 mph, temperature, resistance, mass, particles, lose, thermal, Celsius, Fahrenheit, attraction

- Another word for heat energy is _____ energy.
- If we know the temperature of a gas we can work out how _____ the particles are moving.
- Electronic thermometers often use a change in _____ to measure temperature.
- Digital thermometers show us a _____ for the temperature.

- Objects at the same _____ have more internal energy if they have more _____. This is because they will be made from more _____.
- In a cold bath you _____ heat energy.
- The usual unit of temperature is degrees _____.
- A less often used unit of temperature is degrees _____.
- Particles in a gas move at about _____ at room temperature .
- _____ are used for measuring the temperature of food.
- Internal energy is the energy a substance has due to the _____ of the particles and the _____ between them.
- In a hot bath you _____ heat energy.

3. On the Fahrenheit temperature scale **68°F** is equal to **20°C**. To work this out we use the equation;

   $$°C = 5/9 \times (F-32)$$

   So 68°F gives; 5/9 x (68-32) = 5/9 x 36 = **20°C**

   Convert the following temperatures from Fahrenheit to Celsius and check that they are roughly correct by looking at the thermometers opposite.

   A.   122°F   B.   212°F   C.   77°F

   D.   104°F   E.   113°F   F.   176°F

Heat Transfer

Remember heat energy always flows from hot to cold. It can do this in three ways, by **conduction**, **convection** or **radiation**.

Conduction

This method of heat transfer happens best in solids. In liquids and gases heat transfer by conduction is poor. Hold tightly on a metal climbing frame and the metal 'feels' cold. This is because metal is a good conductor of heat. Heat flows from your hand to the metal bar quickly, so it feels cold. Wood is a poor conductor of heat, if the climbing frame was made of wood, heat flow from your hand would be slow and the climbing frame wouldn't feel cold. Imagine tightly linking arms in a human chain. The person at the end of the chain is tickled so jiggles about. The tickled person, because they are linked, makes the person next to them (neighbour) jiggle, and so on. In this way jiggles are passed on down the chain. In a solid, if one end of the substance is heated the vibrations are passed down the chain (conducted) from particle to neighbouring particle.

Radiation

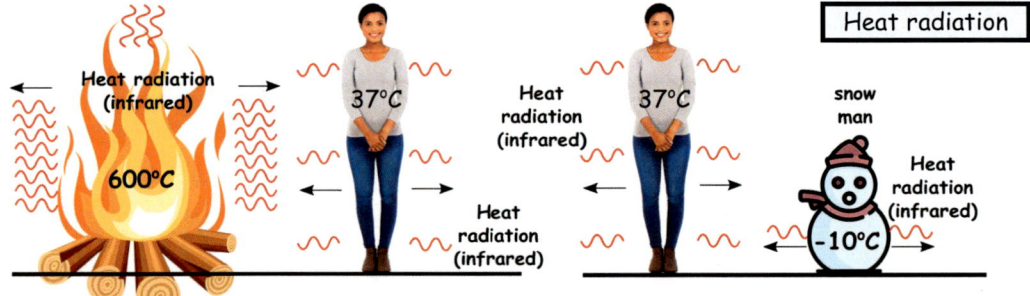

All objects emit **heat radiation** which is **infrared** waves carrying energy. The hotter an object is, the more heat radiation it emits. If an object absorbs more heat radiation than it emits, it gets hotter. If it emits more than it absorbs it gets colder. If we think about **heat radiation only**, standing near to a fire that is emitting lots of heat radiation means we would get hotter. We would absorb more radiation than we emit. Standing near to a snowman means we would get colder, we would emit more heat radiation than we absorb.

Convection

Convection is a method of heat transfer in liquids and gases only. If air is heated the particles gain energy and spread out a little, the air expands and becomes lighter (less dense) than before. It floats or rises on top of the cooler more dense air that falls (or sinks) to replace the risen air. This continues and sets up a current of air flowing towards and away from the heat source, producing

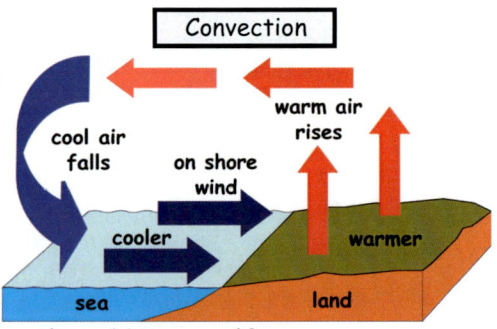

a **convection current**. The wind is a convection current. An 'on shore' breeze (from sea towards land) is often caused by the land heating up faster than the sea. This makes the air above the land heat up **more than** the air above the sea. The air above the land rises and a convection current begins. Put your hand above a radiator and you can feel the warm air rising. Radiators transfer heat mainly through convection so are badly named! They set up a convection current which spreads warm air around the room.

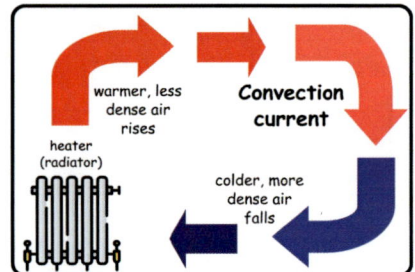

WHAT?

The best conductor of heat is diamond, 5 times better than copper.

Questions on Heat Transfer

Comprehension

1. Which way will heat energy always flow?
2. Where does conduction happen best?
3. How does a metal often feel to touch?
4. Why is this?
5. Why wouldn't a wooden climbing frame feel cold?
6. In the human chain what happens to the person next to the tickled person and why?
7. If one end of a solid is heated what is passed on down the chain?
8. What do all objects emit?
9. What is heat radiation?
10. What sort of objects emit more heat radiation?
11. When thinking about heat radiation **only**, why do we get hot near to a fire?
12. What states of matter does convection happen in?
13. What happens to the density of air when it is heated?
14. What does this cause the warm air to do?
15. What is wind an example of?
16. Why are radiators badly named?

Additional tasks

1. Label the diagram of the onshore breeze. Add your **own arrows** to show the movement of the air.

2. Complete the gap fill to explain what is happening below. Choose from the words in bold.

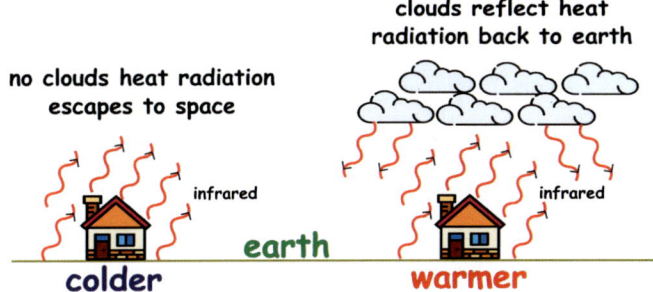

absorbed, day, infrared, heat, space, left, reflect, earth, warmer, blanket

At night, heat _____ by the earth during the _____ is emitted as _____ or _____ radiation. If the heat radiation escapes into _____ it is colder. That is what happens to the house on the _____. Clouds _____ heat radiation emitted from the _____ back down so the house on the right is _____. The clouds act like a _____.

3. State for the ice cubes **A** to **L** below whether they will **warm up**, **melt**, **cool** or **no change**.

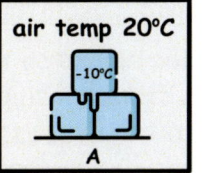
air temp 20°C — A

air temp 0°C — B

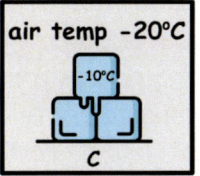
air temp -20°C — C

air temp 1°C — D

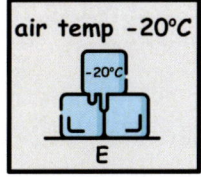
air temp -20°C — E

air temp -5°C — F

air temp 8°C — G

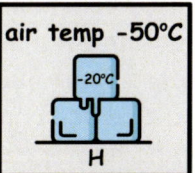
air temp -50°C — H

air temp -20°C — I

air temp -6°C — J

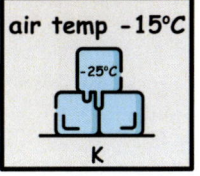
air temp -15°C — K

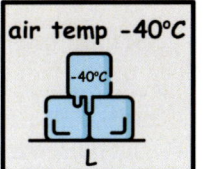
air temp -40°C — L

Photocopiable
135
Only write on photocopied version

Insulators and Insulation

An insulator is a material that is poor at conducting heat. Hold a metal rod in a Bunsen flame and it would soon become too hot to hold. Hold a glass rod in a Bunsen flame and it would take much longer for the glass rod to become too hot to hold. Metals are good conductors of heat, glass is a poor conductor of heat, it is an insulator.

No prob   Ouch!

glass   copper

Material	Conductivity (higher number better conductor)
Copper	410
Aluminium	240
Steel	54
Glass	1.0
Wood (oak)	0.17
Water	0.61
Air	0.026

The bottom of frying pans are often made from copper, copper is a good conductor, it transfers heat to the food quickly. The handles of frying pans are usually made from insulators like wood or plastic to stop our hands getting burnt. When we remove something from the oven we use oven gloves which usually contain an insulator like cotton wool inside the fabric. A winter coat contains an insulating material between the inside and outside of the coat. The warmest coats have down feathers as the insulating material. They are brilliant insulators, great at trapping air.

Insulating down feather

Keeping our Houses Warm: Insulation

It costs money to heat our homes so we want to slow down the loss of this heat. Cavity wall insulation, loft insulation and double glazing are effective methods. They work in a similar way, by trapping air which is a poor conductor of heat so a good insulator.

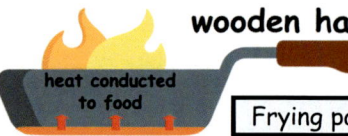
wooden handle

heat conducted to food

copper base

Frying pan

This slows down heat loss by conduction. Since the air is trapped it cannot move so does not allow convection currents to circulate. Heat loss by convection is also reduced. Modern insulating panels for cavity walls are made from a plastic foam that traps air and is often covered in a reflective foil. The foil reflects heat radiation back into the house to help reduce heat loss by radiation. In the summer months, especially in hot countries, this can be useful to keep heat radiation out when it is **hotter outside** the house **than inside,** where the air conditioning is switched on.

Modern double glazing or even triple glazing often has a gas other than air between the glass panes. Argon is an even better insulator than air (worse conductor). It is the most commonly used gas. It reduces heat loss by conduction even more than air. Household fridges are insulated (just like cavity walls) with a plastic foam, rather than stopping heat escaping the insulation stops heat getting into the cold fridge.

WHAT?

On re-entry to earth's atmosphere spacecraft can experience temperatures around 1500°C so have highly insulating panels on the outside to protect the craft. In 2003 the space shuttle's insulation was damaged and the craft broke up on re-entry.

Loft insulation

Insulation panel

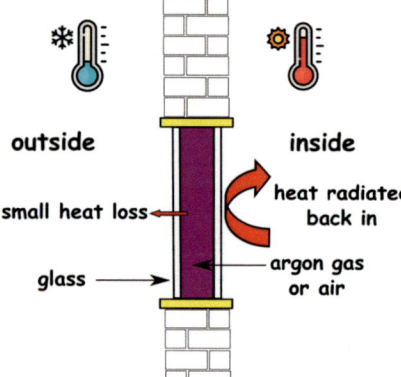

outside   inside

small heat loss

glass

heat radiated back in

argon gas or air

Double glazing

Loft and cavity wall insulation

loft insulation
fibre glass 'traps air'

cavity wall insulation panel
plastic foam 'traps air'

Questions on Insulators and Insulation

Comprehension

1. What is an insulator?
2. Which materials are good conductors of heat?
3. What are the bottom of frying pans often made from and why?
4. Why are the handles often made from wood or plastic?
5. What are some of the warmest coats insulated with and why?
6. Why do we want to slow down the loss of heat from our homes?
7. What are three effective methods of insulating the home?
8. In what similar way do they work?
9. How are convection currents prevented from circulating?
10. What are the modern insulating panels used in cavity walls made from?
11. What does the reflective foil do?
12. Why is this layer useful in hot countries during summer?
13. Why is argon often used in double glazing rather than air?
14. What is the purpose of insulating a fridge?
15. Why do spacecraft have insulating panels on the outside? (WHAT? box)

Additional tasks

1. Solve the clues on insulators and insulation.

1. The gas often used in double glazing? A _ _ _ _
2. What cavity wall and loft insulation rely on to insulate? T _ _ _ _ _ _ _   A _ _
3. The diagram of double glazing doesn't have a ? C _ _ _ _ _ _   W _ _ _
4. Best conductor listed in the table? C _ _ _ _ _
5. Fridges are insulated to stop _____ entering? H _ _ _
6. Brilliantly insulating bird feathers? D _ _ _
7. Trapped air stops _____ _____ circulating? C _ _ _ _ _ _ _ _ _   C _ _ _ _ _ _ _

2. A student carried out an experiment by measuring the temperature every two minutes of 150ml of hot water poured into beakers. One beaker had **no insulation**, one was insulated with **bubble wrap** and the third with **cotton wool**. Plot the results on the graph below, connect the points and **label the lines**.

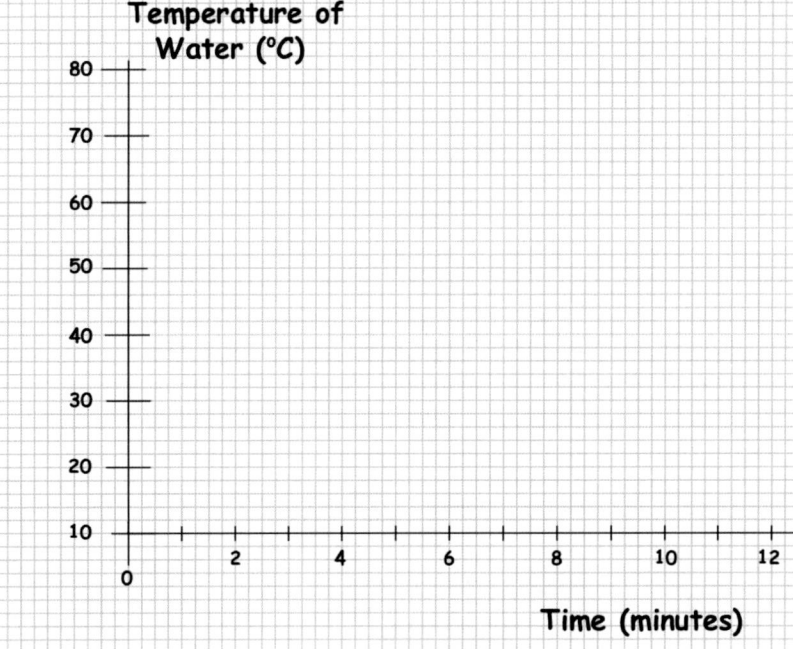

Temperature of Water (°C)

Time (minutes)

3 a. What is the starting temperature of the water?

b. The water in which beaker cools quickest and why?

	Temperature of Water (°C)		
Time (mins)	No insulation	Cotton wool	Bubble wrap
0	80	80	80
2	65	70	74
4	56	62	68
6	48	54	64
8	42	48	60
10	38	43	57
12	35	40	54

c. The temperature in the room is 20°C, what temperature will the water eventually become in each beaker?

Speed

Speed is something that scientists call a **rate**. A rate is a measure of how much something changes in a given time. Speed tells us how much our distance changes (how far we've travelled) in a given time. The 'scientific' unit for this is how many metres we have travelled in one second, metres per second (in symbols

Motion	Typical speed (m/s)	Typical speed (mph)
Walking	1.3	3
Running	2.6	6
Bicycle	6.3	14
Car	17.9	40
Plane	220	500
Sound	340	760
Satellite	3070	6870
Light	300,000,000	671,100,000

$$\text{Average speed (m/s)} = \frac{\text{distance travelled (m)}}{\text{time taken (s)}}$$

m/s). We are more used to how many miles we travel every hour, miles per hour (in symbols mph). We can write speed as an equation. Notice the word average has appeared, this is because when things like cars move they don't always move at the same speed, they speed up (accelerate) and slow down (decelerate). Usain Bolt ran the 100m in an **average** speed of (100 m ÷ 9.58 s = 10.4 m/s) **10.4 m/s.** His top speed though was 12.4 m/s

(27.8 mph). Most runners reach their top speed at about halfway (50m).

Plotting Motion: Distance Time Graphs

When looking at distance time graphs for motion, it is tempting to think that we are going uphill or travelling along the flat! In fact, the steepness of the lines on a graph tell us how fast we are moving and the flat sections tell us that there is no movement. The **steepness** or **gradient** of a line is found by **dividing** how much the **y-axis** (vertical, here distance) **changes** by how much the **x-axis** (horizontal, here time) **changes**. This tells us the speed because dividing

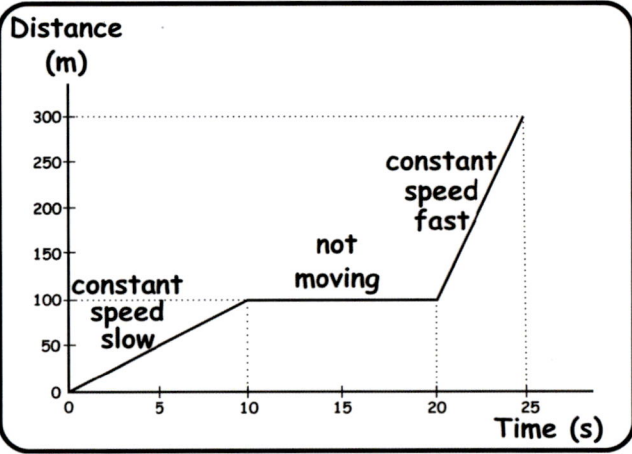

distance by time is speed. The graph shows an object that moves 100 metres (the y-axis change) in 10 seconds (the x-axis change). This means 100 ÷ 10 = **10 m/s.** This is the **gradient** and therefore the speed over the first 10 seconds. Between 10 to 20 seconds there is no change in distance, so there is no gradient so the speed is zero. The object has stopped moving (is stationary). Between 20 to 25 seconds the object is moving again. Here it moves a distance of 200m (300-100), this is the y-axis change. It took a time of 5 seconds (25-20), this is the x-axis change. During this time the object's speed is, 200 ÷ 5 = **40 m/s.** Both speeds are constant.

Speed Cameras

Speed cameras calculate if a car's average speed is over the speed limit. The camera takes two photographs (sometimes you see the two bright flashes) 0.5 seconds apart. The white lines painted 2 metres apart on the road, mean that it is possible to measure how far the car has travelled in the 0.5 seconds by observing the photographs. This provides proof as to whether the car has broken the speed limit. A car is photographed 0.5 seconds apart having covered four white lines of distance (8 metres) in a 30 mph zone. This means they will have been travelling at (8 ÷ 0.5) **16 m/s.** This is equal to **35.8 mph** and they will be receiving a speeding fine, oops!

WHAT?

Earth's orbital speed around the sun is nearly 67,000 mph (30,000m/s). Due to earth's rotation your speed at the equator is about 1000 mph.

Questions on Speed

Comprehension

1. What is speed an example of?
2. What does speed tell us?
3. What is the 'Scientific' unit for speed?
4. Which unit are we more used to?
5. Why does the word average appear in the equation?
6. When running 100m when do athletes normally reach their top speed?
7. What does the steepness (gradient) on a distance time graph tell us?
8. What's happening on the flat section of the graph?
9. How is the gradient (steepness) of the line found?
10. If you move 200m in 10 seconds how fast are you moving?
11. Between 20 to 25 seconds, how far does the object move?
12. What do speed cameras do and how do they do it?

Additional tasks

1. Calculate the speed for sections **A** and **B** on the graphs below.

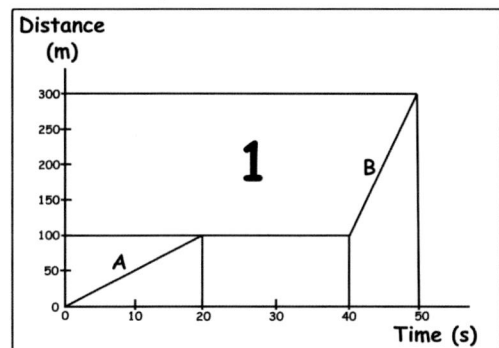

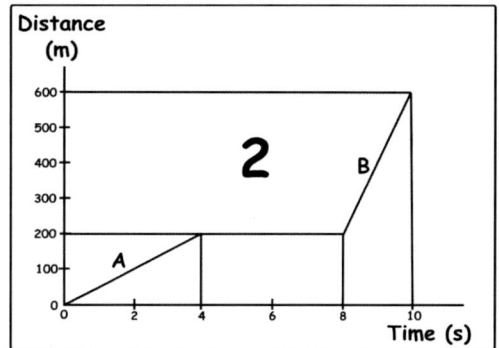

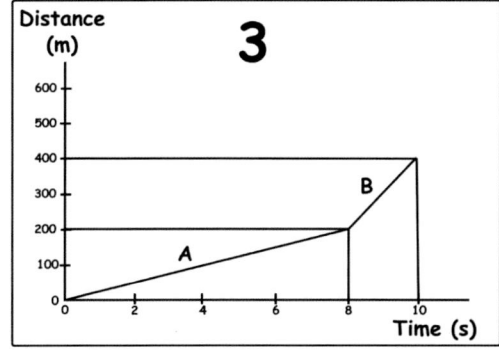

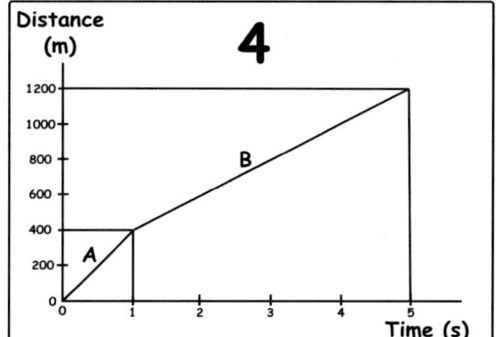

2. Use a calculator to find the speeds of the moving objects below in m/s, then multiply by 2.24 to convert to mph.

What's moving?	Distance travelled (m)	Time taken (s)	Speed (m/s)	Speed (mph)
Bugatti Chiron	272	2		
Skydiver	220	4		
Bus	108	6		
Peregrine falcon	320	3		
A Snail	1	78		
A Bullet	1609	1.8		

3. Choose from the six objects below to label lines **A** to **F** on the graph below.
Bullet, sound, bicycle, fast tennis serve, formula 1 car, a satellite

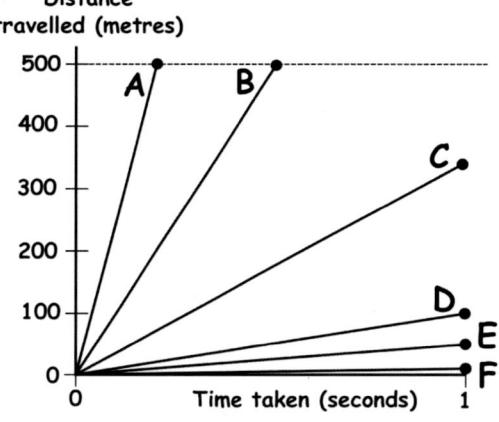

Relative Speed and more Distance Time Graphs

Distance Time Graphs Again

There are two more things that are important to think about with distance time graphs. If we plot our distance in a straight line, from a starting point like the start line on a 100 metre running track, then we can move away from the start line and also back towards it. On a 100 metre running track a man decides to time himself **walking** as fast as he can to the finish line, stop for a 10 second rest before **running** back to the start as fast as he can. The graph then looks like that

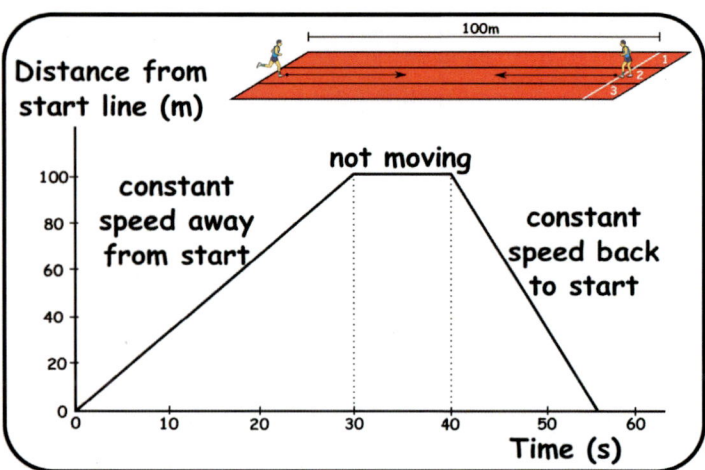

shown opposite. It takes 30 seconds to walk the 100 metres and after a 10 second rest it takes him 15 seconds to run back to the start line. Graphs like this mean we can show which way something is travelling.

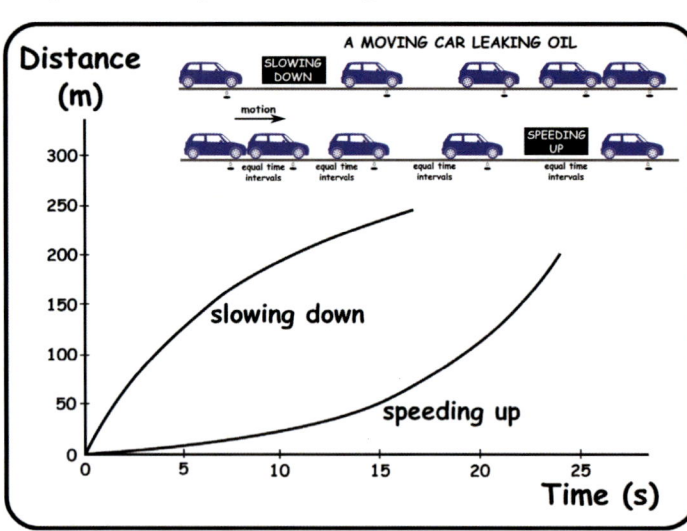

Curves

Most objects don't move at a nice constant speed. They speed up (accelerate) or slow down (decelerate) throughout their journey. Since the steepness of the line is the speed, if a line is getting **steeper** then it means the object is **accelerating** and if it is getting **less steep** it is **decelerating**. This means the distance travelled between equal time intervals changes.

WHAT?
Albert Einstein used relative speed in his theory that gave us the famous equation $E=mc^2$. E = energy, m = mass, c = speed of light.

Relative Speed

It is not a silly question to ask, 'how can you tell you are moving'? On the motorway when the signs tell everyone to travel no more than 60 mph, you may have noticed a car next to you not appearing to move. This is the same as being stopped in traffic and the car next to you really is not moving! We normally think of our speed as how fast we are moving over the ground, but if we compare our speed to another moving object then things are different.

In **A** of the diagram, the black car is approaching the red car at 20 m/s. In **B** the black car is approaching the red car at 40 m/s (20+20). **We add them** because they are moving in opposite directions. In **C** the black car is approaching the red car at 5 m/s (20-15). **We minus them** because they are moving in the same direction. Compared to the ground the black car **always** moves at 20 m/s. It's relative!

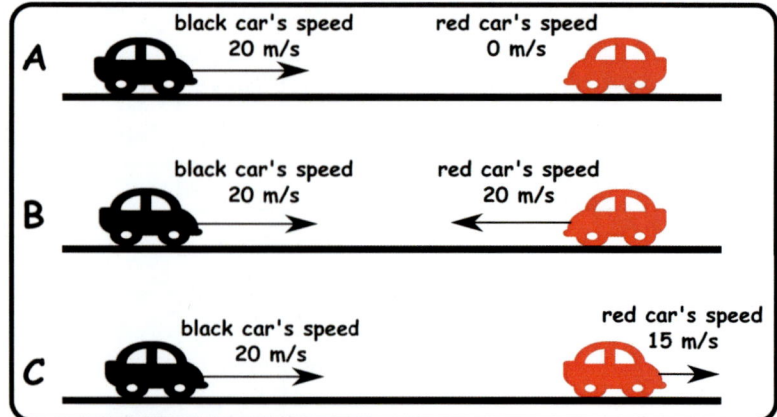

Questions on Relative Speed and more Distance Time Graphs

Comprehension

1. If we plot our distance from a starting point, what can we then do?
2. How long does it take the man to walk 100m?
3. How long did he stop for before running back to the start?
4. What was his walking speed if he walked 100m in 30 seconds?
5. What was his running speed if he ran 100m in 15 seconds?
6. How **don't** most objects move?
7. What usually happens?
8. What does the steepness (gradient) of a distance time graph tell us?
9. If a line is getting steeper what must an object be doing?
10. How does a line show slowing down?
11. What isn't a silly question?
12. When all the cars on a motorway are moving at the same speed what does the car next to you appear to be doing?
13. Is the car in question 12 'really' moving?
14. How do we normally think of our speed?
15. In **B** why are the red car and black car approaching each other at 40 m/s?
16. How do we work out how fast objects are approaching each other if they are moving in the **same** direction?
17. How fast is the black car always moving across the ground?

Additional tasks

1. The table below shows the distance and time data for a boy running to the corner shop to buy an ice cream and walking home as he eats it. Plot the graph below and label the lines with, **running to shop, buying ice cream** and **walking home.**

Distance from the house (m)	0	50	100	150	200	200	200	200	175	150	125	100	75	50	25	0
Time (s)	0	10	20	30	40	50	60	70	80	90	100	110	120	130	140	150

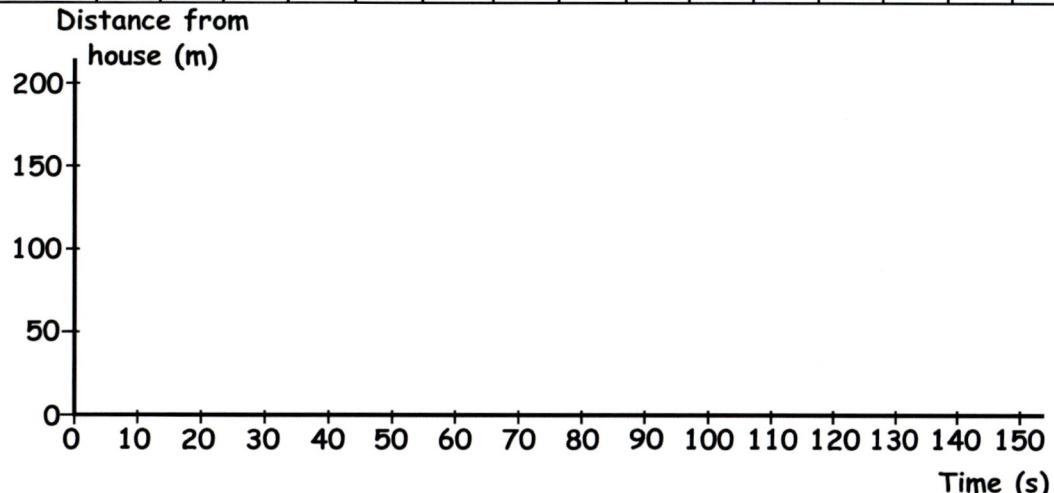

2. Calculate the **walking** and **running** speed for the boy's journey to the shop using the graph. Show your working out.

3 a. Calculate how fast the **black car** is approaching the **red car** in A, B and C opposite.

b. A cheetah is running at 70mph chasing a gazelle for dinner running away at 40mph. How fast is the cheetah approaching the gazelle?

c. A car gets on a dual carriage way the wrong way and has a head on collision with a car coming the other way. One car is travelling at 40mph and the other 60mph. At what speed do they approach each other?

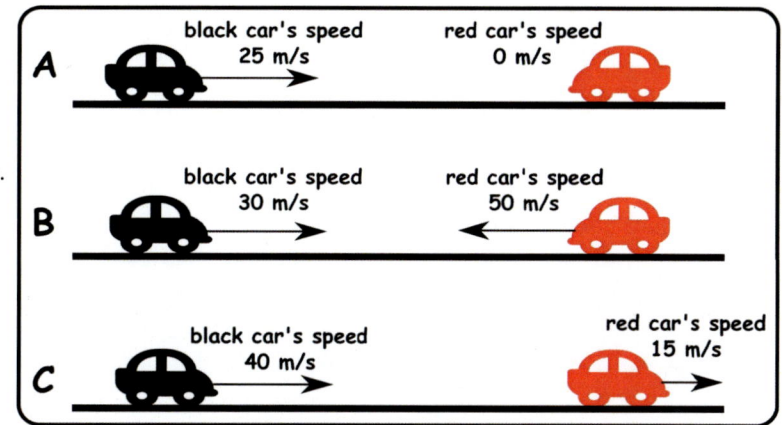

Contact Forces: the Different Kinds

We've all experienced being pushed from behind and have probably noticed that the bigger the **push** the more it affects us in some way. The same is true for holding someone's hand and **pulling** them along. We measure the size of a force in **newtons** and can show forces acting using arrows. All forces are examples of pushes or pulls. In the two examples mentioned above, matter (stuff) actually touch or come in contact. You can't pull someone by the hand without touching them! These are called **contact forces,** when objects must touch each other to have an effect.

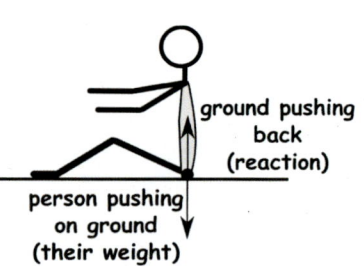

Reaction Force Push as hard as you can against a wall, nothing much happens. However, the wall is definitely pushing back with the same force, the more you push the harder the wall pushes back. The wall 'reacts' to the force from your hand, the **reaction force**. Sit down on your bottom and the ground reacts to the force from your bottom (your weight) by **pushing back** with the **same force**, the **reaction force**.

Upthrust Drop an ice cube into water and it floats. So do huge cruise ships. A force must be pushing upwards against the weight acting downwards. This force is called **upthrust**. Upthrust is the upward force on something placed in a fluid (a fluid is a liquid or gas). If the upthrust is the same as the object's weight, it floats. A helium balloon in air has an upthrust from the air that is **greater** than its weight, so it rises upwards.

Friction Try to move any object along the ground (or any surface) and a force called friction will act in the opposite direction to try and stop it moving. **Friction can be useful**, for example, rubbing your hands together to get warm, climbing a rope or the brakes in a car to stop. Imagine roads made of ice with very little friction, stopping would be scary! **Or not useful**, a rusty bicycle chain can be hard to pedal because there is too much friction. Also skiing wouldn't be much fun if there was too much friction, you wouldn't move! Friction can be reduced with lubrication (oiling). An oiled chain moves much more easily because there is less friction.

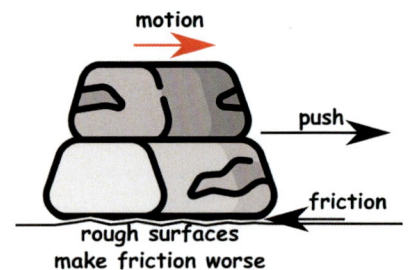

Air Resistance or Drag Like friction, when any object moves through air, a force acts in the opposite direction to try and stop it moving. Air resistance increases with speed. If you've ever put your hand out of the window of a moving car, you will have felt a lot of air resistance. **Air resistance** is **reduced** by making an object **streamlined**, a sports car is streamlined, a van is not. Parachutes create a lot of air resistance using a canopy with a large area, this means a person falls slowly and can land safely.

Tension Whenever we pull anything we create a tension force. This is most obvious in things like hanging a weight on a cable, or pulling on a rope or string. Stretch an elastic band and you can feel the tension force trying to pull your hands back together.

> **WHAT?**
>
> Felix Baumgartner reached 834mph when completing his record breaking skydive from 24 miles above the earth. He was able to reach such speeds because the air is so thin at that height, meaning air resistance is much less. An average skydiver reaches about 120mph.

Questions on Contact Forces

Comprehension

1. What is the size of a force measured in?
2. How are forces shown in diagrams?
3. What do we mean by contact forces?
4. What does a wall do if you push against it?
5. What do we call this force?
6. What is upthrust?
7. How must the upthrust compare to an object's weight for it to float?
8. Why does a helium balloon rise upwards?
9. Try to move an object along the ground and which way does friction always act?
10. Give two examples of friction being useful?
11. Why is a rusty bicycle chain difficult to pedal?
12. What can reduce friction?
13. What is another name for air resistance?
14. What does air resistance increase with?
15. How can air resistance be reduced?
16. How is tension created?

Additional tasks

1. Match and memorise the meanings of the words below.

Reaction force	a force that tries to stop an object moving through air
Upthrust	using oil or grease to reduce friction between surfaces
Friction	a force created when an object is pulled, suspended by a rope, cable or string
Air resistance (drag)	a force that tries to stop an object moving over a surface
Tension	the force pushing back on an object
Lubrication	upward force on an object placed in a fluid

2. A student carries out an experiment to see how the force required to move a plate across a table varies with the amount of food on it. The student uses a force meter to measure how much force is required to pull the plate and measures the weight using a balance that reads in newtons. *Plot the student's results on the graph.*

3a. Connect the points with a line.

Force to slide (N)	1.6	3.2	6.0	8.0	12.0	16.0
Weight (N)	2.0	4.0	7.5	10.0	15.0	20.0

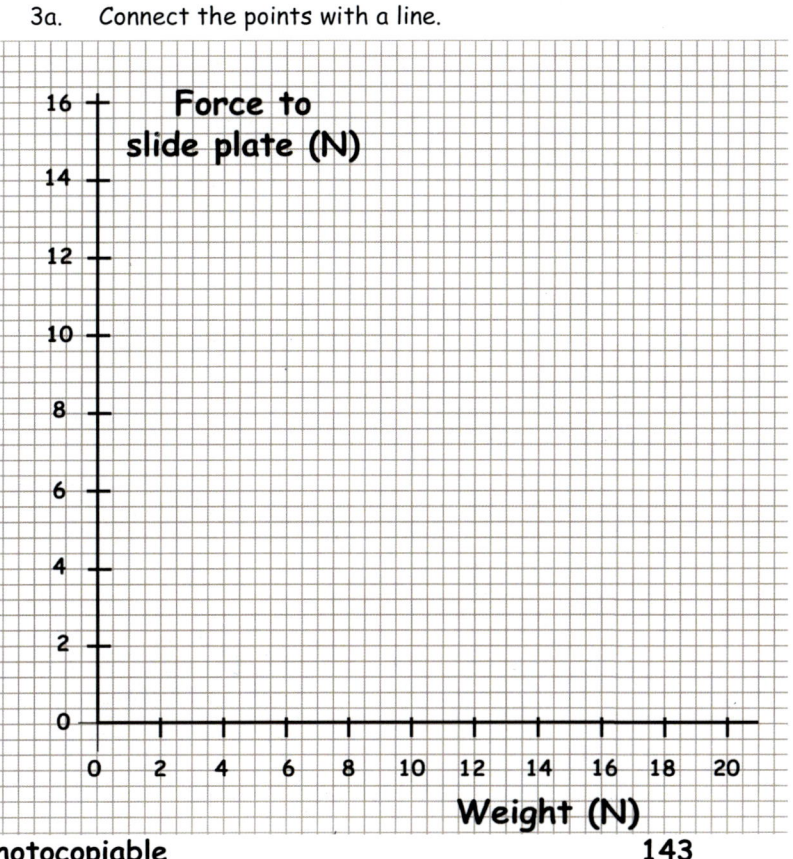

b. The force required to make the plate slide is the same as friction. How does the weight affect friction?

c. The relationship produces a line through the origin (0,0). What do we call this? (see page 152)

d. What could be used to reduce the friction between the plate and table?

e. The experiment was done again on a table that had just been **polished** with **wax** AND is much **smoother**. How might this change the results?

f. Would these new results produce a steeper or shallower line on the graph?

Photocopiable

143

Only write on photocopied version

Non-contact Forces: the Different Kinds

Action at a distance is a way of describing forces that can have effects on objects without touching them. These forces are more simply described as non-contact forces. **Gravity** is the one that we 'feel' all the time and keeps the earth in orbit around the sun. The other two are the **electrostatic force** and the **magnetic force.**

Gravitational Force, Mass and Weight

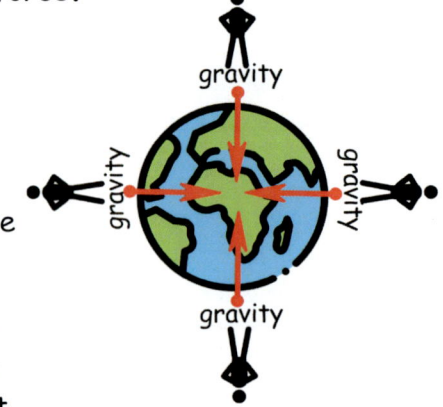

Mass, the amount of stuff (atoms) that you are made from is **measured in kilograms**. This stays the same whether you are on the Moon, Jupiter or Earth.

Everything with mass (made of atoms) attracts everything else with mass. We call this gravity. You are made of atoms and attract the person next to you, but earth's gravity is so big you don't notice it. The more mass an object has the stronger the gravitational pull it exerts. It is always a pull, gravity only attracts. On earth it pulls us towards the centre of the planet.

Earth's gravity has a strength of (called the **gravitational field strength**) 10 newtons per kilogram (N/kg). This means on earth, any object made from enough atoms to have a mass of 1 kg (like a bag of sugar), will have a **weight** of 10 N. An object with a mass of 2 kg has a **weight** of 20 N. An object with a mass of 5 kg has a **weight** of 50 N. To calculate the weight of an object we multiply its mass by the gravitational field strength. *Weight is the pull of gravity acting on an object.* **Its unit is newtons, N.** On the moon gravity has a value of 1.6 N/kg, so on the moon a mass of 1 kg has a weight of 1.6 N, 2 kg has a weight of 3.2 N. On Jupiter, the biggest planet, gravity has a value of 25 N/kg.

Magnetic Force

Not all objects feel the force that **magnetic fields** can exert. Any object that does is said to be magnetic. Objects that always have a magnetic field are called permanent magnets. A 'bar' magnet or fridge magnet is a permanent magnet. The flow of electricity (an electric current) also produces a magnetic field and can be used to make an electromagnetic. These only work when the electricity is turned on. Non-metals are not affected by magnetic fields, the three metals that do feel the magnetic force are, **iron, nickel** and **cobalt**. These metals, like an iron paper clip, become magnets themselves when brought near permanent magnets but don't usually stay magnetic for long afterwards, they are called **induced magnets.**

cotton

Electrostatic Force

This is the force that charged objects feel when they are in **electric fields.** Like magnets have magnetic fields around them, charges have electric fields. If enough charge builds up on an object, the electric field can be strong. The object, like a charged ruler, can exert forces on other charges to attract or repel them. **Opposite** charges **attract, like** charges **repel.** The charged ruler can bend a stream of water because one side of a water molecule is positive and the other side negative. The positive side of the water molecules are attracted to the negative ruler.

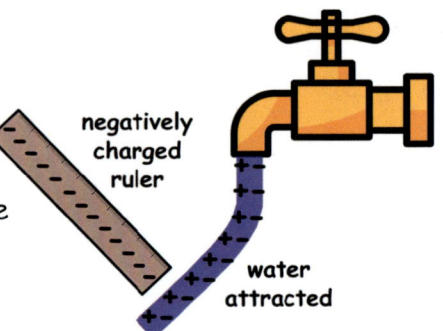

negatively charged ruler

water attracted

> **WHAT?**
>
> If we were able stand on the sun we would weigh 28 times heavier because of the enormous strength of gravity. We'd be crushed!

Questions on Non-contact Forces

Comprehension

1. What is action at a distance a way of describing?

2. How are these forces more simply described?

3. What non-contact force do we feel all the time and what else does it do?

4. What does mass tell us and what's it measured in?

5. What does everything with mass do?

6. Why don't you feel the attraction of the person next to you?

7. Can gravity repel?

8. What size is the gravitational field strength on earth?

9. What is weight?

10. An object that feels the force of a magnetic field is said to be?

11. Permanent magnets always have a magnetic field, what else produces a magnetic field?

12. What are the three magnetic metals?

13. What do charges have around them?

14. Why can a charged ruler bend a stream of water?

Additional tasks

1. Draw a bar chart for the weight of a 1kg bag of sugar on the eight planets using the data below.

Planet	Mercury	Venus	Earth	Mars	Jupiter	Saturn	Uranus	Neptune
Strength of gravity (N/kg)	3.7	8.9	10.0	3.7	25	10.5	9.0	11.7
Mass of sugar (kg)	1.0	1.0	1.0	1.0	1.0	1.0	1.0	1.0
Weight of sugar (N)	3.7	8.9	10.0	3.7	25	10.5	9.0	11.7

Weight of sugar (N)

1 2 3 4 5 6 7 8 9 10 11 12 13 14 15 16 17 18 19 20 21 22 23 24 25

Name
of
planet

2. Write down **true** or **false** in brackets next to the following statements.

Mass is a force (_____)   Gravity repels objects with mass (_____)

The unit of weight is the newton (_____)   Mass is usually measured in stones (_____)

You weigh the same on earth as you do on the moon (_____)   A feather has no weight (_____)

Gravitational field strength is measured in newtons (_____)

On Jupiter you'd be much heavier (_____)

A kilogram mass has the same mass anywhere (_____)   Gravity only attracts (_____)

Gravity is the attraction between masses (_____)   Mass is not a force (_____)

Mass tells us how many atoms we are made from (_____)

There is no gravity on the moon (_____)   Mass is measured in kilograms (_____)

3. One boy said ' *there is no gravity in space because I've seen Tim Peake floating in the space station'*. A girl says '*there must be gravity keeping the space station moving around the earth, like the earth moves around the sun'*. Write a sentence or two saying who you think is correct and why. Ask your teacher who is correct afterwards!

Balanced Forces

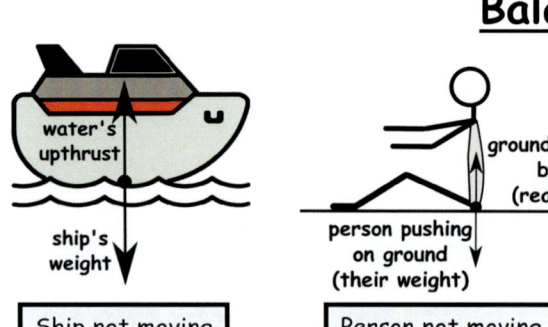

Ship not moving

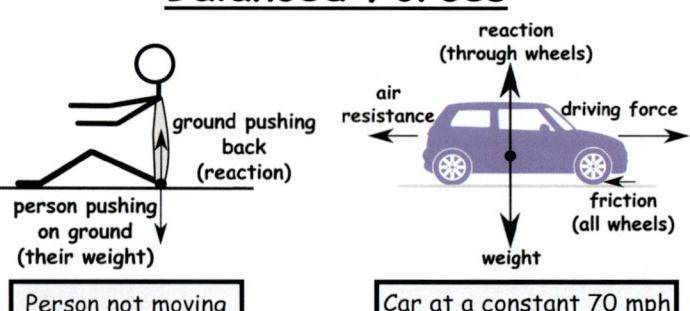

Person not moving

Car at a constant 70 mph

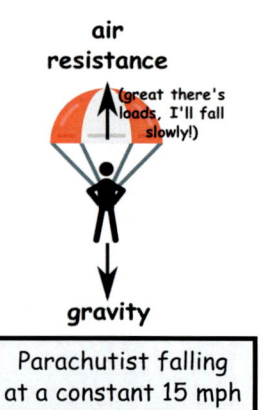

Parachutist falling at a constant 15 mph

In diagrams we use arrows to show the size and direction of the force. When an object has balanced forces acting on it, it means that the size of the force acting **up** is **equal** to the size of the force acting **down**. Also the size of the force acting to the **left** is **equal** to the size of the force acting to the **right**. The **overall force is zero** because we take the forces away from each other if they act in opposite directions. If the forces act in the same direction then we add them. The figure below shows the force diagrams from above with numbers. The arrows are the forces and the black circle the object.

Force diagrams with numbers Object ● Force ⟶

Ship	Person	Car	Parachutist
200,000N	800N	10,000N	800N
200,000N	800N	4,500N 500N 5,000N 10,000N	800N

Overall force

Ship; 200,000 (up) - 200,000 (down) = **0** N
Person; 800 (up) - 800 (down) = **0** N
Car; 10,000 (up) - 10,000 (down) = **0** N
4500 + 500 (left) - 5000 (right) = **0** N
Parachutist; 800 (up) - 800 (down) = **0** N

What happens?

The diagrams above tell us that if the forces acting on an object are balanced, it is either not moving (stationary) or moving at a constant speed. This is called **Newton's first law** named after Sir Isaac Newton. In a car at a constant 70 mph, the **driving force** from the engine is the **same size** as the **air resistance** and **friction** added together. This means the overall force is zero so the car continues to move at 70 mph without slowing down or speeding up. Not long after skydivers open their parachutes, they will fall towards earth at

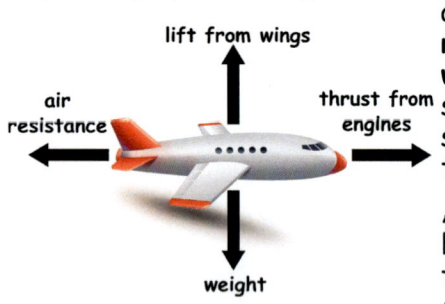

Aeroplane at a constant speed

a constant speed of about 15 mph. This is because the **air resistance** caused by the parachute is the **same size** as their **weight**, there is no overall force and they move at constant speed. The speed they are moving at (15 mph) is about the same speed you would hit the ground with if you jumped from the crossbar of a set of football goal posts.

An aeroplane spends most of its time in flight with the forces balanced since the lift from the wings balances weight and the thrust from the engine is balanced by air resistance, so you fly at a nice steady speed.

Helium balloons experience upthrust from the air. They can be made to 'float' when the weight acting down is the same as the upthrust acting up. Next time you have the chance to play with one try changing the weight with small pieces of Blu tack and see if you can get it to float. Happy birthday!

Helium balloons can be made to float stationary

WHAT?

Sir Isaac Newton came up with his three 'laws of motion' in 1687. They can be used to explain planetary motion or why a car moves at a constant speed.

Questions on Balanced Forces

Comprehension

1. What do the arrows in the diagrams show us?
2. When an object has balanced forces acting on it what does this mean about the up and down and left and right forces?
3. What does this mean for the overall force on the object?
4. If forces are in the opposite direction what do we do with them?
5. If forces are in the same direction what do we do with them?
6. Why is the force to the left 5000N on the car?
7. What happens if the forces on an object are balanced?
8. Whose first law is this?
9. What happens to skydivers not long after opening their parachute?
10. Why is this?
11. Which forces are balanced for an aeroplane at constant speed?
12. Why do helium balloons experience upthrust?

Additional tasks

1. Draw arrows to show the balanced forces on the objects below. The helicopter, jet ski and a bike are **all at a constant speed**. All the rest are **stationary**. Labels needed will be; AIR RESISTANCE, LIFT, WEIGHT, WATER RESISTANCE, THRUST FROM ENGINE, PEDALLING FORCE, FRICTION, REACTION FORCE, UPTHRUST

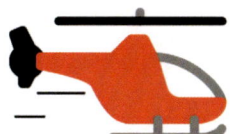

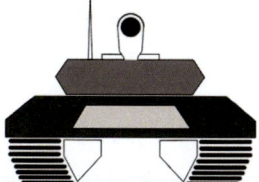

2. Complete the gap fill on balanced forces. Choose from the words below;

air resistance, constant, overall, balanced, parachutist, weight, first, ground, equals, desk, upthrust, laptop, stationary

If the forces acting on an object are _____ it will either be moving at a _____ speed or _____. This is Newton's _____ law. A raindrop and a _____ fall at constant speed because _____ _____ is equal to their _____. There is no _____ force acting. A stationary bus has a reaction from the _____ that is equal to its weight. Float on your back and the _____ from the water _____ the weight due to gravity pulling you down. The reaction from the _____ balances the weight of your stationary _____ when doing school work.

3. Write down **balanced** or **unbalanced** in brackets next to the following examples.

Jumping in the air (_____) A stationary cloud in the sky (_____)
A spider sitting in its web (_____) Bouncing on a trampoline (_____)
Swinging on a swing (_____) Releasing a stretched catapult (_____)
A Speck of dust falling towards the ground (_____)
Lying in bed (_____) Starting to sledge down a hill (_____)

Unbalanced Forces (Newton's 2nd Law)

The motion of an object does not change if the forces acting on it are balanced. The object remains stationary or moving at a constant speed. There is no overall force.

However, if the forces are **unbalanced** then there **is** a change in motion and there **is** an overall force acting. This force is called a **resultant force** and the two main things that a resultant force will do to an object are, speed it up, or slow it down. Examples and diagrams make this easier to see.

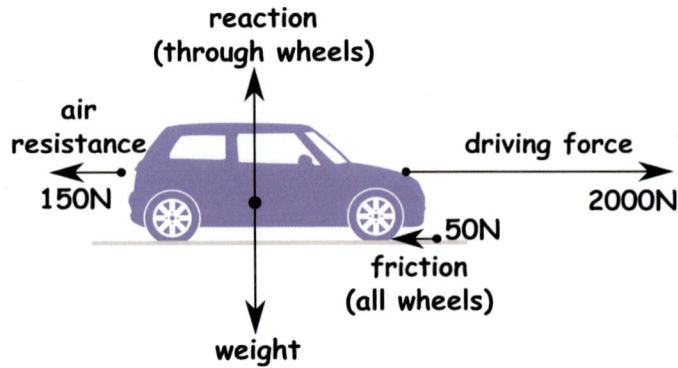

A Car A car will speed up (accelerate) if the forward driving force is greater than the 'backwards' forces (friction and air resistance). The diagram shows the up and down forces are balanced but the driving force is bigger than friction and air resistance added together. The resultant force is, **2000-(150+50)=1800N**. This force will make the car accelerate forwards. The bigger the resultant force the quicker the car accelerates. It can't accelerate forever though, as the car speeds up, air resistance increases and the forces become balanced again and a new constant speed is reached.

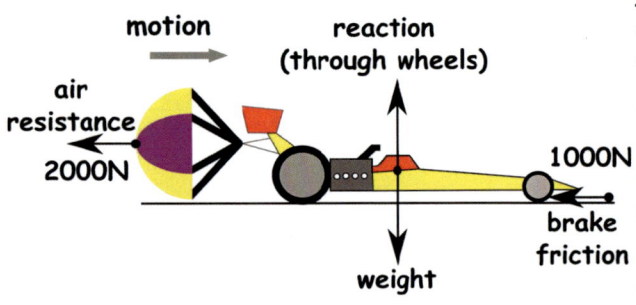

Drag Car Once a drag car has finished accelerating it must slow down. The driver takes their foot off the accelerator, there is no driving force anymore. A parachute is released and the brakes put on. The large air resistance plus braking friction **(1000+2000=3000N)**, produces a resultant force of **3000N** in the **opposite** direction to motion. This causes the drag car to slow down (decelerate) and eventually stop.

Forces Come in Pairs (Newton's 3rd Law)

If we lean against a wall it definitely pushes back (reacts). If we sit on the floor it pushes back (reacts) against our weight. If one object pushes (or pulls) on another there is always an equal reaction back, this is Newton's 3rd law. When a ball is kicked the **boot pushes on the ball** and the ball reacts by **pushing back on the boot**. We are only interested in the ball though, so only have to think about four forces, the ones acting **on the ball**. Weight and reaction (up and down) balance. We can see that from the kick there is a resultant force of **(10-2=8N) 8N**, this will make the ball accelerate whilst the boot is pushing the ball.

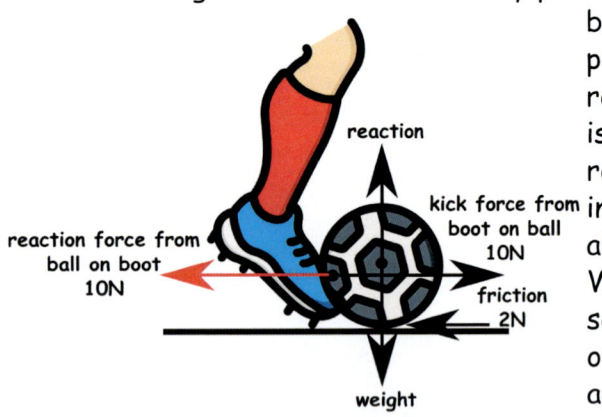

WHAT?
Just like a ball, cliff divers speed up because of the resultant force of gravity, after falling 26 metres they hit the water at over 50mph.

Confusion alert

When we drop a ball, earth pulls the ball downwards (gravity) but the **ball also pulls back on the earth**. That is the force pair or reaction in this example. The tiny force on the earth has no effect but the force on the ball causes it to accelerate downwards. We only want to know what happens to the ball so only consider the forces acting on it.

Questions on Unbalanced Forces

Comprehension

1. What happens to the motion of an object if the forces are balanced? *it does not change* -
2. What happens if the forces are unbalanced?
3. What is the name of the overall force acting on an object?
4. What are the two main things that an object with a resultant force will do?
5. What does accelerate mean?
6. Which are the unbalanced forces in the diagram of the car?
7. Why can't the car accelerate forever?
8. When the driver of the drag car takes their foot off the accelerator, what disappears?
9. What produces the resultant force on the drag car?
10. Which direction does the resultant force act?
11. What does this do to the drag car?
12. What does Newton's 3rd law tell us?
13. Why do we only think about four forces when the ball is being kicked?
14. Complete the sentence.
   After the ball has been kicked and rolls along the ground, the r_ _ _ _ _ _ _ _ force from f_ _ _ _ _ _ _ , s _ _ _ _ it down to a stop.
15. What does the dropped ball do to the earth?

Additional tasks

1. Calculate the resultant force from the diagrams below by taking away the up and down and left and right forces. Say which direction the resultant force is acting.

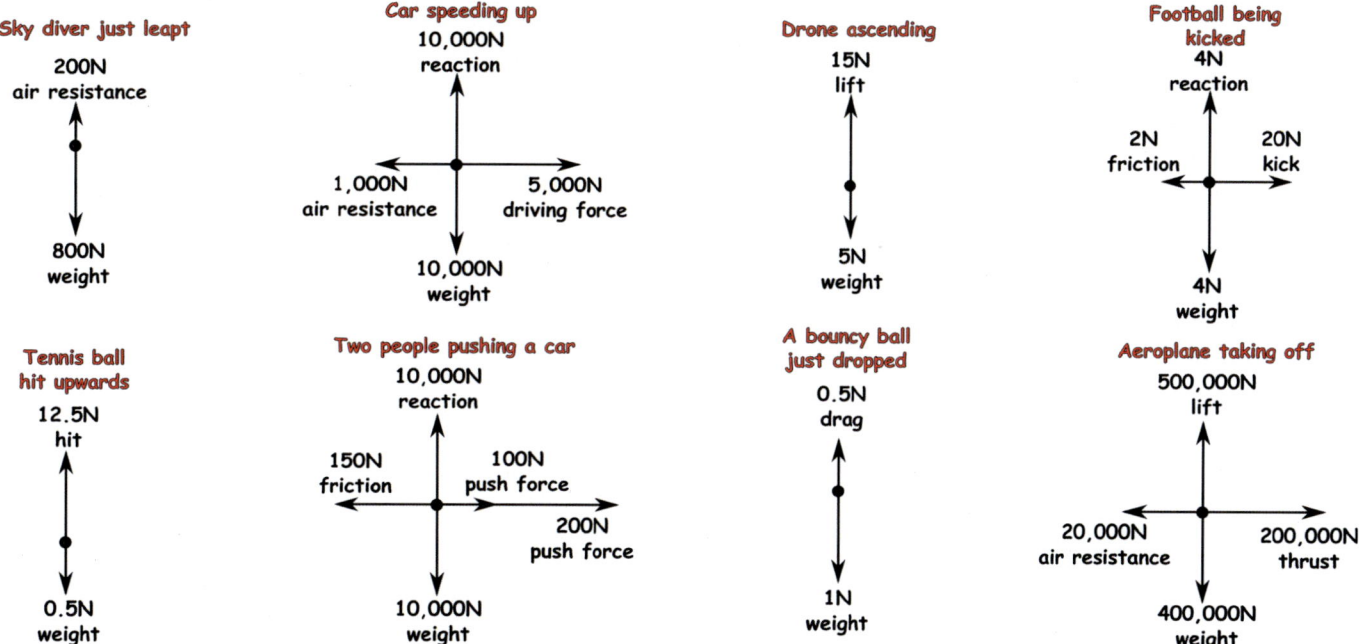

Sky diver just leapt
200N air resistance
800N weight

Car speeding up
10,000N reaction
1,000N air resistance
5,000N driving force
10,000N weight

Drone ascending
15N lift
5N weight

Football being kicked
4N reaction
2N friction
20N kick
4N weight

Tennis ball hit upwards
12.5N hit
0.5N weight

Two people pushing a car
10,000N reaction
150N friction
100N push force
200N push force
10,000N weight

A bouncy ball just dropped
0.5N drag
1N weight

Aeroplane taking off
500,000N lift
20,000N air resistance
200,000N thrust
400,000N weight

2. Complete the sentences about resultant forces below. Choose from the words in bold.
   speeds up, lift, weight, air resistance, driving force, air resistance, weight, foot, opposite, slows, resultant force, opposite, decelerate

a. During take off, a plane _____ ___ until the _____ force from the **wings** is bigger than the _____.
b. Foot to the floor, a car will continue to speed up until the ____ _____ and friction is equal to the _____ _____ from the engine.
c. Drop a cup cake and it speeds up until the ____ _____ is equal to its _____.
d. Kick a ball and it only speeds up whilst your _____ is pushing it.
e. A Resultant force in the _____ direction to motion _____ objects down.
f. Brakes on a bike produce a _____ _____ in the _____ direction to motion to _____ (slow down) the bike.

3. Add force arrows to the parachutist, 1000N for weight (gravity) and 3000N for air resistance.
   a. What will happen to the parachutist and why?

Moments

force

Ever tried opening a door by pushing near to the hinges? You can normally do it but you have to push harder. You are still opening the same door by the same amount so it requires the same amount of energy. Pushing near the hinges requires a larger force for a smaller distance. Pushing on the handle requires a smaller force for a greater distance. The door 'turns' as it is opened because of the force acting at a right angle to the pivot (the centre point of rotation, hinges). The turning effect of a force is called the **moment of a force** and depends on the size of the force and the distance from the pivot. When

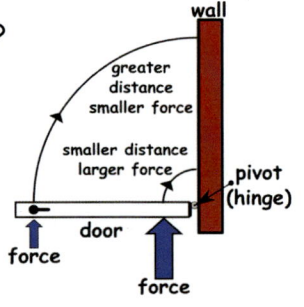

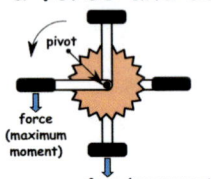

| moment of a force = force × distance from pivot |
| (Nm)   =   (N)   (m) |

pedalling a bike, there is a maximum turning effect when the pedals are horizontal and zero at the bottom when the force acts 'in line' with the pivot. **Increasing the distance** from the **pivot** to produce a **bigger turning effect** has many applications. Car 'wheel braces' are long to undo tight wheel nuts, a short brace wouldn't produce enough turning force. **Nail scissors** have long handles to produce a large turning force to cut your nails. **Crow bars** are long for a large turning force to remove nails or force open doors.

The Principle of Moments

This is the scientific name for **balanced** moments. It means that the **clockwise moments are equal to the anticlockwise moments.** In seesaw **diagram A,** both people have a weight of 500N and are 2m from the pivot so the moments are balanced at **2 × 500 = 1,000Nm** both sides. Clockwise and anticlockwise moments are equal. If the person on the left moved closer to the pivot the seesaw would tip down on the right. The moments are now unbalanced.

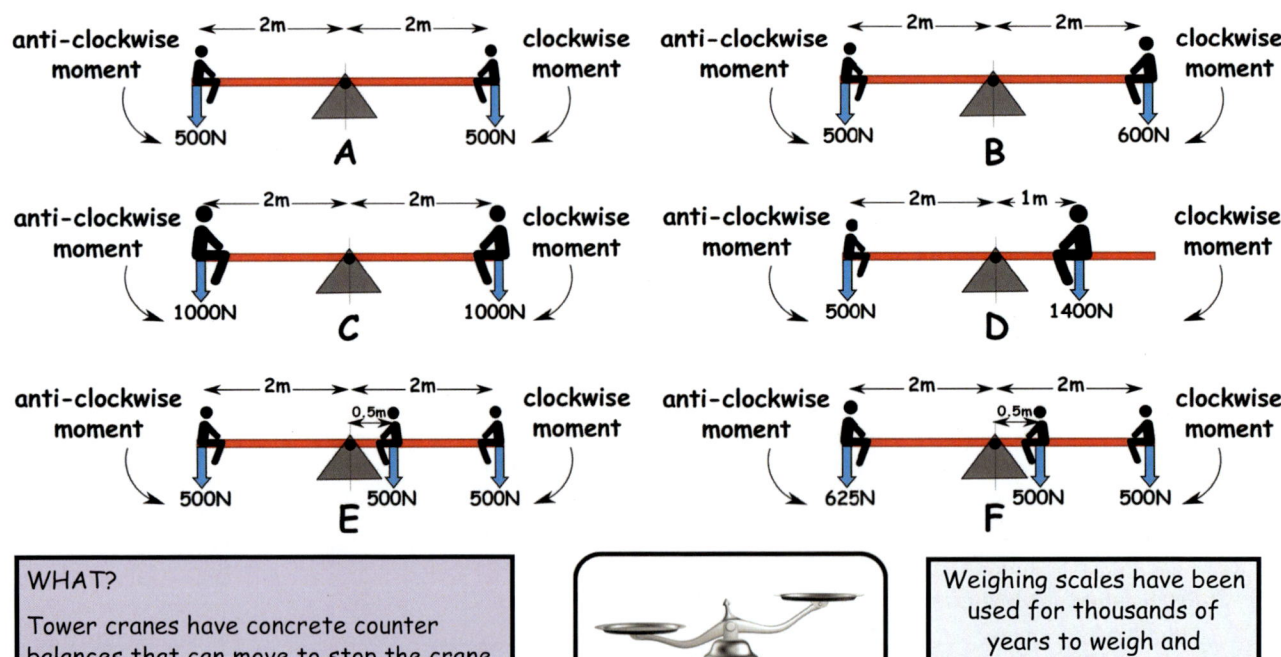

| WHAT? |
| Tower cranes have concrete counter balances that can move to stop the crane becoming unbalanced and toppling over. |

| Weighing scales have been used for thousands of years to weigh and compare objects of value |

0.5 × 10,000 = 5,000Nm   5 × 1,000 = 5,000Nm

not to scale

pivot

0.5m   5m

Weight 10,000 N   Weight 1,000 N

The pivot doesn't have to be in the middle. The diagram of the car opposite shows that it is possible with a long enough bar to use a person's weight to balance a small car. Circus performers use a bouncer to launch a tumbler into the air from a seesaw. Definitely unbalanced!

150

Questions on Moments

Comprehension

1.	What do you have to do if you want to open the door by pushing near to the hinges?	5.	Why wouldn't a shorter wheel brace undo tight wheel nuts?
2.	Pushing on the handle requires a smaller force but greater what?	6.	Why do nail scissors have a long handle?
3.	What is the turning effect of a force called?	7.	What is the scientific name for balanced moments?
4.	How do you calculate the moment of a force?	8.	What does it mean?

Additional tasks

1. Write down what the moment of the force is (force x distance from pivot) for the wheel braces below, remember the units, Nm, newton metres.

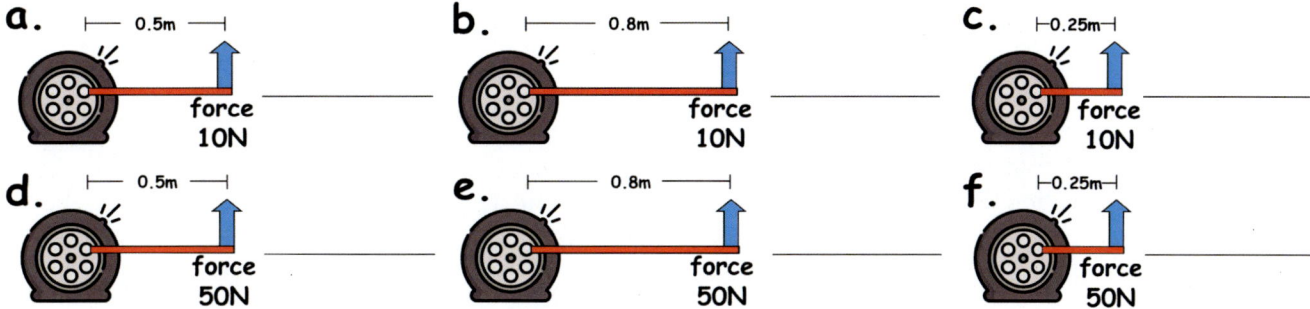

a. 0.5m force 10N

b. 0.8m force 10N

c. 0.25m force 10N

d. 0.5m force 50N

e. 0.8m force 50N

f. 0.25m force 50N

2. Write out what the clockwise and anticlockwise moments are for seesaws A-F and say if they are balanced or unbalanced.

A. anticlockwise = _____ balanced/unbalanced?

   clockwise = _____ _____

B. anticlockwise = _____ balanced/unbalanced?

   clockwise = _____ _____

C. anticlockwise = _____ balanced/unbalanced?

   clockwise = _____ _____

D. anticlockwise = _____ balanced/unbalanced?

   clockwise = _____ _____

E. anticlockwise = _____ balanced/unbalanced?

   clockwise = _____ _____

F. anticlockwise = _____ balanced/unbalanced?

   clockwise = _____ _____

3. The weight of a metre ruler can create an unbalancing moment when it is **not** pivoted in the middle. The situation can be balanced by adding weights on the left of the pivot to balance the ruler's weight.

a. Calculate the **?** weight needed to balance rulers 1 to 6. Use the example to help.

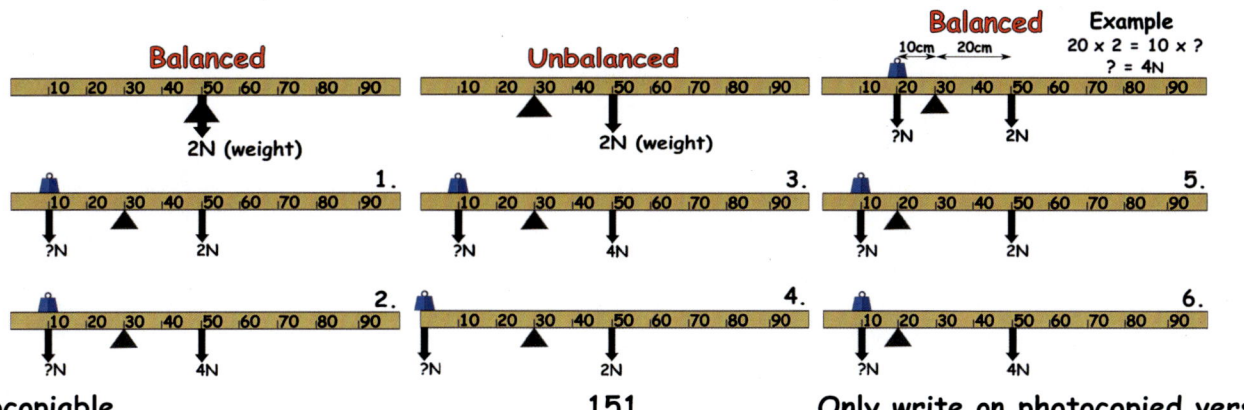

Balanced — 2N (weight)

Unbalanced — 2N (weight)

Balanced — Example
10cm 20cm
20 x 2 = 10 x ?
? = 4N
?N 2N

1. ?N 2N

3. ?N 4N

5. ?N 2N

2. ?N 4N

4. ?N 2N

6. ?N 4N

Hooke's Law

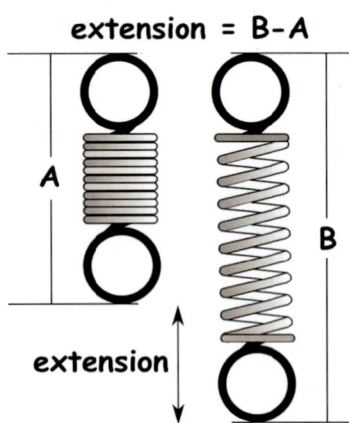

extension = B-A

extension

Hooke's law tells us something you may have already noticed. When you stretch something like an elastic band, the more you stretch it the harder it gets. The table shows a set of results for an elastic band being stretched that is obeying Hooke's law. You can see that as the force increases by 1 N each time the length increases by 4 cm. Or we can say that doubling the force doubles the extension, trebling the force trebles the extension and so on. This relationship (connection) between two quantities is called being **directly proportional**. When an object stretches like this we say it is obeying Hooke's Law. Plotting results that are directly proportional on a graph gives a straight line through the origin (0,0).

Stretching force (N)	Increase in length / extension (cm)
1	4
2	8
3	12
4	16
5	20

Spring Balance or Force Meter

A spring balance or force meter uses Hooke's law. A weight attached to the end of the force meter causes a spring to stretch. The greater the weight added the more the spring stretches. The force meter has a scale on the front. When you pick up an object you can read off the size of the force, this is equal to the weight of the object you are lifting. You can also pull objects with a force meter to see how much force is needed to make them move, this is great for investigating friction.

Force (N)

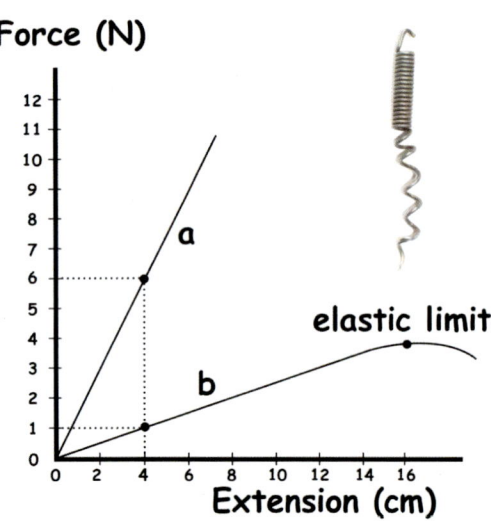

Extension (cm)

elastic limit

a

b

Elasticity and Stiffness

An object like an elastic band, is very elastic, it can stretch a long way and when we remove the stretching force it returns to its original length. We call this **elastic behaviour**. You can also squash (compress) springs like those in your bed mattress and they return to their original length when the force is removed, just like stretching objects. Most objects will stretch and then return to their original length after removing the force even if just a tiny bit. We see elastic behaviour every where; your bed mattress, settee, car seats, your trainers, trampolines …. There is a limit though, if an object is stretched too much it won't return to its original

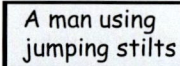
Force Meter

length after the force is removed. This is called the **elastic limit** (see spring above left). Stretch an object too far and it stays permanently longer, we call this **plastic behaviour**. Keep stretching and it will break. Blu tack quickly goes past its elastic limit and shows plastic behaviour by staying stretched when you let go. It also breaks if you keep stretching it.

The graph shows two springs being stretched **a** and **b**, the graph for spring 'a' is steeper, this is because it is **stiffer**. Spring 'a' requires 6N to cause an extension of 4cm, spring 'b' only requires 1N. Stiffness is how difficult it is to stretch an object, by plotting graphs for different objects we can compare them.

A man using jumping stilts

> **WHAT?**
>
> Your skin becomes less elastic as you get older. Ask an older person to pull up some skin on the back of their hand and compare how long it takes to go back to its original length with a young person's, it's very different!

Questions on Hooke's Law

Comprehension

1. What happens the more you stretch an elastic band?

2. When you double or treble one quantity and the related quantity doubles or trebles, what is this called? (like force and extension)

3. If you plot a graph of this sort of relationship what does it look like?

4. What is another name for a spring balance?

5. Inside a force meter, what is it that stretches?

6. If you pick up an object with a force meter, what will the size of the force tell you?

7. If you pull objects along with a force meter, what can you investigate?

8. What do we call it when an object goes back to its original length when the force is removed?

9. What will most objects do?

10. Give two examples of where we see elastic behaviour?

11. What do we mean by the elastic limit?

12. If an object stays permanently stretched after the force is removed what do we call this?

13. Why is the graph for spring 'a' steeper?

14. What does stiffness mean?

Additional tasks

1. Plot the results opposite on the graph below, draw a straight line and predict what extension 2.5 N and 4.5 N will produce by drawing across to your line and down.

2. Look at the numbers in the tables below and decide if the 'Y' values are **directly proportional** to the 'X' values for **A,B,C** and **D**.

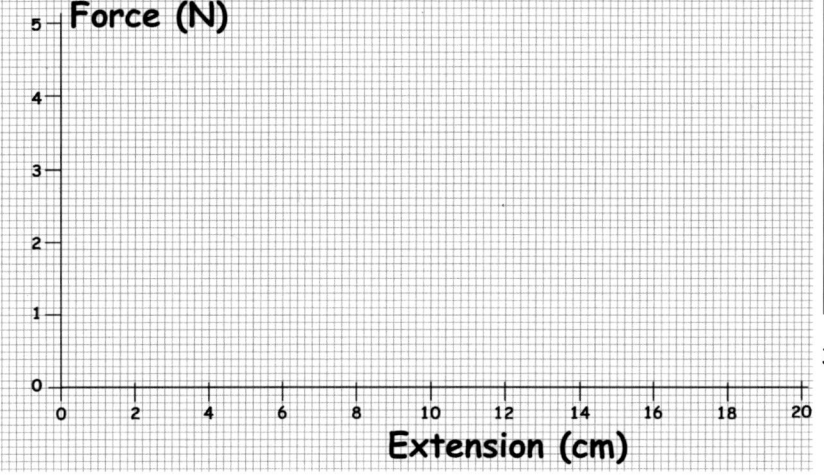

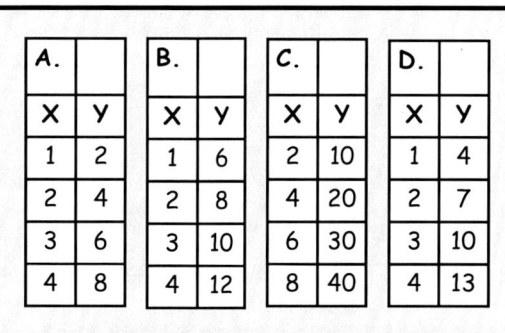

A.		B.		C.		D.	
X	Y	X	Y	X	Y	X	Y
1	2	1	6	2	10	1	4
2	4	2	8	4	20	2	7
3	6	3	10	6	30	3	10
4	8	4	12	8	40	4	13

3. Use the force and extension values **in the table below the graphs** to work out which line **A** to **F** matches the numbers in the table.

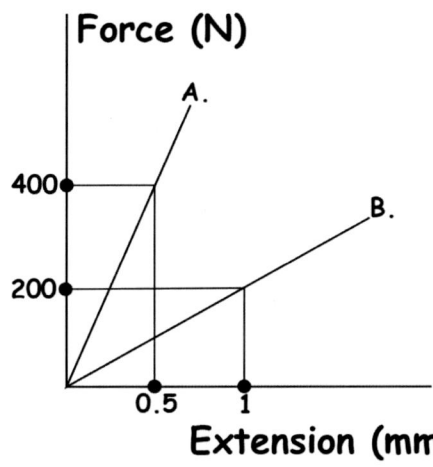

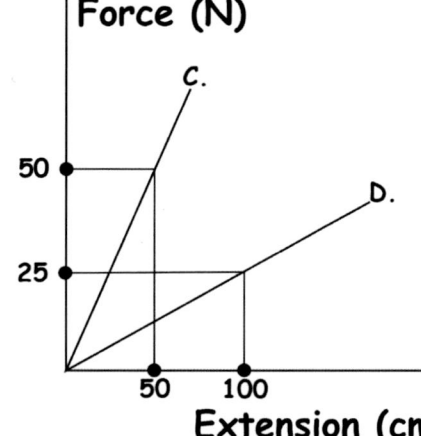

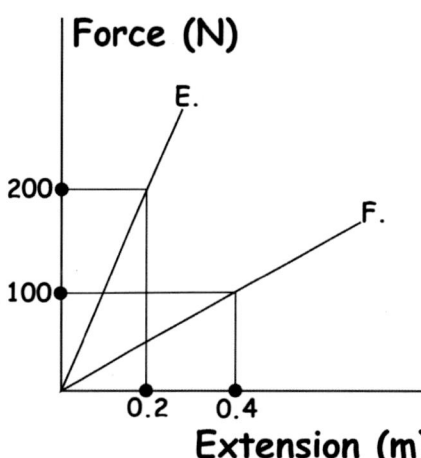

Line?						
Force	400N	25N	12.5N	100N	800N	150N
Extension	2mm	25cm	50cm	0.125mm	0.8m	0.6m

153

Gas Pressure

If you close your mouth tightly and slowly push air from your lungs into your mouth space, you will notice your cheeks move outwards. You can feel your cheeks stretch as the pressure starts to rise inside your mouth as the air pushes outwards. Open your mouth and you can feel the air rush out. This is because the air pressure inside your mouth is greater than the air pressure outside, so air is forced out until the pressure inside and outside are the same.

Pressure = $\dfrac{\text{Force (N)}}{\text{Area (m}^2)}$	$P = F \div A$ (N/m^2)

What's the Cause? Force Over Area

Like any pressure, gas pressure is due to forces. The force comes from the particles (air in this case) hitting the inside of the container (your cheeks) and exerting a force. The gas

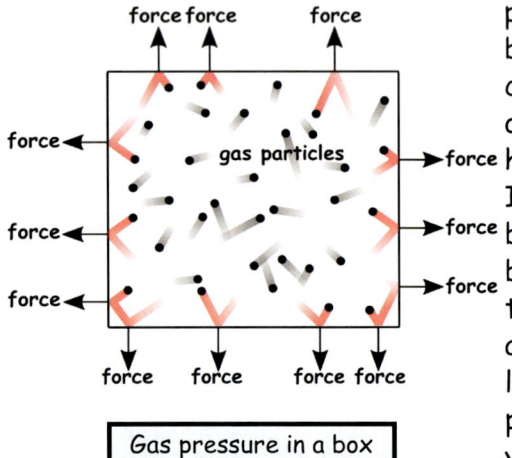

Gas pressure in a box

particles move around randomly inside a container bumping into each other and bumping into the walls of the container. The force they exert on the 'walls' is spread over an area. Pressure is defined as force ÷ area, so we have a pressure. The **pressure acts in all directions**. Imagine being in the box, your front, your back, your sides, the top of your head will all be hit by particles leading to an **equal** pressure all over your body.

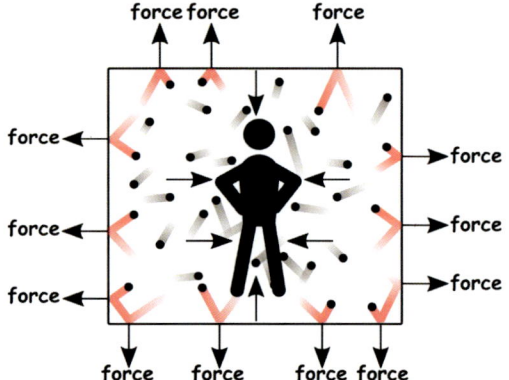

Increasing Pressure

There are three ways in which the pressure of a gas can be increased and they are easy to understand when we know that it is the particles colliding with the walls that causes the pressure.

All three ways involve increasing the force from the particles colliding with the walls.

Pushing air into a tyre increases the pressure

1. Pushing more gas particles into the same space. This is what we did at the beginning with our cheeks, and is what happens when you pump a tyre up. More particles in the same space means the gas particles collide with the walls more often leading to a greater force and pressure.

2. Heat the gas up. This makes all the particles move faster, so they bump into the walls more often and with a greater force. This increases the pressure.

3. Reduce the amount of space (volume) for the gas particles to move. This means the particles collide with the walls more often producing a greater force and increasing the pressure.

> **WHAT?**
>
> A drinking straw works when you use your mouth to create a lower air pressure in the straw. Like when you put your hand into a tub of playdough, it moves up. The pressure on top of the surrounding water pushes the water in the straw upwards because the air pressure above **it** is smaller, just like the playdough when you put your hand into the tub.

Compressing a gas

High temperature particles move faster

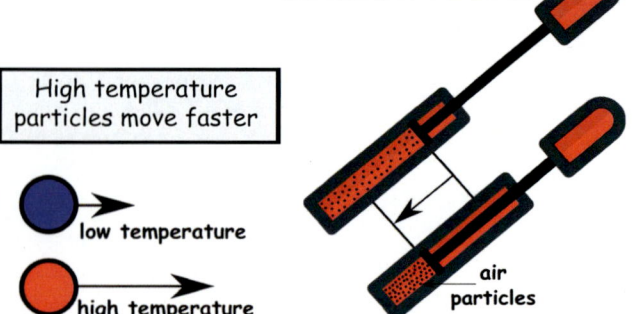

low temperature

high temperature

air particles

Questions on Gas Pressure

Comprehension

1. What happens if you push air from your lungs into your mouth space? *your cheeks move outwards -*

2. What happens to the pressure inside your mouth?

3. Why does the air rush out when you open your mouth?

4. When does the air stop rushing out?

5. Where does the force come from for gas pressure?

6. In what way do the gas particles move around inside a container?

7. How is pressure defined?

8. Which direction does gas pressure act?

9. How many ways are there to increase the pressure of a gas?

10. What makes them easy to understand?

11. What happens when you pump up a tyre?

12. What does this do to how often the collisions occur?

13. What does heating the gas up do to the particles?

14. What's another way of saying reduce the space for the particles?

Additional tasks

1. Label the boxes containing particles with the words **low** and **high**, then write the following statements next to the correct box. *Particles move fast, particles collide with the walls less often, particles move slow, particles collide with the walls more often, particles exert less force, particles exert more force*

_ _ _ _ temperature
_ _ _ pressure

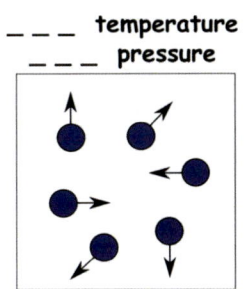

Statements

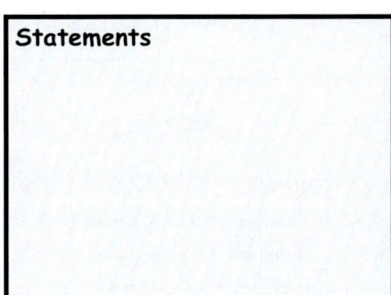

_ _ _ _ temperature
_ _ _ _ pressure

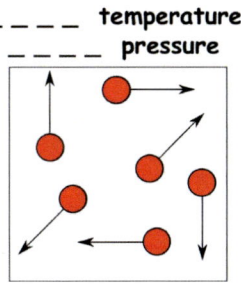

Statements

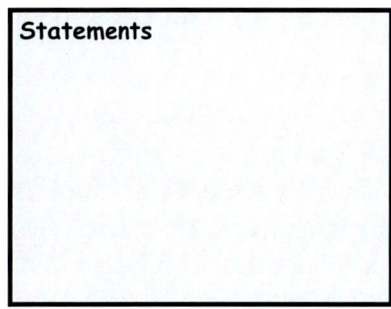

2. Compare 'boxes' **A.** and **B.** below and explain which you think has the highest pressure and why?
Compare 'boxes' **C.** and **D.** and explain which you think has the highest pressure and why?

A. Less particles

B. More particles

Same temperature

C. More space

D. Less space

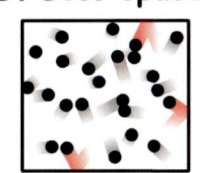

Same temperature and same number of particles

3. Plot the pressure and volume values for compressing a gas like in the pump shown opposite. Draw a smooth line through the points. Explain what the graph shows.

Pressure	Volume (cm^3)
1	80
1.33	60
2	40
4	20

Pressure (times greater than 'normal' air pressure)

4
3.5
3
2.5
2
1.5
1
0.5
0

Volume (cm^3)

0 10 20 30 40 50 60 70 80

Atmospheric Pressure

It can be confusing talking about atmospheric pressure because we don't normally feel it. Atmospheric or air pressure is similar to being in bed! If more covers are placed on top of you, you feel their weight. This force is spread over the area of your body so you feel the pressure this creates. The layers of air above us are miles high and lead to a huge pressure. If we think of an area 1 m² (about 16 A4 sheets of paper) the weight of air above pushing down on this area is 100,000 N. Atmospheric pressure is 100,000 newtons per m² (N/m²). This is about the weight of 10 small cars piled on top of our 16 A4 sheets. We don't 'normally' notice this huge pressure from the air because inside our bodies we have the **same pressure** pushing **outwards** as the air pressure pushing **inwards**.

Diagram labels: layers of air 10 miles high (16,000m); Atmospheric pressure; weight of 1m² 10 mile high air column is 100,000N; EARTH; air particles; area 1m²

Pressure and Height

Look carefully at the diagram (left) and you can see that there are less air particles the higher you go, the air is thinner. This means there is less oxygen to breathe and it is why high altitude climbers wear breathing apparatus. It also means that the air pressure is lower, there are less particles to collide with so the force they exert is smaller. The air pressure at the top of Mount Everest, 8848m above sea level, is only one third of what it is at sea level.

Pressure Difference: the Collapsing Can

When pressure **differences** are created we do see the effects of the large forces involved in atmospheric pressure. Two 'famous' examples of this are the collapsing can and the Magdeburg hemispheres.

A metal can is heated with a little water in the bottom and the lid off. The can fills with steam but the pressure doesn't rise because the lid is off.

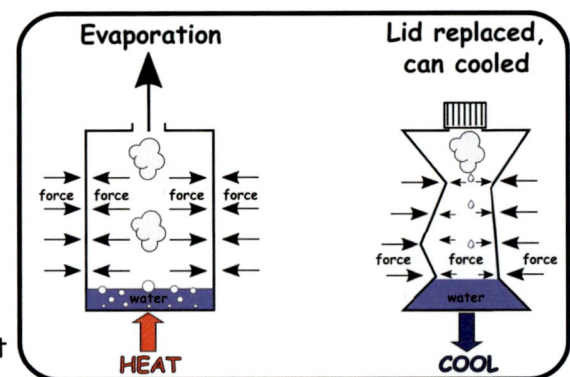

Pressure in and out are the same. The lid is replaced and the can cooled. All the steam that **was pushing outwards** condenses back to water, the force from the steam is now gone and air can't enter the can because the lid is on. The force from the air pushing inwards is now much bigger than the force pushing outwards, so the can is crushed (collapses).

Magdeburg Hemispheres

Two hollow (empty) hemispheres are put together and the air is pumped out of the hollow space inside. A tap is then closed so no air can get back in. Now there is no push from any air inside the sphere to balance the push from the atmosphere outside. This produces a huge force pushing the two halves together and makes it almost impossible to pull them apart. Magdeburg used 16 horses to try and pull them apart but still couldn't. That's a lot of force from the air!

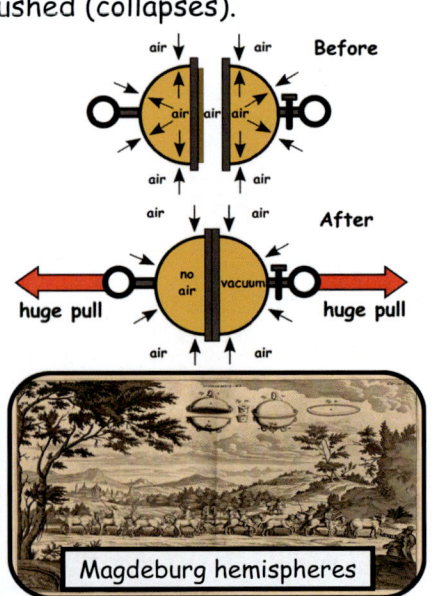

Magdeburg hemispheres

WHAT?

At the altitude (height) of Mount Everest the lower pressure means that water boils at about 70°C not 100°C. The Magdeburg hemispheres were pushed together by a force of over 20,000 N by atmospheric pressure, about the weight of two cars. Vacuums don't suck! Air is **pushed** in due to a pressure difference created by the vacuum's fan.

Questions on Atmospheric Pressure

Comprehension

1. Why can it be confusing to talk about atmospheric pressure?

2. Why is atmospheric pressure similar to being in bed?

3. How high are the layers of air above us?

4. What is the weight of air that is pushing down on $1m^2$?

5. What is this weight about the same as?

6. Why don't we normally feel the huge atmospheric pressure of 100,000 N/m^2?

7. What happens to the number of air particles as you go higher up?

8. Why do high altitude climbers wear breathing apparatus?

9. If the air pressure at sea level is 100,000 N/m^2, what is it up Mount Everest?

10. When do we see the effects of the large forces involved in atmospheric pressure?

11. When the collapsing can fills with steam, why doesn't the pressure rise?

12. What happens to the steam that was pushing outwards when the lid is replaced and the can cooled?

13. Why does the can get crushed?

14. By pumping the air out of the hemispheres and closing the tap, what does this mean for the 'push balance'?

Additional tasks

1. Plot the points from the table below and draw a smooth curve to show how atmospheric pressure changes with height. Use the grid opposite.

Atmospheric pressure (1000s of N/m^2)	Altitude/ Height (kilometres)
100	0 (sea level)
50	5
30	10
16	15
9	20
5	25

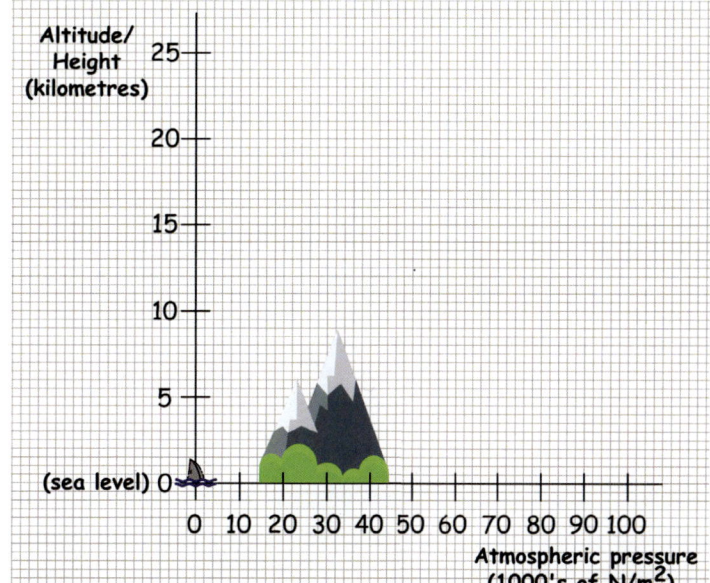

2. Complete the gap fill on atmospheric pressure. Choose from the words below.

higher, decreases, less, pressure, oxygen, thinner, volume, surface, lower, 70, higher, boils

Atmospheric pressure _____ as you move _____ up in the atmosphere. This is because in a certain _____ of air there are _____ particles. Climbers sometimes need to carry _____ tanks when ascending high mountains because the air is _____ which means there is less oxygen. Water _____ at a higher temperature when the pressure on top of the water's surface is _____ this is used to cook foods quicker in a _____ cooker. When the pressure above the _____ of water is lower water boils at a _____ temperature. Water boils at about ____ degrees Celsius on top of Mount Everest because of the lower pressure.

3. Write **true** or **false** in brackets next to the statements on atmospheric pressure.

Gravity stops our atmosphere escaping into space (_____) Air weighs nothing (_____)
Our atmosphere is made mainly from nitrogen and oxygen (_____)
Air can't be frozen (_____) Vacuum cleaners don't suck, air gets 'pushed' in due to a difference in air pressure (_____) 1000 litres of air 'weighs' 1.3 kilograms (_____)
Most of earth's atmosphere is within 10 miles of the surface (_____)

Pressure in Water

You've probably pulled a swimming float underwater and let it go, it races to the surface, leaves the water and then floats back on top. The reason this happens is because of a force called **upthrust**. Any object in a fluid (a liquid or gas) will experience some upthrust. Objects that sink also have upthrust. Objects in air have it too, it's just small.

Upthrust is the upward force exerted by a fluid on an object. Under water if the upthrust is bigger than an object's weight it will head to the surface like the float. If it is less than the object's weight, it will sink. At the surface a partially submerged object like a boat or an ice cube will **float** because the **upthrust** is **equal in size** to the **object's weight**. The pressure can shows that water pressure increases with depth. This is because the weight of more and more layers of water molecules lie above. This increased pressure leads to a greater force. A pressure can shows water spurting out furthest at the bottom.

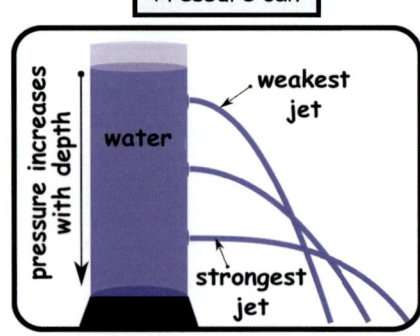

The pressure acts in all directions, it is pushing on the top, the bottom, the left side and the right side of an object in water. It is the difference in pressure with depth that causes upthrust. The force on the sides cancel but the force on the bottom is bigger than the force on the top. This **difference in force** creates the **upthrust**. A submerged object will always displace its own volume in water. Look at **diagram A,** you can see that the water is trying to get back into the space that the metal cube now occupies, so it pushes. If the ice cube in **diagram B** was to be pushed under water it too would displace 100cm³ of water. **Archimedes noticed that the upthrust is always equal to the weight of water displaced.** Objects that sink feel lighter under water because of the upthrust. It is called the **apparent weight.** It is equal to the actual weight minus the upthrust. You can experiment with this by attaching objects that sink to a force meter and placing them into water.

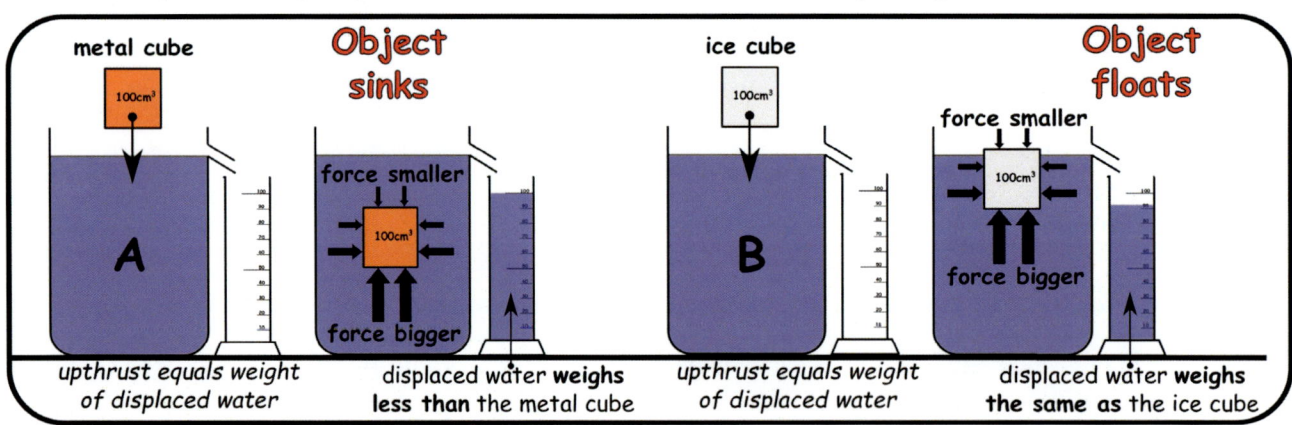

Floating and Sinking

Ice is unusual because it is solid yet less dense than water. Its density is 0.92g of mass for every cm³ of volume, whereas water has 1g of mass for every cm³ of volume. **Any substance that is less dense than water will float.** Huge ships float because although they are made from metal they have a lot of air inside. This means their density overall is less than water so they float, phew!

> **WHAT?**
>
> A steel cube will float on liquid mercury which is more dense than steel! The Mariana trench in the pacific ocean is the deepest on earth, about 11,000m deep (6.8 miles). The water pressure at this depth is over 1000 times more than atmospheric pressure.

Questions on Pressure in Water

Comprehension

1. What force makes a float rise to the surface?

2. What will any object in a fluid experience?

3. What happens if the upthrust is less than an object's weight?

4. What can be used to show that the pressure of water increases with depth?

5. Why is this?

6. This increased pressure leads to a greater?

7. How is this shown with the pressure can?

8. What causes upthrust?

9. What happens to the force on the sides of objects?

10. What will a submerged object do to the water?

11. In diagram **A** what is the water trying to do to the space taken up by the cube?

12. How much water would the ice cube displace if it was pushed under water?

13. What did Archimedes notice?

14. Even if an object sinks, it still feels lighter because of upthrust, what do we call this?

15. Why is ice unusual?

16. Why do huge ships float?

Additional tasks

1. Complete the table to say whether the example will float (yes/no) and whether it will displace its own weight in water.

Example	Density (g/cm^3)	Floats (yes/no?)	Displaces its own weight in water (yes/no?)
Beeswax	0.96		
Aluminium	2.7		
Baking powder	0.72		
Brick	2.0		
Coal	1.5		
Potassium	0.86		
Steel	7.82		
Butter	0.86		
Pencil Rubber	1.1		
Sand	1.6		

2. A boy lifts several objects with string attached to them using a force meter. He records their weights. All have a volume of 100cm^3.

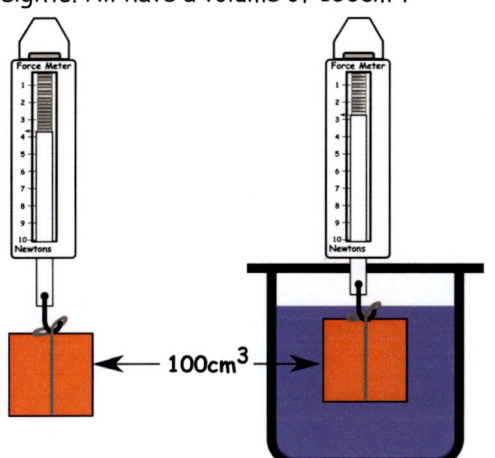

100cm^3

2. (continued) He then measures the apparent weight (the new reading on the force meter) when submerged in water.

His results are recorded in the table below.

a. Calculate the upthrust in each case (weight – apparent weight). What do you notice in each case and why is this?

Material	Weight (N)	Apparent weight in water (N)	Upthrust (N)
Aluminium	2.7	1.7	
Steel	7.8	6.8	
Brick	2.0	1.0	
Copper	8.8	7.8	
Glass	2.5	1.5	
Coal	1.5	0.5	

3. A student drops a clementine orange into a bowl of water and notices that it floats. The student decides that they want to eat the orange so peel it. Before eating it the student wonders if the orange will still float so drops it into the water after it is peeled. It sinks this time!

a. What does this mean for the density of the orange peeled and unpeeled?

b. How might you explain this? (clue; it has to do with the orange peel and air)

Pressure on Solid Surfaces

When two solid surfaces come into contact, pressure is produced. The two factors that affect the size of the pressure produced is:

- The area of the surfaces in contact

- The size of the force exerted

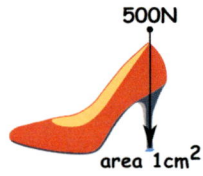

500N

area 1cm^2

500N

area 250cm^2

Pressure = $\dfrac{\text{Force (N)}}{\text{Area (cm}^2)}$ or Pressure = Force ÷ Area
(N/cm^2)

These two factors are connected by the equation that we use to calculate pressure. The units are usually newtons per m^2 (N/m^2), but because cm^2 is more familiar we use that to begin with. Some **simple** numbers help us to understand how these two factors affect the pressure produced. A man and a woman weighing the same (500 Newtons) both stand on one leg. The force they exert on the ground is 500 N (their weight). The man is wearing trainers and the woman stiletto heels. The man's trainers have an area of 250 cm^2 so the pressure under his shoe is, 500 ÷ 250 = **2 N/cm^2**. The woman's stiletto heels have an area of 1cm^2, the pressure she creates is, 500 ÷ 1 = **500 N/cm^2**. Stiletto heels often leave imprints in the floor and they are terrible for walking in mud because the high pressure means they sink in!

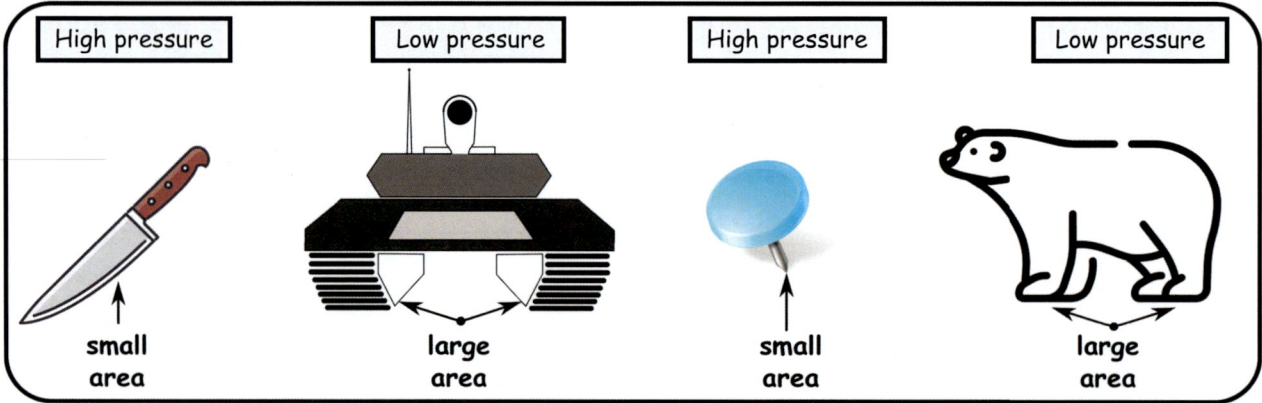

High pressure — small area

Low pressure — large area

High pressure — small area

Low pressure — large area

Knives cut well when they are sharp, this is because a thin edge to the blade means that when you apply a force, it's concentrated on a small area so the pressure produced is high.

A drawing pin has a very small area at its tip, this means that when you apply a force, a high

pressure is produced so the pin will penetrate into walls or wood. A tank is very heavy, so its weight needs to be spread over a wide area so the pressure produced under its tracks is small to stop it sinking into the mud. Polar bears are also heavy and often walk on snow. One of their adaptations is to have large paws, this means their weight is spread over a large area producing a small pressure so they don't sink into the snow. Humans don't have this adaptation so wear snow shoes instead!

Bed of Nails 'Trick'

If we tried to sit on one nail the nail would pierce our skin. Our weight would be

WHAT?

The highest pressure ever reached by scientists is 77 million newtons per cm^2. This is the same as 150,000 women on top of one stiletto heel, get off!

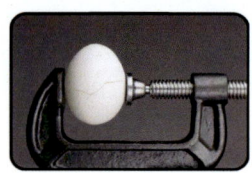

concentrated on a small area to produce a high pressure. If someone sits on a bed of nails, their weight is spread over the area of hundreds of nails, the pressure is low enough not to pierce the skin and it is possible to sit down. It is not comfortable though! G-clamps (opposite) can produce large forces so high pressures to grip or squash objects.

Questions on Pressure on Solid Surfaces

Comprehension

1. What is produced when two solid surfaces come into contact?
2. What two factors affect the size of this pressure?
3. What is the usual unit of pressure?
4. Why use cm^2 rather than m^2 to begin with?
5. How many times bigger is the pressure under stiletto heels compared to trainers?
6. What do stiletto heels often leave in the floor?
7. Why are they terrible for walking in mud?
8. When do knives cut well?
9. Why is this?
10. What does the small area tip enable a drawing pin to do?
11. Why does the weight of a tank need to be spread over a wide area?
12. What is one of the adaptations of a polar bear?
13. What does this stop them doing?
14. What do humans do to stop this happening?
15. What would happen if we tried to sit on one nail?
16. Why are we able to sit on a bed of nails?

Additional tasks

1. Calculate the **pressure** in the table below (divide force by area).

Example	Force (Newtons)	Area (cm^2)	Pressure (N/cm^2)
Knife edge	5	0.02	
Tank tracks	300,000	25,000	
Drawing pin tip	10	0.005	
Polar Bear's paws	5000	800	
Under a **car** tyre	2500	100	
Razor blade	5	0.001	
A punch	400	30	
Pressure of a human bite	500	8	

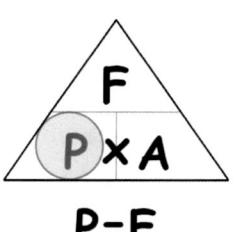

$$P = \frac{F}{A}$$

2. Calculate the **force** in the table below for the slightly different examples (multiply pressure by area).

Example	Force (Newtons)	Area (cm^2)	Pressure (N/cm^2)
Knife edge (blunt)		0.06	133.33
Tank tracks		25,000	10
Drawing pin tip (blunt)		0.01	2000
Polar Bear's paws (cub)		100	6.25
Under a **truck** tyre		250	30
Razor blade (blunt)		0.008	3000
A punch		25	15
Pressure of a human bite		6	50

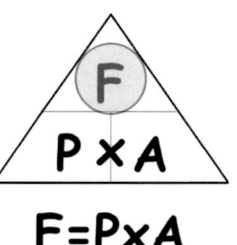

$$F = P \times A$$

3. Complete the gap fill on pressure. Choose from the words below.

weight, area, force, pressure, force, concentrated, bigger, always, penetrates, backpacks, wider, bigger, sharp

The equation for pressure is _____ divided by _____. This means that for a given _____ the bigger the area the smaller the _____ or the smaller the area the _____ the pressure. Also for a given area the _____ the force the bigger the pressure this will _____ be true. You always hit a nail into wood _____ end first. This means that when you hit the nail, the force at the sharp end is _____ on a small area and the high pressure means the nail _____ the wood. The straps on _____ are always wide so the _____ of the backpack is spread over a _____ area and the straps don't dig in due to a high pressure.

Waves and their Properties

Many of us are familiar with the use of the word 'waves'. We wave our hands (move them back and forth), there are water waves on the ocean, also waves on the surface of water called ripples and waves on a skipping rope when you move it up and down. You may also be aware that sound and light are waves.

Waves have common properties (things they all do). They are all made by some sort of 'up and down' or 'back and forth' motion, this is called **an oscillation**. They all **transfer energy** from place to place but do **not** transfer **matter** (atoms). They all **reflect** (bounce off when they hit stuff), they all **refract** (change direction when they move between substances) and they can all **add** together or **cancel** out.

There are two main types of wave motion, **transverse** and **longitudinal**. The most important example of each are: **light** is a **transverse** wave and **sound** is a **longitudinal** wave.

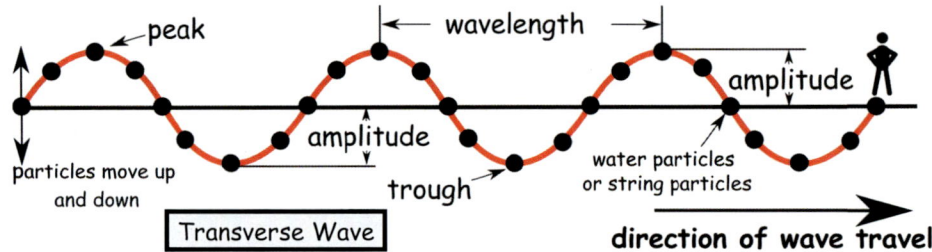

Light waves

Transverse Waves and What We Can Measure

The peak is the top of the wave and the trough is the bottom. The distance **between two peaks** or troughs is called the **wavelength**, it is how long one wave is. The **amplitude** is the distance from the centre line (rest position) to the peak or trough. The bigger the amplitude the more energy a wave carries. The person at the end of the wave just moves up and down as the wave travels to the right, if the amplitude is bigger the person would move up and down more. Another quantity we can measure is the **frequency**, this is the number of wavelengths that pass per second (the unit is hertz, Hz). Notice the particles vibrate at right angles to the direction of the wave's travel. **Transverse** means at a **right angle** to.

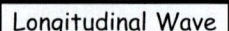
Longitudinal Wave

Longitudinal Waves (sound waves)

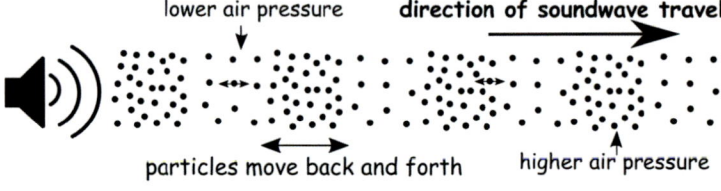

In air these are made by making the air particles vibrate back and forth. We use our voice box or larynx to do this. This causes the air particles to be closer together (squashed) at some points, causing a higher pressure and further apart (stretched) at others, meaning a lower pressure. The vibrations are parallel to the direction the wave is travelling, this is an important difference between longitudinal and transverse waves.

Waves Adding and Cancelling

If two or more waves meet, they add or cancel. You've probably heard of interference on a TV or radio, this is caused by waves meeting. The diagram (right) shows what can happen when waves **a** and **b** meet. They can add together to give a bigger wave or cancel to give no wave at all. What happens depends upon how the waves meet.

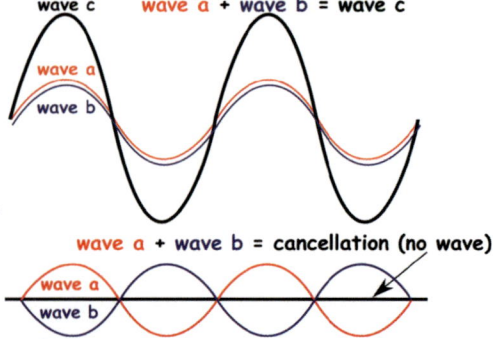

WHAT?
It is possible to cancel noise using more noise! It is called anti-noise and works like wave **a** and **b** above.

162

Questions on Waves and their Properties

Comprehension

1. When we wave our hands what do we do?
2. What are the waves on the surface of water called?
3. When we say waves have common properties what do we mean?
4. What's the name for the up and down or back and forth motion that makes a wave?
5. As well as transferring energy, reflecting and refracting what else can waves do?
6. What are the names of the two types of wave motion?
7. Which type of wave is light and sound?
8. What is the top of a wave called?
9. What is the wavelength?
10. What do we call the distance from the centre line (rest position) to the peak?
11. What does this tell us about the wave?
12. What does the frequency tell us and what is its unit?
13. How do the particles move compared to the direction of travel for transverse waves?
14. What causes the air particles to produce a higher pressure in a sound wave?
15. What's an important difference between longitudinal and transverse waves?
16. What can cause interference on a TV or radio?

Additional tasks

1. Match and memorise the meanings of the words below.

Peak	waves where the vibrations are at right angles to wave travel, e.g. light
Trough	distance from centre line (rest position) to peak or trough
Amplitude	waves adding or cancelling when they meet
Wavelength	waves where the vibrations are parallel to wave travel, e.g. sound.
Frequency	top of the wave
Transverse waves	number of wavelengths that pass per second
Longitudinal waves	distance from peak to peak
Interference	bottom of the wave

2. Label the wavelength, amplitude, peak and trough **in more than one** place on the transverse wave below.

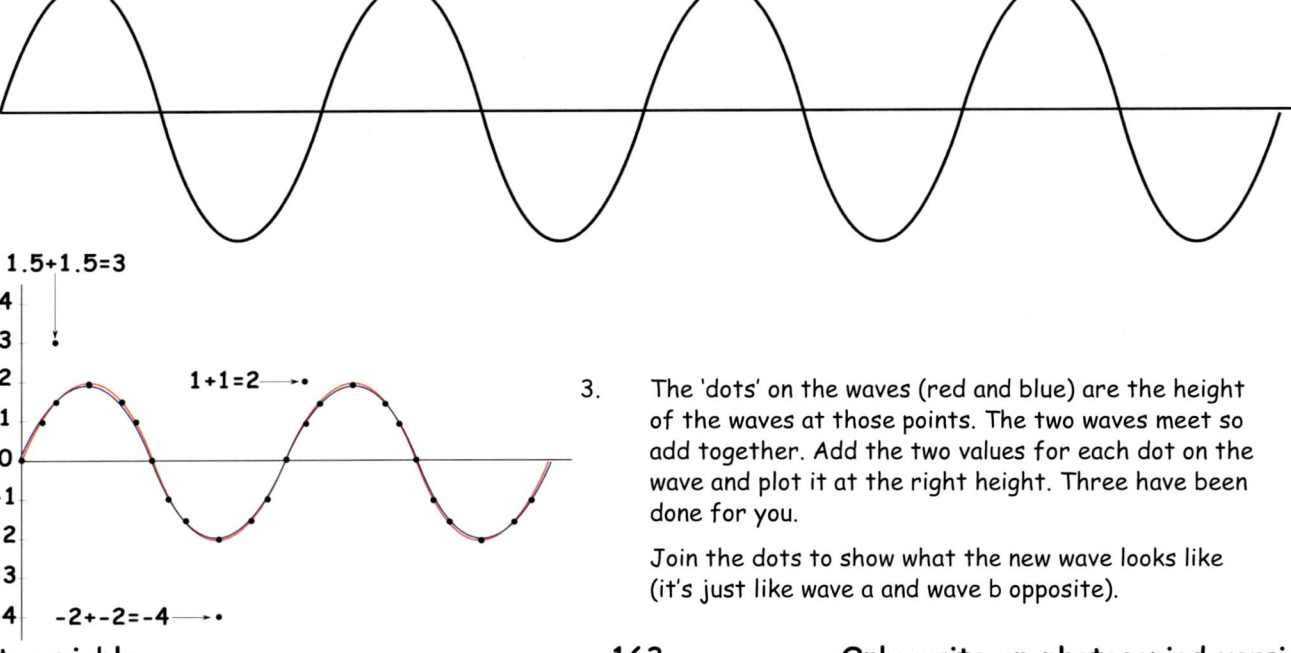

3. The 'dots' on the waves (red and blue) are the height of the waves at those points. The two waves meet so add together. Add the two values for each dot on the wave and plot it at the right height. Three have been done for you.

Join the dots to show what the new wave looks like (it's just like wave a and wave b opposite).

Sound

A sound is made when something vibrates. This could be your vocal cords vibrating (this makes the sound of our voices), or the table top when you tap it, or the vibration of a ruler twanged over the edge of a desk. The way in which an object vibrates changes the sound we hear. Objects can vibrate back and forth a lot or a small amount. The **size** of the vibration is called the **amplitude**. Objects can also vibrate very quickly or very slowly.

Describing Sound

We can describe sounds as being **loud** or **quiet** and as being **high pitched** or **low pitched**. The loudness (or volume) of a sound tells us about the amount of energy carried by the sound. Loud sounds carry a lot of energy and can damage our ear drums, quiet sounds carry less energy. Think about shouting, it takes a lot more energy than talking quietly. The **loudness** of sound is measured in a unit called **decibels, (dB).**

When we say a sound is high pitched, it means the object is vibrating very quickly (it has a high frequency) and with low pitched sounds objects vibrate slowly (have a low frequency). Frequency is the number of vibrations per second and is measured in the unit, hertz, Hz. Ten hertz is 10 vibrations in one second (there and back 10 times in one second), 500 hertz is 500 vibrations per second (faster) and so on.

Aeroplane (*120 dB*)

(loud, big amplitude)

Sleeping baby (*10 dB*)

(quiet, small amplitude)

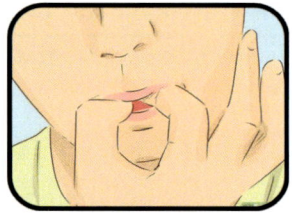
Whistling

(high pitch)

Bass drum

(low pitch)

Sound on the Move

Everything is made from particles (tiny pieces of matter made from atoms). In solids, liquids and gases the particles are arranged differently. Sound (caused by vibrations) can travel from place to place because a vibrating particle passes on the vibration to the particle next to it, which passes on the vibration to the particle next to it, and so on. This happens to the air particles for us to be able to hear (see pg166). The **substance** that sound is travelling through is called the **medium**. Sound travels fastest in solids, then liquids and slowest in gases. About 6000m/s in steel, 1500m/s in water and 340m/s in air. This is because the particles are arranged closer together in solids than liquids and furthest apart in gases. The closer the particles are, the faster the vibrations are passed on.

> **WHAT?**
>
> Sound travels at 770 mph (340 m/s) in air. The crack of a whip happens because the tip moves so fast it breaks the speed of sound and produces a **sonic boom**. Music is just a pleasing arrangement of sounds! Noise is just unwanted sound! Thunder is the sound of lightning rapidly heating the air. The study of sound is called **acoustics**.

Medium Required

If you put a vibrating object like an alarm clock in a bell jar (a glass jar) and pump out all of the air, you can no longer hear the sound. Although the object is still vibrating, the vibrations can't be passed on because there are no particles (air) to pass on the vibrations. This means that on the moon, apart from not being able to breathe, you can't communicate by talking no matter how loud you shout! There is no air to pass on the vibrations.

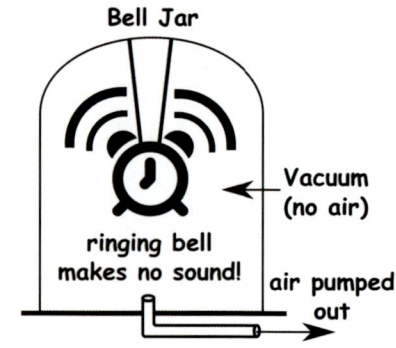

Bell Jar

Vacuum (no air)

ringing bell makes no sound!

air pumped out

Questions on Sound

Comprehension

1. How is sound made?
2. What changes the sound we hear?
3. How can we describe sounds?
4. What is another word for loudness?
5. What do loud sounds carry a lot of?
6. What can loud sounds do to our ear drums?
7. What is the unit for the loudness of sound?
8. What do we mean by high pitched sound?
9. What do we mean by frequency and what is the unit?
10. How can sound travel from place to place?
11. What do we mean by 'the medium' when talking about sound?
12. What substances does sound travel fastest in and why?
13. What happens to the sound of a vibrating object in a bell jar with all the air pumped out?
14. Why can't the vibrations be passed on?

Additional tasks

1. Match and memorise the words and their meanings below.

Vibration	the number of vibrations per second
Amplitude	the substance sound travels through
Medium	the unit of frequency
Frequency	the to and fro or back and forth motion that produces sound
Hertz (Hz)	the unit for the loudness of sound
Decibels (dB)	the size of the vibration

2. Unscramble the words from the clues to reveal the 'sound' words below.

High frequency so high ……. (ITEPDCH)

Also called volume (OUSLENSD)

If this is big the sound is loud (MPDAUIELT)

What sound travels through (MDMEUI)

The study of sound (COCAISSUT)

The unit of frequency (THZER)

This produces sound (IBOVIANRT)

Sound can't travel through this (VCMAUU)

Unit of loudness (ECLDEBSI)

This causes low pitched sounds (OFNLEQYWUREC)

This causes high pitched sounds (IHNHEEYGUFRQC)

A bass drum produces this sort of sound (OPELHTDWCI)

Sound travels fastest in (SLSODI)

The number of vibrations per second (RECFNUYQE)

3. Decide if the following examples are usually loud sounds or quiet sounds and say if you think they would be high pitched or low pitched.

   ➤ An erupting volcano
   ➤ Squeaky brakes
   ➤ The wind rustling leaves
   ➤ A lion's raw
   ➤ A female opera singer
   ➤ A referee's whistle
   ➤ Drilling a hole in the wall
   ➤ A honey bee hovering
   ➤ A bird chirping

4. Put the following mediums in order of what sound would travel through fastest to slowest.

   a. Sound travelling through treacle
   b. Sound travelling through a helium balloon
   c. Sound travelling through the ground

Picturing Sound

Sound travels in a wave motion, this means that the energy of the sound wave travels outwards but no matter (usually air particles) actually moves from place to place. What the air particles do is vibrate back and forth making the air pressure slightly higher or lower as the particles get closer or further apart. It is a kind of wave called a **longitudinal wave.**

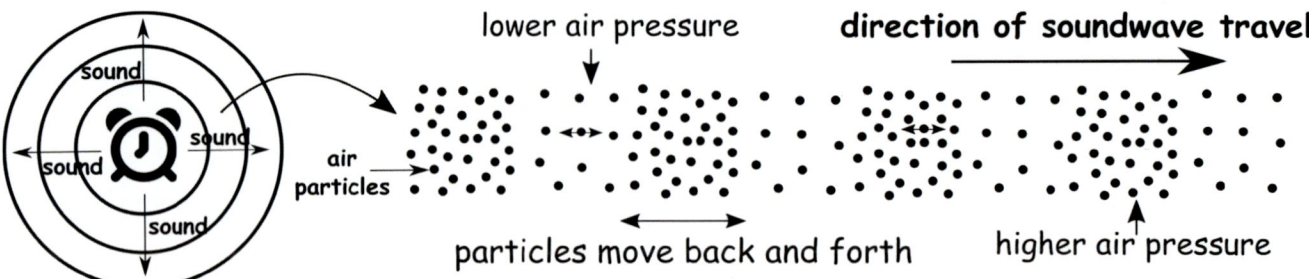

We know that it is not possible to see the sound wave, but we can detect the vibration using a microphone. Microphones convert sound waves into electrical signals. This just means we get a voltage that changes in the same way that the sound wave does. To display this we use a voltmeter called an oscilloscope. Oscilloscopes leave a trace on a screen, the **higher** the **trace**, called the amplitude, the **louder** the **sound**. The **smaller** the **height** of the trace the

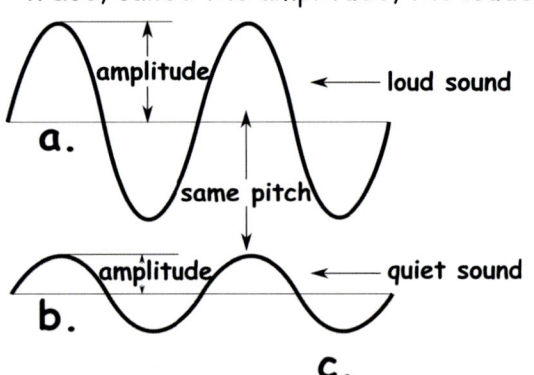

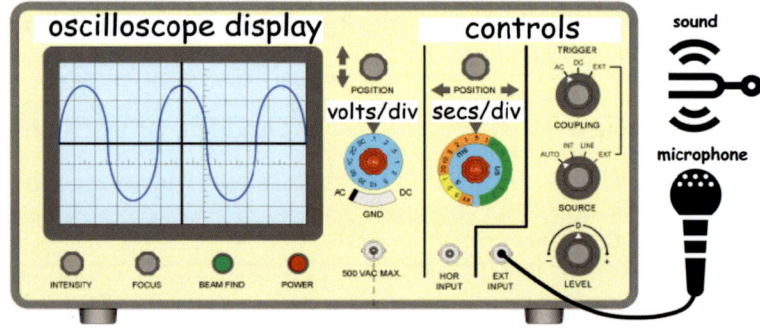

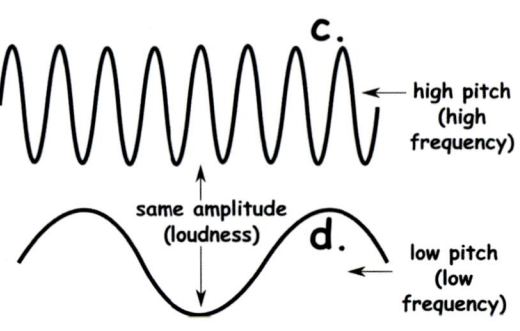

quieter the **sound**. In the diagram opposite, **wave a** is a **loud sound** because it has a **big amplitude** and **wave b** is a **quiet sound** because it has a **small amplitude**. We can also see if a sound is high pitched (high frequency) or low pitched (low frequency). The tops of the waves (called the peaks) are close together if the sound is **high pitched (wave c)**, this means there are a lot of vibrations every second. The frequency is high.

If the peaks of the wave are more spread out (**wave d**), the sound is **low pitched**, there are less vibrations per second. The frequency is low.

Echoes, Absorption and Transmission

Sound can bounce off objects (reflect) and travel back towards you, we call this an echo. If you face a building 340 metres away and shout, you will hear your own voice

> **WHAT?**
>
> The loudest ever sound was that of the eruption of a volcano called Krakatoa in 1883. It ruptured the ear drums of people 40 miles away!

(echo) 2 seconds later, 1 second to get there and 1 second to get back. A person inside the building would hear the sound too, some of the sound's energy would transmit (pass through the walls), some would reflect (the echo) and some would be absorbed (taken in) by the building.

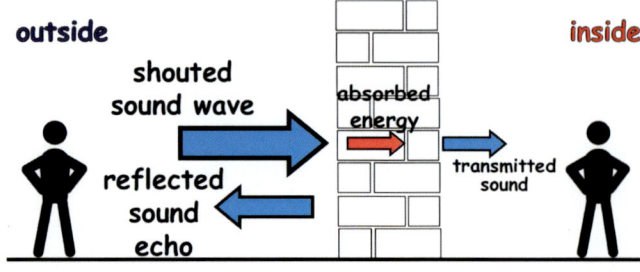

Questions on Picturing Sound

Comprehension

1. The energy of a sound wave travels outwards in all directions, but what does not move from place to place?

2. What kind of wave is a sound wave?

3. How can we detect the vibration of a sound wave?

4. What do microphones convert sound waves into?

5. What do we use to display sound waves?

6. How can we tell a sound is loud by looking at the trace on an oscilloscope?

7. How can you tell by looking at a trace that a sound is high pitched?

8. If the pitch is high what else must be high?

9. What does it mean when the peaks of a wave are more spread out?

10. What do we call it when sound bounces off an object?

11. When you shout towards a building 340m away why do you hear your echo 2 seconds later?

12. Why would someone inside hear the sound?

Additional tasks

1. Two students stand 250m away from the gym wall. One student shouts and when he hears the echo shouts again. The other student times how long it takes the sound to go there and back between shouts for a different number of times. They then calculated the speed of sound. Plot six bars on the chart below for each speed value.

Number of times there and back	1	2	3	4	5	6
Distance (m)	500	1000	1500	2000	2500	3000
Time (seconds)	2.0	3.3	4.7	6.1	7.5	8.9
Speed (m/s)	250	300	320	330	330	340

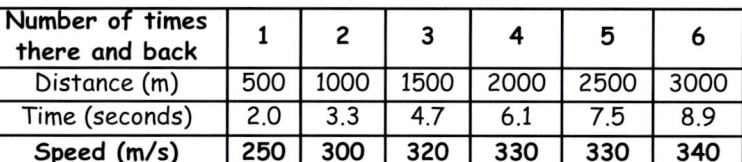

Speed of sound (m/s)

350
300
250
200
150
100
50
0

Number of times there and back

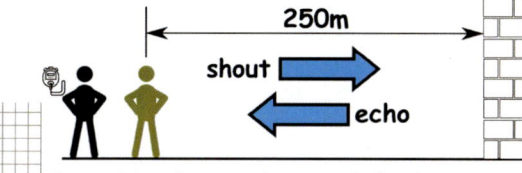

2 a. The diagram bottom left shows six wave traces of sounds with different frequencies and amplitudes (loudness). Complete the table for the frequency of each wave, remember frequency is the number of waves in one second **so count the waves!**

Wave number	Frequency (waves per second, Hz)
1	
2	
3	
4	
5	
6	

b. Which is the *highest pitch, lowest pitch, loudest* and *quietest* out of waves 1 to 6 ?

c. A student puts a buzzer in a box connected to a battery. The student has six layers of cotton wool to cover the box and an oscilloscope with a microphone that shows the amplitude of the sound on the display.
Explain how the student could investigate how the number of layers of cotton wool affect the loudness of the sound? Think about;

• What to change? What to keep the same? What to measure?

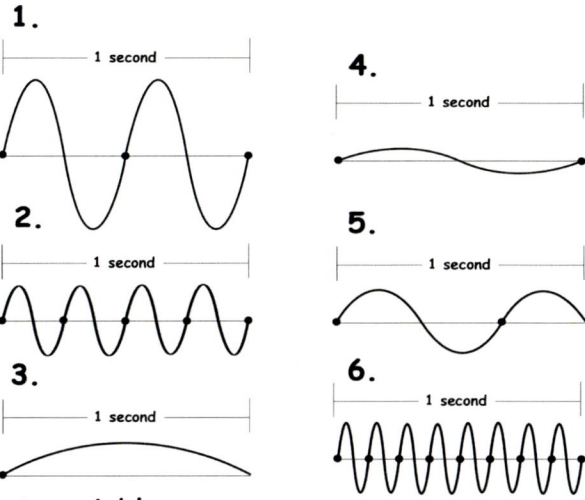

1. *1 second*
2. *1 second*
3. *1 second*
4. *1 second*
5. *1 second*
6. *1 second*

Hearing and Using Sound

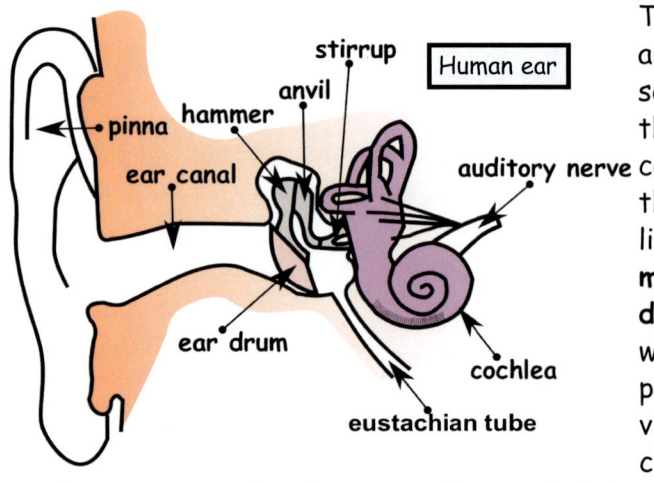

Human ear

The two main ways to detect sound are your ear and a microphone. Both convert the energy of a sound wave into an electrical signal. It works like this. The **outer ear** or **pinna** is shaped to help collect sound and direct it down the **ear canal**. At the end of the ear canal is the **ear drum** which is like a thin piece of skin (**a membrane**). In a **microphone** a thin piece of paper called a **diaphragm** does the same job. The sound wave which is a series of high and low pressures, pushes the drum back and forth (makes it vibrate). The vibrations are passed onto the cochlea through three tiny bones called the **hammer, anvil and stirrup** (also called the **ossicles**). These bones amplify the vibrations by acting as levers to produce a larger force. The **cochlea** contains a liquid with tiny hairs inside. As the liquid vibrates the hairs are made to move back and forth. The bottom of the hairs have special cells for converting the **vibration** into an **electrical impulse** (a short burst of electricity). These impulses are then sent along the **auditory nerve** to the brain where we 'hear' them.

Hearing Ranges

Range means the difference from lowest to highest. Different animals have different frequency ranges they can hear, with moths thought to have evolved the highest range. This enables them to escape their high pitched predator the bat. Humans have a range of 20Hz to 20,000Hz. Frequencies **above 20,000Hz** we **can't hear** and are called **ultrasound**. Many animals such as dogs, cats and bats can hear ultrasound.

Animal	Lowest audible frequency (Hz)	Highest audible frequency (Hz)
Dog	65	45,000
Cat	45	64,000
Dolphin	80	150,000
Elephant	15	12,000
Mouse	1,000	90,000
Owl	20	12,000
Moth	50	300,000

Uses of Sound

Our main use of sound is for communication, talking. However, high frequency ultrasound has many uses too. Bats use ultrasound for **echolocation** to find their prey. They send out high frequency squeaks and then listen for the echo reflection from potential prey. The shorter the echo time, the closer the prey. Ultrasound is used to **scan unborn babies**. A transducer sends ultrasound waves into the uterus and the different echo times are used to build a picture of the baby. They are completely harmless to the baby. Ultrasound is also used by **physiotherapists**. The vibrations that pass deeper into the flesh can gently heat and improve circulation for healing after an injury or operation.

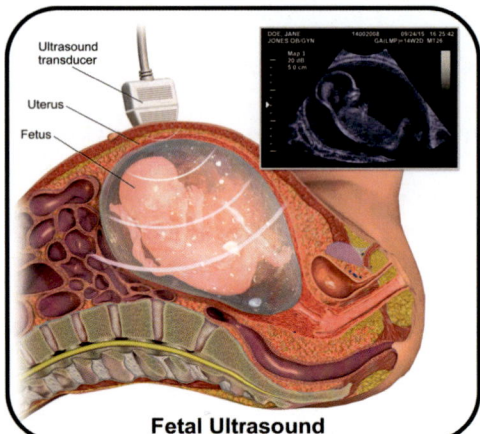

Fetal Ultrasound

WHAT?

Submarines use SONAR (**so**und **na**vigation and **r**anging) to detect targets and navigate. Another form of echolocation. A 'ping' of sound is emitted and the echo time recorded to calculate distances. It stops submarines bumping into stuff!

Questions on Hearing and Using Sound

Comprehension

1. What are the two main ways to detect sound?	9. How do the electrical impulses get to the brain?
2. What do both methods do?	10. What does range mean?
3. What does the pinna help direct the sound down?	11. How does a moth's large hearing range help it?
4. What is the ear drum like?	12. What are frequencies above 20,000Hz called?
5. What does the sound wave do to the ear drum?	13. How do bats find their prey?
6. What are the ossicles?	14. How does a bat know if the prey is close?
7. How do these bones amplify the vibration?	15. How is ultrasound used to build a picture of an unborn baby?
8. What does the cochlea contain?	16. Why is ultrasound used by physiotherapists?

Additional tasks

1. Label and memorise the diagram of the ear below.

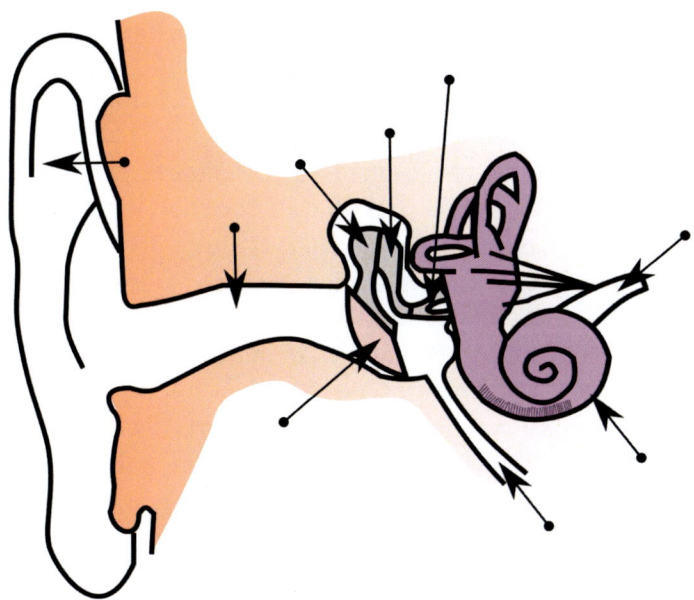

2. Complete the gap fill on echolocation.

echolocation, hear, emitting, echo, frequency, closer, Longer, 20,000Hz

Ultrasound is sound of _____ above _____. Humans can't _____ ultrasound.

Bats, dolphins, submarines and ships use ultrasound for _____.

This means _____ ultrasound and listening for how long it takes the _____ to return.

Shorter echo times mean an object is _____. _____ echo times means an object is further away.

3. The speed of sound in water is **1500m/s,** this means that an object 1500 metres away will have an echo time of 2 seconds. One second for the sound to get there and one second for the sound to get back. In each of the examples in the table calculate the **distance** to the object. Use the example below. Reminder, the speed of sound in water is **1500m/s.**

EXAMPLE
echo time = 4 seconds

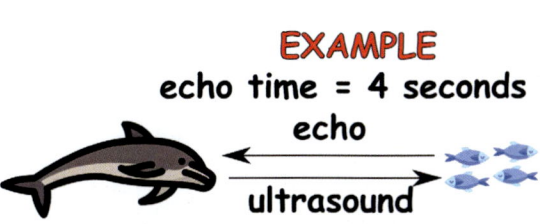

echo

ultrasound

distance to fish = speed x (echo time/2)
= 1500 x 4/2
= 3000m

Example	Echo time (seconds)	Distance (m)
A Ship testing the depth of water	0.6	
A whale hunting squid	8	
A submarine detecting a ship	6	
A dolphin hunting a shoal of herring	1	
A bat hunting moths **speed of sound in air = 340 m/s**	0.2	

Light and Reflection

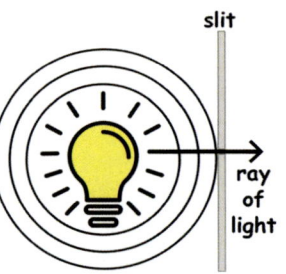

Light travels as a wave and in straight lines. Look at the diagram of the lamp, light travels out in all directions. When we want to investigate how light is going to behave we just use a thin beam of light called a ray.

Light travels really fast, nothing goes faster. It travels 186,000 miles in one second, sound only travels 0.2 miles in one second.

Transparent, Translucent and Opaque

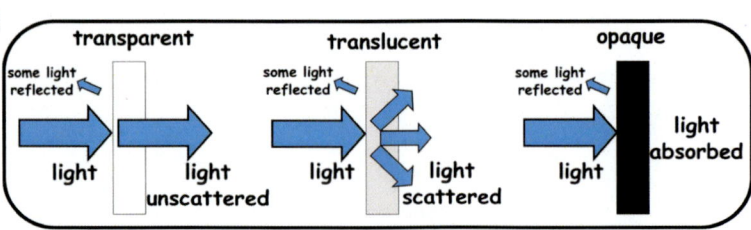

As well as reflecting, light can **pass through** materials like glass, these materials are called **transparent**. Light can also **partially** (not completely) **pass through** materials like tracing paper, these materials are called **translucent**. We don't see objects clearly through translucent materials. Light can also be blocked by objects so we **can't see through** them at all, these materials are called **opaque**. A piece of paper is opaque.

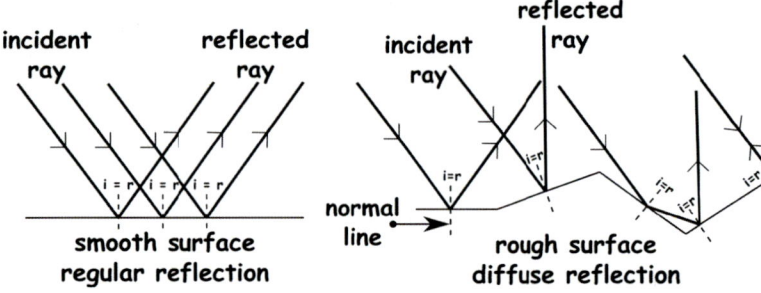

The Law of Reflection

This tells us the way in which light bounces off a substance. It always bounces off the surface (reflects) at the same angle that it meets the surface. Just like a football kicked against a wall. Kick it straight at the wall and it comes straight back at you. Kick it at an angle and it goes away from you at the same angle. We use a ray of light and a smooth surface like a mirror to show this. We say that the angle of **incidence, i** (angle of the light travelling towards the mirror) **is equal to** the angle of **reflection, r** (angle of light travelling away from the mirror). This is shown as **i = r** in the diagrams. We always draw a dashed line at right angles (90°) to the surface to measure the angle from, called the **normal line**. The law of reflection is true for all surfaces rough or smooth. Smooth surfaces like mirrors give a **regular** reflection and we can see ourselves in them. Rough surfaces like a piece of paper give **diffuse** reflection so we don't see ourselves in them.

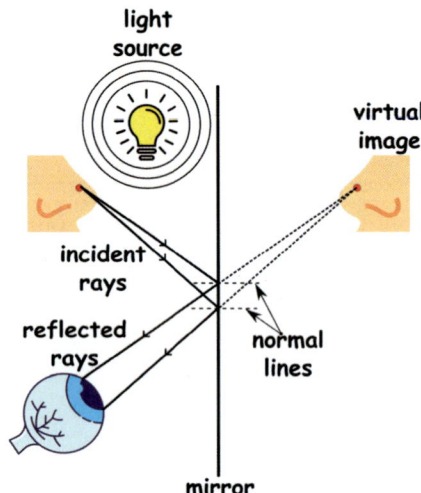

Virtual Image in a Mirror

To see an object, light must travel from the source (a bulb/the sun) reflect off the object and enter our eyes. Imagine a spot on someone's nose. Light will bounce off the spot and travel in **all directions**. If we look at **two rays** of light that **will reflect off** the mirror and **into the eye**, we can see why the image is virtual. Our brains have learned to form images from light that has travelled in a straight line. The brain 'thinks' the light has come from behind the mirror so we see the spot on the person's nose appear to be behind the mirror. The image appears the same distance behind the mirror as the object is in front, it is also **laterally inverted**, meaning your left appears to be your right. Being a virtual image you cannot touch it.

WHAT?

Real images exist too! The image on your retina and the image projected onto a screen are real images, you can touch them.

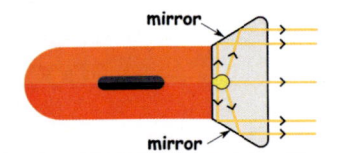

Torch mirror reflects light into a beam

Questions on Light and Reflection

Comprehension

1. How does light travel?

2. When we want to investigate how light is going to behave, what do we use?

3. How far does light travel in one second?

4. What do we call a material that light passes through?

5. What can light do to a translucent material?

6. What does the law of reflection tell us?

7. What do we use to show the law of reflection?

8. Complete the following sentence describing the law of reflection.
The angle of **i** _ _ _ _ _ _ _ _ is **e** _ _ _ _ **t** _ the angle of **r** _ _ _ _ _ _ _ _ _.

9. What is the normal line?

10. What sort of surface is the law of reflection true for?

11. To see an object what must light do?

12. When light is shone on the person's spot, in which direction will the reflected light travel?

13. How many rays do we use to show the image produced?

14. Why does the brain 'see' the spot behind the mirror?

15. How far behind the mirror does the image appear to be?

Additional tasks

1. Using a protractor measure the angles **a**, **b** and **c** below and draw in the reflected rays.

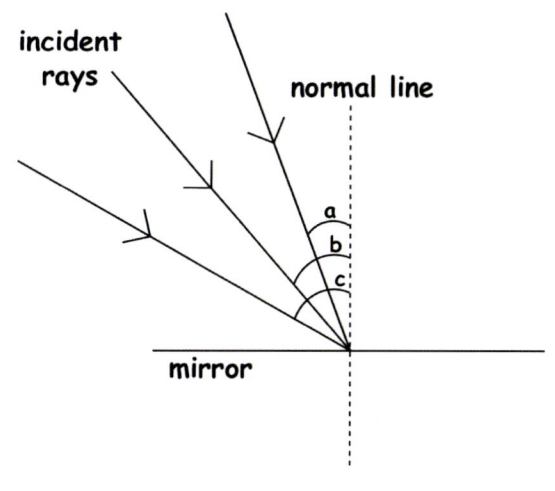

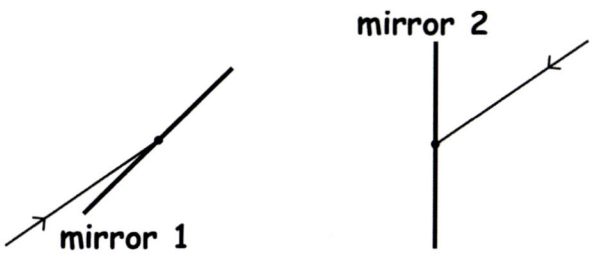

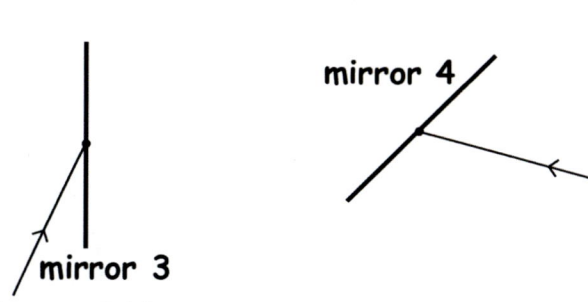

2. Complete the ray diagram (as shown opposite) to show how a virtual image of the stiletto heel is formed.

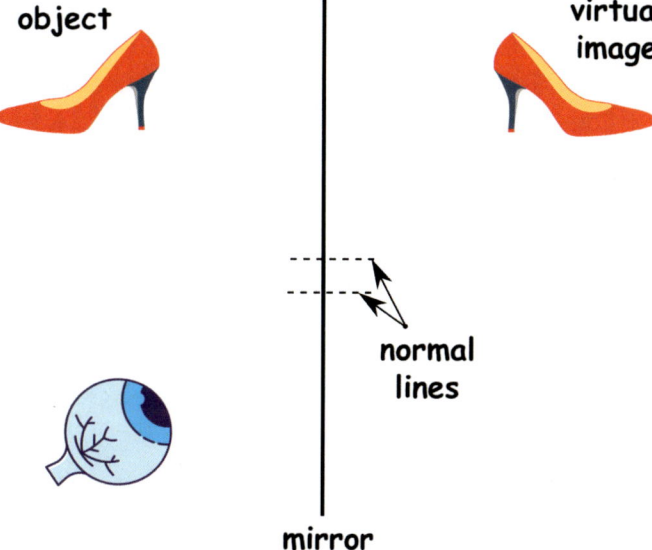

3. Draw in a **dashed normal line** for each of the mirrors **1** to **4**. Measure the angle of incidence and draw in the reflected ray at the correct angle.

4. Show the path of a ray of light from the dolphin into the eye to demonstrate how a periscope works.

periscope

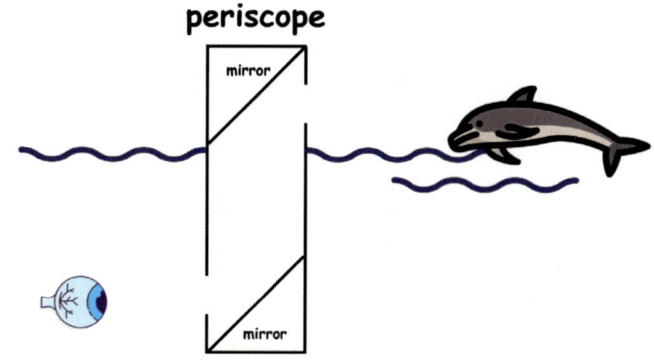

Refraction, Lenses and the Eye

Sound waves in air, water waves and waves on a string all transfer energy by making the substance they are travelling through (the medium) vibrate. If there is no air, water or string there is no wave. Light is also a wave but **doesn't need anything to travel through**, it reaches earth after travelling from the sun across the emptiness (vacuum) of space. On hitting the earth's atmosphere light slows down a tiny bit. If light travels through water or glass it slows down much more. This slowing down can cause light to **change direction**. If light does change direction as it moves from say **air** into **glass** it is called **refraction**.

Refraction and Convex Lenses

Using a ray box and a glass block we can observe refraction. If light hits the glass block 'head on' it slows down and speeds up but doesn't change direction. If light hits the glass

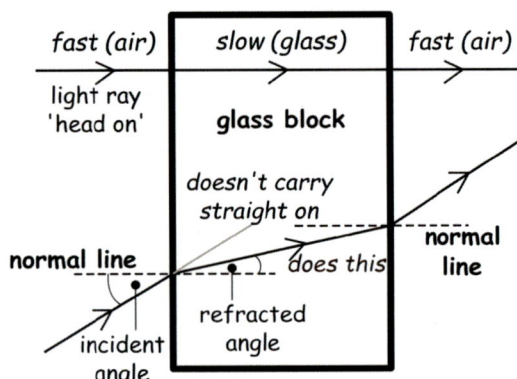

at another angle it is made to take a new path through the glass which is **closer** to the **normal line** (the dashed line at 90° that angles are measured from). When the ray leaves it takes a new path **further away** from the **normal** as it speeds up. Your eye has a **convex lens** (converging lens) which is able to focus light to form a **real image** on the retina. Real images can be touched, like on a screen. Parallel rays of light are refracted by the lens and pass through a **focal**

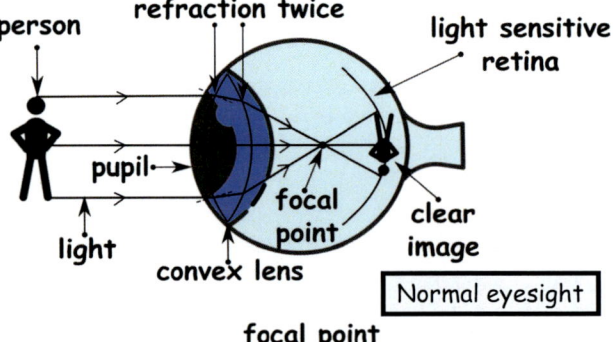

point. The image is upside down because light from the bottom of the object is refracted upwards and light from the top is refracted downwards. The light energy is converted into an electrical signal, which for humans is sent to the brain. A camera works in exactly the same way. In a camera the electrical signal is sent to the camera's memory.

Short sightedness (myopia) is the most common eye defect in people under 40 years old. It occurs when the focal point is short of where it should be. It can be corrected using another lens called a **concave** lens (diverging lens) that is placed in front of the eye (**glasses, see diagram opposite**). This makes the light rays move apart,

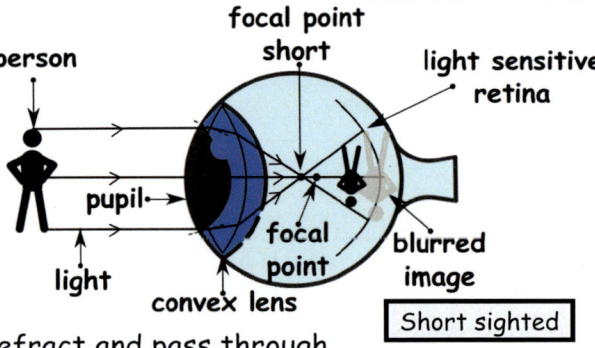

so when they do pass through the eye's lens, they refract and pass through the correct focal point and the image formed is clear.

Virtual Images

Refraction can cause objects to seem to be in a different position. Your brain is used to forming images from light that has travelled in a straight line so continues to do the same with the coin on the bottom of the swimming pool. The light has actually come from lower down so the coin appears to be shallower than it is.

Lost his head!

WHAT?

Dragonflies have the most lenses in their eyes, some have more than 28,000.

Questions on Refraction, Lenses and the Eye

Comprehension

1. How do sound waves in air, water waves and waves on a string transfer energy?
2. What **doesn't** light need to travel?
3. What is another word for the emptiness of space?
4. What happens when light hits earth's atmosphere?
5. What can the slowing down of light cause?
6. What is this called?
7. If light hits the glass block at a 0° angle (head on) what doesn't happen?
8. If light hits the glass block at another angle, what happens to its path?
9. What happens to light's path as it leaves the glass block?
10. What sort of lens does your eye have and what is it able to do?
11. Where do parallel rays of light pass through after being refracted by the lens?
12. What is myopia?
13. How can myopia be corrected?
14. What does a diverging lens do to light rays?
15. Refraction can cause objects to seem to be....?

Additional tasks

1. Complete the ray diagrams below by 'joining the dots'. **A**, **B** and **C** show how the focal point changes with lens thickness.

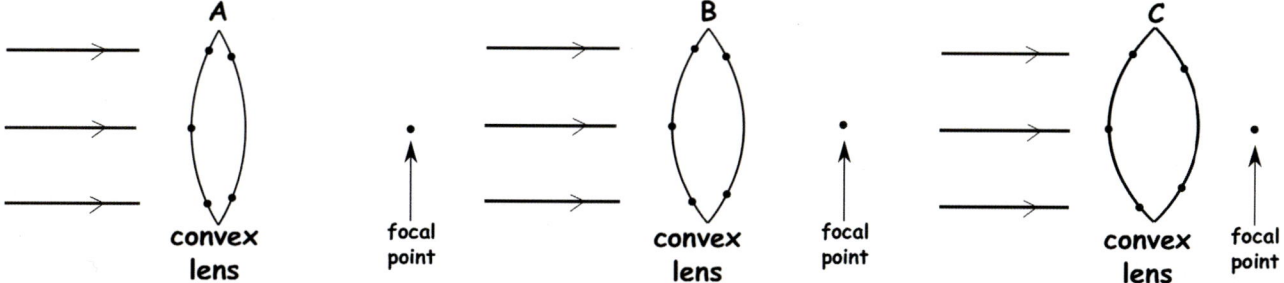

2. Draw in the refracted ray at the correct angle to show the ray passing through the glass block (as shown opposite). The ray leaves the block **parallel** to the incident ray. Draw a normal line where it is about to leave the glass block and show it leaving at the correct angle (i.e. 30°, 50° and 60° from the normal on the opposite edge).

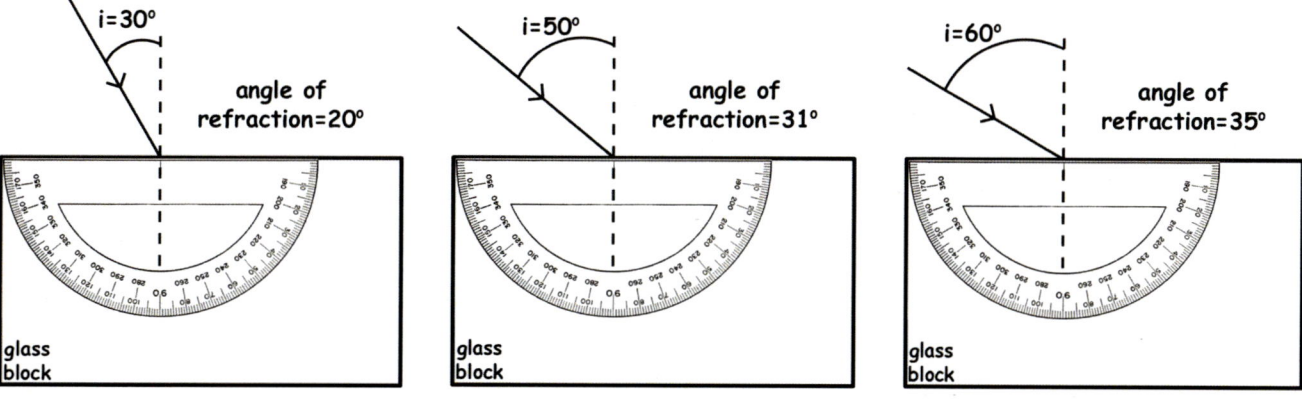

3. The right hand diagram shows how a concave lens can be use to correct short sightedness. Complete the path of the three rays showing how short sightedness can be corrected. Join the dots!

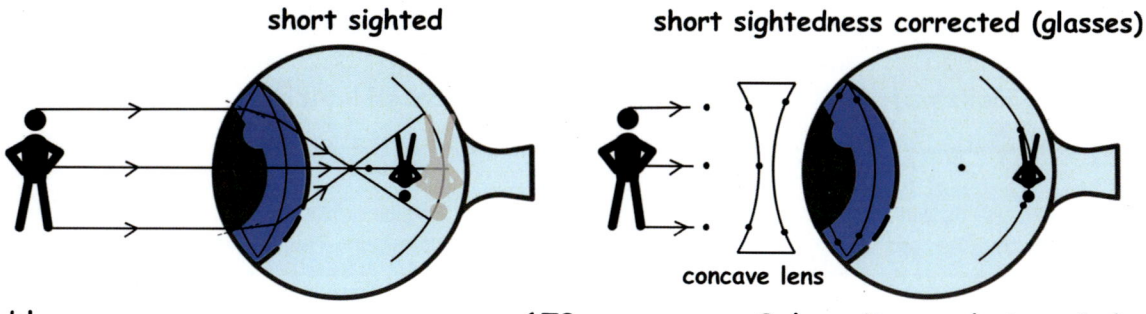

Dispersion and Colour

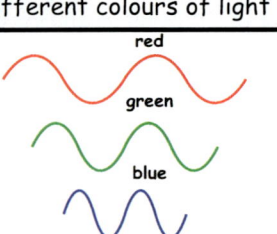

Different colours of light

Rainbows show us that sunlight must contain many different colours. Scientists call light that contains all the colours of the visible spectrum, **white light**. These are red, orange, yellow, green, blue, indigo and violet (**ROY G BIV** as a memory aid). The different colours of light have different wavelengths (distance between peaks). Sources of white light include the sun or an ordinary lamp. You may have seen other sources of light that are a different colour like the LED's of Christmas lights or the standby on the TV which is normally red (also an LED).

Dispersion

Sir Isaac Newton studied light using a prism (triangular glass block). On a sunny day he made a small hole in his window shutters to allow a ray of light into his darkened room. He

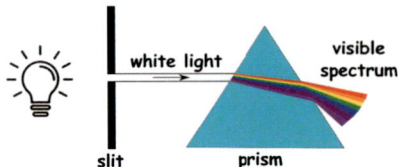

placed a prism in the path of the light and observed the visible spectrum produced. Using another prism the spectrum can be recombined to give white light. Dispersion means to spread or split white light into its component parts. That is the seven colours of the visible spectrum. It happens because the different colours are refracted different amounts. Red is slowed down least so refracts the least. Violet slows down most so refracts (changes direction) the most. In this way white light is split into the individual colours we see. 'Blue Bends Best' can help you to remember which colours refract most.

Colour

The reason an object looks a particular colour is that it reflects that colour (wavelength) of light. The T-shirt **looks red** because it **reflects** the **red** wavelength of light but **absorbs all other colours** of light. The shorts **look blue** because they **reflect** the **blue wavelength** of light but **absorb all other colours**. The socks look **white** because they

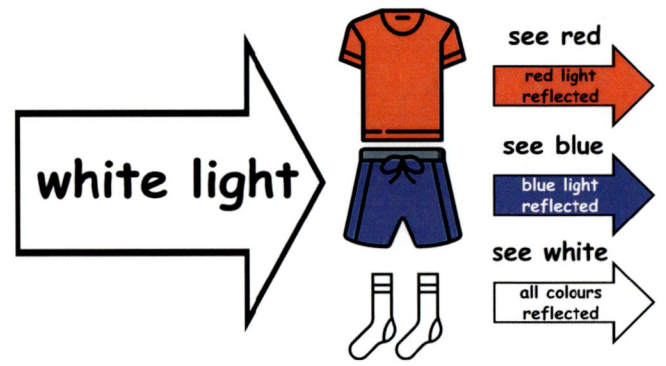

reflect **all wavelengths of light**. Objects that look **black** do so because they **absorb all wavelengths** so we don't see any light reflected and they appear black or dark to us.

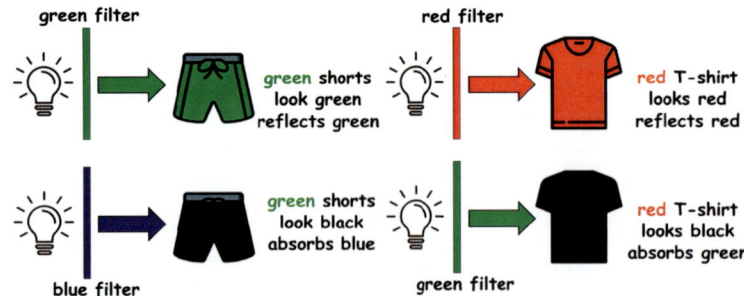

Filters

If white light is directed at a green filter, the filter only allows green light through, the other colours are absorbed. This is the same for a red filter or a blue filter that only allow red or blue light through. Green shorts look green under green light because they reflect green. Green shorts look black under blue light because they absorb blue. The red T-shirt looks red under red light but black under green light since it absorbs green light.

WHAT?

Light sensitive cells called cones in the retina are responsible for detecting red, green and blue wavelengths. The primary colours that can combine to give all colours. If the cones are faulty a person can be colour blind.

Questions on Dispersion and Colour

Comprehension

1. What do rainbows show?

2. What do we call light that contains all the colours of the visible spectrum?

3. What is a useful memory aid for the colours in the visible spectrum?

4. What did Sir Isaac Newton place in the path of a light ray entering his room?

5. Using another prism what are you able to do to the spectrum produced?

6. Why does dispersion happen?

7. Why does an object look a particular colour?

8. What does a red T-shirt do to all colours apart from red?

9. Why do the socks look white?

10. Why do objects look black?

11. What colour light does a green filter allow through?

12. Why do green shorts look black under blue light?

Additional tasks

1. Write down what each of the coloured shorts will look like under the different coloured light.

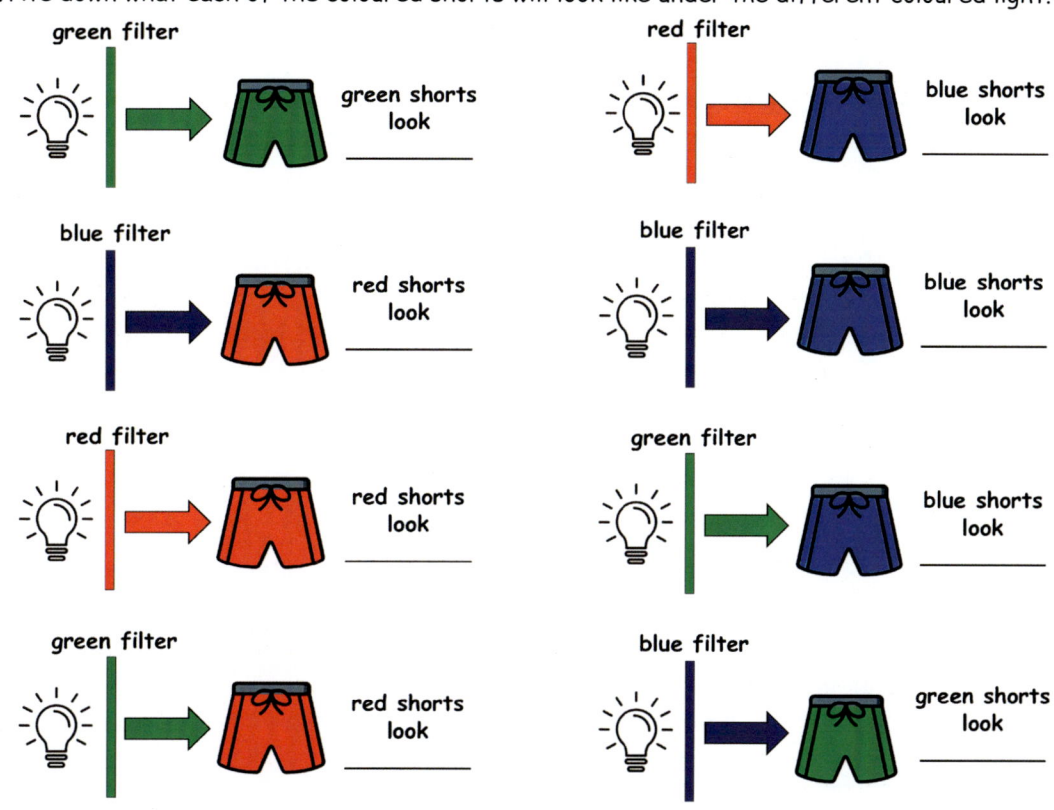

2. State what colour the eye will see in examples **A** to **F** below.

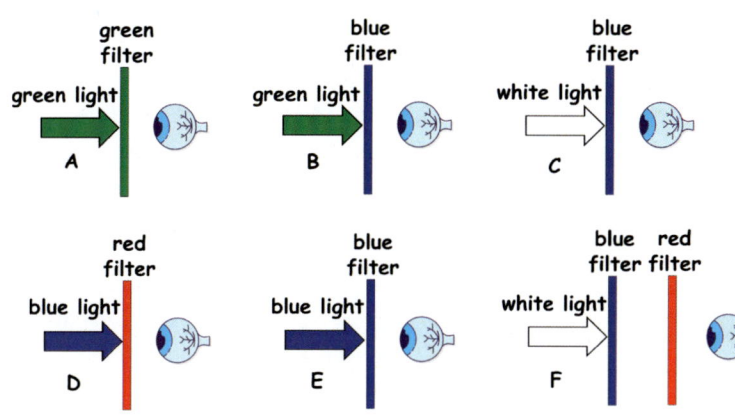

3. Think of your own mnemonic for the colours of the visible spectrum.
   An example of a well known one is;

   Richard Of York Gave Battle In Vain

   Red, Orange, Yellow, Green, Blue, Indigo, Violet

Electric Circuits

Electric circuits allow energy to be transferred from the source (usually batteries or a mains socket) to the appliance. Electricity is so useful because it can transform into many other forms of energy, e.g. light (from a bulb), heat (from a heater), sound (from a speaker), kinetic (from a motor) and chemical (when recharging batteries).

What's Happening Inside a Wire?

The circuit opposite shows a wire connected to the ends of a battery. The negative charges (electrons) in a metal are free to move, they just need a push. This push comes from the negative terminal of the battery because negative repels negative. The electrons flow (like water in a pipe) to the positive terminal of the battery which they are attracted to (opposites attract). The wire must touch both ends of the battery making a **complete circuit**, otherwise there would be a 'dead end' (incomplete circuit) and no current would flow.

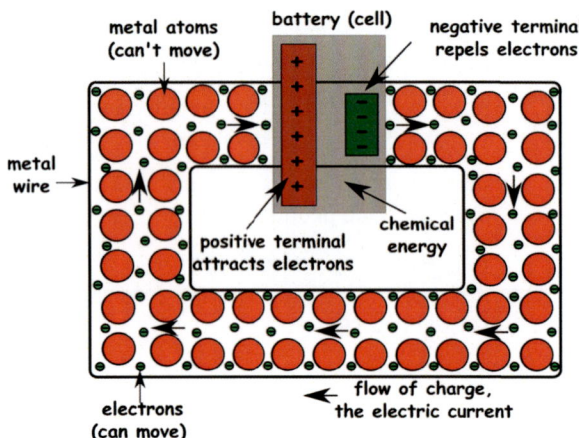

Voltage or Potential Difference Voltage tells us the amount of push or energy the electrons are given. The bigger the voltage the bigger the push the electrons are given, so they can move faster, giving us a bigger electric current. The **unit** for voltage is the **volt**. We measure **voltage** with a **voltmeter** and the symbol for voltage is '**V**'.

Current

A current is the flow of charge (electrons). The size of the current tells us how much charge has passed in one second. If we could shrink in size and get inside a wire, we could count how many electrons pass us in one second. This would tell us the size of the current. The more electrons (and hence charge) that passes per second the bigger the current. Fewer electrons per second the smaller the current. The **current carries the energy** given to it from the battery. The **unit** for current is the **amp**. The symbol for current is '**I**' and we measure **current** with an **ammeter**.

Resistance

This tells us how easy or hard it is for the current to flow. We measure resistance in **ohms** and its symbol is '**R**'. Some components like a voltmeter have a very high resistance and some components like an ammeter have a very low resistance. The equation connecting current, voltage and resistance is given below, putting numbers into the equation helps us to see the effect of resistance. Imagine I connect a **12V** battery to a **6 ohm** bulb and make a complete circuit. The current flow will be: **current = 12 ÷ 6 = 2 amps**. If I connect my **12V** battery to a **12 ohm** bulb and make a complete circuit, the current flow will be: **current = 12 ÷ 12 = 1 amp**. This means making it harder for current to flow (increasing the resistance) decreases the size of the current, which makes sense.

Current = Voltage (volts)	I = V ÷ R
Resistance (ohms)	(amps)

Voltmeters have very high resistance
10,000,000 ohms

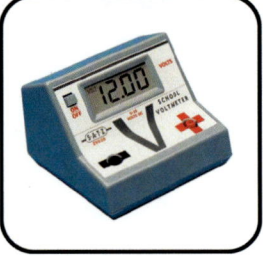

WHAT?
The metal with the lowest resistance is silver. The highest voltage ever achieved is 25.5 million volts using a kind of Van de Graaff generator, don't touch! The symbol for current, **I**, comes from the French word 'Intensite de Courant' meaning current intensity, now just current.

Questions on Electric Circuits

Comprehension

1. What do electric circuits allow?
2. Why is electricity so useful?
3. When can electricity increase a chemical energy store?
4. What do electrons need to get them moving?
5. What is the flow of electrons like?
6. What's another name for voltage?
7. What does voltage tell us?
8. What is the unit of voltage and what do we measure it with?
9. What is a current?
10. What does the size of a current tell us?
11. What does the current carry?
12. What is the unit of current and what is it measured with?
13. What does resistance tell us?
14. What is its unit and what is the symbol for resistance?
15. What component has a very high resistance?
16. What does increasing the resistance do to the current?

Additional tasks

1. Use current = voltage ÷ resistance to calculate the current in each case.

$$I = \frac{V}{R}$$

6 Ohms
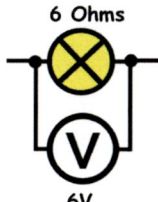
6V

I = _____

12 Ohms
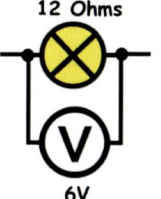
6V

I = _____

2 Ohms
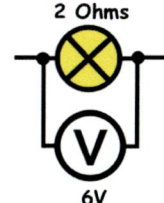
6V

I = _____

1 Ohm

6V

I = _____

24 Ohms

6V

I = _____

60 Ohms

6V

I = _____

2. Complete the gap fill below. Choose from the words;
bigger, fixed, smaller, bigger, inversely, smaller

If the voltage has a _____ value then as the resistance gets _____, the current gets _____. Or as the resistance gets _____, the current gets _____.
This relationship is called being _____ proportional.

---

3. Find the 'circuit words' below in the word search opposite.

POTENTIALDIFFERENCE	VOLTAGE
CURRENT	RESISTANCE
ELECTRONS	BATTERY
VOLTMETER	AMPS
OHMS	VOLTS
CIRCUIT	FLOW
AMMETER	CHEMICALREACTION

```
A  B  C  D  E  F  G  H  I  T  J  K  L  M  N  O  P  Q  R  S
T  U  V  W  X  Y  Z  U  I  A  A  P  B  N  V  C  O  U  O  O
L  G  V  C  L  S  T  U  T  G  J  X  W  Q  I  L  R  H  D  X
P  D  Z  J  R  Z  C  E  R  F  V  S  G  Q  A  R  C  S  M  B
Q  V  H  M  D  R  H  E  F  I  C  U  R  R  E  N  T  F  J  S
T  W  E  K  I  G  T  P  V  S  E  F  K  T  P  C  P  L  N  W
X  G  X  C  H  E  M  I  C  A  L  R  E  A  C  T  I  O  N  R
B  M  P  I  M  U  D  P  S  Q  M  M  J  Q  U  H  R  W  Y  E
R  A  X  M  C  A  U  P  C  L  T  P  Y  W  X  T  H  Y  L  S
N  F  A  L  P  W  K  V  E  L  V  V  S  U  C  K  R  C  A  I
V  N  Z  L  B  J  Y  M  O  Y  C  O  R  E  T  E  W  L  H  S
Y  B  Q  M  X  V  D  V  E  L  K  Y  L  B  T  X  W  U  W  T
F  N  Z  A  Z  B  C  A  X  M  T  E  Z  T  U  N  L  O  R  A
S  K  D  F  T  D  X  F  E  S  I  S  A  P  A  N  Z  M  B  N
S  C  W  D  T  W  M  F  V  A  S  B  A  Y  A  G  Q  S  W  C
G  P  O  T  E  N  T  I  A  L  D  I  F  F  E  R  E  N  C  E
```

Series Circuits

Series Circuits

Series means one after the other. A series circuit has one component connected after the other. This could be one component, two, three or more. There are four important facts to learn about series circuits and then looking at examples is the best way to understand.

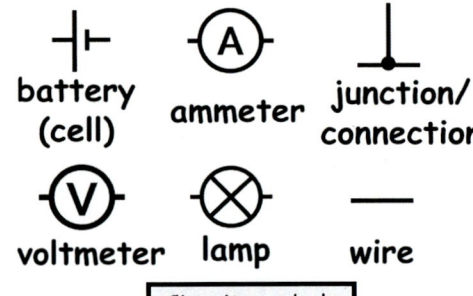
Circuit symbols

- In series circuits the **current is the same everywhere**

- The **voltage** or energy from the battery **is shared** between the components

- If the **circuit breaks** (no longer complete) then **all components stop working**

- The **resistance** of components in **series adds up**

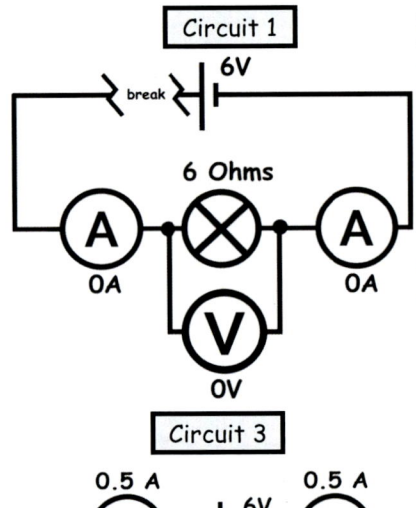

Voltmeters and Ammeters

Notice in the circuits the **ammeter** can be connected before or after the components or even in-between. It must **always** be connected 'in series'. The two wires from the voltmeter are always connected one before and one after the component (a bulb here). This means that **voltmeters** are **always** connected **in parallel**.

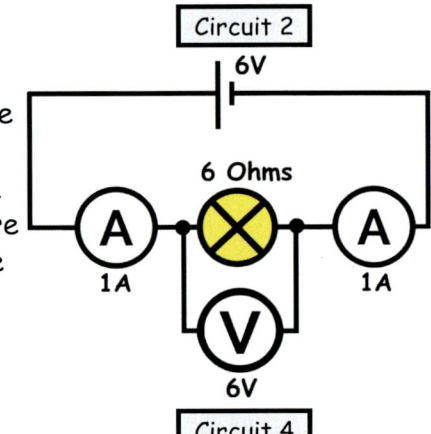

Circuits

Circuit 1 is incomplete, there is a gap so no current flows and the bulb does not light. **Circuit 2** has a resistance of 6 ohms which means the **current = 6 ÷ 6 = 1A**. Since there is only one bulb, it gets all of the energy (voltage) from the battery, so the voltmeter tells us there is **6V for the bulb**. The bulb is bright. **Circuit 3** has a resistance

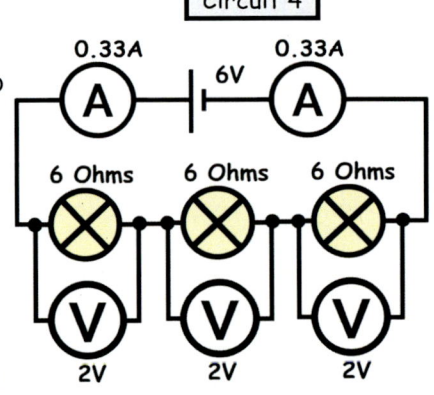

of 12 ohms (6 + 6) which means the **current = 6 ÷ 12 = 0.5A**. This is because it is twice as hard for the current to flow now, so it's only half as big as when there is one bulb on its own. The energy carried by the current (the voltage) now has to be **shared** between the two bulbs so they get **(6 ÷ 2) 3V** each. The bulbs are dimmer. **Circuit 4** has a resistance of 18 ohms (6 + 6 + 6) which means the **current = 6 ÷ 18 = 1/3A (0.33A)**. It is now three times harder for the current to flow compared to circuit 2, so the current is one third of what it was then. The energy carried by the current now has to be shared between three bulbs so they get **(6 ÷ 3) 2V** each. The bulbs are dimmer than in circuit 3.

WHAT?

The first battery was invented by Alessandro Volta an Italian physicist in 1800. He used layers of copper and zinc which were separated by cloth soaked in salty water. The unit of voltage was named after him. If 6,250,000,000,000,000,000 electrons pass by in one second then this is 1 amp of current, try counting that!

Questions on Series Circuits

Comprehension

1. What does series mean?
2. How many important facts are there to learn about series circuits?
3. What happens to the voltage in a series circuit?
4. Where can the ammeter be connected in a series circuit?
5. How are voltmeters always connected?

6. Why does no current flow in circuit 1?
7. Why does the bulb in circuit 2 get 6V?
8. How much harder is it for the current to flow in circuit 3 compared to circuit 2?
9. Why do the bulbs in circuit 3 get 3V?
10. What is the total resistance of circuit 4?

Additional tasks

1. Calculate the voltage **across** the bulbs below (multiply current by resistance).

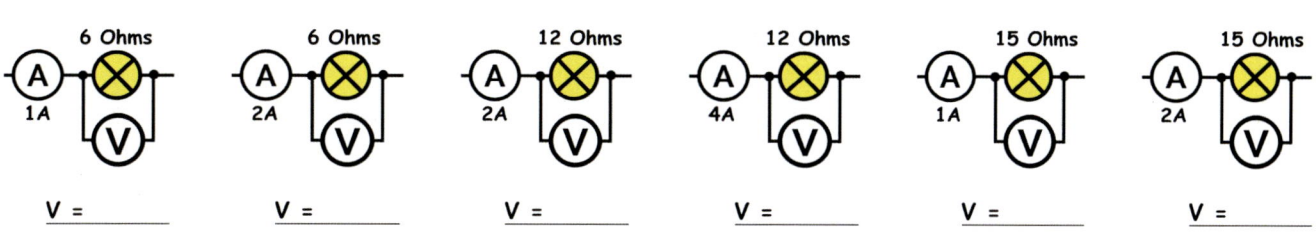

2. Calculate the current **through** the bulbs below (divide voltage by resistance).

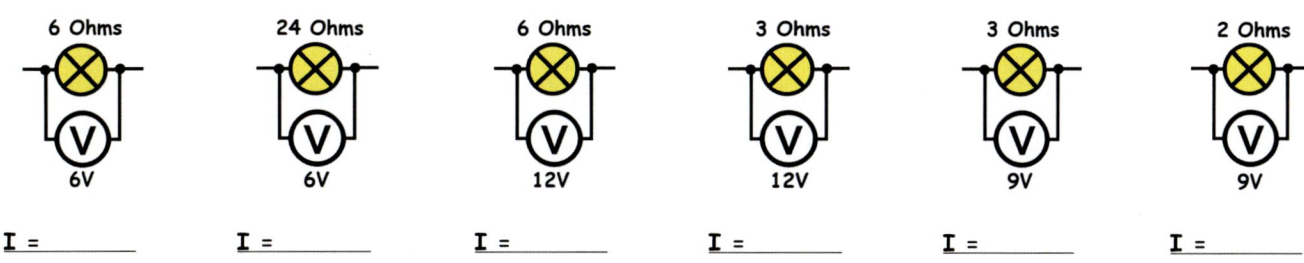

3. Calculate the resistance **of** the bulbs below (divide voltage by current).

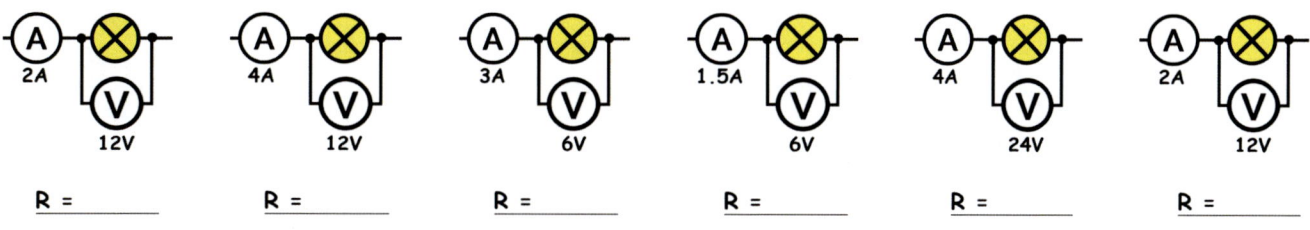

Parallel Circuits

What makes parallel circuits different from series is that they have junctions where the current can split and flow along a different branch of the circuit. This is just like arriving at a 'T' junction in a car, you can take the left path or the right path. The more paths or branches that the current has to flow along, the easier it is for the current to flow. So the resistance is lowered with more paths.

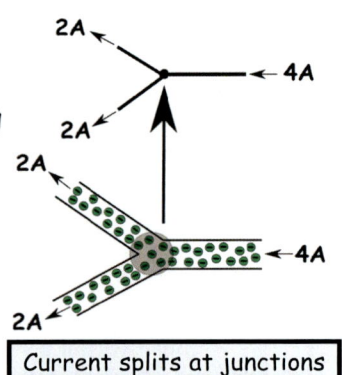

Current splits at junctions

There are four important facts to know about parallel circuits and then looking at examples is the best way to understand them.

Parallel Circuits

Circuit 1

4A   6V   4A
2A
3 Ohms
3 Ohms
2A
6V

Circuit 2

6A   6V   6A
6V
3 Ohms   2A
3 Ohms   2A
3 Ohms   2A

Circuit 3

8A   6V   8A
6V
1.5 Ohms   4A
3 Ohms   2A
3 Ohms   2A

- The current **splits at junctions** so the **total current** is the **sum** of the **current flowing** along **all branches**

- The **voltage** across **each branch** is the **same**

- If **one branch fails** (say a bulb), the **components** in the other branches **still work**

- **Adding** more branches **reduces** the **total resistance** of the circuit.

Circuit 1 has two branches, each branch has 6V because the voltage across each branch is the same, it's the battery voltage. This means each branch has:
current = 6 ÷ 3 = **2A**. Both branches have 2A, so the **total current** being the sum of the branches is, **2 + 2 = 4A.**

Circuit 2 has three branches, each branch has 6V because the voltage across each branch is still the battery voltage. This means each branch has: **current = 6 ÷ 3 = 2A.** All three branches have 2A, so the **total current** being the sum of the branches is, **2 + 2 + 2 = 6A.**

Circuit 3 also has three branches, each branch has 6V because the voltage across each branch is still the battery voltage. Here two of the branches have a resistance of 3 ohms (the bulb) so the current through them is 2A each. The third branch has a bulb with a smaller resistance of 1.5 ohms, so this branch has: **current = 6 ÷ 1.5 = 4A.** This means the **total current** is, **2 + 2 + 4 = 8A.**

Resistance

Dividing **voltage** by **total current** tells us the **total resistance** of the circuit.
Circuit 1 has a total resistance of:

WHAT?

The sockets in your house are all wired in parallel so that they all provide the same voltage, 230V (mains).

R = 6 ÷ 4 = **1.5 ohms. Circuit 2** has a total resistance of:
R = 6 ÷ 6 = **1 ohm.** We can see that more paths means lower resistance and a bigger current. Adding more branches with 3 ohm bulbs to circuit 2 would mean **more equally bright** bulbs. However, this would decrease the resistance of the circuit further, meaning an even bigger current and the battery draining more quickly.

Questions on Parallel Circuits

Comprehension

1.	What makes a parallel circuit different from a series circuit?	6.	How do we know what the voltage across each branch is in the example circuits?
2.	What does this mean that the current can do?	7.	Why is the **total current** in circuit one 4A?
3.	What is this just like?	8.	Why is the current bigger in circuit 2 compared to circuit 1?
4.	What do more paths do to how easily the current flows?	9.	Why does the 1.5 ohm bulb have 4A of current flowing through it?
5.	The current splits at junctions, how do we know the total current?	10.	What does dividing voltage by total current tell us?

Additional tasks

1. Use I = V/R to calculate the current along **each** branch and **total** current for circuits **1,2,3** and **4** below.

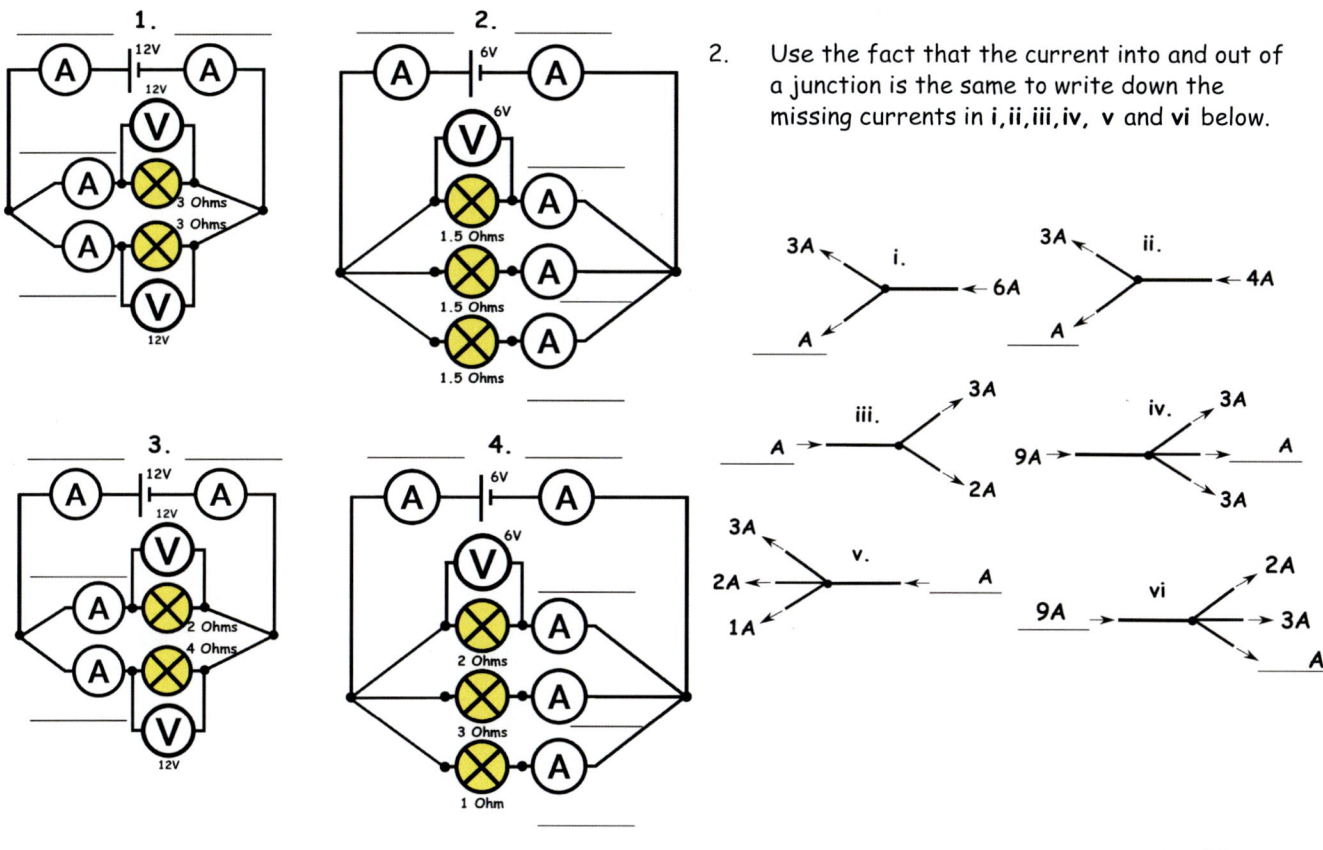

2. Use the fact that the current into and out of a junction is the same to write down the missing currents in **i,ii,iii,iv, v** and **vi** below.

3 a. Write down the missing currents in circuits **W**, **X**, **Y** and **Z**.

b. In circuit **W**, out of the two **parallel bulbs** which has the highest resistance and why? Top or bottom?

c. In circuit **X**, out of the two **parallel bulbs** which has the highest resistance and why? Top or bottom?

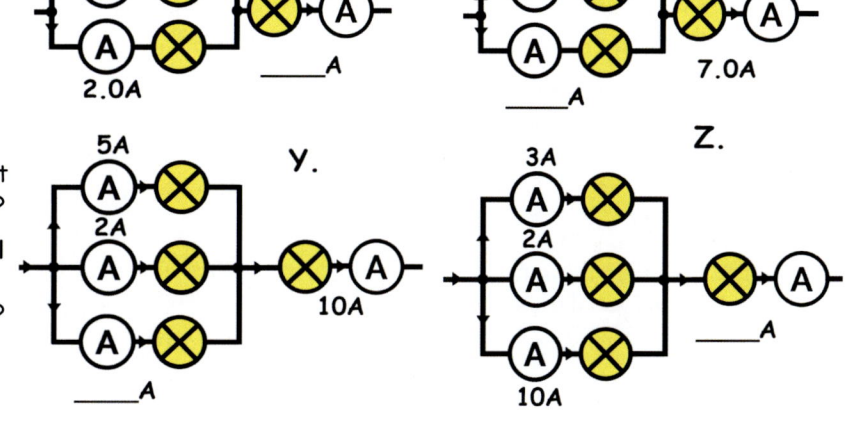

Photocopiable

Only write on photocopied version

Electric Fields

Just like magnets have magnetic fields around them, electric charges have electric fields. We can draw lines to show they are there. If a charge enters **another** electric field it **experiences** a **force**. This can happen when charges are close enough together that they enter **each others** electric field and push or pull on each other. We can make an electric field like the one shown below. The lines point away from the positive towards the negative, downwards as shown. The diagram shows that when charges are in an electric field

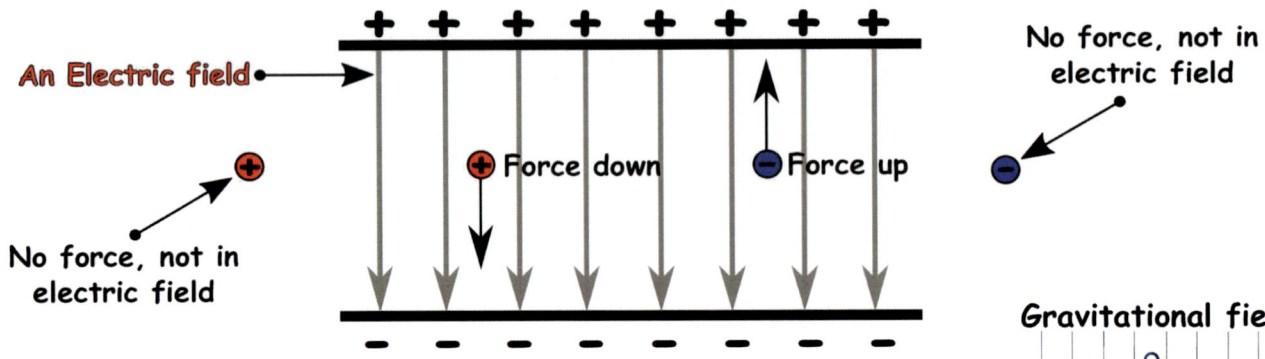

they experience a force and when they are not, they don't. The forces that electric fields exert are **non-contact**. The charges don't have to touch to experience the force. Gravity and magnetism are the other two non-contact forces. The diagram opposite shows a kilogram mass experiencing the pull of earth's gravitational field. This is just like charges experiencing the force of an electric field shown above. Charges **attract** each other if they are **oppositely** charged (+ and -) or **repel** each other if they have the **same** charge (+ and + or - and -). We say **opposites attract** and **like repel**. We often see the shape of a magnetic field drawn around a bar magnet. We can do the same for electric fields around charges.

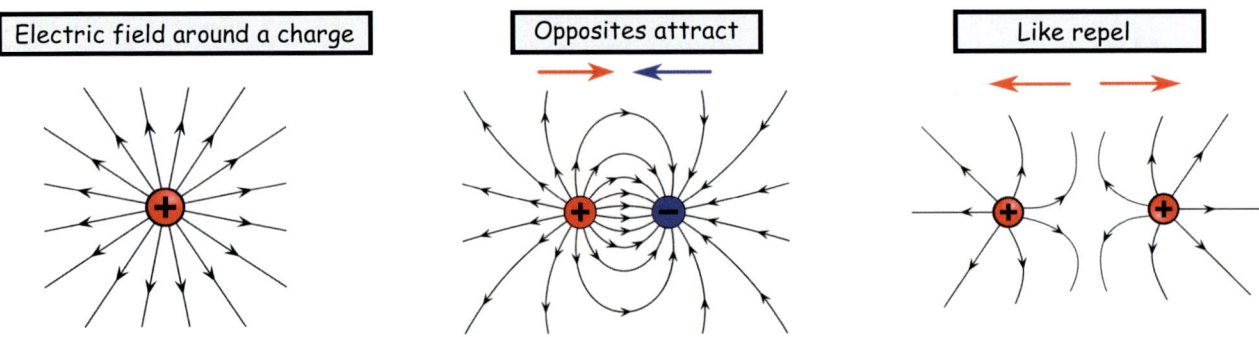

The electric field lines point outwards for positive charges, just like the spines of a puffer fish, and inwards for negative charges. Similar to gravity, where large masses like the sun, for example, have strong gravitational fields. A **large amount** of **charge build up** produces a **strong electric field**, the stronger the field the bigger the force it can exert. Strong electric fields are why we get lightning. During storms, rain and ice crystals bumping into each other, can cause a build up of charge. Air doesn't normally conduct electricity, but if the electric field is strong enough it can be made to conduct. A very strong electric field

between the cloud and the ground (earth) forces the charges in the air (electrons) to move towards the ground creating a brief spark that we call lightning. The thunder is the noise the lightning 'spark' makes.

> **WHAT?**
>
> Don't forget the electric fields from charges and the forces they exert are responsible for holding all atoms and molecules together so it holds us together too!

Questions on Electric Fields

Comprehension

1. What do electric charges have around them?
2. What happens if a charge enters another electric field?
3. How can this happen?
4. What does the diagram show?
5. The forces electric fields exert are what kind?
6. What is the diagram of a KG mass experiencing earth's gravitational field just like?
7. What do oppositely charged particles do to each other?
8. Which direction do electric field lines point for positive charges?
9. What can strong electric fields do?
10. During storms what can cause the build up of charge in clouds?
11. What doesn't air normally do?
12. What is thunder?

Additional tasks

1. Choose from the words below to match to the statements.

> **Electric fields, attract, gravitational fields, repel, magnetic fields, air**
>
> Normally doesn't conduct _____
>
> Opposite charges _____
>
> Magnetic materials experience forces in _____
>
> Like charges _____
>
> Charges experience forces in _____
>
> Masses experience forces in _____

2. Underneath each of the adjacent charges write down whether they will attract or repel.

a_____ b_____ c_____ d_____ e_____ f_____

3. Complete the gap fill. Choose from the words below.

balloons, repel, force, close, electric, attract, field, atoms, inwards, inside, static, stands, electric, outwards

All charges have _____ fields around them. The electric field lines point _____ for positive charges and _____ for negative charges. If a charge is _____ another electric field (not its own), then it experiences a _____. If two charges are _____ enough they experience the force of each other's electric field. This means two close positive charges will repel and two close negative charges will _____. Close positive and negative charges will _____ when in each other's electric _____. It is the force from electric fields that holds _____ and molecules together so it also holds us together! Electric fields are responsible for the effects of _____ electricity, when your hair _____ on end, getting an _____ shock and sticking _____ to walls.

Static Electricity

Ever had a shock when you've touched a car door, when you've taken off a jumper or even when you touch someone else? This is because of static electricity, in fact it is only static before you get the shock! Atoms have **negative charges** called **electrons** that can move from one object to another (it's only the electrons that can move!). This effect can be increased by rubbing different materials together, using **friction**. If an object **loses electrons** (negative charge) it has more positive than negative charge so **becomes positive** overall. The object that **gains electrons becomes negative** overall. Rub a plastic ruler on your clothes and then bring it near to a **tiny ripped** piece of paper, magic!

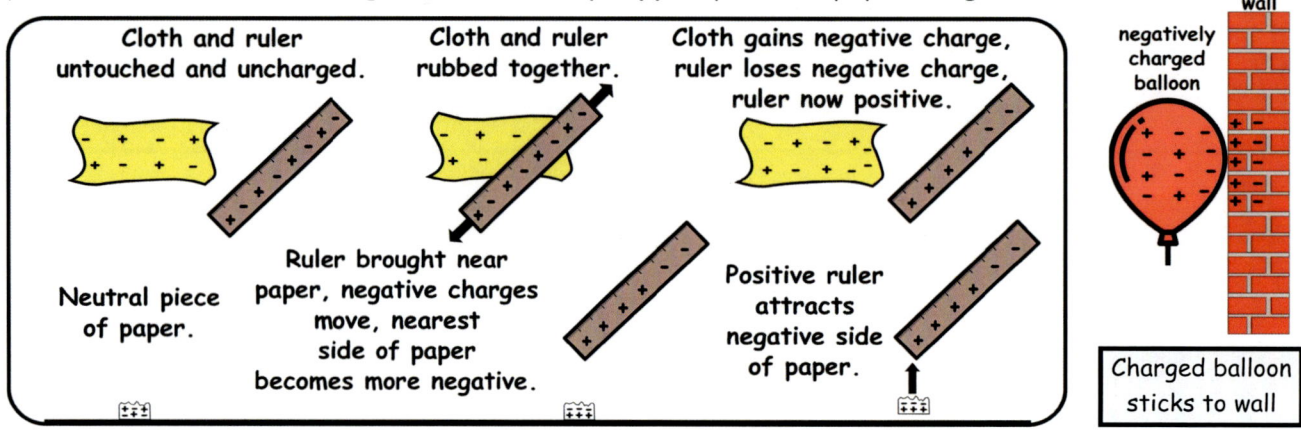

The diagrams above show what's happening. A charged balloon sticks to the wall for the same reason the piece of paper is picked up.

Shocking

If a lot of negative charge builds up on an object, like, for example, a car, the charges push away from each other. The more charge that builds up the greater the push. We can say the voltage of the object increases as the charge increases. If the voltage of the car becomes large enough, when we touch the car we can get a shock. This is because we are connected to earth. When we touch the car we create a path for the excess charge on the car to flow down to earth and spread out. As it flows through us we get an electric shock. Since the amount of charge that flows is small and for such a small period of time, it doesn't normally cause us any harm. It is just a bit of a shock!

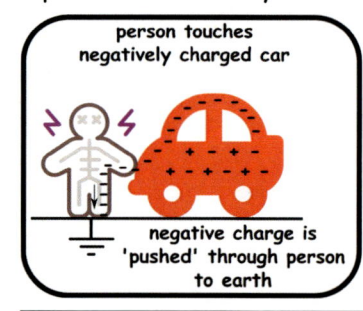

Shock from a charged car

The Van de Graaff Generator

This device makes it possible to build up a lot of charge onto a metal dome using a rotating rubber belt. If you stand on an insulator (like a rubber mat) and put your hand on top of the dome, charge builds up on your body. This can make your hair stand up. Each strand of hair gains the same charge and so are repelled by each other **and** away from your head.

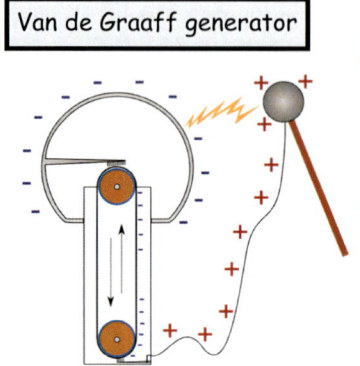

Van de Graaff generator

WHAT?

Photocopiers use static electricity, the negatively charged toner is attracted to the positively charged image on a drum before being rolled onto the paper. More worksheets! Air doesn't normally conduct but if enough charge builds up on an object the voltage becomes big enough to push charge through the air and we get a spark (lightning).

Hair standing up due to static charge

Questions on Static Electricity

Comprehension

1. When might you get a shock from static electricity?

2. What is the name of the negative charges that atoms have?

3. What can these charges do?

4. What can increase this effect?

5. Why does an object become positive if it loses electrons?

6. What happens to the cloth when it is rubbed with a ruler? (diagram)

7. What happens to the charges in the paper when the positive ruler is brought near? (diagram)

8. What increases as the charge on an object increases?

9. What happens if the voltage of the car becomes large enough?

10. When we touch a car that is charged what do we create for the excess charge?

11. What happens as this charge flows through us?

12. What does a Van de Graaff Generator make possible?

13. If you stand on an insulator and touch the dome what happens?

14. Why do the strands of hair stand up and repel each other?

Additional tasks

1. The red polyethene ruler below gains negative charge when rubbed with a cloth. Complete the gaps to explain what is happening. Use the opposite page to help.

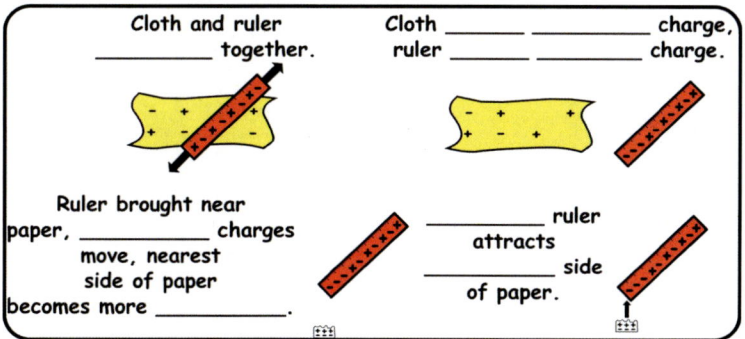

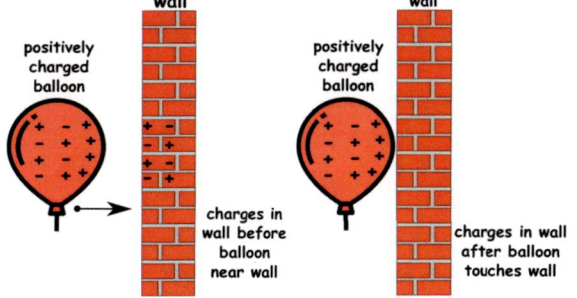

2. A balloon is rubbed and one 'side' of the balloon becomes more positive. The balloon is brought near to a wall and sticks to the wall. Draw the **new arrangement** of the charges in the wall after the balloon sticks to the wall (look opposite for help).

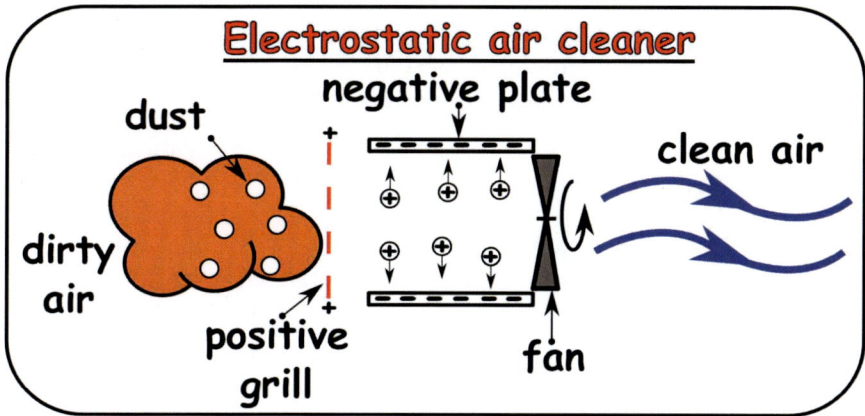

3. Complete the gap fill below explaining how an **electrostatic air cleaner** works.

   Choose from the words in bold and look at the diagram to help.

   negatively, dust, positive, Clean, brushing, charged, attracted, stick, lose

Dirty air containing _____ particles is blown over a _____ grill. This makes the neutral dust particles positive because they _____ electrons. The now positively _____ dust particles pass between _____ charged plates. The positive dust particles are _____ to the negative plates and _____ to them. _____ air leaves the other end of the air cleaner. The plates can be taken out and cleaned by _____ the dust off.

Magnets and Magnetic Fields

Lucky for us the earth has a giant magnetic field that looks just like a bar magnet's field. We can't see magnetic fields but we can see their effects on the three magnetic metals, **iron**, **nickel** and **cobalt**. A nice way to observe the shape of a magnetic field around a bar magnet is to use plotting compasses. Placing compasses at different positions around a bar magnet and observing the direction in which they point

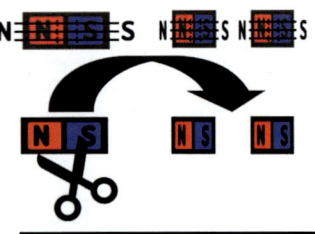

Cutting a magnet in half

enables us to 'see' the shape. Drawing dots in line with the needles then 'joining up the dots' means we can draw the shape of the field. The magnetic field lines continue to run through the magnet. So if you cut a magnet in half you have a new north and new south pole. The same is true if you were to cut the magnet in half again. The magnetic field is strongest near to the poles of a bar magnet.

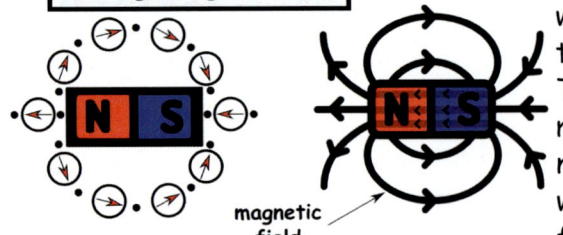

Plotting a magnetic field

magnetic field

When we draw the magnetic field lines around a bar magnet, we show the field lines leaving the north pole and curling around in a squashed circle shape to enter the south pole. Bar magnets are normally coloured red for the north pole and blue for the south pole.

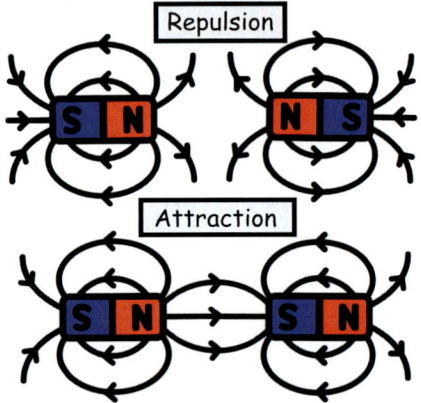

Repulsion

Attraction

Attraction and Repulsion

Like (the same) poles repel and opposites attract. The diagram shows the magnetic field for two north poles repelling each other. It's a bit like pushing the tips of your fingers together, you can feel them pushing back as they rise up.

When a north pole is brought near to a south pole, the field from the north travels to the south of the nearby magnet attracting it. When they come together they form one new longer magnet with one north and one south pole.

induced

Induction

An iron paper clip is not 'normally' a magnet. When you pick it up with a permanent magnet though, it becomes an **induced magnet**. One end of the paper clip becomes a north pole and the other a south pole, it is then attracted to the permanent magnet. It stays a little bit magnetic afterwards but not normally for long. This is how the magnetic metals are attracted to permanent magnets.

unmagnetised

The Earth's Magnetic Field

The earth's magnetic field comes from the earth's core and looks just like that of a bar magnet. **Earth's geographic north pole** (the top) is a **magnetic south pole**. The needle

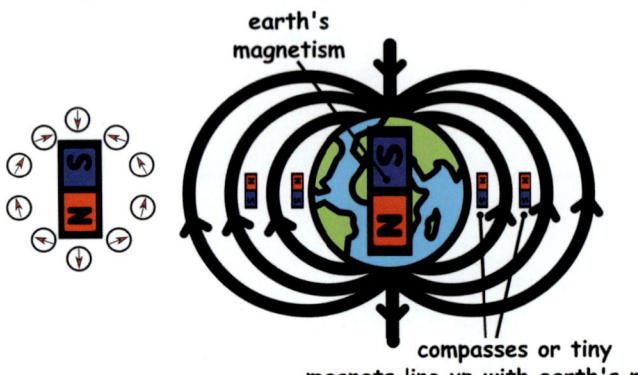

earth's magnetism

compasses or tiny magnets line up with earth's magnetic field so point north-south

of a plotting compass 'lines up' with the earth's magnetic field so always points in a north-south direction (never east-west). The red of a compass needle is attracted to the earth's geographic north pole (magnetic south).

WHAT?

Apart from not being able to use a compass, without the earth's magnetic field we wouldn't be alive. It deflects the damaging charged particles from outer space that would make life impossible.

Questions on Magnetic Fields

Comprehension

1. It's lucky for us that earth has what?

2. What are the names of the three magnetic metals?

3. What is a nice way to observe the magnetic field around a bar magnet?

4. What do the magnetic field lines continue to do through the magnet?

5. What happens if you cut a magnet in half?

6. The magnetic field lines leave the north pole then what?

7. State what like and opposite magnetic poles do to each other?

8. What happens when a north and south pole of a magnet come together?

9. An iron paper clip is not normally what?

10. What does the paper clip become when picked up by a permanent magnet?

11. Where does earth's magnetic field come from?

12. What does the needle of a plotting compass do with the earth's magnetic field?

Additional tasks

1. Practise drawing the shape of the magnetic field around a single bar magnet and pairs that are repelling, use pencil in case of mistakes.

MAGNET ON ITS OWN

TWO MAGNETS REPELLING

2. Write underneath the magnets below whether they will attract or repel.

3. Write **yes** or **no** next to the whether the following items can be picked up by a **permanent magnet**.

Item	Can pick up?
Paper clip	
Plastic ruler	
Permanent magnet	
Rubber	
Nickel coin	
Paper	
Iron nail	
Plotting compass	
Aluminium Can	
Chewing gum	
Piece of wood	
Cobalt cube	

4. Try drawing the magnetic field lines around a horse shoe magnet. The same rules apply, field lines come out of the north and into the south. Inside they flow from south to north as shown, same as a 'normal' magnet.

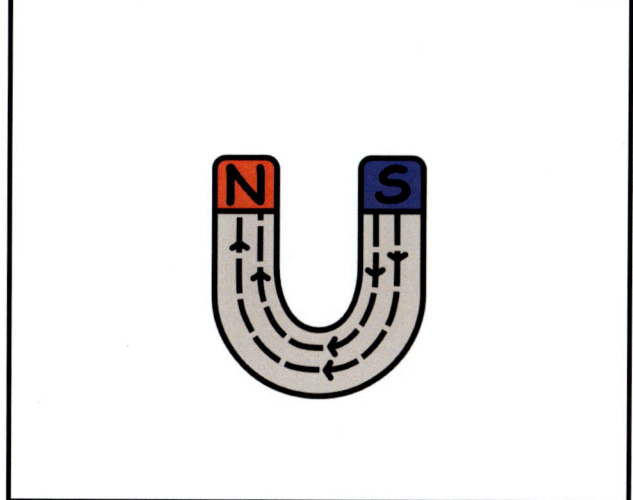

Electromagnetism

The magnetic field around a permanent magnet is exactly that, permanent. However, an **electric current** also produces a **magnetic field** which can be turned on or off with the current. This connection between electricity and magnetism we call **electromagnetism**. It is really useful and many devices use electromagnetism. A straight wire carrying a current produces a circular magnetic field. A loop of wire produces a field **like** a bar magnet is in the middle. If we continue to loop the wire round we make a **solenoid** that produces a magnetic field just like that of a bar magnet. We can make a solenoid's magnetic field stronger by:

- Increasing the size of the current
- Having more coils of wire closer together
- Adding an iron core to the centre of a solenoid which makes an electromagnet.

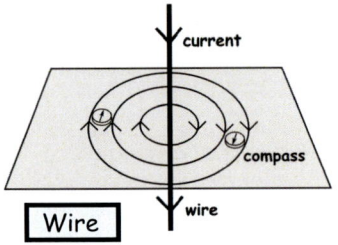

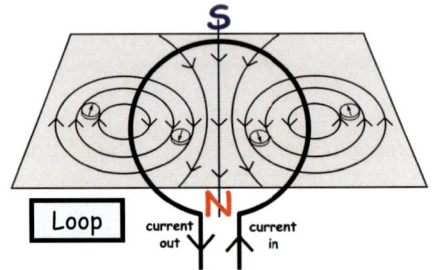

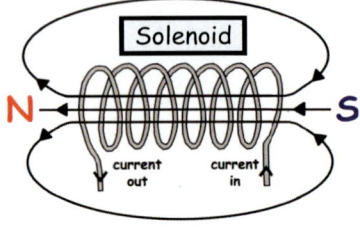

Solenoids and electromagnets have many uses. **Electromagnets** can be made strong enough to **pick up cars** and then drop them again when the current is switched off. They are used in safety devices called **circuit breakers** that turn off the electricity when too much current flows. An **electric bell** uses an electromagnet that is made to turn on and off so that a small hammer hits the gong and 'rings the bell'.

The Electric Motor

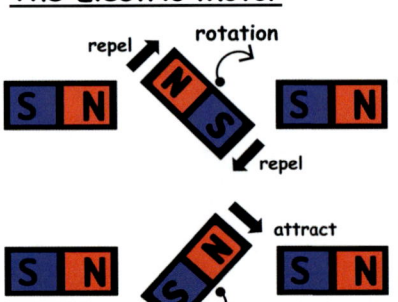

Electric motors convert the energy carried by an electric current into kinetic (movement) energy. This is really useful and has loads of applications. It's easy to understand how they work if we remember opposite poles attract (north-south) and like poles (north-north or south-south) repel.

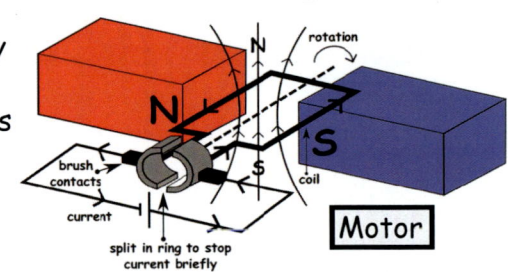

When a current flows through the coil one end becomes a north pole and the other end a south pole. The coil is made to rotate until the poles **line up** (1/4 of a turn in the diagram). At this point the split in the ring (grey) briefly stops the current flowing, the coil's magnetic field turns off so the coil keeps moving (just like you do when you stop pedalling your bike). The contacts then touch the ring again, a current flows again and the coil carries on turning. **A loudspeaker** has a coil attached to a diaphragm (or skin). The **current** into the speaker coil **changes direction**, so the north and south poles keep flipping, this forces it to be pulled towards or pushed away from a permanent magnet. This vibration produces the sound.

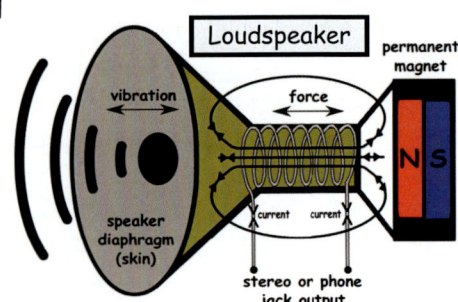

WHAT?
A loudspeaker is effectively a microphone in reverse, and vice versa!

Questions on Electromagnetism

Comprehension

1. What also produces a magnetic field?
2. What can we do with this magnetic field that can't be done with a permanent magnet?
3. What shape magnetic field does a straight wire carrying a current produce?
4. What is the magnetic field *like* for a loop of wire carrying a current?
5. What does the magnetic field of a solenoid look like?
6. What does increasing the current do to the strength of the magnetic field?
7. If we add an iron core to the solenoid, what do we make?
8. Electromagnets can be made strong enough to do what?
9. What safety device are they used in?
10. What do electric motors do?
11. What happens when a current flows through the coil of an electric motor?
12. When the poles line up what does the split in the ring do?

Additional tasks

1. The solenoid below has a current of 2.0 amps and 10 coils of wire over 10cm. Complete the table to say whether the magnetic field will be **stronger**, **weaker** or the **same** with the changes given below.

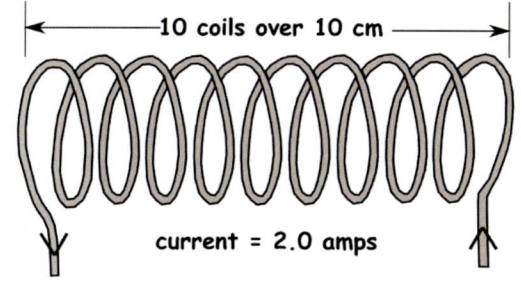

←————10 coils over 10 cm————→

current = 2.0 amps

split in ring to stop current briefly

3. Use the **logic of opposites** i.e. swap magnets over, motor turns the other way, change current direction, motor turns the other way. To complete **same way/other** way column. Use the current column to decide if the motor turns **faster**, **slower** or the **same speed**.

Coils	Current	Magnetic field Stronger/ Weaker/ Same
10 coils over 10cm	3.0 amps	
20 coils over 20cm	2.0 amps	
5 coils over 10cm	2.0 amps	
10 coils over 10cm	0.5 amps	
40 coils over 10cm	2.0 amps	
20 coils over 10cm	2.5 amps	
6 coils over 10cm	1.0 amp	

Magnets' position	Current	Faster/ Slower/Same	Same way/ Other way
same as above	**smaller** than above same direction		
north south swapped over	**same size** as above same direction		
same as above	**bigger** than above same direction		
same as above	**bigger** than above opposite direction		
north south swapped over	**bigger** than above same direction		
north south swapped over	**same size** as above opposite direction		

2. Complete the gap fill on how a loudspeaker works. Choose from the words below.

phone, magnetic, output, current, magnetic, pulls, field, coil, changes, forces, vibrate, direction

A speaker works because an electric current makes a _____ field. Two magnetic fields can exert _____ on each other. The coil of a loudspeaker is connected to the _____ of a source like a _____ jack. This forces a _____ to flow in the speaker _____ that changes _____. The current in the coil makes a _____ field. As the current flows back and forth, the permanent magnet of the loudspeaker pushes or _____ on the magnetic _____ from the coil as it _____. This forces the speaker to _____to and fro in time with the music. This produces the sound we hear.

The Day, the Year and the Seasons

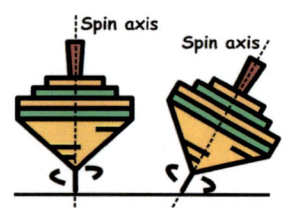

The earth spins like a spinning top. About 4.5 billion years ago, it was hit by a huge rock, so instead of spinning 'upright' it spins at an angle (a tilt) of 23.5°. This **tilt causes our seasons**, without it there would be no seasons (spring, summer, autumn and winter). It takes the earth one day (24 hours) to spin around once. When our 'bit' of the earth is facing the sun it is day time for us. When our 'bit' of the earth is facing away from the sun it is night time for us. So when one half of the earth is in daylight the other half is in darkness. The earth stays in orbit around the sun because of the pull of the sun's gravity. The shape of earth's orbit is a slightly squashed circle shape called an **ellipse**. It takes the earth **365** and a **quarter** days (365.25) to make one complete orbit of the sun (**a year**). Every fourth year, called a **leap year**, we add an extra day to February to stop the seasons moving position on the calendar.

The Seasons

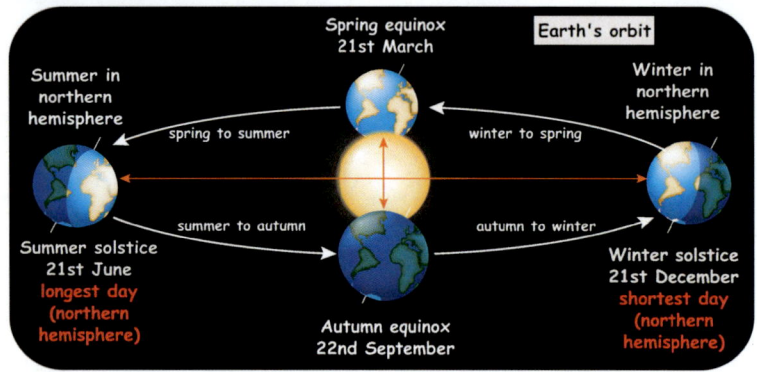

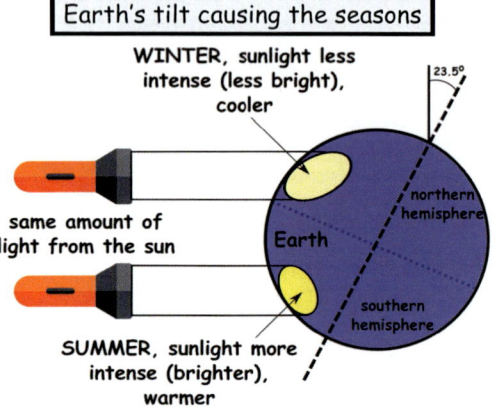

If the earth was not tilted we would have equal day and night. However, because of earth's tilt, during the **summer** the top half (northern hemisphere) of earth is tilted **towards** the sun. This gives us longer days and more light. In **winter**, the northern hemisphere is tilted **away** from the sun and we have shorter days and less sunlight (diagram above). The torches pretending to be the sun's light in the diagram, show that **in winter**, the same amount of light from the sun is spread over a larger area in the **northern hemisphere**, it is colder. The **southern hemisphere** where it is **summer**, the same amount of light is concentrated on a smaller area, so it is warmer. During the summer, the path of the sun across the sky is more directly over head rather than being much lower in the sky as it is in the winter.

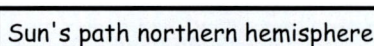

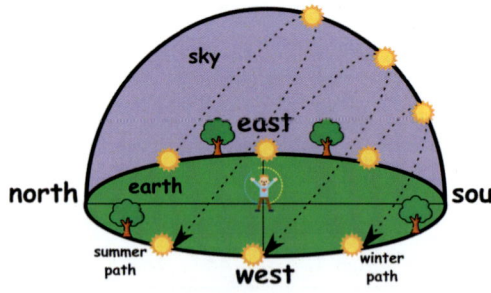

The Orbit and Spin

Looking down from above the earth's north pole, the earth orbits the sun anticlockwise and at the same time rotates anticlockwise. This means that the sun always **rises** in the **east** and **sets** in the **west**. Look carefully at the earth's orbit diagram above, you will notice that at the **north pole** in **winter** the sun doesn't rise above the horizon (can't see the sun) during the daytime. In the summer the sun doesn't drop below the horizon **day** or **night** (you can always see the sun). It's still cold though!

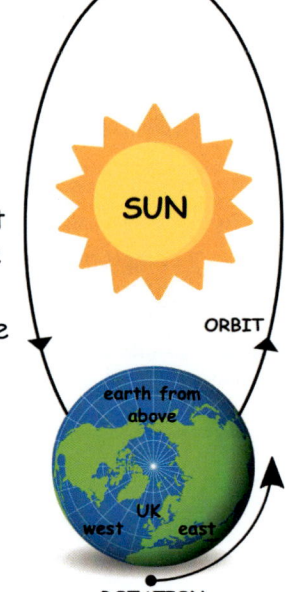

> **WHAT?**
>
> If we didn't have a leap year every four years then after 730 years, the 22nd June (longest day in summer) would be the same weather as the 22nd December (shortest day in winter). Earth would be on the opposite side of its orbit.

Questions on The Day, the Year and the Seasons

Comprehension

1. What happened to the earth about 4.5 billion years ago?
2. What does the earth's tilt cause?
3. How long does it take the earth to spin round once?
4. When 'our bit' of the earth is facing away from the sun is it daytime or night time?
5. What keeps the earth in its orbit?
6. What shape is an ellipse?
7. How long does it take the earth to orbit the sun?
8. During summer in the **northern hemisphere**, which way is earth tilted?
9. What do the torches show for winter in the northern hemisphere?
10. In the southern hemisphere when it is summer, what happens to the same amount of light?
11. When is the sun's path more directly overhead?
12. Looking from above the north pole which way does the earth rotate?
13. In which direction does the sun always rise and set?
14. At the north pole in winter what can't you see during daytime?

Additional tasks

1. Match and memorise the meanings of the useful terms below.

Equinox	the half of earth north of (above) the equator
Solstice	the half of earth south of (below) the equator
Equator	every fourth year in which an extra day is added to February because the earth takes 365 and 1/4 days to orbit the sun not 365
Northern hemisphere	spring 21st March and autumn 22nd September, when **day** and **night** are **equal** length (12hrs of day and 12hrs of night)
Southern hemisphere	**summer solstice** is the **longest day**, 21st June. **winter solstice** is the **shortest day**, 21st December
Leap year	an imaginary line drawn around the centre of earth half way between the north and south pole

2. Plot a bar chart of the average hours of daylight for each month in Britain.

Month	Jan	Feb	Mar	Apr	May	Jun	Jul	Aug	Sept	Oct	Nov	Dec
Average Hours of daylight	8	9	11	13	15	16	16.5	16	14	11	10	8

3. Match the statements to the correct answers.

When it's summer in the northern hemisphere	360⁰
The sun is lower in the sky during	it's summer in the southern hemisphere
The angle of the earth's tilt is	summer
In one day the earth rotates	it's winter in the southern hemisphere
When it's winter in the northern hemisphere	23.5⁰
The sun is more directly overhead during	winter

4. During the summer at the north pole it stays light 24 hours of the day. During the winter it stays in full darkness all day long. Write about what you think this would be like and what would be the advantages and disadvantages.

Our Solar System, Galaxies and the Universe

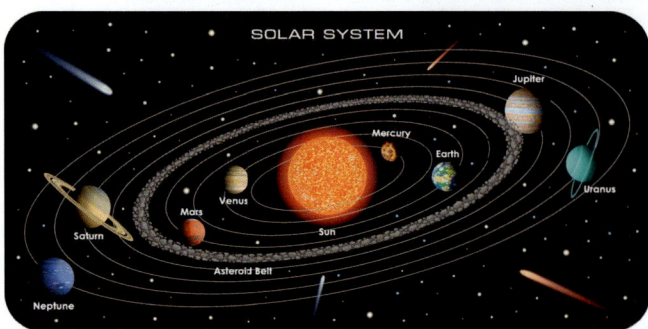

SOLAR SYSTEM

It's our solar system rather than the solar system because there are many. At the centre of ours is a <u>star called the sun.</u> The sun is so massive that its gravity is strong enough to keep all of the planets in their elliptical (squashed circle) orbits. The planets are satellites (smaller objects in orbit around larger objects) of the sun. Earth has its own **natural satellite** called the **moon** and thousands of other man-made ones used for communication, remote monitoring and meteorology (weather forecasting).

	Mercury	Venus	Earth	Mars	Jupiter	Saturn	Uranus	Neptune
Distance from sun (millions of kms)	60	110	*150*	230	780	1400	2900	4500
Orbit time (earth years)	0.2	0.6	*1*	2	12	30	84	160

The further a planet is from the sun the longer it takes to orbit, so a year on some planets (earth's is 365.25 days) is longer or shorter than others. An easy way to remember the order of the planets is the mnemonic **M**y **V**ery **E**asy **M**ethod **J**ust **S**peeds **U**p **N**aming **P**lanets. Although Pluto is no longer classed as a planet!

Galaxies and the Universe

Our solar system is part of the **Milky Way galaxy**. This is **our galaxy**. It is a 'flat' spiral shaped disk with arms, think of it like a spinning star fish with bent arms!

As we look out at the night sky we can see a milky band of light across the sky, this is where our galaxy gets its name from. We are looking **across our own galaxy** to see this band of light. Look above or below this and we are **looking out of** our galaxy to deep space (see below). The stars that we see in the night sky are **all** part of our own galaxy, the **Milky Way**. There are around 250 billion stars in our galaxy (250,000,000,000). A **light year**, which is a measure of **distance**, is how far light travels in one year (nearly 6 million million miles). Our nearest star (not counting the sun) is **Alpha Centauri** 4.4 light years

|— 100,000 light years —|

We are here

Milky Way galaxy from above

WHAT?

Our Milky Way galaxy rotates, it takes our solar system 250 million years to complete one rotation. Scientists don't know what most of the universe is made from!

Hubble telescope image

away. The Milky Way is 100 thousand light years across. Our nearest major galaxy is **Andromeda**, it can be seen as a smudge of light in the night sky. It is also a spiral galaxy like our own (the Milky Way). It is 2.5 million light years away. To get there you would have to travel at the speed of light (186,000 miles a second) for 2.5 million years. The **universe** is **all** known **space** and **matter**. It is made up of hundreds of billions of galaxies. An image from the Hubble space telescope shows the galaxies in one small patch of night sky, a tiny fraction of the universe.

Milky Way from earth

Looking across and out of the Milky Way galaxy

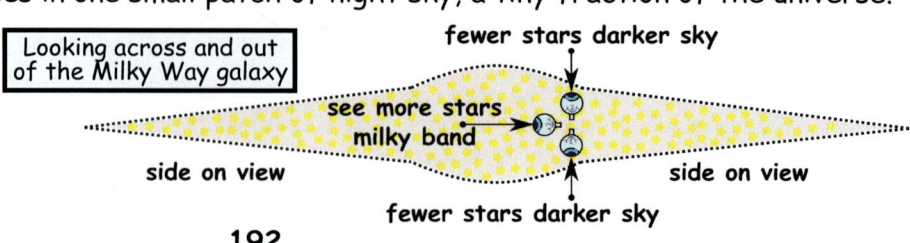

fewer stars darker sky

see more stars
milky band

side on view

side on view

fewer stars darker sky

Questions on Our Solar System, Galaxies and the Universe

Comprehension

1. What is at the centre of our solar system?
2. Why is the sun's gravity strong enough to keep the planets in their orbits?
3. What is the shape of the planets' orbits?
4. What is a satellite?
5. What happens to the amount of time needed to orbit the sun as you move further away?
6. Use the mnemonic to write out the order of the planets that starts closest to the sun.
7. What is the name of the galaxy we are in?
8. Where does our galaxy get its name from?
9. How many stars are there in the Milky Way?
10. What is a light year?
11. What is the name of our nearest major galaxy?
12. What is the universe?

Additional tasks

1. Plot a bar chart below of orbit time in earth years for each planet. You will need eight bars at the correct height for the eight planets.

2. Put the following objects in order of size starting with smallest first.

> THE MILKY WAY GALAXY, JUPITER, INTERNATIONAL SPACE STATION, THE SUN, OUR SOLAR SYSTEM, THE UNIVERSE, THE MOON, THE EARTH

3. Write **true** or **false** next to the following statements to do with space.

A light year is a measurement of speed (false) The Milky Way doesn't rotate (false)
There are only a few man-made satellites orbiting earth (false) The sun is a star (true)
There has been a manned mission to Mars (false) No one lives in the space station (false) true
Our nearest star is Alpha Centauri (true) The moon has no air on it (false)
Andromeda's our nearest galaxy (true) There are billions of galaxies in the universe (true)
Pluto is classed as a dwarf planet (true) An ellipse is like a squashed circle (true)
It takes 365 days for earth to orbit the sun (true) Venus is closest to the sun (false)
Scientists don't know what most of the universe is made from (false)

Index

Acknowledgements

Image, **author**, source

Adobe Stock images

Acacia Tree, **Parkheta**; African women, **michaeljung**; Bat, **Perysty**; Bee Orchid, **creativenature.nl**; Bleach, **Alex Yeung**; Blood cells, **designua**; Bonefire, **Alfmaler**; Burnt toast, **petert2**; Cannabis leaf, **klickit24**; Car battery, **shashkin**; Cell division, **Kateryna_Kon**; Chemical formula, **konstruktor1980**; Champagne, **Rogatnev**;Chips, **Peter Polak**; Circulatory system, **blueringmedia**; Diffusion, **wahoo**;Disposable cup, **Shashkin**; DNA, **designua**; Electric car, **Aldeca Productions**; Electric car renewables, **mast3r**; Engine oil, **artegorov3@gmail**; Fox, **Milan**; Fruit basket, **valeriy555**; Gases dissolving, **photGapHie**; G-clamp, **Kenjo**; Germination, **Bogdan Wankowicz**; Glow sticks, **catherinelprod**; Golf ball, **mumindurmaz35**; Gut bacteria, **sakurra**; Headache,**PeterSchreiber.media**; Ice, **Yeti Studio**;Insulation panel, **srki66**; Loft insulation, **Kuchina**; Lungs(smoking), **fdsmsoft**; Jumping stilts, **shmel**; Microbes, bubbles, **Yummy Buum**; Moth, **dule964**; Mouse, **Happymonkey**; Muscle cell, **topvectors**; Oxygen tank, **mrkevvzime**; Persil, **Alenkadr**; Planting trees, **AS photo project**; Pollinating plants, **elina33**; Pond ecosystem, **Kazakova Maryia**; Rabbit, **Stefan Andronache**; Recycle, **Good studio**; Red blood cell, **MicroOne**; Scales, **Sergey Ilin**; Smell (bad), **nicoletaionescu**; Sunscreen, **cosmic_pony**; Water (girl drinking), **Riccardo Niels Mayer**; Wolf, **andamanec**; Yogurt, **HstrongArt**; adobe.stock.com.

Free vectors

Abstract Colourful Light Waves (cover), **Vector Art**, free vectors

Flaticon;

Pharmacy, **catkuro**, Butter, Nail scissors, **creaticca-creative-agency**, www.Flaticon.com; Van, Tree, Strong (muscles), Weak, **darius-dan**, www.Flaticon.com; Chromosome, **ddara**, www.Flaticon.com; DNA, **dimitry-miroliubov**, www.Flaticon.com; lion, **Dinosoft labs**, wwwflaticon; Antibiotic, Cement mixer, Heatwave, Lawnmower, Sewer, Stopwatch, Tidy (Closet), **Eucalyp**, www.Flaticon.com; Ant, Apple, Banana, Bath tub, Beer, Bleach, Bolt (lightning), Bonfire, Bread, Bush, Cabbage, Can, Caterpillar, Chair, Chimpanzee, Clip, Cocaine, Cola, Cold, Cow, Cucumber, Dandelion, Dolphin, Door handle, Draw (writing), Eat plate, Eye, Feather, Flashlight, Flat tire, Food and Restaurant, Football, Frying Pan, Generator, Geothermal, Glow, Grasshopper, Hammer, Hamburger, Happy (face), Hawk, Headache, Healthy, Helmet, Herring, Hot, Insect, Insecticide, Jet ski, Kg mass, Kilogram, Knife, Ladybird, Lying down, Magnetic field (earth's), Magnetic field, Match, Meat, Milk, Motivation (hand), Mountain, Music (tuning fork), Nail, Nausea, Newton's cradle (pendulum), Orange, Peas, Planet earth, Pot (plant), Potato, Pregnant, Puffer, Radiator, Rain Cloud, Recycle bin, Rice, Rocks, Ruler, Running, Seeds, Smell, Snow man, Soap, Socks, Solar cell, Sneakers, Sparkler, Sparrow, Spoon, Sugar, Sun, Swimming, Tarantula, Tea, Thermometer, Tidal (water), Tomato, Tree, Truffle, Walk, Washing machine, Washing powder, Wasp, Weed, Weight lifting, Wind energy, Wine glass, **www.Flaticon.com**; Drug, **geotatah**, www.Flaticon.com; Thermometer, **fps-web-agency**, www.Flaticon.com; Idea (light bulb), Ship cargo, Tuna, **Goodware**, www.Flaticon.com; Gravity, **Icongeek26**, www.Flaticon.com; Pipeline, **Itim2101**, www.Flaticon.com; Ammeter, Bike, Car battery, Orange, Pasta, Pregnant, Sheep, Shorts, Top, Voltmeter, Water (tap), **monkik**, www.Flaticon.com; Yogurt, **mynamepong**, www.Flaticon.com; Crowbar, Helicopter, Tire, Wrecking ball, Funeral, **Nikita Golubev**, www.Flaticon.com; Kettle, Meter, **pause08**, www.Flaticon.com; Population (climate change), Inhaler, **Surang**, www.Flaticon.com; Coal, **pause08**, www.Flaticon.com; T-shirt, **photo3idea-studio**, www.Flaticon.com; Champagne, Nose,**pixelmeetup**, www.Flaticon.com; Helicopter, **pixelperfect**, www.Flaticon.com; Smart phone, **Roundicons**, www.Flaticon.com; Beer,house, **smalllikeart**, www.Flaticon.com; Exercise, Cheese, Ladybird, Melting (ice), Pendulum, Steel girder, **smashicons**, www.Flaticon.com; Coffee pot, shine, **srip**, www.Flaticon.com; Bleach, Egg, Fish, Four Leafed Clover, Pump, **those-icons**, www.Flaticon.com; Scissors, **tomas-knop**, www.Flaticon.com; Climbing, **turkkub**, www.Flaticon.com; Motorbike, Toaster, **ultimatearm**, www.Flaticon.com; Stilettoes, **vectors market**, www.Flaticon.com; Bowling ball, **Vitaly Gorbachev**, Power plant, **wanicon**, www.Flaticon.com;

Iconfinder

Airplane, **Iconnice studio**, Iconfinder; Brocolli, **Ionescu Georgiana Lavinia**, Iconfinder; Camel, **Rizalul Ammar**, Iconfinder; Car, **Jim Caesar**, Iconfinder; Cruise ship, **Visual pharm**, Iconfinder; Drawing pin, **Icons land**, Iconfinder; Human, Microphone, **Chamestudio Pvt Ltd**, Iconfinder; Polar bear, **Chanut is industries**, Iconfinder; Shark, **Emojious.com**, Iconfinder; TV, **Oxygen team**, Iconfinder; Shock, **Webalys**, Iconfinder;

Pixabay

Freckles, **Mohamed Chermiti**; Lizard, **Monkik**; Weighing scales, **Open clipart-vectors**; Pixabay

Shutterstock

Condensation on the window, **Olga Narcissa**, Shutterstock; View under the grey bridge in the city (concrete), **Lijphoto**, Shutterstock; Cool gel, **Andrey_Popov**, Shutterstock; Small intestine, **BlueRingMedia**, Shutterstock; Our Solar System, **D1min**, Shutterstock; Earth globe, **Pyty**, Shutterstock; Man shooting a gun, **Xtremest**, Shutterstock; Silver star balloon, **Dmitry Lobanov**, Shutterstock; Girl screaming, **Hanaha**, Shutterstock; Sun illustration, **Juergen Faelchle**, Shutterstock; Elastic band on hands, **Africa Studio**, Shutterstock; Earth's Seasons, **Designua**, Shutterstock; Taking Toy, **AnggaR3ind**, Shutterstock; Peristalsis, **Sakurra**, Shutterstock, Tired child (lethargy), **ViDI Studio**, Shutterstock; Broken spring, **Aurre**, Shutterstock; Pick n Mix, **Limolida design Studio**, Shutterstock; Foetus, **Stephen Barnes**, Shutterstock; Plastic waste, **StockSmartStart**, Shutterstock; Model lungs, **Aldona Griskeviciene**, Shutterstock; Food probe, **PCH.Vector**, Shutterstock; Acid rain damage, **Axel Jung**, Shutterstock; Venus fly trap, **Usenko Oleksandr**, Shutterstock, male reproductive system, **Blue ring media**, Shutterstock; female reproductive system, **Spreadthesign**, Shutterstock; Drug addict, **US 2015**, Shutterstock.

Wikipedia

Alveoli, **ladyofhats**, Animal cell, **domdomegg**, Apple bitten, **Dan Gerhards**, Bass drum, **Wikivisual**, Calcium oxide, **Leiem**, Cane toad, **Bidgee**, Carbon fibre bike, **Glory Cycles**, Cat and mouse, 197, Charges alike, 197, Cola, **National Institute of Korean Language**, Coleshill Church, **Amanda Slater**, corrosion, **Gralistair**, Dandelion, **Greg Hume**, Drops of sweat, **bibikoff**, Ear diagram, **Ian at English Wiki**, Earth, **Isaac Grant**, Explosion, **John Sullivan**, Fire triangle, **Gustavb**, fossil, **Ghedoghedo**, Greenhouse effect, **A loose necktie**, Human Skeleton,**LadyofHats Mariana Ruiz Villarreal**, Ice block, **Sharon Mollerus**, Intestine cells, **Jamil Baza**, Lime Kiln, **Greg Goebel**, Marakkanam Salt Pans, **Dey.sandip**, Magnesium ribbon burning,**Capt.John Yossarian**, Milkyway, **ESO/Y Beletsky**, Okapi, **Raul654**, Oscilloscope, **Brian S. Elliott**, Ouzo, **Phoney**, Plant cell, **domdomegg**, Jumping stilts, **Pagenfairie**, Presssure can Torrecelli's law, **Matt Cook**,Refraction (swimming pool head), **Bugpower**, Rickets Xray, **Michael L. Richardson**, Salt farming, **JJ Harrison**, Separating funnel, **Shakki**, Ship wreck of Cabo de Santa Maria,   **Ximonic (Simo Räsänen)**, Sleeping baby, **Stephanie Pratt**, Taj Mahal, **Yann**, Van de Graaff, 197,Whistling, **Wikivisual**, World map, **Strebe**; Wikipedia.

Every effort has been made to appropriately acknowledge the use of any images in this book. Any omissions that may become apparent will be rectified in subsequent printings.